MINOR ETHICS

Minor Ethics

Deleuzian Variations

Edited by

CASEY FORD, SUZANNE M. MCCULLAGH,
AND KAREN L.F. HOULE

McGill-Queen's University Press
Montreal & Kingston • London • Chicago

ISBN 978-0-2280-0563-6 (cloth)
ISBN 978-0-2280-0564-3 (paper)
ISBN 978-0-2280-0699-2 (ePDF)
ISBN 978-0-2280-0700-5 (ePUB)

Legal deposit first quarter 2021
Bibliothèque nationale du Québec

Printed in Canada on acid-free paper that is 100% ancient forest free
(100% post-consumer recycled), processed chlorine free

Funded by the Financé par le
Government gouvernement
of Canada du Canada

Canada

Canada Council Conseil des arts
for the Arts du Canada

We acknowledge the support of the Canada Council for the Arts.

Nous remercions le Conseil des arts du Canada de son soutien.

Library and Archives Canada Cataloguing in Publication

Title: Minor ethics: Deleuzian variations/edited by Casey Ford, Suzanne
McCullagh, and Karen Houle.

Names: Ford, Casey, 1987– editor. | McCullagh, Suzanne, 1975– editor. |
Houle, Karen, editor.

Description: Includes bibliographical references and index.

Identifiers: Canadiana (print) 20200380885 | Canadiana (ebook) 20200381180 |
ISBN 9780228005643 (paper) | ISBN 9780228005636 (cloth) |
ISBN 9780228006992 (ePDF) | ISBN 9780228007005 (ePUB)

Subjects: LCSH: Ethics. | LCSH: Deleuze, Gilles, 1925–1995.

Classification: LCC BJ1012 .M56 2021 | DDC 170—dc23

This book was typeset by Marquis Interscript in 10.5/13 Sabon.

Contents

Acknowledgments

We want to thank everyone whose support, contributions, and participation made this project possible. We are especially grateful to the chapter authors for sharing their writing, their willingness to work with our suggestions, and their graceful patience. We thank Mark Abley and Khadija Coxon at McGill-Queen's University Press, whose careful attention, advice, and support was invaluable in shaping and seeing the manuscript through the publication process. We are thankful to the Guelph Philosophy Administrators – including Patricia Sheridan, Janet Thackray, and Pam Armitage, and the team in the College of Arts – who supported the Minor Ethics Workshop in 2016, and who have also done so much to support us as scholars and to care for the Guelph philosophy community. We are grateful to all those who attended and participated in the Minor Ethics Workshop – whose comments and questions helped shape the chapters at an early stage – and to all the Guelph Philosophy students who helped organize it with us. We are grateful for the financial support of Social Sciences and Humanities Research Council, which made the workshop possible by enabling us to bring the authors of this volume together to share and discuss their work. We owe so much to the intellectual community fostered by all those who have participated in the City Seminar, and especially to Daniel Griffin, Lindsay Lerman, Jacob Singer, and Sasa Stankovic through their many yeared co-organization. We would also like to acknowledge that an early spark of this project was ignited during the *Difference and Repetition* Reading Group and Workshop at Guelph with Daniel Griffin, Kelly Jones, Susannah Mulvale, and Jacob Singer. Finally, we want to give a huge thanks to Dianne McCullagh for letting us hatch the idea for the volume in her garden with the fresh air, whiskey, and mosquitoes.

Note on References

All references to Gilles Deleuze's major works are included in-text according to the following scheme of abbreviations. We hope this will make reference convenient for those in Deleuze studies and allow general readers immediately to differentiate the concepts in Deleuze's work from those of others that are being read simultaneously. Full citation information for the following works are in the bibliography, with the standard English publications first, followed by the original French publication information. When pagination refers to two pages separated by a slash (e.g. DR, 12/20), it refers to the English/French editions respectively.

WORKS BY GILLES DELEUZE

B	*Bergsonism*
CC	*Essays Critical and Clinical*
D	*Dialogues* (with Claire Parnet)
DI	*Desert Islands*
DR	*Difference and Repetition*
EP	*Expressionism in Philosophy*
ES	*Empiricism and Subjectivity*
KCP	*Kant's Critical Philosophy*
LS	*The Logic of Sense*
N	*Negotiations*
NP	*Nietzsche and Philosophy*
PS	*Proust and Signs*
SPP	*Spinoza: Practical Philosophy*
TRM	*Two Regimes of Madness*

WORKS BY DELEUZE AND FÉLIX GUATTARI

AO   *Anti-Oedipus*
K   *Kafka: Toward a Minor Literature*
TP   *A Thousand Plateaus*
WP   *What Is Philosophy?*

MINOR ETHICS

Toward a Minor Ethics

Casey Ford and Suzanne M. McCullagh

This book is an experiment in the practice of philosophical ethics. Our hypothesis is that there are complex "minor" lines of problems, concepts, and interlocutors that subtend the "major" narrative of ethics in the tradition of Western philosophy. This project is rooted in the innovative spirit of Gilles Deleuze's thought, particularly the idea of philosophy as the "creation of concepts" (WP, 2–6/8–11).[1] Rather than a collection on Deleuze's philosophy itself, this is an attempt to put his philosophical concepts to work, to make them operative as tools of discovery, creation, and variation in the ways we approach philosophical ethics and think about the generation of intellectual narratives. What we want to bring forth with this work is not a new, alternative *system* of concepts and theses that would oppose those of major ethics. Rather we envision a new spirit or practice of thinking that knows that the "creation of concepts" is never *ex nihilo*, but always an implication and inflexion of a long, labyrinthine path of production – in short, a "history" (WP, 17–19/23–5).This experiment is footed firmly in ethical texts with an eye to the vague and the peripheral, to the turbulent and shifting side of decisions, to the messy material from which natures or forms are extracted, and to concepts that move along "lines of flight" away from the demands of systematicity and clarity that come from without – that is, from a plane of organization (TP, 269–70/329–30) that seeks to suppress that which cannot be systematized.[2]

Our Introduction elucidates the theoretical aims of the project of minor ethics. In §1 we outline the significance of the "minor" generally as an element to be analyzed in discourse, systems, and practices, focusing specifically on the examples of language and science. This allows us in §2 to explain why it is imperative to pursue investigations of the minor specifically in the domain of ethical thought. In §3 we outline the practice of reading that guides the different projects of this book and map the sets of thinkers, concepts, and claims that the book develops. The book's "postscript" considers the potential the project has as a perspectival practice for approaching the history of thought.

In *A Thousand Plateaus*, Deleuze and Félix Guattari propose a practice – at once linguistic, aesthetic, and political – for elucidating "minor" lines of thought to challenge "major" narratives, languages, and forms of expression. Rather than regarding the "minor" as the trivial, we differentiate the *minor* and the *major* as two functions or powers to be parsed out in fields ranging from politics to musicology: the minor "power of variation" and the major "power of constancy" respectively (TP, 101/128) (see §1). The minor can be defined as an element or set of elements that introduces variations into a system (of thought, expression, etc.), at once necessary for that system's functioning and resistant to the tendencies toward systemization and rigid organization that systems tend to produce. We take up the "minor" as an experimental practice: a new way of doing and studying ethics, politics, or literature that is attentive to the errant lines of thought that are at once presupposed, occluded, and subordinated by systems of thought that become normative by way of generality, regularity, and a certain force. There is no strict "methodology" of the minor, no rigid system of rules or procedures, beyond an incentive to enliven the divergent lines of thought that are frequently suppressed in the ethical texts we study and teach, and to activate texts and ideas that have been excluded from or downplayed in the Western ethical canon.

The minor is not another version of the major; it is not simply what the major misses, forgets, or ignores. The minor is the dynamic from which the major is derived and which the latter obstructs in establishing a set of norms for thought and action. The minor follows life in all its complexity and variability, while the major represents life systematically and uniformly. We are not proposing a disjunctive choice here between opposed perspectives or principles, but rather a reorientation that will implicate us further in the complexity of concepts: "By making [a] system more flexible," Michel Serres notes, "it is made more complex, more dynamic; it is saved, given life, multiplied."[3] At a certain point, any life faces a "rigor mortis," the stiffening and final sounding of its body before death. Although "ideas do not die" (TP, 235/287)[4] in the same way physical bodies do, perhaps like bodies they too sometimes face a rigor mortis, a kind of ossification that renders them rigid and incapable of movement. Such a state may be prolonged indefinitely, but the "reusability" of a concept, its potential to be reactivated in new "modes," attests to a chance, with the right conditions, to turn in another direction, toward a flexibility that will return it to life.[5]

The chapters in this volume forge engagements and conjunctions between texts in the history of ethical philosophy (both minor or major) and concepts offered to us by Deleuze's work (alone and with Guattari). The goal is to see what these new conceptual configurations can do and produce, and how they allow us to think differently about what ethics is and what thoughts it needs in order to do its work adequately and in more expansive ways. These staged encounters thus aim to amplify *minor* strands of thought within the history of ethical philosophy, to accentuate the conceptual otherness that has often been foreclosed within a certain history of ethical thinking predominant in the Western academy (see §2). Our proposal, following Deleuze and Guattari, is that for any system of thought there are intrinsic lines of inquiry that are incapable of being systematized yet which remain as important conditions and potentials for thinking differently. As we will see, while these elements or concepts have not exactly been included in the official canon of ethical philosophy – for instance, as foci of scholarship and teaching on major thinkers – they are also not excluded entirely from the canon, since they remain nested in major texts and thus indirectly constitutive of the major systems of interpretation that have covered them over. Our concerns are which concepts, problems, and texts in the history of ethics have occupied marginal and obscured positions, and the reasons for these minoritizations. We explore what can happen to our understanding of a text or thinker if there were a shift of focus onto these marginal elements.

This collection is a conjunctive practice for reapproaching the history of philosophy in a theatrical way, as a way of staging conceptual encounters that are not predetermined by a prior system of normative, "canonical" valuation. While the volume is attentive to a fundamentally open set of concepts, there are some that take centre stage: the concept of "affect," which links a subject to a world of formative forces, at once determining and capacitating; of "affirmation," which compels the will to strive for and accept something other than itself, destining yet enriching in possibility; and of "multiplicity," which sees the acting individual in a necessary relation with an assemblage of other beings with common and heterogeneous origins. Yet even this line-up of leading concepts involves a cast of other minor, conceptual relations: the relation of "affective" life with the generation of "habits" and "becomings"; a "will" that, in relation to the conditions of natural necessity, comes to resemble "destiny"; or the "multiplicity" of a collectively human life or "community" of members defined by both identity and difference, inclusion and exclusion. Approaching ethical thought as a "theatre" of concepts (DI, 98/137–38),[6] we propose, reveals it to be more dynamic and complex than traditional academic philosophy may sometimes lead us to believe. If the results are problematic, this is in relation to concepts generated from the problems of life and living rather than merely in the abstraction of thought.

I. THE POWER OF THE MINOR

What does it mean to speak of the "minor"? The proposal to develop a minor ethics will inevitably invoke a sense of the trivial, the insignificant, or what has little interest. The minor might then be seen as what has only secondary importance: as a painter's preparatory sketches set alongside her masterpieces, as a quantitative disadvantage in the cases of electoral mandates or statistical deviations, or as an inconsequential blip in a causal series of historical events. To study the minor side of something thus might be understood as highlighting those elements that do not make a difference as we attempt to grasp the "uniform," "consistent," or "dominant" nature and power of the phenomenon. Whether these values are necessary to, or in fact detrimental for, "rigorous" thought is a central question for us in what follows. Our proposal, following Deleuze and Guattari, is that the minor is not what is most negligible in a system, but rather what is most profound in it.

The concepts of the *major* and the *minor* are introduced by Deleuze and Guattari for the sake of more adequately understanding systems that show distinct tendencies toward "constancy" and "variation" respectively (TP, 101/128). The major and the minor in a given system are therefore not static elements, but dynamic "powers." They involve an analytic difference, but from this it does not follow that they are oppositional in essence or substance; rather, they are mutually implicating and formative forces. While the primary examples that demonstrate this distinction in *A Thousand Plateaus* are drawn from literature, language, music, politics, and science, our proposal is that the terms apply to systems generally: "You will never find a homogenous system that is not still or already affected by a regulated, continuous, immanent process of variations" (TP, 103/130). In short, the minor is not simply the "other" excluded by a major system as such, but rather the other existing *within* a major system. What constitutes the minor are the necessary variables in a dynamic system that major variables exclude, obstruct, diminish, marginalize, or obfuscate in order to make a system appear regular, homogeneous, and unified. Yet by this specific mechanism, the minor elements of a system are what remain unassimilable, ineradicable, and indirectly constitutive of the system itself, even if they lack "official" recognition or endorsement. In this sense, the distinction between the major and the minor, even at its most abstract, is political, that is, a question of power.[7] Before we turn to the question of power more directly, we offer a number of examples to illustrate the term.

The mutually constitutive nature of the minor and the major is most visible in the reality and study of language.[8] On the one hand, language becomes a "system" through the agreement of signs, the establishment of an official lexicon, and the regimentation of grammatical rules. We can call these the "major" elements of a language. These provide a multiplicity of speakers with a common and structurally *constant* medium of communication: the association of words and phrases with understandable meanings, an index of referenceable words, and the intuitively "normal" conjugation of verbs or order of phrases. On the other hand, there is no need for *constants* to be established except in a system that is subject to *variation*. While diachronic- and sociolinguistics study more what the proponents of universal grammar tend to de-emphasize in favour of the universal and structural properties of human language,[9] it is clear that no concrete development of language is closed to the contingencies of local and historical developments, such as geographic and cultural dialects, or to the political formations, identities, communities, and collectives that develop around these variations (cf. TP, 102–3/129–30). We can call these latter the "minor" elements of a language system. While it can be argued that linguistic elements such as dialects and idioms are mere aberrations of a system of rules, it is also the case that no systemization of language would emerge except by transforming a more open or "disorganized" multiplicity of enunciation into a unity of regime.[10]

Yet these minor differences always refer to a major language that, through the power of its systemization, gives differences in speech a universal invariability. When one passes from American slang in Brooklyn to the Queen's English of Buckingham Palace, one does so without leaving the major English that envelops both and thus makes communication possible; understanding will happen even amid sneers and snide remarks. "Constants and constant relations" confer on a system its coherence and unity, but variations subsist and remain irreducible to the regimes of permissible articulation: the twang of the voice, the proliferation of idioms, idiosyncratic phrasing and nominations (idiolects), the enunciations born in palaces and ghettos (sociolects and topolects). Speech remains tied to the earth, to place, to a situation, but each singularity of origin also inclines beyond itself toward a universality that tends to unite differences. We see this irreducibility of minor variations clearly in the innovations of dialects. The point is not that dialects within a single major language are multiple – for instance, when we compare Eastern New England English in Boston to the variety of confluent accents in New Orleans – or that they are simple "deviations," aberrations, or falsifications of a pure mother tongue. Rather, dialects proceed in terms of a process of variation within and of a major language. A dialect is an assemblage of geographic, social, political, and *stylistic* realities that constitute lines of becoming or "flight" even while they are inseparable from a mother tongue. Dialects are veritable creations, innovations, and, in an important sense, *anti-systemic* forms of enunciations; they are "deterritorializations" of language itself.[11] Beyond the scientific prerogative of producing a pure system of language, or the discovery of a universal "grammar" beneath the contingent multiplicity of linguistic styles, at a fundamental level every concrete language presupposes an assemblage of encounters between "heterogeneous" forces and systems.

Québécois well attests to this geohistorical specificity of the dialect and its link to normative, political, and cultural relations of power. While it derives from a major French tongue, it simultaneously puts French into variation with English phrasing and inflections, phonetic speed, and contractions of words, producing an unmistakable variant. Beyond phonetics, to live the reality of Québécois is to know that a "dialect" is not linguistically neutral, but a pejorative employed by speakers of a mother tongue: "You do not have *a language*, you have *a dialect*; you *only* speak Québécois." The result is both a linguistic innovation and a cultural sense of "minorness" and linguistic insecurity.

If dialects involve a "minoritization" of language, it is not simply for the smallness of their specificity compared to a larger standard, but because of the multiplicity of their forms, their capacity to inject variation into a language beyond permissible rules of enunciation, and the normative lack of recognition by a major system. As minor, the position of the dialect is inseparable from modes of cultural and political supremacy.

The struggles between the minor and the major in language are not far removed from those we find in the history of Western philosophy. We know well that philosophy has, at least in large part since its inception, striven toward a common goal of knowledge, just as some contemporary philosophy of science takes unity to be an important ideal for the theoretical explanation of the physical world.[12] Yet these traditions have developed historically through a multiplicity of competing and at times diverging and incommensurable ways of knowing.[13] If Thomas Kuhn's concept of "paradigms" draws our attention to the historicity of scientific knowledge, which involves breaks or shifts (for instance, between pre-Copernican and Copernican astronomy) in incommensurable paradigms of knowing the world,[14] this fact raises a pressing normative or dispositional problem for modern scientific thought. Particularly relevant to us in this regard is Paul K. Feyerabend's diagnosis of the tendency in modern scientific empiricism to enforce a dogmatism that it originally intended to overcome – for example, in orthodox metaphysics[15] – by disregarding any mode of thought that does not conform to what he identifies as two "dogmas" of science: the "consistency condition" and "meaning invariance."[16] Feyerabend contends that the consistency condition, operative arguably in any domain of systematized knowledge, serves to eliminate alternative theories and hypotheses, not because they disagree with the "facts," but because the alternatives disagree with theories that have achieved dominance in a given field, or in our major and accepted terminology by which we conceptualize facts themselves. As such, the requirement of theoretical consistency "contributes to the preservation of the old and familiar not because of any inherent advantage in it but because it is old and familiar."[17] Thus, far from overcoming the dogmatisms that were thought to stunt the progress of scientific inquiry, we see within science itself a "new tyranny" of "facts" and "confirmation" that makes "dogma and metaphysics respectable" and "progress impossible."[18] There is, in short, a "self-deception involved in all uniformity."[19]

Feyerabend's normative proposal is that the scientific mindset should be oriented *toward*, not away from, the different, the dissymmetrical, the inconsistent, and the variant – in short, the minor. Arguing for the significance of the power of the minor in scientific thought and discovery, he ultimately advocates for an "epistemological" or "theoretical pluralism" as "an *essential feature* of all knowledge that claims to be objective."[20] This plurality of knowledges and approaches allows "for a much sharper criticism of accepted ideas than does the comparison with the domain of 'facts' which are supposed to sit there independently of theoretical considerations." He thus advocates for a fundamental procedural openness to *maximally* alternative approaches and hypotheses that are inconsistent with currently dominant theories: "Alternatives will be the most efficient the more radically they differ from the point of view to be investigated."[21] Increasing understanding of the complexity of the world "demands complex procedures and defies analysis on the basis of rules which have been set up in advance and without regard to the ever-changing conditions of history."[22]

This activation of the power of the minor is an antidote to the tendency toward the simplification and unification of ways of knowing the world, a tendency that, rather than improving our knowledge of the world, in fact runs counter to capacities for understanding worldly complexity. Feyerabend argues that the history of science, and scientific ideas themselves, are and ought to be "complex, chaotic, and full of mistakes."[23] Attention to these elements, rather than to theoretical unity and consistency, increases the adequacy or "progress" of thought to and in the world. Knowledge is full of presuppositions that shape and, in Feyerbend's estimation, frequently block our capacity to grasp the world sufficiently in terms of its magnitude of complexity. Such presuppositions need to be critically examined, but, as Feyerabend notes, this leads to a problem: "How can we possibly examine something we are using all the time? How can we analyse the terms in which we habitually express our most simple and straightforward observations, and reveal their presuppositions? How can we discover the kind of world we presuppose when proceeding as we do?"[24] His answer is that we need to confront our familiar ways of thinking with hypotheses and theories that come from outside our established ways of thinking: "We must invent a new conceptual system that suspends, or clashes with, the most carefully established observational results, confounds the most plausible theoretical principles, and introduces perception that cannot form part of the existing perceptual world."

At the fore of the minor and major as analytic and normative concepts is the struggle between the constancies of systems and the diverse forms of otherness that inhere in them. The minor involves elements that propagate and constantly produce variations, that deviate and create while resisting the tendency to be stabilized and homogenized. The minor often indicates something significant even if less dominant within a canon: an openness to the heterogeneity, difference, and contingency that contributes to the formation of things. The "minor works" of an author are customarily less read, though they tend to reveal a process of experimentation, youthful errors and dead ends, the rumblings of creation not yet consummated, and the unripe fruits of later blossoming styles. In music, the function of the minor is more technical but no less revelatory. The major and the minor (scales, keys, chords) refer to different musical intervals, but more consequentially, they also reflect different moods, with the minor producing softer tones and darker, more subdued melodies. The minor thus manifests itself in aesthetic affects beyond mere technicalities or classifications. Politically, the minority signifies a political disadvantage in decision-making and representation that, at certain points in the history of democracy, has been marked as a dimension to social life that must be safeguarded. As the potential target of exploitation or oppression – by elected despots or through the force of social conformity – the minority is a counterforce to what the early American republicans called the "tyranny of the majority,"[25] or to what Deleuze and Guattari call the "state of domination" intrinsic to the form of the major as such (TP, 291/356).

The distinction between the minor and the major, for Deleuze and Guattari, is therefore not merely an analytic one; it is not simply a matter of identifying the varying and the constant as predicates to be attached to respective elements within a system. Rather, the minor is foremost an activity, a power, a tendency toward creation in its own right. In a world confronted by constancy in social, political, and linguistic modes of expression, the minor is a creative resistance *against conformity*: the minor is always political because the political saturates speech no less than the personal affects from which all enunciation emerges. By generalizing the concept of the "minor" from Deleuze and Guattari's idea of "minor literature," we can make the following three points. First, the difference between the minor and the major is not a substantial or essential difference (K, 16/29). Rather, what defines a "minor" practice – be it in literature or ethics – is what a "minority constructs *within a major language* ... affected with a high coefficient of deterritorialization" (K, 16/29, our emphasis). What constitutes a minor expression is the movement an individual or a multiplicity makes in light of and against a major tendency that minoritizes the former in the attempt to establish a system of rules, regimentation, or invariability (of language, behaviour, expression, etc.). What is important for Deleuze and Guattari is the moment of "impossibility" in minor expression. This impossibility is expressed, for instance, in Kafka's attempt to write in German, which distanced him from the Czech and Jewish modes of his expression while simultaneously allowing him to inflect the major German language with minor linguistic valences, that is, to cause it to go beyond its "national" and linguistic "territory" toward new formulations. Ultimately, in situating itself at the threshold of the impossible, the minor is not reactionary but creative; its primary concern is not opposition but rather the creation of new modes of existence and expression.[26] "Becoming is always double" (TP, 305/374). Second, if "everything [in the minor] is political" (K, 17/30), it is because the immanent system of which the minor is an expression, its whole field of possible life, has already been territorialized or been laid claim to politically by a force other than itself (by a nation, a people, a mother tongue, a theoretical system). Third, as a consequence, for the minor "everything takes on a collective value" (K, 17/31). This is especially true if a person or group is marginalized and deprived of a community, since it is here that expression concerns the creation or anticipation of a new community, a "people to come," a "new earth" (AO, 131/155–56, 299, 318–19/355–56, 321/384, 382/458).[27] Minor expression is oriented toward the potentiality of a new world and a new conceptual vocabulary rather than the conformity to a sedimentary one.

We can thus understand the claim that, for Deleuze and Guattari, there is always a "becoming-minor" but never a "becoming-major" (TP, 106/134): this is because "becoming" belongs properly to the minor side of reality, the part of the world that tends toward change, differentiation, or diversification, while the major sediments, ossifies, homogenizes, and represents reality into the "being" of stable, solid, rigid forms. "What is real is the becoming itself, the block of becoming, not the supposedly fixed terms through which that which becomes passes" (TP, 238/291). The task, for Deleuze and Guattari, is to "know how to create a becoming-minor" in opposition to the dream of assuming "a major function in language" (K, 27/50). Doing so entails a commitment to the new, to variation, to becoming.[28]

If every system – ranging from the production of language to the operations of political systems – can therefore be analyzed in terms of its major and minor structures, or through tendencies toward constancy and powers of variation, then our questions are the following: What are the modes of variation that subtend and subsist in the history of ethics? What are the subterranean problems and elements at work in ethical philosophy that cannot be assimilated into the major form of ethics, and why? Are these unassimilable problems not in fact essential to the major ethical inquiries that have relegated them to the margins of consideration and to the depths of a surpassed history? This volume aims to approach the history of ethics in such a way as to bring to life these minor elements that have constituted the study of ethics.

2. MINOR ETHICS

This is not a book about Deleuze's ethics, for there are already several philosophical resources for exploring the difficulties and potentials of reading Deleuze as an ethical thinker.[29] This work explores what happens when concepts, given a certain inflexion by Deleuze's philosophy, are placed into relation with a range of texts and thinkers in the history of ethics: What resonances occur? What problems and questions about ethical life, action, and subjectivity arise? What greater complexity for thought is generated? Which concepts and considerations do and do not work for thinking about ethics? How might we do ethics differently?

Deleuze's concept of "common sense" can help us think about the status of ethics as a philosophical discipline. An exploratory thesis of this volume is that there is a "common sense" about the content and aims of philosophical ethics, just as there are common establishments to the thinking and teaching of schools or traditions of thought generally. This manifests itself in the way we determine ethical problems, establish curriculums of learning, and exclude those problems, questions, materials, affects, ideas, and thinkers deemed extraneous to ethical scholarship. This common sense manifests itself in the classroom, where we might dismiss a student's question about "human nature" because it is "meta-ethical" rather than "ethical," or a question about "social class" as "sociological." Professionally, it manifests itself when a colleague questions our inclusion of a "political" text in a course devoted to the "Introduction to Ethics," or our inclusion of portions of *The Diagnostic and Statistical Manual of Mental Disorders* in a course devoted to "Ethical Theory." In short, there is a certain common understanding of what constitutes the historically sanctioned domain of ethical philosophy, a common sense that maintains the canon of permissible philosophical approaches, texts, and questions on the subject. It is, we contend, the "codification" or systematization of a major tradition of ethics that dictates which questions matter and are necessary to learn: "What is the *good* life? What action *ought* I to perform? To whom am I *obligated*? Is euthanasia a *moral* choice?" However rich these questions are, they refer to an irreducible set of values (the good, the compulsory, the obligatory, the moral), the status, origin, and philosophical weight of which matter and warrant questioning even before they are evoked. Furthermore, when taken in isolation as given, accepted, and constant conceptual values, they inevitably establish relations of codified rivalry: the Platonic "Good" versus Stoic "necessity," deontology versus consequentialism, or virtue ethics versus contractualism. From centuries of rich philosophical inquiry, and from texts mired in the problems of human action in a complex world, is derived a system of concise positions, theses, and principles. To speak of Aristotle is to speak of "achieving virtue," to speak of Kant is to "employ the categorical imperative," to speak of Mill is to "calculate utility," to speak of Rawls is to "invoke a veil of ignorance." In each case, there is an overarching demand for the simplicity of a solution that disavows the complexity of the problem's source: life and the world itself. We maintain that if there is a pedagogical "efficiency" to this approach, there is also a risk of overemphasizing ethical positions and principles that obscure many of the philosophically rich reflections on the conditions and limits of ethical questioning and ethical life contained in the texts from which these positions and principles emerged. Has the study of ethics, as a consequence of this mode of selection, not passed too far from the original conditions of its significance, from the life of its inquiry? How much philosophical and human complexity has been lost or obscured in the texts that serve as the wellsprings of our now canonical theories of ethics?

Where major ethics propagates a common sense about the form, aim, and content of ethics, a minor ethics risks not knowing what everyone is already supposed to know: "it is a question of someone – if only one – with the necessary modesty not managing to know what everybody knows, and modestly denying what everybody is supposed to recognise" (DR, 130/171).[30] Why this emphasis on not knowing what others claim to know in common, on what is "recognized"? While there are clear demarcations between the different theoretical approaches in the major tradition, they nonetheless share certain presuppositions, that is, they share a common sense. For instance, while theories of ethics might offer or appeal to different accounts of human nature, they tend to presuppose a necessary homogeneity of the ethical subject in terms of the attributes of human agents capable of being ethical: rationality, shared affectivity, the capacity to recognize or empathize with like others, and so on. The fact that "everybody knows" that human life and action is the proper focus of ethics is an irreducible common sense of ethical questioning. Rather than focusing attention on the structures and assemblages that give rise to differing cognitive, affective, and dispositional capacities, we find in major ethics an overemphasis on the *human* (at least, on certain conceptions of the human) and the *rational*. This pre-emptively forecloses consideration of the non-human and irrational elements of situations that prompt and shape certain actions rather than others.

It might be objected that the proper domain of ethics applies fundamentally to those beings capable of intending and planning their actions and who can thus be held responsible for them. In the major tradition of ethics we thus see an overemphasis on the individual at the expense of pre- and trans-individual, ecological, and collective dimensions of life, action, and experience. We also see a privileging of what are considered to be purely human capacities (thought, rationality, communication, and calculation) over those capacities that humans share with other beings (desire, affect, becoming). Humans and dogs, for instance, are both capable of being trained; they are both receptive to behavioural modification through disciplinary systems, including but not limited to systems of punishment and reward. The common sense that is operative in major ethics thus risks occluding from view the real affects, desires, capacities, and associations we have with other human, non-human, inorganic, and political beings – associations that are ethically significant and that have the capacity to generate thought. Moreover, it risks ignoring the concrete assemblages (material, social, technological, and linguistic) through which our reality is constituted and which determine the affects, desires, and capacities that structure the meaning our thoughts and actions have in the world. Emphasizing ethics as a solely human attribute, and employing concepts derived from the presupposed form of the autonomous, rational self, thus separates the ethical agent from the world itself. The consequence is an undervaluing of the heterogeneous and problematic origins of ethical agency, and a philosophical simplification of the very subject matters of ethics. We are foremost concerned about the loss of the world in the attempt to render solvable the actions of a constant, intelligible, abstracted subject capable of acting ethically in it.

We thus propose to return ethics to the rich and problematic domain of life from which its inquiry originally drew the force of its significance. If our "minor ethics" echoes Theodor Adorno's *Minima Moralia*,[31] it is precisely in the sense that no philosophy with a fundamental prerogative to the world – as is the case with what has variously been called "ethics" and "morality" – can continue to operate without allowing its form of thinking to be shaped by the world and, most importantly, to reflect critically on this shaping. The question is not how to make thought mirror the world, but how to make theoretical content adequate the problematic shapes of the world it needs to address. The alternative, as Adorno recognized, is dire: "The more passionately thought denies its conditionality for the sake of the unconditional, the more unconsciously, and so calamitously, it is delivered up to the world."[32]

3. THE PRACTICE OF READING THE MINOR

The chapters in this volume engage with texts in the history of philosophical ethics and forge interventions in the ways these texts have been framed, passed on, and canonized in and for the present. These interventions are created by reading thinkers and texts from the history of ethical thought with specific Deleuzian concepts that, the contributors argue, occupy and carve out a minor status in the tradition. The analyses of these historical texts are, in each case, given an inflection by how those concepts are developed in Deleuze's own work. If intellectual history is generally interested in making sense of the ideas of the past as they were held by thinkers in their historical contexts, and if the (philosophical) history of philosophy is oriented more toward engaging with philosophers of the past in terms of present philosophical problems and ideas,[33] then *Minor Ethics* has greater affinity with a philosophical approach to the history of philosophy. However, while *Minor Ethics* takes a philosophical approach to the history of philosophy that renders texts from the past responsive to

the present, it does not necessarily aim to create philosophical conti-
nuity between past philosophical problems and questions and present
ones.[34] The present volume takes an irreverent approach to the history
of philosophy that aims most precisely at questioning and transforming the history of philosophy that has been bequeathed to us in the
present.[35] This volume is guided by the following question: what
minor elements in the history of philosophy (that have been ignored,
silenced, and/or obscured by major narratives) can be amplified, when
assembled with Deleuzian concepts, so that they speak to the present?
We address insights generated by this experimental collective work
in the history of ethical philosophy in the postscript of this volume.

The question of how texts and figures are "paired," in research and
teaching, points to certain assumptions about the nature of texts and
their compatibility. It also has important intellectual and pedagogical
consequences for what we notice and prioritize in texts or between
texts. In short, the reading of a text is determined by the relations and
assemblages in which it finds itself. For instance, reading or teaching
a text like Descartes's *Meditations* within a certain lineage of epistemological thinkers may lead us to ignore certain elements (such as the
"weaker" proofs for the existence of God). The point is that the "primary" materials of teaching and studying the history of philosophy
are texts that are themselves fundamentally assemblages of concepts,
and that the formation of their history entails the complex construction of larger assemblages. Experimenting with new textual assemblages
aims to produce new resonances, different configurations of problems,
and different modes for thinking. A text never stands on its own, and
no text has only one position in a coordinate system of intellectual
history; texts are, in a real and concrete sense, multiplicities. If assemblages "function," it is in relation to a milieu in which any function
may take on a new capacity, meaning, or way of working given the
composition of its field of interaction. Of course, the experimentation
with assembling and reassembling can be inefficacious in its results,
can fail to activate new capacities, or worse, may diminish capacities
for thinking; multiplicities can hook up in haphazard ways, or fail to
connect meaningfully and only sediment the isolation of each. The art
of assembling is never guaranteed to produce new thought, yet the
results can only be determined through the process itself.

A predominant feature of the ethics of reading taught in philosophy
classes is the *principle of charity*: in their study, readers are admon-
ished to attribute to the author of a text the strongest, most coherent

argument possible, that is, regardless of what is actually stated in the text. Such an approach to reading aims foremost to instil in students the capacities to think as robustly as possible about any given argument, even beyond the "historical" limitations of what an author may have achieved. However, there is another consequence of the attempt to be "charitable," as Yitzhak Y. Melamed has argued: it erases the errors and discontinuities of texts in order to present coherent and consistent arguments.[36] A charitable reading of a text works with the assumption that the author would herself want to make the strongest argument possible, that a text should, beyond its historical circumstances, be rendered systematically and uniformly as an integral, functional, building argument. It therefore privileges such a reading over one that would attend to the aberrations, deviations, quirks, and variations that are a dimension of all philosophical texts.

While the principle of charity recommends a method of reading that is undeniably useful in teaching argument analysis and reconstruction, we should be wary of its widespread adoption in philosophical scholarship, for it can also promote a way of reading and thinking that eschews nuance and complexity. "[W]e should consider the possibility," Melamed proposes, "that the internal inconsistency in the text may result from unresolved deliberation by the author."[37] We propose that there is a rich potential for thinking about the products (concepts) of unresolved deliberations that are often dismissed as "errors," "deviations," and "inconsistencies." Rather than attempting to form a coherent whole from a philosophical text that *always* has gaps, discontinuities, tensions, incompatibilities, and surprising statements, one can maintain a vigilant alertness to vibrations and resonances that are activated in the encounter with a text and in the coupling of texts that facilitate the emergence of new questions, new problems, and new trajectories for thinking. Where the principle of charity urges the suppression and explaining away of tensions, gaps, and discontinuities in texts, a minor reading of texts holds, as Serres reminds us, that a "system has interesting relations according to what is deemed to be its faults or depreciations."[38]

There are certainly many ways to read a text – with different procedures, interests, modes of selection – and there is definitely more than one way of reading to be found in this collection. Yet here we would like to emphasize two possibilities when reading a text: one interpretative, the other intensive. The *interpretive* way of reading a text is, Deleuze suggests, to "see it as a box with something inside" and to "start looking for what it signifies" (N, 7/17).[39] Alternatively, the *intensive* "relates a book directly to what's Outside" in a way that makes the book itself "a little cog in much more complicated external machinery," a "flow meeting other flows, one machine among others, as a series of experiments for each reader in the midst of events" (N, 8–9/18). The practice of this work is therefore principally conjunctive rather than explicative. If we aim to reread the history of philosophy here, it is not merely to uncover the truths of texts that have remained hidden or undiscovered, but also to activate their elements in new conceptual assemblages of thinking.

The chapters in this book are organized by way of three conceptual pairings: affect and becoming, repetition and affirmation, and assemblage and multiplicity. Each section opens with a short *intermezzo* that speaks to these Deleuzian concepts and affords opportunities for multiplying the layers of meaning with which the subsequent chapters can be read.

AFFECT AND BECOMING

The constitution of ethical subjectivity is the common element that links this first assemblage of works on Aristotle, Saint Augustine, and David Hume and Adam Smith. Casey Ford (chapter 1) brings together Aristotle's "practical ethics" with Deleuze and Guattari's account of "habituation" and "becoming" to examine the origin of ethics in the concrete constitution of the ethical subject as a habituated, affective being in the world. Through analyses of Aristotle's ideas of the soul, habituation, and the "mean," Ford draws attention to the "inexact" nature of ethical decision making that cannot be determined by way of rational speculation alone; rather, our very capacities for determining the point between excesses are affected by the habits and desires that define us and simultaneously often pull us away from the mean to which we strive. As such, ethical becoming involves that which exceeds rational determination. While Aristotle's ethics is sometimes regarded as seeing "habit" as a "second nature" in the process of becoming virtuous, the ethical self or subject read through the lens of Deleuze and Guattari *is* its habits. Insofar as habits are what Ford calls the "contractions of a world," habits bring that which is other into the constitution of the self. To illustrate this point, Ford draws from the experiences and literature on substance addiction to suggest, for instance, that addiction to opiates occurs at a cellular and not

merely a behavioural level, and thus how withdrawal is experienced
as a withdrawal from one's very self. Ethical consideration and judgment are thus broadened to include attention to the way the world
constitutes the subject's capacities and limitations for action.

This question of the capacity for becoming-different is at the core
of Suzanne M. McCullagh's (chapter 2) reading of Saint Augustine's
Confessions alongside Deleuze and Guattari's concept of the "body
without organs." *Confessions* is, McCullagh argues, fundamentally
an account of the ethical becoming of the self in the world. A theological reading of *Confessions* might emphasize Augustine's experience
of disavowing worldly, embodied, and sensual habits as impediments
to a knowledge and love of, and communion with God. However,
McCullagh makes the case that Augustine shows a profound involve-
ment with the habits of the self, rather than a simple rejection of them,
and she interprets this as a fundamental concern for increasing the
self's capacity for experience, for the process of changing the determinate functions of its organism, and for an expanded openness to
alterity. In these senses, Augustine's account of the self, and his theological account of the "formless matter" from which all beings are
generated, resonates strongly with what Deleuze and Guattari call
the "body without organs." In both cases, McCullagh argues, we see
an interest in the "unformed" or "formless," not as a deprivation of
being, but rather as a greater potential for change and becoming that
may allow us to develop more capacities and relations with the world
of human and non-human others.

The role of habit in the formation of our epistemological, social,
and ethical conventions is taken up by Jeffrey A. Bell (chapter 3),
who draws together the work of David Hume, Adam Smith,
Wittgenstein, and Deleuze and Guattari. Bell appeals to Deleuze to
critique a tendency in the practice of philosophy to presuppose the
nature of the subject who pursues it – to assume that the subject has
an innate capacity and "good will" to seek and discover the truth and
the good. Bell urges us to recognize that classical Empiricists like
Hume and Smith, to the contrary, begin with a conception of the
subject as fundamentally prone to affects like madness, error, suspicion, and disagreement that always risk thwarting the desire to pursue
the true and the good. Rather than making ethical dispositions
impossible, Bell argues, this ground of an affective subject in fact
serves as the basis for the development of many key ideas in major
ethics and politics about customary accords, such as Smith's "impartial

spectator." These concepts are intended not as abstractions of the subject but rather as means to mitigate the errant tendencies that always remain in our potential as humans. Drawing from Deleuze and Guattari's reflections on the role of affect in art, Bell concludes by proposing that a minor ethics should orient our major ethics to the affective nature of subjectivity it presupposes.

REPETITION AND AFFIRMATION

This assemblage of chapters concerns the link between the will's power of *affirmation* in the world and the form of *repetition*. This link between the will's affirmative activity (e.g., to decide, to accept, to consent) and repetition (to do or happen again) may not be obvious. In one sense, the process of repetition may seem antithetical to what we normally call the "will." Ethical decision, it may be asserted, necessarily involves a capacity to decide for oneself freely in relation to both an open set of possible outcomes (to harm or not to harm) and a set of rationally reflected principles or considerations (e.g., will *this* harm produce more *overall* benefit than detriment?). In short, the decision of the will seems to be a power independent of mere repetition, for instance, when a habitual decision simply repeats a behaviour based on custom rather than rational, ethical reflection. Repetition suggests a determinism, a "mechanical" and lifeless process, that would negate ethical capacities for freedom, creativity, affirmation, and the commitment to the new over the repetition of the old. To the contrary, these chapters distinctly show the significance of the process of repetition for values of affirmation, willing, and creativity. They consequently problematize the way we conceive the ethical will in relation to a world in which our will is activated and in which it plays itself out.

Ryan J. Johnson (chapter 4) takes up the tradition of Epicurean atomism to determine which ethical values, and what type of affirmation or disposition toward the world, should be understood as following from a system that sees the physical composition and organization of the world in terms of the movement, collision, and composition of atoms. Through a debate in classicism on the authenticity of the ending of Lucretius's *On the Nature of Things* in the pestilential plague of Athens, Johnson argues that such an ending represents a falsification of the affirmative, creative spirit of atomism. By connecting atomism with the contemporary linguistic procedure of Louis Wolfson, Johnson compels us to re-examine the structure and possibilities of language to act and express in the world, that is, as a repetition of an infinite set of modal elements and relations rather than a finite number of rules and forms for conduct and expression.

This question of the "making of sense" is central to Henry Somers-Hall's (chapter 5) reconsideration of Plato's epistemology and Kierkegaard's call to return "sense" from a transcendent realm of forms to an immanent domain of life. Rather than seeing Plato's theory of sense as grounded simply in the knowledge of "forms" beyond the world of sense itself, Somers-Hall argues that Plato's philosophy takes its point of departure from an ethical and "selective" decision regarding how to determine "claims" to knowledge *within* the worldly immanence of sense itself. To develop the ethical nature of this position, Somers-Hall takes up Kierkegaard's account of time to show that our models of epistemic representation are ontologically secondary to the "ethical stance we take in the face of a world of becoming."

Continuing the study of the relation between ethical decision and the reality of time, Bruce Baugh (chapter 6) closely studies Nietzsche's concept of the "eternal return" as an ethical test of affirmation for the individual when faced with events of a life that problematize this affirmation. Baugh traces the interpretation of Nietzsche's eternal return through Lev Shestov, Benjamin Fondane, and Deleuze to determine whether the ethical demand necessarily entails a submission to necessity and fate, or rather an affirmation of difference and becoming, that is, the return of the world as the eternal repetition of difference itself. Returning the question of the nature of the will to one of its more prominent instantiations in the history of philosophy, Saša Stanković (chapter 7) reads Kant's moral philosophy, specifically the concept of the "categorical imperative," as fundamentally grounded in the critique of "dogmatic moral values" and as a "pragmatic" ethics of the will. The consequence, Stanković argues, is that the will's desire for universality has less to do with the imposition of a set of rules than it does with the freeing of the will from values so that it may become active in the creation of both values themselves and an immanent world in which the will can be actualized.

ASSEMBLAGE AND MULTIPLICITY

In these chapters we find a shared concern with ways of resisting organizations of life and relations that deplete capacities for ethical responsiveness to and engagement with different others. This concern motivates explorations of alternative modes of assembling that arise from the reworking of social and political organizations. When considering the suffering and plight of others, major ethics asks: *what ethical actions are called for?* The chapters in this section, however, shift the locus of consideration to the assemblages that constitute us as beings capable of ethical attention and response. The question becomes: *how can we assemble?* While not eschewing the need for action, these chapters invite us to consider that ethical concern for others involves reworking the assemblages that enable certain encounters and disable others, and which allow some voices to be heard and render others inaudible. The present political tendency toward the management of human life, action, and association is manifest in institutions ranging from factories, hospitals, and universities to national and international political and humanitarian bodies. Loosening, and in moments letting go of, the unified, individualized actor that major ethics requires facilitates awareness of multiplicities that exceed the individual and that are virtual potentials for new forms of association. Creating and experimenting with different forms of association with an eye to enhancing ethical responsiveness is a minor ethical task with a political orientation.

Sophie Bourgault (chapter 8) reads Simone Weil's "politics of attention" through the lens of Deleuze and Guattari's concept of "deterritorialization." This concept helps elucidate the political significance of Weil's suggestion that attention to minor voices requires both a "decreation" of the self and an "uprooting" of the self from homogeneous and hierarchical groups. The capacity to hear and acknowledge minor or marginalized voices is activated in Weil's practice of attention through loosening our majoritarian identities. It is not, however, only the strength of the ego and the identity of the self that need to be worked on in becoming attentive. Bourgault argues that Weil's call for a political practice of attention requires the deterritorializing of majoritarian systems such as political parties and factories. Political parties, Weil thinks, inhibit the hearing of minor voices by calling for party allegiance over justice, promoting homogeneity of thought, and producing toxic passions that nourish intolerance. The excessive "noise" that is produced by our social media environments, Bourgault suggests, is as problematic for the cultivation of attention as the noise generated in the large-scale factories with which Weil was concerned.

Antonio Calcagno (chapter 9) continues the reflection on politics and ethical receptivity by exploring Roberto Esposito's concept of the body and Deleuze's concept of "a life." Calcagno argues that while contemporary regimes of "governmentalization" individualize people and cut them off from what they can do together, the "life of the impersonal" is shared between individuals and resists governmentalized determination. Such resistance is important for the cultivation of ethical responses that are not and cannot be determined by political regimes. When refugees and their allies come together to form a body that appeals to other bodies for help, Calcagno asks us to consider such appeals as appeals for impersonal life, for the recognition and support of indeterminate and transindividual life. Rather than considering such appeals in terms of the provision of resources and the management of populations by governmental regimes, these appeals can call forth new assemblages capable of ethical response.

Simone Bignall (chapter 10) also attends to political assemblages, but with a focus on postcolonial assemblages as means for the ethical communication of differences. She elucidates Aimé Césaire's and Léopold Senghor's ways of envisaging forms of political association in which cultural differences are valued and able to interact free from the constraints of state boundaries and national identities. Difference, Bignall argues, for both Senghor and Deleuze, is not negative or oppositional, but rather a creative power that is part of the potential of different bodies to combine so as to produce more complex bodies with more affective power. The colonial assemblage (in this case, the transnational assemblage of the French Republic), Césaire thought, could be complexified through a reconstruction that would enable equitable participation and bilateral communication of difference. Rather than independence for the colonies, Césaire envisaged alternative forms of transnational assemblage that would maintain different cultures in contact but in a "non-coercive process of shared becoming and individuation."

NOTE ON INTERMEZZOS

An intermezzo exists in between, in the middle, in a space that belongs neither to the before or to the after, to one or to the other, forming a third space of communication or resonance or disjoining. As such, it constitutes another style of thought, another pace and duration of thinking. In them we often find a strange cast of elements, differing in nature from the longer and more dramatic (musical and narrative) works that adjoin them: mythology, comedic routines, quotidian dialects, irreverence, the play of disguises and jest. The intermezzos below were commissioned on the basis of two, and only two, concepts, rather than the chapters or sections between which they mark thresholds. In this sense, their composition is owed to other milieux. If an essay, a chapter, or a book inevitably carves a major territory, the intermezzo is a minor interjection and expression. They do not, for that matter, lack seriousness; their seriousness concerns an outside.

NOTES

1   Deleuze and Guattari, *What Is Philosophy?* Hereafter w p.
2   Deleuze and Guattari, *A Thousand Plateaus.* Hereafter t p.
3   Serres, *The Parasite,* 94. Cf. Paul K. Feyerabend's claim: "Flexibility, and even sloppiness in semantical matters is a prerequisite of scientific progress." "How to be a Good Empiricist," 99. See §2 below for a further discussion of Feyerabend.
4   "Not that [ideas] survive simply as archaisms. At a given moment they may reach a scientific stage, and then lose that status or emigrate to other sciences. Their application and status, even their form and content, may change; yet they retain something essential throughout the process, across the displacement, in the distribution of a new domain. Ideas are always reusable, because they have been usable before, but in the most varied of actual modes" (Deleuze and Guattari, t p, 235/287). For an example of a scientific idea that has been minoritized – denigrated as a "logical," "mechanical," and "physical absurdity" – while also surviving in new forms in modern scientific thought (e.g., in Newtonian or Leibnizian physics, or contemporary subatomic particle theory), see Serres's account of classical atomism in *The Birth of Physics.* See also Ryan Johnson's ethical account of Epicurean atomism concerning this historical problem (chapter 4 below).
5   Deleuze and Guattari note that Kafka's "minoritization" of language, rather than entailing a "poverty of a language" by a Jew from Prague (mixing Czech and Yiddish) against the standards of German literature, takes up a "new expressivity, a *new flexibility,* a new intensity" through which language "*stops being representative* in order to now *move toward its extremities* or its limits." *Kafka,* 23/42 (our emphasis). Hereafter K.
6   Deleuze, *Desert Islands.* Hereafter d i.
7   Feminist and postcolonial theorists have analyzed the operation of exclusionary inclusion whereby women and non-Western subjects are excluded

from Western philosophical rationality by way of inclusions that mark
them as different and inferior, thus bolstering the power of a particular
vision or form of philosophical rationality. In other words, it is not simply
that women and non-Western subjects have been left out of the history
of Western philosophy, but that they are included so that they may be per-
formatively excluded. We find throughout texts in the history of Western
philosophy numerous references to women and non-Europeans who are
represented as less rational and less civilized than the rational male
European subject; these references serve to reinforce the power of a certain
kind of rationality and civilization. For an analysis of how philosophical
ideals of reason were constructed by way of a male–female distinction
and the exclusion of women, see Genevieve Lloyd, *The Man of Reason*.
Two important postcolonial texts that critically analyze the exclusion
of indigenous people's philosophical knowledge from legal and political
discourse are Dale Turner, *This Is Not a Peace Pipe*; and Glen Sean
Coulthard, *Red Skin, White Masks*. For an analysis of the entwinement
of European colonial power and the exclusionary inclusion of non-
Europeans in European discourse, see Edward W. Said, *Orientalism*.

8   For Deleuze and Guattari's own account of the role of power in the formation of language and in linguistics, see "Postulates of Linguistics" and
"On Several Regimes of Signs" in TP.

9   Noam Chomsky defines "universal grammar" as "the system of principles,
conditions, and rules that are elements or properties of all human languages not merely by accident but by [biological, not logical] necessity."
"Reflections on Language," collected in *On Language*, 29. Whether the
development of a primary language can be accounted for solely in terms
of the behavioural contingencies of experience, or rather requires generative structures based in the constancy of human cognition, was the stakes
of the debate between Chomsky and Skinner, which marked the transition
from structuralism to generative grammar in linguistics. For Deleuze and
Guattari's critique of Chomsky, see TP, 7–8/13–14, 12/19–20,
92–110/116–138. For the approach of sociolinguistics, see Louis-Jean
Calvet, *La Sociolinguistique*.

10 The history of the formalization of the French language during the
sixteenth century is particularly telling of a process of moving from the
minor to the major. At stake was the consolidation of a multitude of
diverse regional dialectics into a "universal language" by "royal" interests
of state and cultural consolidation. "The French language of the early
sixteenth century," Freeman G. Henry notes, "viewed inside the realm as
culturally and linguistically inferior to Latin and Greek and outside the

realm as deficient and aesthetically inferior to Italian and Spanish, in less than two hundred years, by dint of similar national resolve and sustained collective impetus, ascended to the status of 'universal language of Europe.'" *Language, Culture, and Hegemony*, 10.

11 "A semiotic chain is like a tuber agglomerating very diverse acts, not only linguistic, but also perceptive, mimetic, gestural, and cognitive: there is no language in itself, nor are there any linguistic universals, only a throng of dialects, patois, slangs, and specialized languages. There is no ideal speaker-listener, any more than there is a homogenous linguistic community. Language is, in Weinreich's words, 'an essentially heterogeneous reality.' There is no mother tongue, only a power takeover by a dominant language within a political multiplicity … A language is never closed upon itself, except as a function of impotence" (Deleuze and Guattari, TP, 7–8/14).

12 Philip Kitcher, "Unification as a Regulative Ideal."

13 Feminist epistemology has developed a significant body of work that demonstrates how multiple ways of knowing have been covered over or erased by dominant forms of knowledge that claim universality, value neutrality, and objectivity. Against assertions of the universality of knowledge, feminist epistemologists foreground knowledge as a contested site of struggle and multiplicity. For just two of several examples, see Donna Haraway, "The Science Question in Feminism"; and Lorraine Code, "Taking Subjectivity into Account," in *Women, Knowledge, and Reality*, 192. Charles W. Mills analyzes the "whiting out" of black perspectives in the development of conceptual and theoretical knowledge in "White Ignorance."

14 For Kuhn, these changes of paradigm are shifts not merely in the content of empirical observations, but also in the conceptual structures of systems themselves (i.e., in the theoretical suppositions about the nature of the world). Thus, for Kuhn in *The Structure of Scientific Revolutions*, it is untenable to hold on to a purely major, constant, and universal system of knowing that has been developing linearly and progressively throughout history, since any system refers necessarily to other minor paradigms that precede it and make it possible.

15 Feyerabend, "How to Be a Good Empiricist," 78–9.

16 Ibid., 83–5.

17 Feyerabend, *Against Method*, 25.

18 Feyerabend, "How to Be a Good Empiricist," 78–9.

19 Ibid., 94.

20 Ibid., 78–80; *Against Method*, 10–11.

21 Feyerabend, "How to Be a Good Empiricist," 81.

22 Feyerabend, *Against Method*, 10–11.

23 Ibid., 11.

24 Ibid., 22–3.

25 The notion of the "tyranny of the majority" developed from James Madison's cautions in "Federalist Paper 10" (1787) regarding a potential "violence of a majority faction" (Hamilton et al., *Federalist Papers*, 41–7), to John Adams's coinage of the phrase proper in 1788, and popularized in later works such as Edmund Burke's *Reflections on the Revolution in France* (1790) and John Stuart Mill's *On Liberty* (1859).

26 "In a sense, all signification takes place within the orbit of the compulsion to repeat; 'agency,' then, is to be located within the possibility of a variation on that repetition. If the rules governing signification not only restrict, but enable the assertion of alternative domains of cultural intelligibility, i.e., new possibilities for gender that contest the rigid codes of hierarchical binarisms, then it is only within the practices of repetitive signifying that a subversion of identity becomes possible." Butler, *Gender Trouble*, 185.

27 Deleuze and Guattari, *Anti-Oedipus*. Hereafter A O.

28 For Deleuze and Guattari, a "minority" is not defined against a "majority," for instance, as the smallness of a sum (of people or identities) existing in relation to a larger body that outnumbers. What defines the "minoritarian" is their innovative and problematic capacity in relation to majoritarian tendencies. As Jay Lampert notes, "[m]inorities create 'innovations' as 'problems' that cannot be resolved on any terms whatsoever; they are the human material of instability ... The problem is not whether or not a minority is integrated into an axiomatic; the point is that the minority always creates '*another* co-existing struggle' [TP, 471/588]. The logic of co-existence is that as soon as a regime signs a compromise deal with a minority, the minority splits off into factions that refuse to comply ... In short, the challenge of the minority is that 'it is the formula of multiplicities' [TP, 470/588]." *Deleuze and Guattari's Philosophy of History*, 167–8.

29 Among those thinkers who assert the ethics in Deleuze's thought, there is general agreement that it is different from traditional approaches in that it reinvents the concept of normativity, redeploying it as "immanent" rather than "transcendent" and rendering it "pragmatic" rather than "theoretical." In short, these readings concern the critique and transformation of norms rather than what norms ought to be followed; see Nathan Jun's "Deleuze, Values, and Normativity" in Jun and Smith, *Deleuze and Ethics*, 101. For an excellent account of the situation of Deleuze's ethics in the history of philosophical "immanence," see Daniel W. Smith's "The Place

of Ethics in Deleuze's Philosophy" in ibid. Rather than telling us what to
do or how to live, Deleuze's ethics facilitates new modes of affecting
and being affected; see Simone Bignall, "Affective Assemblages." For an
account of Deleuze's ethological ethics, attentive to the affects and capacities of creatures, that pushes ethics beyond the traditional concern with
the exclusively human and rational, see Keith Ansell Pearson, *Germinal
Life*. For the political element and its relation to subjectivity, see Braidotti,
"Nomadic Ethics."

30 Deleuze, *Difference and Repetition*. Hereafter DR.

31 Adorno, *Minima Moralia*.

32 Ibid., 247.

33 While the terminology differs, this distinction between two modes or orientations toward philosophical texts in the past is addressed by a range
of scholars concerned with how the history of philosophy should be done.
Richard Rorty, J.B. Schneewind, and Quentin Skinner differentiate
between two ideal types of thinkers interested in the history of ideas: the
intellectual historian, and the philosopher interested in the history of philosophy; *Philosophy in History*, 5. While they acknowledge that no one
can entirely embody either type, they maintain that this general typology
facilitates the recognition of differing orientations and sets of concerns.
The intellectual historian is concerned with understanding the historical
context in which the author wrote and thus understanding the meaning of
his texts within his historical and cultural milieu, whereas the philosopher
approaching the history of philosophy is interested in understanding the
relevance of past thinkers in order to present philosophical problems. This
broad characterization of two different orientations is echoed by Mogens
Lærke, Justin E.H. Smith, and Eric Schliesser in their characterization of
"contextualists" who study the history of philosophy "for its own sake
and on its own terms" and "appropriationists" who look to the history of
philosophy as "a source of ideas and arguments that may be of use in current philosophy." *Philosophy and Its History*, 1. Michael Frede also recognizes this broad distinction but names the philosophical approach to the
history of philosophy as part of a "doxographical" tradition, stating that
"from Aristotle onward, there have been philosophers who have studied
the history of philosophy for philosophical reasons. They were interested
in philosophical views or positions of the past, because they thought that
at least some of them were still worth philosophical consideration."
"History of Philosophy as a Discipline," 666–8. While Frede claims not to
object to the "philosophically oriented study of the history of philosophy
in the doxographical tradition," he is concerned that this kind of history

of philosophy "which imposes our philosophical views and interests on the history of philosophy, ultimately presupposes the second kind of history of philosophy, i.e., a study of the history of philosophy in its own right, on its own terms, quite independently of our philosophical views, interests, and standards."

34 Alasdair MacIntyre, "The Relationship of Philosophy to its Past," 45.

35 In this regard, the approach of this volume shares with feminist philosophical work in the history of philosophy the concern that the history of philosophy, as it is canonically constructed, is problematic and that reinterpreting texts in the history of philosophy can change their relationship to the present by activating different elements in the texts than those given to us by history. See Cynthia A. Freeland, "Feminism and Ideology," 365–7.

36 Melamed, "Charitable Interpretations," 260.

37 Ibid., 275.

38 Serres, *The Parasite*, 13.

39 Deleuze, *Negotiations*. Hereafter N.

Affection and Becoming

Leonard Lawlor

Both emotions and affections are passive experiences, experiences
that come over us. However, while emotions seem to be based on
an already formed subject or character, affections seem to be part
of the latter's formation. For example, one feels fear (an emotion)
in the face of a consequence that will negatively affect one's goals
and ambitions without destroying them. In contrast, one may feel
pain (an affection), especially an intense pain, that seems to unravel
all goals and ambitions. If one survives the pain, the experience
leads one to transform who one is: to become otherwise. It is affection, which seems to be a kind of super-passivity – not passivity felt
in relation to a thing but rather, as Deleuze would say, a passivity
in the face of "the being of the sensible" (DR, 140) – that really
opens the way for genuine thinking and for thinking-otherwise,
that is, thinking other than the ways we have been trained to think.
How do we truly reach genuine thinking and thinking-otherwise?
Since Plato's *Protagoras*, we have defined thinking as interior
monologue. Generally, we experience our everyday monologue as
a pleasant experience. However, if we examine the experience more
closely, or better, "deconstruct" it, as Derrida would say, we see
that the relation between me speaking to myself and me hearing
myself is a non-identical relation. Time and space, an interval and
a distance, separate me from myself. Even more, we see that the me
speaking is unable to identify itself with the me hearing. The inability to make the identity happen is a kind of super-passivity, and this
inability results in pain. But it is only through the pain of another
within me that I reach genuine thought. It is only through the pain
of another in me that I can suffer with the pain of others outside of

me (com-passion). Then, not only am I now really thinking-otherwise, but also I will be motivated (by the affection of pain) to act otherwise. We must add one more comment. Becoming-otherwise is a becoming that is non-teleological. There is no model toward which the becoming approximates; there is no stopping point. Becoming is therefore interminable. And if we are constantly being driven to change because of the painful experience of separation, then the real feeling we are undergoing in thought is mourning.

The Affective Milieu of Ethical Life in Aristotle and Deleuze

Casey Ford

Never fail to ask thyself this question ... What relation have I to this part of me they call the ruling Reason [ἡγεμονικὸν]? And whose soul have I got now? The Soul of a child? Of a youth? Of a woman? Of a tyrant? Of a domestic animal? Of a wild beast?

Marcus Aurelius

[The] appetite for pleasures, which is very strong and grows by being fed, can be starved ... if the body is given plenty of hard work to distract it.

The Athenian, Plato's Laws

Nothing straight can be constructed from such warped wood as that which man is made of.

Immanuel Kant

A central insight of Aristotle's ethics is that ethical problems and norms are grounded in the concrete nature of the human being rather than in abstract and speculative terms removed from the messiness of life. Ethical decisions are a concern precisely because we are human, and it is the form of humanity that provides the normative measure for "virtuous" conduct.[1] Our question is what ethics entails when it begins, as it does with Aristotle, from the ground of life and being in the world? In one sense, there is something major to Aristotle's thought insofar as the diverse considerations he offers about ethical life are measured in terms of the human "form." In another sense, the process of achieving "virtue" (ἀρετή) – that is, of fulfilling and actualizing a fully human life – is possible only through a complex process of habituation. Habituation presupposes, we will argue, a heterogeneous and differential self that is worked on and fashioned in and through a world that is fundamentally more than human.

Emphasizing this minor dimension to ethical determination in Aristotle's thought allows us to appreciate how major ethical norms are realized through – and limited by – a pragmatics of life, desire, and embodiment. By reading Aristotle's *Nicomachean Ethics* from the perspective of its second book on habit formation,[2] this chapter situates ethical judgment in terms of what Aristotle calls the "practical" and what Deleuze and Guattari call "pragmatics" as an "experimentation in contact with the real" (TP, 12/20). The wager of this chapter is that the primacy given to "affect" and "becoming" in Deleuze's work can allow us to see a deeper and more challenging dimension to Aristotle's own "practical" ethics in which worldly habituation is an essential ethical activity rather than a nature that is secondary to the more primary form of being human.[3] We thus aim to push Aristotle's insightful premises about life to some of Deleuze's consequences.

In the intersection between Aristotle and Deleuze, the sections of this chapter make four sets of claims. (1) The "practical" ethics conceived by Aristotle hinges on a conception of human nature that is realized and analyzable only in the context of a living and temporal world. (2) The ethical development of the self toward virtue requires a logistical deliberation in its habitual life among the heterogeneous forces constitutive of who we are in our desire. The guiding principle or "mean" of ethical judgment is thus oriented in terms of bodily and affective situations. (3) While Deleuze's thought also takes the habituated body, as a contraction of differential elements, as its ontological point of departure, it also extends the domain of habit significantly beyond the human actions in which Aristotle locates it. Here we raise the issue of the experience of addiction as a way of problematizing the models of the atomistic individual and autonomous choice in ethical action. (4) Deleuze's conception of "becoming" effectively reverses the priority of form over becoming that we find in Aristotle. Consequently, the goal of ethical life ceases to be the perfection of a particular form of life and becomes the experimentation on and production of new forms of life. Deleuze and Guattari thus redefine the normative principle of the "middle" as a "milieu" of ethical interaction rather than a "mean" of moderation. This reversal, we argue, creates the condition for an expansion of ethical values.

I. ARISTOTLE AND AN ETHICS FOR LIFE

What Aristotle designates as "ethics" (ἠθικός) is a field of study that "does not aim at theoretical knowledge like the others,"[4] for instance, in the way the thought of a triangle's geometric properties can remain indifferent to the imprecision of physical bodies or the use-value of geometry. Rather, ethics is concerned with the "actions" and "states" of being human in the world.[5] As Aristotle cautions, "we are inquiring not in order to know what excellence is, but in order to become good, since otherwise our inquiry would have been of no use."[6] Our aim in this section is to frame the central insights of Aristotle's ethical thought in terms of its existential and practical bases. We show how, for Aristotle, ethical judgment emerges from, and intends to remain concerned with, the complex situation of human life.

If the vital and practical development of human life forms the special object of ethical inquiry, it is because human nature is foremost the site of a problem: the "goodness" we seek is not a mere predicate or given of our nature but rather a task to be accomplished.[7] Insofar as an ethical state is something we aim to achieve, it is not something we already possess or are guaranteed to achieve. This makes us different from beings or events in the world that can be explained in terms of constitutive or efficient causality.[8] For instance, the glass's fall downwards can be accounted for by the factors of weight, trajectory, and gravity, or by the external impact of the errant hand that sends it off the desk (*primum movens*). Yet the course of a human being's life – and the life of the species through which its individual existence is brought to fruition – is irreducible to mere causal determinations. Human beings are not simply determined by an extrinsic state of affairs; we have a defining capacity to act, decide, and deliberate between possibilities, and this capacity offers us a world and a self to be arranged and fashioned rather than terms to which we must resign ourselves. Yet while ethical thought allows us to investigate the principles by which we should act and behave in a world, and thus become different than we are, it does so in relation to a world that is not wholly our own. Ethics allows us to step beyond the actuality of existence by seeing that human life is oriented toward a future in each moment of decision, toward unrealized possibilities to which we are answerable and through which we will accomplish what it means to be ourselves. Yet as we will see, the paradox of the ethical self is that of a living actuality oriented to its *own* indeterminacy, which is determinable through the principles of its own nature.

Every being – or what Aristotle designates as "substance" – strives to bring into "actuality" the form constitutive of itself and that at its inception is only a potential to be realized or not. In fact, this "movement" of "becoming"[9] is ultimately what it means to "be."[10] For instance, it would be inadequate to take the child in its present moment of crying as a finalized reality that simply "is," since the cry is both the result of a preceding, efficient cause (e.g., the withdrawal of the mother's breast) and the anticipation of a future state of relief or calming (the return of sustenance). The "being" of a reality must take into account the complex causal logic whereby something "is" only in its multi-causality; a sapling is thus "caused" both by the insect that carried its seed to the place of growth and by the constitutive teleology that determines its development into a maple rather than an oak tree.[11] In short, explaining any reality must take into account how something becomes different in the course from rudimentary state, through the contingencies of an environment, toward the "actuality" of maturation.

Two points in Aristotle's insight about the nature of things are of interest here. First, the analysis of living things must take up the temporality in which life unfolds.[12] If personal, physical, and social histories concern the past development leading to the determinacy of who we are in the present, ethics is one type of concern with what we may and should become beyond our present self. While the ethical prescriptions regarding any decision indicate a certain determinacy about a possible life that will follow, the disjunction between the present moment of decision and its future outcome retains a certain indeterminacy; drought may prevent a sapling from partaking the nourishment it needs to become a tree just as much as the contingency of a situation may send a human life to a place where prior plans and aspirations are stunted or forfeited. In this sense, Aristotle cautions us not to treat the "subject-matter" of ethical life within a theoretical framework that demands "exactitude," since "matters concerned with conduct and questions of what is good for us have no fixity, any more than matters of health."[13] Second, like organic life, ethics recognizes that individual reality is possible as an existence only through a complex and vital interaction with its world.[14] Something can be said to be living only to the extent that it relates to and exists through an environment of otherness as the conditions of its being.[15] For ethics to inform the practical life of the individual, it must thus consider the constitution of the person (its "character") in this physical and social space.[16] In short, ethics must begin with the condition of life in the same gesture that it expands and makes human life possible.

If one existential side of ethical thought is oriented toward the indeterminacy or openness of something's environment and future, it is also determinatively guided by a principle endemic to the human being that strives to realize itself. For Aristotle, the study of ethics requires, first, that we apprehend the appropriate "end" of ethical activity, and second, that we examine the nature of the thing to which ethical judgments apply and for which they have meaning.[17] Our understanding of Aristotle's ethics is clear on this first point: the chief and supreme end – that is, the principle and "human good" that should guide the development of our character in its worldly becoming – is determined and measured by our own nature. What is designated by "happiness" (εὐδαιμονία) is thus "the activity of the soul in conformity with excellence."[18] Just as the excellence of the hammer is determined by its ability to "hammer" well, human life excels ethically by realizing what it means to be and do itself. Yet given the functionally complex nature of what a human life entails, the ethical determination of an individual life requires more than something like a unifunctional tool. The state of happiness is thus "the best and most complete" insofar as it reflects the holistic demands of a human life, and not merely one of the many (personal, occupational) ends we may pursue to the detriment of others; "one swallow does not make a summer,"[19] and in the same way, one determinate goal does not make a human life. Thus, for Aristotle, it is not simply a matter of realizing something like a leisurely "contemplative life" of the mind at the expense of the degeneration of physical health, familial or civic obligation, or artistic sensibilities. There is a demand for holism in Aristotle's thought precisely because human life is not reducible to a simple, homogeneous essence or activity. Its "function" is "fulfilled" through a balance of a multiplicity of needs and capacities.

The problem at the heart of the opening chapter of Aristotle's *Ethics* is twofold: to recognize human nature's complex and shared constitution with the non-human world while also identifying the singular, defining capacity of the human soul. The problem with identifying the humanness of the soul is that a significant portion of the soul's activity involves both an organic life and a perceptual one. For all the given diversity of the natural world, with its plethora of species and functions, the human soul finds a profound complicity with nature. The bodies of the human swimmer, the galloping racehorse, and the spreading vine are all individually and distinctly encased in similar layers of material flesh – skin, muscle tissue, plasma, functionally analogous membranes and fluids – and organized in ways that facilitate the common task of surviving and growing. To develop we must extend beyond ourselves to acquire, consume, and metabolize the organic material of an exterior world that sustains us. Furthermore, Aristotle notes that for both rational and non-rational animals, these organic elements and processes are indissociable from perceptual experience.[20] Thus we do not simply consume the material world; we also smell and taste it, just as our capacity to move and navigate our environments is made possible by sight and touch. The domesticated dog, in the home no less than the forest, charts the course of its body based on discovered and placed scents – a veritable cartography of sense – just as humans choose things to engage based on their perceptual qualities. In short, there is no singularly human life without the being material of an organic body or the being perceptual of an experiencing subject. Yet the essence of the human cannot be reduced to these parts of the soul, since they also define the capacities of different forms of life.[21] Rather than formally distinguishing the body from the soul in terms of substance,[22] Aristotle recognizes that the form of the human soul must be grasped as a multiplicity of formally distinct but vitally holistic elements integrated into a single, moving life.[23] There are two important points to note before we move in §2 to define this complex constitution and situation of human nature more precisely.

First, if the human being were reducible to its changing body, or to its capacity to passively perceive the effects of other bodies upon its own, there would be no capacity for ethical consideration. Life would be fully determined by the material situation in a world, and consciousness would be no more than a registration of effects.[24] What is needed is a principle of decision. Second, what Aristotle identifies as our "rational principle" (ἐπιπειθὲς λόγῳ) and defining human essence[25] is precisely our capacity to act or make decisions in the world in conjunction with a thought capable of standing apart from, and deliberating about, the quality of decisions themselves. Ethics concerns practice or action rather than mere knowledge, and when the study of it involves a kind of knowledge (as it does in the knowing of human nature), this is precisely to enable ethical action. "Thought by itself moves nothing; what moves us is goal-directed thought concerned with action," and this is why "decision is either understanding combined with desire or desire combined with thought; and this is the sort of principle that a human being is."[26] What should be emphasized here is the necessity of "combination," the conjunction of thought and desire, or what Deleuze, below, will call "contraction." Decision extends us beyond mere determinacy, suspending us in a present defined by a multiplicity of potential outcomes. In this sense, for Aristotle, it demands a logistical deliberation that combines "desiderative thought" with "intellectual desire."[27] The converse relation expressed in these formulations serves to make a crucial point about both the nature of ethical inquiry and its subject matter. Ethical judgment does not originate beyond or stand apart from the embodied reality of desire to which it is subsequently applied, as a despot might arbitrarily impose obligations on an unruly population. Nor does desire present a reality substantially irreverent to intellectual thought. The relation between thought and desire is one of mutually implicated capacities of the same moving, growing reality. Desire reaches outside itself insofar as it is informed by a thought that is irreducible to external stimulus, and thought is incited in its activity by a desiderative motive itself. When I desire food or drink, it is never as a mere mechanism; the desire is always conjoined with the anticipation of satisfaction, body images and plans, or the indecision concerning the efficacy of the act itself. Conversely, no thought, however abstract, occurs without a motive power that compels it further in its intellectual activity (whether it is a desire for intellectual credentials or the need for a solution). Yet desire and rationality still represent distinct capacities despite the way they mutually inform and implicate each other. Human life becomes both distinct and alive in this problematic moment of mutual dependence and adjustment between capacities that assert a simultaneous difference and identity.

For Aristotle, ethics is an essentially *practical* discipline whose primary concerns are the nature, parameters, and ends of action. Aristotle reminds us, in a paramount passage, that knowledge of the "supreme goods" serves to have a "great practical importance *for the conduct of life*."[28] But more importantly, ethics is meaningful in this endeavour because it is situated at this nexus in which the desires and thoughts of a being enter into an existential encounter, as at once

confluent faculties of a single organism and antagonists in a battle
that is a life that can live only by becoming different than it has been.
Since ethical thought itself emerges from and is activated by desire,
it is necessary to consider the field in which embodied, desiderative
life operates.

2. THE MEAN AS THE LIVED, VOLATILE MIDDLE

By virtue of the physical and living environment from which the human
organism draws both its sustenance and its fragility, the soul essentially
involves more than human reality. The human soul entails a duplicity.
On the one hand, we require the acquisition and metabolizing of
foreign material in order to simply be the organisms that we are. On
the other hand, Aristotle draws our attention to the fact that the holism
of the human organism is defined by more than propriety, coherency,
and unity: the organism is itself the site of a differential and antagonistic relation in which our very bodily and desirous life is other than
the intellectual processes that attempt to guide it. In short, ethics
pertains to a life, and as we will see, life can go awry. The differential
relationship between the principle of ethical striving and its embodied
enactment means that ethical judgment is necessarily situational and
relational.[29] In this section we will consider how Aristotle concludes
from these insights that the achievement of ethical virtue is a "mean"
of activity, and how the required habituation is, for reasons endemic
to human nature, difficult to achieve. But on what precise aspect of
our being does our rational capacity come to bear?

Just as it is meaningless to speak of "governance" except in relation
to something that is regarded as needing to be "governed" or managed
differently than it is inclined to behave, there can be in the soul a
"rational principle" (λόγος) or capacity only insofar as there is also
present in the soul something to manage or bring into conformity
with this principle. Aristotle thus recognizes that the soul is constituted
by a tension between different tendencies. However, Aristotle notes
an important complication when analyzing the human body that runs
counter to a basic dichotomy between the rational mind and the
irrational body. On the one hand, the organic body operates by its
own laws. Just as the rock cannot be habituated to stay in the air by
repetitive tossing,[30] neither can the physical processes of the body
(the beating heart, the reproduction of cells) be trained to operate
differently than determined by their own natures. Just as "in the body

we see that which moves astray" from our capacity to determine it, "in the soul too there is something beside reason [λόγος], resisting and opposing it [ἄλογος]."³¹ Aristotle distinguishes further that in the a-logical or "irrational elements" of our being (ἄλογος) there is that which "in no way shares in reason" (the "vegetative") and that which importantly has the capacity to listen to and thus be guided by principled reflection (the "appetitive").³² Strictly speaking, it is not that the vegetative elements of the soul lack function or purpose, but rather that they are incapable of being persuaded to act contrarily: no amount of argumentation or habituation will get the heart to stop pumping blood throughout the circulatory system. The vegetative can be externally affected by decisions effected upon the body – as when the consumption of excessive amounts of cholesterol increases the stickiness of the blood, leading to plaque accumulation and a stroke or stoppage of circulation. However, it cannot be incited to change internally and of its own accord; it is thus purposive while being deaf to the power of persuasion. Rather than being a mere contemplative capacity to think the world, the rational (λόγος) functions as a principled or regulative power of the a-logical that moves our bodily and appetitive life. We are thus defined by a complex organic and appetitive existence that does not reflexively think or regulate itself but that can nonetheless *by its nature* be brought into conformity with and *obedience to* rational judgments. The appetitive is grounded in organic processes (as hunger is by digestion), but it is by nature malleable and persuadable. Insofar as desire constitutes an intermediary between the rational and the vegetative, desire is thus the site of ethical and rational governance. Yet as we will see for Aristotle, desire presents a power of operating in the world of its own accord if principles fail to habituate it toward proper ends.

For Aristotle, virtue is neither a static predicate of our nature nor a guarantee that our characters will achieve such a state. "Moral excellence comes about as a result of habit [and] none of the moral excellences arises in us by nature; for nothing that exists by nature can form a habit contrary to its nature … Neither by nature, then, nor contrary to nature do excellences arise in us; rather we are adapted by nature to receive them, and are made perfect by habit [τελειουμένοις δὲ διὰ τοῦ ἔθους]."³³ Habit is not contrary to our essence, but rather designates the extrinsic development of our character through growth to a point of "completion." Yet the scope of habits of which we are composed is extensive and modulating. Conditions of health require

physical habits of diet and exercise, while communicative and intellectual tasks require habits of thinking and study. The physical and
cognitive aspects of our being are united by our capacity to grow
through habituation, education, and training, and they are also cut
through by habits of desire that integrate our life with a world of
projects, distractions, aspirations, failures, and growth. On their own,
habits do not entail states of ethical excellence: a habit is only as good
as a principle that guides it, and a principle is only efficacious insofar
as it can apprehend the complexity of a body's situation, inclinations,
and needs. Behavioural habits may lead to sickness, and to stunted
capacities for action and thought, and in extreme cases they may
render us more akin to vegetative existence (the "couch potato") than
to a philosophically and culturally capacitated member of the world.
Yet it is only through habituation that we can achieve a state of virtue
and become anything more than unformed potential; it is through
developing new habits that we pass from inadequate states of being
to adequate and fuller ones. Habit is not blind mechanism, but a vital
adjustment and adaption to a world as the condition of existence.[34]

The goal of ethics, for Aristotle, is not simply to determine which
habits we should acquire, as if it was a matter of choosing intellectual
or spiritual desires over those of the body. The prior task is to understand the existential situation of human desire itself and the necessary
logistical means for navigating the field of forces in which an embodied
life is always entangled. Aristotle's famous formula here is a strongly
normative and deceptively simple one: in any activity, we should strive
to reach a "mean" or "intermediary" state. "Thus the master of any
art avoids excess and defect, but seeks the intermediate and chooses
this."[35] What is the nature of an ethical mean in relation to desire?
Mathematically, the mean designates the point of a line segment that
is equidistant from the endpoints. There is thus no middle point
without opposed extremes, and every relation between extremities
entails its own intermediary. In terms of activity, the mean approximates a degree that is neither *too much* (eating till the point of
engorgement) nor *too little* (starvation). Despite their opposition (e.g.,
between a deficiency or excess of food), the extremes lead to a common state of inadequacy marked by sickness, while the intermediary
point promises the opportunity for nutrition, energy, and growth.

Despite the simplicity of this formula, Aristotle notes further that
the intermediate of ethical activity, as it pertains diversely to the decisions of life, is "not *in* the object but relatively *to us*."[36] This point

complicates the *exactitude* of ethical determination for two reasons. First, the intermediate for any given activity cannot have the character of a generalizable rule, precisely because the intermediary is not determined by the object or activity itself. The point of moderation, for instance, does not inhere in the food one consumes; there is no predicate in alcohol that denotes a point of excess. The intermediary and its precise extremities are constituted in the relation between the body of the consumer and the organic world to be metabolized. The points of moderation or excess are determined by the quality and power of the situated body and will thus vary between bodies of different constitutions in the way that the necessary food to sustain the power of a swimmer's body will be quantitatively greater than that for a writer. In a similar vein, the habituation or acclimation of an alcoholic's body to the quantity of alcohol can diminish or delay the behavioural manifestation of drunkenness in comparison to those of unaccustomed bodies. While quantity is an important component for judging the intermediary point of an action, it is significantly relative to the quality of the embodied and affective life at the agentive centre of the activity.

Second, while the terminology of the mean suggests a mathematical exactitude, it is not a mathematical concept (at least not in the logic of Euclidean geometry). The mean is a dynamic concept, a fluxion of habituated and vital life. The mean is determined not simply by physical need, but by the complex desires that activate our bodies in the world. Our desires are constituted in part independently of norms of excellence, by habits that push and pull our decisions toward and away from things. Aristotle thus notes that "it is no easy task to be good. For in everything it is no easy task to find the middle ... Hence he who aims at the intermediate must first depart from what is the more contrary to it ... We must consider the things towards which we ourselves also are easily carried away ... We must drag ourselves away to the contrary extreme; for we shall get into the intermediate state by drawing well away from error, as people do in straightening sticks that are bent."[37] Aristotle's crucial insight here is that if rational reflection (thought, cognition, understanding) were sufficient to recognize the location of the mean, then an adequately rational agent could achieve virtue simply by knowing the state to be achieved, in the way a satellite might triangulate a destination. This procedure, however, is problematized by the fact that ethics is a conjunction of both knowing and desire as quasi-independent faculties. Our very capacity to determine the intermediary point occurs while always being affected by inclinations away from it.[38] The decision to eat more moderately must be made simultaneously with the hunger to consume excessively, and the mean must function as a counterforce to this excess by which we are affected. Thus the point of departure for the journey to virtue is one that is affected by the state of being capacitated or debilitated by extremes. Hence Aristotle's point that, rather than approximating the mean directly, it may often be necessary to overshoot the mean, to aim for a contrary excess, as a way of counteracting the excess one is.[39] Like the alcoholic who quits "cold turkey" rather than by immediate moderation, one tries to straighten the warped, habitual self by pulling it not to a position of straightness, but rather far away from the inclination of the warp.

If our primary nature involves the capacity for intellectual coordination and end-oriented development, then this nature plays itself out always in relation to desires that affect us independently of our capacity to coordinate them. From inception to maturation, we are a plexus of habits and desires held together or contracted by the embodied soul. We may experience certain needs, habits, and behaviours as foreign to us to the extent that they present us with undesirable or harmful tendencies, but they are nonetheless apprehended negatively only by virtue of being modulations of the self that we have become, that we sustain, and that we anticipate the possibility of augmenting. Practical ethics must thus be an ethics of embodiment, since, as Aristotle notes importantly in *On the Soul*, "all the affections of the soul involve a body – passion, gentleness, fear, pity, courage, joy, loving, and hating."[40] The "concurrent" unity of affections that condition our actions and body means that both ethics and the "study of the soul" must be "enmattered accounts" and thus "must fall within the science of nature." Changing desire requires changing the habits that have sedimented our choices and actions. Ethics opens us to the possibility of becoming something other than determined by a finite set of affections. It is insufficient to oppose thought to desire as much as it is to separate an active desire from passive habits. Habit may sediment us in past choices or behaviours, but desire also gives habit a direction, a purpose, a goal. Desire orients us toward an outside.

Through modes of habituation, the living being is an envelopment of the world. Habits of taste develop from the ingestion of alien material that is metabolized into our own physical constitution. What results is not merely nutrition and the closed fulfilment of need, but the restructuring of our senses of both need and the future: our desire is shaped and reshaped by intensive pleasures and repulsions, repeated and compounded associations, expectations, and the desire for what is foreign to us. For instance, the eye is not merely a passive organ; it both shapes or contracts the perceptual data it processes as much as it is shaped by the visions it has. Through habitual need, the eye remakes the territory of the foraged forest according to vectors of possible affections to be plucked or avoided: the ripeness of the berry, the poison signalled by the spines of a leaf. Habits are the product of our stepping outside ourselves, our becoming relational with and reliant on a world. If ethics is irreducible to theoretical knowing, it is foremost because it originates in a geography or "mapping" of sense and affection, in the logistics of the self and its worlds.[41]

3. DELEUZE AND THE HABITS THAT WE ARE

Before turning to Deleuze's account of the habitual and differential self, it is necessary to outline a problem at the centre of the encounter between Aristotle and Deleuze. We have argued that habit formation is the essential process of ethical becoming and development, and that habituation attests to a reality of the human self in which it involves other realities that exceed its human form. However, in the interpretation of Aristotle's ontology no less than in our common ways of approaching reality, there is a tendency to mark a distinction between the primary and secondary natures of something. For instance, we might say that an individual remains a human despite developing a cellular or behavioural dependency on an organic or synthetic material, as is the case in substance addictions ranging widely from sucrose to opiates. In these cases, behaviour, perception, judgment, need, pleasure, and pain – in short, the affective terms of ethical decisions – are rooted in a foreign material that has come to define the self. However, we do not ordinarily conclude, for instance, that the human individual has "become-heroin" or "become-fructose." We envision human nature as split between an enduring form of our humanity or selfhood, and a level of change where we engage with and become defined and influenced by a foreign world. In short, we subordinate our becoming different to our remaining the same. In this section we show how a significant part of Deleuze's work on habituation aims to free habit from being simply an inessential component or afterthought in the accounts we give of the reality of things, and how this insight is anticipated in Aristotle's own ethics.

With reference to David Hume's moral psychology, Deleuze notes that "the real dualism ... is not between affection and reason, nature and artifice, but rather between the whole of nature which includes the artifice and the mind affected and determined by this whole ... Justice is not a principle of nature; it is an artifice. But to the extent that humanity is an inventive species, even the artifice is nature" (ES, 44/32–3).[42] The ethical self does not stand independent of the culture that only shapes it secondarily.[43] Ethics proceeds from a position of immanence that grasps nature, the affections of the body and mind, and consequential actions in a common process of modulation. The natural (biology) and the artificial (culture) collapse into an immanent world without losing their difference in series. The question is no longer what there is naturally given to be known, but rather: how have I come to be given as I am? (ES, 87/92).[44] We thus find a thesis in Deleuze, attributed to Henri Bergson, that reflects an important insight into Aristotle's account of ethical life: "[Habits] are not themselves natural, but what is natural is the habit to take up habits. Nature does not reach its ends except by means of culture, and tendency is not satisfied except through the institution. History is in this sense part of human nature. Conversely, nature is encountered as the residue of history ... Nature and culture form, therefore, a whole or a composite" (ES, 44/33–4).[45] It is insufficient to posit what the nature of a form demands over and against the inessential and contingent properties that will affect a subject capable of acquiring behavioural or cultural habits. A crucial task of ethics is to determine how the form of something realizes itself in a milieu of historical and cultural acclimation and adaptation. Moreover, it requires seeing how the "natural" posture of an ethical being is this very adaptation and "contraction" of a world in which it realizes anything at all.

The self, Deleuze argues, is primarily a "synthesis" (DR, 73–9/99–108) of contracted habits and elements that are "passive" before they "render possible both the action and the active subject" (DR, 75/103). The syntheses of habit are the "the primary sensibility that we *are*" (DR, 73/99), the "thousands of passive syntheses of which we are organically composed" (DR, 74/101). The smoker often does not contract her addiction on first contact, but only after a long repetition in which a milieu of social association overpowers the disgust of the smoke. It is only after the fact that one realizes that what was at its inception disgust and indifference has become, below the level of perception, a pleasure or a need; for the addict, at a certain threshold, "becoming conscious counts for little" (DR, 19/30). Thus the experiential self is foremost a "multiplicity," an "assemblage" of relations, for instance, between nicotine, membranes, the affective rush, the image, and the external arrangement of supply and occasion. The multiplicity is "machinic" insofar as its "assemblage" (*agencement*) defines a determinate system of bodily configuration (TP, 406/506, 257–8/314–15), that is, a "system of the self" (DR, 78/107). However, every assemblage is also open to, interactive with, and reconfigured by outside milieux (TP, 313/384–5). As Deleuze and Guattari insist, every assemblage is also an "inter-assemblage" (*inter-agencement*) (TP, 323–33/397–412). The taste of tobacco in the mouth might deter a partner, or the erratic actions of an addict might ruin other possible relationships. Whatever the situation, the fact is that every action or disposition happens between milieux, between the multiplicity of a self and the multiplicity of an outside encountered. Rather than being an abstract and focal centre that grounds and stabilizes experience, the self is always a decentred set of relations, a bundle of otherness whose "unity" of composition is defined only by the force or "contractile power" (DR, 70/96). "We speak of our 'self' only in virtue of these thousands of little witnesses which contemplate within us: it is always a third party who says 'me'" (DR, 75/103). It is easy to synthesize all our experiences as *ours*, but more difficult to recognize what was *other* in all that happened in us.

The physical sciences recognize the significance of this more than philosophical ethics has prepared itself to. For instance, when molecules of hydrogen and oxygen are destabilized under the conditions of heat, they agitate, speed up, and pull apart to change the state of liquid water into steam. It is thus not merely in relation to the world that we form habits; the habit is not merely an effect of some inhuman material on us and to which we stand both opposed and distinct in our influenced state. Habit pervades both our levels of action and our molecular composition. "The self does not undergo modifications, it is itself a modification" (DR, 79/107). To contract a habit in the world is to become that world and thus to become other than oneself. Addiction, as an intensified habit, is thus not merely the habit of repeating the consumption of a substance. The opiate addict does not merely *use* heroin with a quantitative regularity, but has, at the threshold of addiction, in part become molecularly defined by the substance itself; the neural and cellular levels of the addict's brain, demonstrating its "plasticity," become "adapted" to the effects of the drug on cellular reception, leading to symptoms of need, withdrawal, and tolerance.[46] At an experiential level, withdrawal symptoms attest to this confluence of habit and the cellular body in which the absence of the contracted material is experienced as a becoming vacant of the self, of the self's own inadequacy, its "withdrawal" from itself under the condition of being "held" together by a foreign element. What Deleuze and Guattari allude to as "becoming-plant" (TP, 4/10, 275/339; cf. 10/17) here gains a literal value, not as an exercise of "imitation," but as the lived reality of organic and habituated life. In the moment of habituated action – when action is "contracting that from which we come" (DR, 74/101), that is, when we are effectuated from heterogeneous becomings or compositions – the "*I* is an other" (DR, 86/116).

Deleuze's reading of the ethical import of Spinoza's ontology provides us an important illustration of this point. The "consciousness" that the self maintains an autonomy from nature, according to Deleuze, attests to a kind of "illusion" in which the self, in taking itself as a fundamental cause, fails to see the extent to which it is an "effect" of a complex world of ulterior causes and processes:

> When a body "encounters" another body, or an idea another
> idea, it happens that the two relations sometimes combine to
> form a more powerful whole, and sometimes one decomposes
> the other, destroying the cohesion of its parts. And this is what
> is prodigious in the body and the mind alike, these sets of living
> parts that enter into composition with and decompose one
> another according to complex laws. The order of causes is
> therefore an order of composition and decomposition of
> relations, which infinitely affects all of nature. (SPP, 19/29)[47]

Spinoza's claim that "nobody as yet has learned from experience what the body can and cannot do, without being determined by the mind, solely from the laws of its nature"[48] should be understood as a fundamental insight that our understanding of ethical action is wedded to an "inadequate" conception of mental autonomy. As Spinoza illustrates, the gossiper has already disclosed the other's secret before having cognitively decided to do so, and in the clamour of the bar, the drunk believes that what he is doing or saying is a free and conscious act. The point is not that freedom is impossible, as interpreters have long held, but rather that localizing freedom solely in the mind fails to grasp the extent to which the habitual body itself acts below the level of consciousness. The theft executed in the pangs of withdrawal, the drink consumed past the point of moderation, the outburst under waves of grief, cannot be divorced from the "decompositions" of bodily and mental relations, whether it is cellular dependency, intoxicated euphoria, or crippling loss. This is not to suggest that action and ethical judgment be reduced to these causes; in fact, this is rendered impossible since every action is open to a future, to multivalent consequences, and to possible deviations. If freedom and decision are to have any meaning, ethically or otherwise, they must proceed from the situation in which they are effectuated. Ethical consciousness must be grasped in its "constitution," that is, in relation to the causes of its affections (of hunger, desire, fatigue) and its capacities for action. It is from this position that action is grounded. The ground is the world of differential processes that give rise to individuated situations of actions. The question then, for Deleuze, is not whether the ethical subject is the autonomous agent of her own actions or a mere habitual effect of determinate conditions outside her (cf. TP, 130/162). When the ethical self is apprehended in an effectuated and affected state, what matters is whether she has an "active" or "reactive" power of action (NP, 40-2/63–7, 53–5/82–6, 176/276–7)[49] and whether this action is capable of leading to a more diversified life.

Habit is not the passive derivative of determinate life. Habit is the limit that links the living being to the world, the experiential hinge between a "larval subject" (DR, 78/107) and its conditions for difference. Félix Ravaisson, drawing from the early struggle to conceptually define the terms of the calculus, provides a resonant account of habit that emphasizes its differential character within an immanent "*naturing* nature": "Like effort between action and passion, habit is the dividing line [*la commune limite*], or the middle term, between will and nature; but it is a moving middle term ... which advances by an imperceptible [*insensible*] movement proper to habit. Habit is thus, so to speak, the infinitesimal *differential*, or, the dynamic *fluxion* from Will to Nature."[50] When we take on a new habit or break an existing one, difference is introduced into the self. We contract the tic of another person in our prolonged contact with them – the twitch of an eye, the turn of the jaw, the wisp of a hand. This is not a matter of imitation primarily, even if it may appear so at certain moments. It is properly a "contagion" between things (TP, 241–3/295–7), the "communication" or communion that links the terms of life in a "double" becoming (TP, 293–4/358–60, 305/374). Habit is not brute mechanism, but a vital and differential reality. If habits have the character of the involuntary and inactive, this attests first to the intensive nature of the body to be shaped by its world, the degrees in which an affect is stronger or weaker given the force of the original encounter or the strength of its hold. Habit is "affect," and the affect is the differential relation between the self and its world: "Affects are becomings" (TP, 256/313). Every habit is a sort of "claim" (*pretension*) on the constitution of the self (DR, 79/107), determining the intensity of sensations, responses, and expectations. In short, the self is less a mere receiver of habits than it is a territory that is carved out in experience; it is the process of habituation that defines this experiential zone in which the scope of our choices and decisions are "territorialized" and determined. Yet by virtue of being a contraction, every habit is also a "deterritorialization" (TP, 306/375–6), that is, a change of the assemblage that the self is. Even mechanical habits or repetitions intensify the degree of our need or expectation, while the acquisitions of new habits change the capacity of the organism for new tasks or desires. Every contraction introduces a difference into the self. What would it mean for ethical judgment to operate in terms of a subject that is foremost a complex, differentiated product or "fold" of a world?

4. A MILIEU WITHOUT A MEAN

We do not wish to resolve the problem of primary and secondary natures in Aristotle's thought, nor to dismiss the distinction altogether. For Aristotle, this problem is at once ontological and experiential: in the course of an individual's life, from childhood education to adulthood, we are compelled to assert that she remains the same individual through the diverse habits acquired and abandoned. Moreover, the significance of her life cannot be divorced from the human faculties that capacitate and define the scope of her actions (whether it is language, sociability, or responsibility), nor from the human communities in which these actions will materialize. In terms of the changes that will affect her, the "essence" of a substance can endure "accidental" changes to its body and desires; her being subtends, supports, and determines her becoming. Rather than accept the mutual opposition of these sides of reality, what we aim to underscore is the fact that for Aristotle's ethics, the primacy of forms can be realized only through habitual becomings in a world. It is with this insight that we can appreciate the ethical value of Deleuze and Guattari's appeal to a "milieu" of ethical becoming.

Yet to this double account of things, in which the being of a substance undergirds and limits becomings, Deleuze and Guattari pose a philosophical reversal: "A body is not defined by the form that determines it nor as a determinate substance or subject nor by the organs it possesses or the functions it fulfills" (TP, 260/318). Prior to becoming a determinate subject (a self that recognizes all of its experiences as its own) or an organized system (a biologically normalized body), a body is defined by a variable assemblage of elements with a certain degree of power of acting, that is, of being affected by and affecting things in the world based on its composition. In this way, for Deleuze and Guattari, habitual embodiment is a condition for the generation of determinate forms themselves. Becoming attests to an independent reality that occurs "between" that of "substantial forms and determined subjects," a "whole operation" or "natural play of haecceities, degrees, intensities, event, and accidents that compose individuations totally different from those of the well-formed subjects that receive them" (TP, 253/310). The central thesis here is that processes of "becoming" are not derivative of stable, enduring forms or substances that can hold them together. For Deleuze and Guattari, becoming presupposes neither an ideal, enduring form nor a foundational subject; becoming is prior to, independent, and constitutive of forms:

> Becoming produces nothing other than itself ... What is real is the becoming itself, the block of becoming, not the supposedly fixed terms through which that which becomes passes ... [A] becoming lacks a subject distinct from itself [and] has no term, since its terms in turn exists only as taken up in another becoming of which it is the subject, and which coexists, forms a block, with the first ... Becoming is a verb with a consistency all its own. (TP, 238–9/291–2)

With this ontological or meta-ethical account, we face a distinct problem for the condition of ethical action as Aristotle conceives it. Without a determinative form, are we not left without a stable object of normative concern, without a principle to which the diversity of our actions can be guided, oriented, or "meaned"? As we saw for Aristotle, the mean of ethical life requires a form to determine its approximation. The twist is that, rather than abandoning the notion of a "middle" along with form, Deleuze and Guattari mobilize it in a different way. "A becoming is always in the middle; one can only get at it by the middle" (TP, 293/359). Becoming is not the unfolding, realization, or actualization of a pre-given form. By virtue of occurring always in relation to a world of otherness, becoming occurs in the relation itself, in the encounter between things. "Becoming is always double" (TP, 305/374), and the determination is relational and shared. Becoming happens between things while also giving rise to the terms that constitute the relation. "The middle is by no means an average: on the contrary, it is where things pick up speed. *Between* things [designates] a transversal movement that sweeps one *and* the other away, a stream without beginning or end that undermines its banks and picks up speed in the middle" (TP, 25/37). The middle is no longer a goal of moderation or the perfection of a form, but rather the orientation that allows a body to change. Becoming, taken universally, is a vector of change, just like the acquisition of habits orients us beyond our current and settled dispositions and characters toward something else. For both Aristotle and Deleuze, ethical life involves becoming, and this becoming plays itself out in a world where we must become other than ourselves, to uproot the self from its situatedness and to live out something where our present form is not guaranteed.

There are two consequences to Deleuze and Guattari's approach that are confluent with and of interest to Aristotle's account. First, this account of a milieu of becoming emphasizes that the ethical life, decisions, and capacities of an individual are fulfilled, in any fashion, only through a world. At a social level, an adequately nutritional body, differently "meaned" for the athletes and intellectuals of a society, requires adequate conditions of harvest, market values proportionate to incomes and standards of living, and production regulated to align with health and distributive ideals. At an individual level, this means recognizing that the habits we acquire are more than our own personal properties; they are also becomings with natures different than our own, adaptations in a plexus of "intra-assemblages." Viruses do not simply produce symptoms in us, but also mutate as they infect our bodies and transmit between species members. It is possible that our prolonged metabolic becoming in relation to ethanol or diamorphine may not only affect our ethical judgments, but also fundamentally alter our sense of and capacity for being human. We may retain the potential for achieving virtue, but it is equally possible that our behaviours in the world may leave our bodies too fatigued, bent, and poorly affected to achieve this.

Second, Deleuze and Guattari's suggestion is that a life lived at the extremity of form, at the "cutting edges [*les pointes*] of deterritorialization" (TP, 57/74, 88/112, 109/138, 191/233, 244/298), has an ethical quality. It is from their redefinition of the body that Deleuze and Guattari define ethics as a "pragmatics" of "experimentation" according to the following problem: "[H]ow can we unhook ourselves from the points of subjectification that secure us, nail us down to a dominant reality?" (TP, 160/198). As we have seen, we are continually "subjectified," or made into subjects, by the complex milieux in which we are embedded: biological, familial, social, and political worlds that habituate us to the distinct norms of being a particular kind of self in a territory or a world. What movements of "deterritorialization" or "desubjectification" indicate in terms of a pragmatics of working on the self, for Deleuze and Guattari, does not involve a wholesale destruction or demolition, but rather "necessary caution" and

> the art of dosages, since overdose is a danger. You don't do it with a sledgehammer, you use a very fine file. You invent self-destructions that have nothing to do with the death drive. Dismantling the organism has never meant killing yourself, but rather opening the body to connections that presuppose an entire assemblage, circuits, conjunctions; levels and thresholds, passages and distributions of intensity, and territories and deterritorializations measured with the craft of a surveyor. (TP, 160/198)

Why dismantle, break down, or harm the self? Every self, as a living thing, is capable both of growth and of becoming rigid in the habits that define it. There is no becoming virtuous, whatever we decide this means in the end, without the venture out to both comprise and compromise the self: to file away at the frivolity of the child's play, the teenager's stubbornness, the adult's ideology, or the elderly's rigidity. Ethics needs virtue, ends, a goal, but it also needs a pragmatics of tools for dismantling the self in all the ways it risks becoming ossified, for the sake of the becoming-different entailed by every growth.

5. CONCLUSION: THE WARP THAT WE ARE

There are a number of philosophical questions that follow. First, the traditional concern is whether Aristotle and Deleuze provide distinct accounts of the grounds of ethical action. Should the human form be understood as the regulative origin and goal of ethics, or should ethical becoming be grounded in a world of life decentred from the fixity of essential forms themselves? Second, how does the latter thesis push our thinking beyond the limits of an exclusively human ethics, and what can be accomplished by doing so? Rather than stripping ethics of its normative appeal, we argue that Deleuze gives us a broader relational ontology for ethical consideration. How can one understand the violence of the inmate when the action reflects and repeats, in conjunction, the violence of the guard's club and the walls of the enclosure? Or the drug addict's relapse when the experience of an autonomous self has been overridden by cellular need? Ethics, we argue, needs a more complex, dynamic, and relational conception of the "world." Third, the stakes of Deleuze's thought are to replace the question of what the "right" action is with the following: What kind of life does an action or decision make possible, not just for the individual, but for the worldly milieux in which the individual is assembled? As we have shown, this is a question that is hardly foreign to Aristotle's ethical thought. Yet answering this question requires being attuned continually to the minor foothold of ethical decision in a world that is, at every moment, a constitutive limit of our action and our judgment. When ethics abandons the false security of foundations that transcend the world of becoming, it can open as an experimental site for the production of new ethical values "beyond morality" (SPP, 17–29/27–42).

Perhaps Kant is correct that the warp of our nature is irremediable. Perhaps the promise of straightening ourselves to a perfect mean of character, to which Aristotle's ethics directs us in principle, can remain only an indefinite project or orientation bereft of absolute fulfilment. But this impossibility is not the more profound point about an ethical subjectivity that is by nature warped, distorted, bent out of shape, irreparable in its empirical life. Before it becomes a moment of despair, or a limit of ethical accomplishment, this warp is also the malleability that opens us onto difference, the capacity that inclines our becoming in a world. Is it not this warp that inaugurates the question of ethics most perennially?

My soul itself may be straight and good;
ah, but my heart, my bent-over blood,
all the distortions that hurt me inside –
it buckles under these things.
It has no garden, it has no sun,
it hangs on my twisted skeleton
and, terrified, flaps its wings.

Rainer Maria Rilke, "The Dwarf's Song"

NOTES

1 "The excellence of a thing is relative to its proper function." Aristotle, *Nicomachean Ethics*, in *Complete Works*, vol. 2, 6.2.1139a17. Hereafter *Ethics*. All references to Aristotle's works are to the Barnes edition and translations, unless otherwise noted. Page references are to the Book. Section.Bekker numbers preceded by the title of the work. References to the Greek are to the Loeb Classics collection.

2 Aristotle, *Ethics*, 1103a14–1109b26.

3 The positive connection between these thinkers is challenging because Deleuze situates his project as a departure from the "organic" model of life, the teleology of ends, and the "representational" determination afforded by what he characterizes as classical Aristotelian thought (DR, 29–35/44–52). Somers-Hall provides a rigorous analysis of Deleuze's engagement with Aristotle's thought in *Hegel, Deleuze, and the Critique of Representation*, 41–66; and *Deleuze's* Difference and Repetition, 21–30.

4 Aristotle, *Ethics*, 2.2.1103b25–30.

5 Ibid., 1103b30–31.

6 Ibid., 2.2.1103b25–30.

7 Ibid., 1.6.1096a12–1098b8.

8 Aristotle makes this distinction between "things that exist ... by nature [and] some from other causes" – that is, between self-moving and inanimate things – in *Physics*, 2.1.192b9–23.

9 Aristotle, *Metaphysics,* 9.3.1047a14.

10 For Aristotle, "being" is equivocal or "said in many ways," that is, in terms of substance, quality, quantity, and so on (*Metaphysics*, 4.2.1003a33; 7.1.1028a10; and *Categories*). Cf. Deleuze's critique of the categorical nature of this account of being (DR, 29–35/44–52). For Aristotle in the *Metaphysics*, what "is" fundamentally is "substance" (7.1.1028a10–35), the "indwelling form" (7.11.1037a29) of independent things in their

"becoming." The point we wish to emphasize here is that to "be" a substance involves a "movement," the potential or "matter" in a process of
self-fulfillment of the "form" or "actuality" that is logically, temporally,
and substantially prior (ibid., 9.8.1049b1–1051a3).

11 For Aristotle's account of causality, see *Physics*, 2.3.194b16–195b30.

12 See Aristotle, *Parts of Animals*, 1.1645b25–37.

13 Aristotle, *Ethics*, 2.2.1104a3-5; cf. ibid., 1.3.1094b12–27.

14 John Dewey notes succinctly that "experience" entails an "active and alert
    commerce with the world." *Art as Experience*, 18. "[Life] goes on in an
    environment; not merely *in* it but because of it, through interaction with
    it. No creature lives merely under its skin; its subcutaneous organs are
    means of connection with what lies beyond its bodily frame, and to which,
    in order to live, it must adjust itself ... The career and destiny of a living
    being are bound up with its interchanges with its environment, not exter-
    nally but in the most intimate way." Ibid., 12.

15 Cf. one of Aristotle's many accounts in *On the Soul* of the self-moving
    soul (ψυχή) and its reliance on its environment: we can speak of things
    as "living" insofar as they "possess an originative power through which
    they increase or decrease in all spatial directions," and this "holds for
    everything which is constantly nourished and continues to live, so long
    as it can absorb nutriment" (2.2.413a22–413b4; cf. his account of
    "reproduction" at 2.4.415a22–30).

16 See Aristotle, *Ethics*, 1.8.1099a32: "[Happiness] needs the external goods
    as well; for it is impossible, or not easy, to do noble acts without the
    proper equipment." The examples of the external conditions of happiness
    include: the health and fate of one's family and friends (1.8.1099b9–17),
    one's reputation after the death of the body (1.10.1100a10–b11), and
    social and material accessibility (1.8.1099a32).

17 Ibid., 1.7.1097b20–1098a20.

18 Ibid., 1098a16–17.

19 Ibid., 1098a18–19.

20 While Aristotle provides one of the most sustained investigations of the
    animal and plant world in Western philosophy, it is necessary that we con-
    tinue to think deeply about how our metaphysical and normative thinking
    relies on a categorical exclusion of certain forms of life and a failure to
    grasp their singular complexities non-analogically. See Karen Houle's
    important intervention in "Animal, Vegetable, Mineral."

21 For Aristotle's definition of "capacity," see *Metaphysics*, 5.12.1019d15–30.

22 Aristotle's account of substance is nuanced, sophisticated, and central to
    his wide-ranging thought, and we do not aim to do justice to it here.

Substance as the "form" or "actuality" of a being is primary over the "potentiality of matter" (*Metaphysics*, 9.8.1049b1–1051a3). As a self-generative activity, however, it is not indifferent to either its "matter" or to its process of self-actualization in which its potential to be itself reaches, or fails to reach, its "fulfillment" in life; "actuality in the strict sense is identified with movement" (ibid., 9.3.1047a31). The "soul is inseparable from its body" (*On the Soul*, 2.1.413a4) in the way that one cannot separate the "wasp" from its buzz or sting. The substantial and formal distinction of thought or essence from matter later finds an expression in Cartesianism, and Spinoza's "substance monism" has significant consequences for how Deleuze's project mobilizes an immanence of being against the Aristotelian and Cartesian traditions (DR, 35–42/52–61).

23 See John Russon's "Aristotle's Animative Epistemology." Russon charts the importance of holism as "life" between Aristotle's metaphysics and epistemology: "In the natural body one and the same subject is present throughout, and it is the simple genus of which all the organs are species. The natural substance, then, is a whole as an organized, active, self-moving totality," that is, an "activity of self-actualization" (242). "Animate existence," according to Russon, is thus "desire" insofar as it is a "situation which is an activity of a complex, organized body opposing itself to an other where this other is the *immediate* object of its desire and the desire is *ultimately* the desire of self-maintenance" (ibid., 244).

24 It is clear to Aristotle that ethical capacity does not pertain to all beings in the world, as is the case with merely physical things that cannot act "contrary to [their] nature" (*Ethics*, 2.1.1103a20). Consequently, it would be inappropriate to pass ethical judgment on the behaviour of a thing that lacks the agency and possibility of doing otherwise: "It is natural, then, that we call neither an ox nor horse nor any other of the animals happy; for none of them is capable of sharing in such activity" (ibid., 1.9.1099b32–1100a9). Aristotle later claims that desirous, sensuous animals without intellect have "no share in action," as the "origin of action – its efficient, not its final cause – is choice, and that of choice is desire and reasoning with a view to an end" (ibid., 6.2.1139a18–35).

25 Ibid., 1.7.1098a3.

26 Aristotle, *Nicomachean Ethics*, trans. Irwin, 87 (6.2.1139a35–1139b5).

27 Aristotle, *Ethics*, 6.2.1139b5.

28 Aristotle, *Nicomachean Ethics*, trans. Rackham, 5 (1.2.1094a22, our emphasis). For a systematic study of *Nicomachean Ethics* in terms of practical philosophy, see Francis Sparshott, *Taking Life Seriously*. Rather than reading the text according to the more speculative concerns of "morality,"

Sparshott follows Aristotle in terms of the "straightforward problem of how to live a lifetime" given a "social set-up and political organization and the necessary psychophysical equipment of humanity" (ibid., 8–9).

29 We refuse the connotation of the term of "relativism" here to emphasize that judgment always occurs in a worldly context from which it draws both a condition of relevance and a limit of achievement. Howard J. Curzer argues in "Aristotle's Mean Relative to Us" that Aristotle's relativity of the mean entails a "situational relativity" and not a relativity to character or social role, with the latter two running the risk of unjustifiable asymmetries in ethical action (like those between members of social classes). See our discussion of the mean's "relativity" below. For an excellent discussion of relativity and Aristotle's virtue ethics, see Martha Nussbaum, "Non-Relative Virtues."

30 Aristotle, *Ethics*, 2.1.1103a20.

31 Ibid., 1.13.1102b15–25. Cf. Aristotle's analysis of the soul in *On the Soul*: "if there be a movement natural to the soul, there must be a countermovement to it, and conversely" (1.3.406a21).

32 Aristotle, *Ethics*, 1.13.1102b29–35.

33 Ibid., 2.1.1103a15–25.

34 In "Personality as Equilibrium," Russon importantly interprets Aristotle's "mean" in terms of the human "self" that, rather than being a neutral substratum, is a "supple mode of plastic responsiveness" to the norms of its natural and interpersonal environment (627). As Russon demonstrates, this plasticity involves not simply "thresholds" of change but also the potentials of rigidity and fragility. The key for our analysis here is that the "identity" of the self is, according to Russon, a "dynamic" process of "interpreting" ourselves "in a way that is inseparably interwoven with how we interpret the world" in a "dynamic system of lived equilibrium" (ibid., 629).

35 Aristotle, *Ethics*, 2.6.1106b1–5.

36 Ibid., our emphasis.

37 Ibid., 2.9.1109b1.

38 J.R. Urmson argues that Aristotle's mean should not be understood as "moderation," since exhibiting something like a moderate amount of anger might situationally be absurd. For Urmson, the mean is a "settled state of character" that is "without friction." "Aristotle's Doctrine of the Mean," 224–5. Our point is to emphasize that the achievement of this state is one that must continually negotiate the tensions that one's desire necessarily entails, that stasis emerges from an original friction.

39 Aristotle, *Ethics*, 2.9.1109d30–35: In order to reach the mean, we must "first depart from what is the more contrary to it, as Calypso advises

– 'Hold the ship beyond that surf and spray' – For of the extremes one
is more erroneous, one less so; therefore, since to hit the mean is hard in
the extreme, we must as a second best, as people say, take the least of the
evils." For the source of this image, see Homer, *Odyssey*, Book XII.

40 Aristotle, *On the Soul*, 1.1.403a15–30.

41 Deleuze and Guattari designate affects in terms of an experiential "cartography" (see TP, 253/310; cf. TP, 160/198). For Aristotle, this means
recognizing that the isolated individual is "not self-sufficing" (*Politics*,
1.2.1253a25), but realized in and through a social world. It is in this sense
that we should interpret Aristotle's claim that the study of ethical life is
also the "study of politics" (πολιτική) (*Ethics*, 1.2.1094a25–1094b12). In
light of our account of habituation here, it would be necessary to explore
two important points made by Aristotle. First, that the social formations
identified at the beginning of the *Politics* are confluent levels of a single
reality, rather than a hierarchical order. Each represents the individual's
becoming integrated in, dependent on, and fulfilled through a wider and
more extensive environment of living. Second, that the art of politics, for
Aristotle, is a "master-art" (μάλιστα ἀρχιτεκτονικῆς) rather than a bureaucratic set of governing procedures. This is to say, the object of politics,
Aristotle notes in multiple texts, is the "moulding" of the citizen "to suit
the form of government under which he lives" (*Politics*, 8.1.1337a10),
and thus "legislators make the citizens good by forming habits in them"
(*Ethics*, 1.2.1103b1–5).

42 Deleuze, *Empiricism and Subjectivity*. Hereafter ES.

43 "[Hume] shows that the two forms under which the mind is *affected* are
essentially the *passional* and the *social*. They imply each other, assuring
thereby the unity of the object of an authentic science" (ES, 21/1).

44 What matters for Deleuze in Hume's empiricist "constructivist logic" is
not what defines the mind or subjectivity as a uniform object of knowledge (ES, 21/1), but rather how the mind can *in experience* "become
human nature" and a "subject" as a "system" (ES, 22–3/3).

45 While Aristotle's metaphysics maintains this formal distinction between
enduring essences (of self, character, or species) over accidental properties
(which are acquirable and losable), his ethics complicates it by seeing that
the human is "adapted by nature to receive [habits]" (*Ethics*,
2.1.1103a24).

46 See Nestler, "Molecular Basis of Long-Term Plasticity"; and Nestler and
Aghajanian, "Molecular and Cellular Basis of Addiction." The neurobio-
logical basis for drug addiction is an extensive and ongoing field of
research and should not be taken as an exclusive model for explaining
the phenomenon or as overriding sociological, genetic, psychological, and

subjective approaches. We highlight it here to emphasize the molecular
level of socially consequential decisions.

47 Deleuze, *Spinoza: Practical Philosophy*. Hereafter SPP.

48 Spinoza, *Ethics*, in *Complete Works*, 280 (III.P.2.Sch.). Deleuze reads
Spinoza's thesis of the "parallelism" between the mind and the body not in
the traditional terms of a reduction of freedom to causal determinism, but
rather as "the reversal of the traditional principle on which Morality was
founded as an enterprise of domination of the passions by consciousness
… It is a matter of showing that the body surpasses the knowledge that
we have of it, *and that thought likewise surpasses the consciousness that
we have of it*" (SPP, 18/28). For Deleuze, this entails a "devaluation of
consciousness in relation to thought: a discovery of the unconscious, of
an *unconscious of thought* just as profound as *the unknown of the body*"
(SPP, 18–9/29).

49 Deleuze, *Nietzsche and Philosophy*. Hereafter NP.

50 Ravaisson, *Of Habit*, 59. Elizabeth Grosz traces a lineage of vital conceptions of habit, from Ravaisson through Bergson to Deleuze, that contests
traditional mechanistic accounts. For these thinkers, according to Grosz,
"habit is regarded not as that which reduces the human to the order of the
mechanical … but rather as a fundamentally creative capacity that produces the possibility of stability in a universe in which change is fundamental." "Habit Today," 219.

2

Undoing the Self:
Augustine's *Confessions* as a Work
of Ethical Becoming

Suzanne M. McCullagh

Undo this creature!

> Anne Carson, *Decreation*

I do not venture to deny that the human body, while retaining blood circulation and whatever else is regarded as essential to life, can nevertheless assume another nature quite different from its own ... It sometimes happens that a man undergoes such changes that I would not be prepared to say that he is the same person.

> Baruch Spinoza, *Ethics*

[The] body assimilates and retains the various differences experienced during travel and returns home a half-breed of new gestures and other customs, dissolved in the body's attitudes and functions, to the point that it believes that as far as it is concerned nothing has changed.

> Michel Serres, *Troubador of Knowledge*

In his *Confessions*, Saint Augustine narrates the intense struggle of a self divided and dissociated from itself in the throes of becoming other than what it is. His attempts at conversion and self-transformation involve a struggle with his habituated self; his habits, ever resistant to change, impede his becoming. In depicting the way that habits hold the self in place, enhancing tendencies toward the repetition of acts, tastes, and experiences, *Confessions* offers rich material for considering the ways that working on one's habits can be considered an ethical task to facilitate an ethical becoming and an increase of the self's capacities for action and responsibility. Insofar as Augustine disavows the significance of his self's multiplicity as enabling his capacity to convert, he comes short of providing us with an account of the self's capacity for change. It is on this point that reading *Confessions* with Deleuze and Guattari's concept of "the body without organs" (a term that describes creative experimentation with forms of life and subjectivity) helps deepen our insights into the self's becoming.

Separating Augustine's account of ethical becoming from its theistic ground could appear either impossible or a patent misinterpretation of the meaning of the text and the intentions of its author. There are, however, significant structural features of his account that can enable us to gain insight into a non-theistic ethical becoming, one that does not involve a transcendent God and a hierarchy of being. By illuminating these features we gain a view of ethical becoming and subjectivity that is not just open to, but constituted by, heterogeneity. In other words, we get a view of ethical becoming that is attentive to the dispositional tendencies, forms of the self, and capacities for experience and action that find their genesis, maintenance, and potentials for alteration in milieux and assemblages composed of different entities, elements, and forces: ideas, norms, cities, friends, books, stories, voices singing, fruits, trees, institutions, discourses, weather, political currents, geography, et cetera. Such a minor reading of *Confessions* can be achieved by extracting the concept of "formless matter" (a term Augustine uses to designate the primacy of the capacity for mutability in creation) from his reading of Genesis in order to bring it to bear on thinking through the *work of the self* that enabled his capacity for conversion. The account of his conversion, or ethical becoming, invokes the capacity for change inherent to forms of self and creatural life. Augustine's ethical becoming is brought about through his relation to alterity, to a God that is absolutely other than he is; his capacity to enter into that relation is dependent upon his capacity to change the form of his self, that is, to change his habits. The focus of this chapter is to push on the structural position that God plays in Augustine's transformation by foregrounding the incommensurability of beings, the otherness the self relates with but also contains within itself, and the work of the self that consists in undoing or dissolving aspects of one's self. This shift in orientation will show that Augustine has important conceptual and theoretical resources for reflecting upon how we can cultivate and develop ethical capacities called for by our contemporary world, one in which there is anxiety around how to relate and respond to alterity (culturally different others, different species, ecologically different entities). Reading Augustine in this way provides insight into how "to act tactically upon yourself to recode to some degree culturally embodied tendencies ... and to cultivate new sensitivities to human and nonhuman agents of multiple sorts."[1]

One way of thinking about human capacities for action and experience is to focus on bodily organs and the role or function they play in a given body's ability to act. There is some debate in the philosophy of science surrounding the distinction between function and capacity, whether they are equivalent or whether one is primary over the other. The entities that most commonly figure in these debates are organs and tools. What the function of an organ is and how it is able to be determined is of concern to those thinkers who are trying to explain the function[2] or purpose[3] an organ serves within a given system. Conversely, others are interested in focusing on the multiple and dynamic capacities of organs and tools and how they may come to take on different roles or functions at different times depending on how they are assembled.[4] Deleuze's Spinozist question, "What can a body do?" (EP, 226) – rather than "What is it?" – prioritizes capacities and thus places him in the latter camp.[5] In fact, Deleuze and Guattari, in their repetition of Artaud's proclamation "[to] be done with the judgement of god" (TP, 150), urge an active resistance to the functionalist view of organs that decrees that eyes are for seeing, ears are for hearing, mouths are for swallowing, tongues are for talking, and brains are for thinking (TP, 151). This is reason itself to be skeptical that Deleuzian concepts could offer anything in terms of reading Augustine's *Confessions*, especially when it is there that we find the opposing proclamation that God has decreed the functions of each organ.[6] The situation is not that simple, however, for *Confessions* is a complex text with multiple layers and twists and turns. Surprising though it may seem, we also find in those pages the freeing of the organs from their functionalist determinations: the heart has ears,[7] the soul has a mouth,[8] the tongue has a hand.[9] In describing his conversion, Augustine's organic concepts enter into a "line of flight" (TP, 55) as he enters into association with alterity. Careful consideration reveals that while he claims to privilege stable and enduring entities above the changing and transient, his own conversion is an experiment in becoming that involves undoing the stability of habit and an activation of the capacity for change. Beneath the theological account that privileges heaven, because of its changeless "cleaving to God,"[10] over the ever transient creatures of the earth, there lies an ontological account wherein formless matter, the capacity to change, plays a pivotal role in ethical becoming and capacitation. In his process of conversion, Augustine breaks his habituated patterns of sensing and makes himself into a "body without organs" in order to be capacitated by alterity, and in so doing enables a *becoming different* that takes place with and through difference.

I. HABIT AND THE FORMS AND FORMATIONS OF THE SELF

The form of the self – that is, experience and action of which a self is capable – is to a significant extent a result of the habits the self has acquired. Habits form the self into a being with certain capacities; they give shape and structure to the lives we lead and determine our experiences by propelling us toward some environments, relations, and experiences while foreclosing others. Consider our habits of eating. Those who are habituated to eating with a knife and fork may experience revulsion and anxiety when, for instance, experiencing Ethiopian cuisine for the first time: one is confronted with a broad platter of *injera* (flatbread) topped with a colourful variety of stews, which are most often shared and eaten by tearing off pieces of the *injera* and scooping up portions of the stew with one's hands. The habit of eating with utensils may have so strongly shaped the self that one may be incapable of tasting and enjoying the meal, or simply avoid the experience altogether. Another person, habituated to eating in the company or presence of others – for instance, in the commotion of a local pub – may be unable to enjoy a meal alone at home or at a fancy restaurant. The self's taste, mannerisms, desires, and capacities for relaxation and enjoyment are shaped by the repetition of particular environments and ways of eating. Catapult someone habituated to taking meals at a pub into a fancy restaurant and they become anxious and lose their appetite; put them alone in their kitchen and they may find themselves bored and listless. One's desire to eat and modes of eating are conditioned by the habits one is – by habits of corporeality and intercorporeality, habits of subjectivity and communality, and habits of culture and class (to name only a few). Furthermore, our habits implicate us in different social and ecological systems. For example, the habit of eating meat every day tends to implicate one in systems of large-scale factory farming that are both resource-intensive (and so ecologically harmful) and cruel to non-human, animal life. To return to someone who is repulsed with eating with their hands, they may find themselves both a product and a perpetuator of social and political aversions to cultural difference that under certain conditions may give rise to forms of ethnic nationalism that threaten the rights, livelihood, and safety of those conceived to be culturally different. This is not, however, to argue for some kind of ethical imperative to eat differently; rather, the point is to illustrate how habits of eating form the self and implicate the self in larger systems of different others (living species, human cultures, social classes, ecological systems). Habits have ethical and political implications and as such are an important site for ethical work.[11]

The habituated self and its problematics are the focus of Augustine's analysis of his ethical becoming. The narrative of his conversion consists of a reflective analysis of the ways that habits maintain the form of the self even when the self's conscious desires oppose them. Ethical becoming is revealed to be a complex event consisting of much more than a rational decision about how best to live. While he consciously desired to turn toward God and live a monastic Christian life, his habits held him back, rendering him incapable of taking up the life he desired. His enjoyment of God, he confesses, was unstable: "I was caught up to you by your beauty and quickly torn away from you by my weight ... This weight was my sexual habit."[12]

While he did not doubt that he should attach himself to God, he "was not yet in a state to be able to do that."[13] His soul, latched to the "treadmill of habit," resisted turning toward God and converting. His habits had a grip on his will, imprisoning him within the grooved paths created by his habitual tendencies. The will to serve and enjoy God as "the only sure source of pleasure" was emerging within him, but he confesses that it "was not yet strong enough to conquer my older will, which had the strength of old habit."[14] We should bear in mind that Augustine uses the term "habit" (*consuetudo*) to refer primarily to what he considers to be bad habits: sensuous living, care for material things, lust, swearing, and so on.[15] While his concern in *Confessions* is primarily with the difficulty he encounters in trying to give up his sexual habit in order to take up a monastic life, his account is relevant to the broader consideration of the role of habit in the formation of the self and the resistance the self experiences when attempting to change.

Habits resist change and as such they generate and maintain the forms we are and the formations we are in. Consider an urban dweller, in the habit of using their car to drive to work even though it is within walking distance, who determines (for bodily, community, and environmental reasons) that they ought to walk instead. Determining what they *ought* to do, however, fails to be effective in altering their habit. In spite of making a conscious determination to walk instead of drive, our urban dweller finds themselves continuing to drive and most likely now feeling either guilty for doing so or defiant toward their will to do otherwise, muttering: "What difference does it make anyways?" As such, they find themselves seemingly locked into a pattern of behaviour that prevents them from experiencing the world in new and more ethical ways. This scenario occurs, according to Augustine, because our habits are almost necessities for us and as such are profoundly difficult to alter. "By servitude to passion, habit is formed, and habit to which there is no resistance becomes necessity."[16] And yet, he thinks, we are responsible for them. It is the "the violence of habit by which even the unwilling mind is dragged down and held, as it deserves to be, since by its own choice it slipped into the habit."[17]

He accused himself, but he confesses: "[M]y soul hung back ... The only thing left to it was a mute trembling, and as if it were facing death it was terrified of being restrained from the treadmill of habit."[18] His soul is terrified of being without its habits because an alteration at the level of habit is a fundamental alteration of the self. Deleuze identifies the self with habit and as such can help us understand Augustine's struggle with his habituated self. "Underneath the self which acts are little selves which contemplate and which render possible the action and the active subject" (DR, 75). These "little selves" or "souls" contract habits; our existence consists in "contracting that from which we come" (DR, 74). This is not just the case for human selves, for according to Deleuze, all organisms are composed by what they contract. "What we call wheat is a contraction of earth and humidity," Deleuze notes. "What organism is not made of elements and cases of repetition, of contemplated and contracted water, nitrogen, carbon, chlorides and sulphates, thereby intertwining all the habits of which it is composed?" (DR, 75). Augustine experienced an intense conflict within himself because his self was composed of the contraction of pleasure through bodily engagement with his lover. Any alteration of this habit would have been a fundamental alteration of the composition, or what we have been calling the form, of his self. Deleuze argues that "one is only what one has: here, being is formed or the passive self is, by having. Every contraction is a presumption, a claim – that is to say, it gives rise to an expectation or a right in regard to that which it contracts, and comes undone once its object escapes" (DR, 79). Augustine's soul clings to habit, resists its undoing, in order to maintain his form, integrity, unity, stability, and identity. The self comes undone in letting go of its contractions, its habits.

In Augustine's estimation, habit is one of three forces that determine the form of the self: God, the individual, and the individual's habits. God has determined the human body, Augustine tells us, such that each organ performs a particular function: "the eye to see and the ear to hear."[19] God is also responsible for the capacities one has; he acknowledges to God that "quick thinking and capacity for acute analysis are your gift."[20] In rendering each creature with a determinate body and capacities, God plays a significant role in the form the self takes. Furthermore, since all beings have their "ground" in God, the stability of the self's form is increased when one is turned toward God and decreased when one is turned away or strays from God.[21] For Augustine, God is the being that inspires praise and fills the self with joy. In this way, then, God plays a role in the form of the self by calling forth certain actions and dispositions such as praise and confession. This aspect of God's role in the formation of the self is different from the first, since there is more space here between the creature and God, and the formation is less determinate. While God, according to Augustine, created the world and its creatures in a determinate way, decreeing functions for organic forms and endowing creatures with capacities, the activation and exercise of capacities and the orientation of the self toward God are the work of the individual who is inspired by God. We could say that God makes it possible for the self to love him, but he does not decree it in the way that Augustine thinks God decrees the ear to hear and the eye to see. Individuals are free to become; the individual is responsible for their self-formation insofar as they make certain choices about how to live and how to act; the self is shaped by the life one lives. "I was responsible for the fact that habit had become so embattled against me; for it was with my consent that I came to the place in which I did not wish to be."[22] While God has determined him in significant ways and given him certain capacities, it is Augustine who makes choices about how to live; as such, his will is free and not fully determined by the ground from which he came.

Just as there is a direct and indirect aspect to God's role in the formation of the self, there are two aspects to the individual's role in the form of the self. While the individual actively makes choices that lend determination to the course of their life (Augustine's teaching of rhetoric, his decision to go to Rome), the life one leads and the relations one has with others cultivate tendencies and dispositions of the self. In living, the self becomes habituated to certain modes of life, and this habituation is a significant aspect of the form of the self. In fact, Augustine suggests that the form the self takes when it is enchained by habitual modes of being is a kind of malformation or deformity: "Our good is life with you for ever, and because we turned away from that, we became twisted. Let us now return to you that we may not be overturned. Our good is life with you and suffers no deficiency."[23]

The point at which he desires to turn toward God is, as we have seen, not the point at which he undergoes his conversion; ethical becoming is not an act of the will, or at least it is not simply an act of the will. The self does not become other than what it is without ceasing to be what it is, without undoing itself. "I fall into my usual ways under my miserable burdens. I am reabsorbed by my habitual practices. I am held in their grip. I weep profusely, but still I am held. Such is the strength of the burden of habit. Here I have the power to be, but do not wish it. There I wish to be, but lack the power. On both grounds I am in misery."[24] Augustine's capacity for ethical becoming hinges on the undoing of habits, that is, on the undoing of the self. The problem becomes: how does one change the form of the self? Augustine approaches this problem through reflective judgment; habits become less integral to the self through a consideration of how they came to be. Rational reflection on the self produces or activates capacities for change. Ethical becoming involves taking responsibility for one's habits, for the form of one's self, and this calls for understanding the emergence of that form. Augustine attempts to will his conversion and discovers that he possesses more than one will, a situation he finds "monstrous."[25] "The mind commands the body and is instantly obeyed. The mind commands itself and meets resistance."[26] In this situation, Augustine reasons, it is not the case that there is a lack of will but that there are *two* wills, both incomplete: "We are dealing

with a morbid condition of the mind which, when it is lifted up by
the truth, does not unreservedly rise to it but is weighted down by
habit." He diagnoses this condition as a conflict within himself: while
he is one self, he is actually dissociated from himself. He both wills
to serve God and is unwilling to do so: "the self which willed to serve
was identical with the self which was unwilling. It was I. I was neither
wholly willing nor wholly unwilling. So I was in conflict with myself
and was dissociated from myself. The dissociation came about against
my will."[27] This monstrous condition is a condition of ethical becoming; the self is no longer entirely held by the stability of habit but is
a multiplicity with no centre of control.[28] While Augustine interprets
this situation in terms of morbidity, he overlooks the necessity of this
dissociation for his ethical conversion. His oversight stems from his
faith in the unity and endurance of the self.[29] A more complex account
of his conversion would attend to the significance of instability, multiplicity, and mutation in ethical becoming.[30]

Augustine comes to this fracture in his self, this dissociation, by
way of the habits he has accumulated from the manner in which he
has lived his life, and also by way of his strengthening desire to convert; the habits constitute one will and his desire for conversion constitutes another will. Thus his wills are in conflict and his self (while
according to him is still unified)[31] is divided against itself. Deleuze
argues that this kind of split, or fracture, in the self arises when the I
that "thinks" is unable to directly determine its being because it is
also a self that is passive and determined within time:

[M]y undetermined existence can be determined only within
time as the existence of a phenomenon, of a passive, receptive
phenomenal subject appearing within time. As a result, the spontaneity of which I am conscious in the "I think" cannot be understood as the attribute of a substantial and spontaneous being, but
only as the affection of a passive self which experiences its own
thought – its own intelligence, that by virtue of which it can say
I – being exercised in it and upon it but not by it. Here begins
a long and inexhaustible story: I is an other, or the paradox of
inner sense. The activity of thought applies to a receptive being,
to a passive subject which represents that activity to itself rather
than enacts it, which experiences its effect rather than initiates it,
and which lives it like an Other within itself. (DR, 86)

For Augustine, the conscious self that wills in the world is "passive
and unwilling," receiving its habits from without, rather than the
"active and willing" and spontaneous being that he thinks he ought
to be.[32] This fracture in the self, however, is a necessary condition of
the self's capacity to become, rather than something to be lamented.

2. FORMLESS MATTER AND ETHICAL BECOMING

We are not the source of our capacities, according to Augustine, yet
we are responsible for them.[33] Good actions and achievements are
not by one's own resources,[34] but rather are owing to God's grace.
The work of the self consists in cultivating one's capacity for receptivity (to alterity), and this, according to Augustine, is done by getting
outside of habit. Habit, as we have seen, is the form the self takes and
as such the self needs to be undone so that one becomes capable of
ethical receptivity and becoming (which for Augustine is the capacity
to receive God's grace). While Augustine gives a robust account of a
divided self struggling to change form by undoing the habits that it
is, he does not in those passages provide an account of how a self can
change form. His narrative aims at becoming and elucidates it as a
complex problem, but it does not provide an ontological account of
the self's capacity to change. Later in *Confessions*, however, in his
reading of Genesis, he introduces the concept of "formless matter"
(*informem materiam*) – which he takes from the *Book of Wisdom* – as
the capacity for mutability and the capacity to receive form[35] that is
ontologically prior to creation.[36] Bringing this ontological concept to
bear on his account of ethical becoming can deepen our insight into
the fecundity of undoing or dissolving aspects of our self-formation.

Augustine's interpretation of creation is that the first thing that God
created, prior to creating the visible earth that we see, was formless
matter. We should understand this priority of the formless over the
formed, however, as ontological rather than temporal. There is no
time prior to creation,[37] he argues, as time cannot possibly "exist
without changes and movements. And where there is no form, there
can be no changes."[38] God "created the world out of formless matter"
(*Wisdom* 2:17), but formless matter was also made by God out of
nothing.[39] He interprets the opening passage of Genesis, that "[in]
the beginning God made heaven and earth. Now the earth was invisible and unorganized and darkness was above the abyss" (Gen. 1:1),
to mean that in the beginning God created formless matter and that

this is what is referred to by the "earth" (or the material) being "invisible and unorganized." While his reading puts him at odds with those who believe that the earth we experience was created out of nothing on the first day of creation,[40] Augustine thinks that this account cannot make sense of the mutability of created things. To account for the inherent mutability of creatures, Augustine reasons that the capacity for mutability must have itself been created by God, and furthermore that nothing with form could be created prior to the existence of the capacity to receive form. This receptive capacity is what makes mutability possible, as "everything mutable implies for us the notion of a kind of formlessness, which allows it to receive form or to undergo change and modification."[41]

Augustine does not connect his account of his conversion with his account of genesis, but arguably we can ascertain significant similarities and shared problems in both his account of ethical becoming and the creation of the earth. The problem of formation is at the heart of the narrative of his conversion: how he has malformed himself through his habits and how these habits are resistant to change such that they block his capacity to convert. In his eyes, habituation has depleted his capacity for change and thus impedes his turning toward God, his becoming Christian. In order to deepen and clarify his insight into ethical becoming, we need to understand the self's "capacity to change," and this is precisely what "formless matter" is. Now, in addition to nothingness and formed matter (creations), there is something that is almost nothing (because it does not really exist yet) without being nothing (since it is implied by all mutable creatures that move from being to non-being). It is this third element, or "formlessness," that forms the very capacity for change and mutability. Without such a capacity for change, Augustine implies, nothing could be formed, because formation involves changes in form. The forms or determinations of creatures involve formlessness, the capacity to take on new forms. "You made it not because you needed it, but from the fullness of your goodness, imposing control and converting it to receive form."[42] The capacity to receive form (formless matter) is a core element that enables Augustine's conversion. In other words, formless matter is an important component of ethical becoming, and a concept that helps shed light on how an undoing of the self could be an ethical task.[43]

Considering his account of formless matter as the capacity to change and to receive form, we can see that the form of Augustine's self needs

to be undone so that he can take on a new form, so that he becomes
a being with different capacities, desires, modes of living, and relations. While Augustine embraces an account of hierarchies of being
from changing matter to unchanging ideas and a divine eternity that
"suffers no variation and experiences no distending in the successive-
ness of time,"[44] he is also attentive to the complexities involved in
processes of self-formation (de-formation, incompatible wills, undoing,
and reformation) and to the relevance of the capacity to change for
the kind of ethical becoming he undergoes and recommends (conversion to Christianity). Our habits are necessary in maintaining the
form of the self, but that formed self is one that emerged because of
the self's fundamental capacity to take on form. In other words, while
our habits seemingly lock us into repetitive or automatic modes of
being, they are themselves the result of the capacity to take on habits,
and as such they are indicative of the self's capacity for change and
not simply impediments to change.

3. BECOMING A BODY WITHOUT ORGANS

Bringing Augustine's account of genesis to bear on thinking through
ethical becoming reveals that formlessness, as the capacity to change,
is a key ingredient of ethical becoming. How then to cultivate or
activate such a capacity? Arguably through degrees of de-formation:
the more rigidly one is constituted by particular forms of life and
within social-material formations, the weaker one's capacity to change
will be. Augustine's ethical becoming is a de-formation of the self that
involves the undoing of habits (forms of self) in order to make a place
for the emergence of different desires and capacities. We cannot simply
become other than what we are; rather, undoing is a core element of
becoming. It is here that Deleuze and Guattari's concept of the "body
without organs" provides us with a conceptual resource for thinking
ethical becoming as an experiment in the dissolution of form (or the
invocation of formlessness).

The concept of the body without organs (BwO) expresses the activities of dissolution and disarticulation of psycho-physical formations
of self, body, and subjectivity – or what Deleuze and Guattari call
"stratifications" – activities that activate new becomings by enabling
the emergence of new forms and facilitating new connections.
"What does it mean to disarticulate, to cease to be an organism? ...
Dismantling the organism has never meant killing yourself, but rather

opening the body to connections that presuppose an entire assemblage, circuits, conjunctions, levels and thresholds, passages and distributions of intensity, and territories and deterritorializations measured with the craft of a surveyor" (TP, 160). The BwO is not *before* the organism; it is contemporaneous with it and "expresses the pure determination of intensity, intensive difference" (TP, 164). The BwO is what one makes in order to activate becomings. It is a work of the self, an ethical unmaking of the self as a desiring being. Just as formless matter, or mutability, subsists with the formed creature, the body without organs subsists with the organism.

Deleuze and Guattari assert that the BwO is "nonstratified, unformed, intense matter" that "causes intensities to pass" and "produces and distributes them in a spatium that is itself intensive, lacking extension" (TP, 153). There are echoes of Augustine here: before God "gave form and particularity to that 'unformed matter' (Wisd. 2:18), there was nothing – no colour, no shape, no body, no spirit? Yet it was not absolute nothingness. It was a kind of formlessness without any definition."[45] Insofar as ethical becoming is a work of the self that involves an undoing of the form of the self through alteration of habit, we can conceive of the BwO as that which enables us to activate formless matter, the capacity to change and to take on new forms. Making a BwO, experimenting with the forms and formations of one's self, produces an intensification of desires and affects such that one becomes capable of new connections, of entering into new formations.

> We are in a social formation; first see how it is stratified for us and in us and at the place where we are; then descend from the strata to the deeper assemblage within which we are held; gently tip the assemblage, making it pass over to the side of the plane of consistency. It is only there that the BwO reveals itself for what it is: connection of desires, conjunction of flows, continuum of intensities. (TP, 161)

We might say that the experimental undoing that comprises the body without organs is what makes possible the contraction of new habits.

Augustine clearly insists that human creatures are better and less changing when they are closer to God and are lowlier insofar as they are variable and farther from God. Nonetheless his narrative of conversion is one that invokes becoming and the capacity to change. "The

nearer approached the moment of time when I would become different, the greater the horror of it struck me."[46] He disparages the mutable nature of earthly creatures, yet it is this very mutability that enables
them to become. Thus, Augustine's account of ethical becoming is a
move away from instability of self toward increasing stability. Yet at
the same time, his narrative rests on the significance of undoing forms
of self and life (habits) in order to become capable of change and of
being capacitated by alterity (in his case, God is the absolutely other).[47]
Augustine strives to develop a narrative of evolution in which he
moves from a multiplicitous self that is consequently unstable toward
a unified self that is stable: "I turned from unity in you to be lost in
multiplicity."[48] Whereas Deleuze and Guattari prioritize multiplicity
and becoming over unity and being:

> A multiplicity is defined not by its elements, nor by a centre of
> unification or comprehension. It is defined by the number of
> dimensions it has; it is not divisible, it cannot lose or gain a
> dimension without changing its nature. Since its variations
> and dimensions are immanent to it, it amounts to the same
> thing to say that each multiplicity is already composed of hetero-
> geneous terms in symbiosis, and that a multiplicity is continually
> transforming itself into a string of other multiplicities, according
> to its thresholds and doors. For example, the Wolf-Man's pack
> of wolves also becomes a swarm of bees, and a field of anuses,
> and a collection of small holes and tiny ulcerations (the theme of
> contagion): all these heterogeneous elements compose "the" mul-
> tiplicity of symbiosis and becoming. If we imagined the position
> of a fascinated Self, it was because the multiplicity toward which
> it leans, stretching to the breaking point, is the continuation of
> another multiplicity that works it and strains it from the inside.
> In fact, the self is only a threshold, a door, a becoming between
> two multiplicities. (TP, 249)

Deleuze urges an attention to the transient nature for which Augustine
thinks our physical sense is inadequate. Augustine wants to halt the
changeability of *his own* human being by orienting himself toward
God, whereas Deleuze wants us to attend to the multiplicity of becomings running through us. Augustine gives becoming a *telos* whose end
is being, or resting with or near Being: "My desire was not to be more
certain of you but to be more stable in you."[49] Whereas for Deleuze

and Guattari, "becoming has neither beginning nor end, departure nor arrival, origin nor destination" (TP, 293). While this is undoubtedly a major point of opposition between the sets of thinkers, they share the insight that mutability, the capacity for mutation and transformation, is a necessary condition for becoming and that degrees of de-formation are necessary in order to activate this capacity.

On the one hand, Augustine's view of the human body is that it is organized by God in such a way that each of the organs has determinate functions ordained by God. It is the "judgement of God," Augustine tells us, that has decreed that the eye is for seeing and the ear is for hearing, that the ear does not see nor the eye hear. On the other hand, when he expresses his relation to God he starts to endow his psychic/spiritual "organs" with different capacities: the soul sees, the heart hears, and so on. Thus the "senses" are dis-organized as Augustine stretches to express a relation with alterity, a relation by which he is differently capacitated. In order to relate with alterity, in order to be constituted by otherness, one makes a body without organs, dismantles the stratified self by dissolving the current organization of one's "organs."[50]

Deleuze and Guattari urge an active resistance to the organization of the organs by God, medicine, society, and call upon us to "make a body without organs" that, properly understood, is a non-organized body. Life and desire, they tell us, depend on dismantling the organism, dismantling the self. "[Y]ou can't desire without making one" (TP, 149). As we saw earlier, the desires one has are a critical element of one's ethical capacities; they are determining forces in our lives and relations with others and with the world. The desire for affluence and social status in an individualistic, capitalist society may impede one's capacity to attend and respond to social and material inequalities in one's neighbourhood. If the desire for affluence is stronger than the desire for social equality, one will be determined by concerns for the maintenance and growth of affluence, and as such one may act to "protect property values" at the expense of improving the quality of education for those who are differently situated socially and economically. The construction of a body without organs, then, is a way of unmaking the structures by which we desire and enabling the formation of new modes of desire.

The importance of working on habitual forms of life and subjectivity in order to activate capacities for the emergence of new affects, desires, and subjectivities is recognized in environmental ethics, where habituated forms of life (dependence on fossil fuels for light, warmth, manufacture, and transportation) are linked with environmental problems (sea level rise, intense weather, forest fires, toxic waste, pollution of groundwater, etc.). Many believe that addressing these issues calls for the transformation of habits as a kind of ethical becoming. The habit of working indoors rather than out in the elements weakens, and in some cases extinguishes, capacities for ethical responsiveness toward non-human worlds.

> Now, living only indoors, immersed only in passing time and not out in the weather, our contemporaries, packed into cities, use neither shovel nor oar; worse yet, they've never even seen them. Indifferent to the climate, except during vacations when they rediscover the world in a clumsy arcadian way, they naively pollute what they don't know, which rarely hurts them and doesn't concern them. Dirty species, monkeys and motorists, drop their filth fast, because they don't live in the space they pass through and thus let themselves foul it.[51]

Ethical becomings involve degrees of desubjectification and designification, and dissolving aspects of oneself through the alteration of habits enables the emergence and development of new capacities. In the case of the environment, a dissolution of habituated forms of living can enable the emergence of capacities for noticing, knowing, appreciating, and being concerned with the more than human world outside.

Experimenting with the dissolution of form as an aspect of ethical becoming can also be done with institutions. Guattari's work at La Borde (a private psychiatric clinic about an hour south of Paris) in the mid- to late 1950s is an example of activating becomings through disorganizing and experimenting with institutional forms. The staff at La Borde developed a practice of changing roles: medical staff took up material chores such as cleaning, cooking, and dishwashing, and service staff collaborated in the care of the patients. "An old washerwoman proved very capable at running the print workshop and editorial committee of the newspaper; another excelled in sporting activities, a former metallurgist showed great talent in leading mime shows."[52] This shifting of individuals' functions, Guattari thinks, activates new subjectivities; "subjectivity, at any stage of the socius worth considering, did not occur by itself, but was produced by certain conditions,

and that these conditions could be modeled through multiple procedures in a way that would channel it in a more creative direction."[53]
Similar to the disorganization of the organs, the people at La Borde
practised an experimentation with ordained functions (medical staff
care for patients, and service staff do material chores) that enabled
the emergence of new desires and connections; this opened up spaces
of becoming rather than adhering to the reproduction of social relations and subjectivities: "under such conditions ... the body without
organs has replaced the organism and experimentation has replaced
all interpretation, for which it no longer has any use. Flows of intensity,
their fluids, their fibers, their continuums and conjunctions of affects,
the wind, fine segmentation, microperceptions, have replaced the
world of the subject. Becomings, becomings-animal, becomings-
molecular, have replaced history, individual or general" (TP, 162).

The experimentation at La Borde activated a becoming that was
not simply individualistic; rather, individuals were swept up by a
becoming of the assemblage within which they were situated. With
the alteration of the assemblage, all the people were consequently
altered and capable of new connections and desires. The institution
of the mental hospital was deformed from "an empty repetition"[54]
in a "molecular revolution" to a "permanent reinvention" that enabled
the constituents (doctors, nurses, cooks, launderers, gardeners, and
patients) to discover "a whole new relationship with the world."[55]
De-formations of selves, institutions, and social structures can be
capacitating insofar as they free us from habituated forms of life that
block us from ethical engagements with ourselves and with the world.

Augustine gives us an account of ethical becoming that involves
the undoing of one's habits, and as we have seen, insofar as the self
is formed by its habits (or the self *is* its habits), ethical becoming
involves a de-formation or dismantling of the self as an ethical work
of the self. This de-formative work calls for an ontological account
of form and habit: how does something come to have form? Augustine's
interpretation of Genesis rests on the concept of "formless matter"
that is "almost nothing," the very capacity of things to change.
Underlying all forms, or formed matter, is the capacity to change; the
capacity to change thus has ontological priority over formations
themselves. The habituated self is only possible because of the capacity
for change. One cannot, however, completely undo oneself (for that
would result in death, both psychic and physical). Instead, one must
dip into "formless matter," make oneself a body without organs, in

order to dismantle aspects of one's habituated self so that one becomes capable of contracting new habits. Experimentations with formlessness, however, preclude the unity of the self. Insofar as unforming habits is an ethical task, what is called for is the embracing of the self in its multiplicity.

NOTES

1 Connolly, *A World of Becoming*, 26.
2 Cummins, "Functional Analysis," 763.
3 Millikan, "In Defense of Proper Functions," 299.
4 Gould and Vrba, "Exaptation," 13; Preston, "Why Is a Wing Like a Spoon?," 237–8; Canguilhem, "Machine and Organism," 19, 57.
5 Deleuze, *Expressionism in Philosophy*. Hereafter cited as EP.
6 Augustine, *Confessions*, X.vii.
7 Ibid., I.v, IV.v, IV.xv.
8 Ibid., I.xiii.
9 Ibid., V.i.
10 Ibid., XII.ix.
11 José Medina develops this idea in terms of pragmatism's concept of social learning: "The experiential disruptions that arise in interaction with significantly different others are precious opportunities ... By seeking these experiences of perplexity and disruption and using them as mechanisms of learning, we can cultivate a social sensibility that opens our eyes, ears, and hearts to other ways of thinking, feeling, and living." *The Epistemology of Resistance*, 19.
12 Augustine, *Confessions*, VII.xvii.
13 Ibid., VIII.vii.
14 Ibid., VIII.v.
15 Prendiville, "The Development," 29, 62.
16 Augustine, *Confessions*, VIII.v.
17 Ibid.
18 Ibid., VIII.vii.
19 Ibid., X.vii.
20 Ibid., IV.xvi.
21 Ibid., XII.x.
22 Ibid., VIII.v.
23 Ibid., IV.xvi.
24 Ibid., X.xl.

25 Ibid., VIII.ix.

26 Ibid., VIII.ix.

27 Ibid., VIII.x.

28 James J. O'Donnell invites us to consider that while Augustine held fast to the idea that the "human personality is at its best single, unified, and subject to rational control," we should resist taking his account of a linear self-transformation at face value. Instead we should consider whether Augustine uses this biographical technique in order to make a new past for himself by effacing and moving his real experience "into the shadow world of the things that were unconfessed." "Augustine's Unconfession," 214–19.

29 William James sees Augustine's conversion and religious experience more generally as a movement from division to unity: "the process, gradual or sudden, by which a self hitherto divided, and consciously wrong interior and unhappy, becomes unified and consciously right superior and happy." *Varieties of Religious Experience*, 189.

30 Mary-Jane Rubenstein counters James's conception of Augustine's conversion as a movement from division to unity, arguing that there "is a constitutive multiplicity at the heart of the Christian will-toward-oneness" and that "remnants of multiplicity" remain after Augustine's conversion. Exploring a polydox theology (in contrast with orthodoxy), she asks readers to consider that "perhaps conversion does not bring about the static unity it promises. Perhaps, far from annihilating multiplicity, the confessional journey uncovers and reconfigures it." "Undone by Each Other," 106–9.

31 William Connolly argues that the ambiguity between Augustine's claim that his will is divided yet unified is indicative of larger theological problems at work in Augustine's thought. "He requires the doctrine of two wills to cope with the experience of dissonance in the self and to make grace indispensable to salvation. But he must stifle a danger opened up by this very formulation that would (a) threaten the goal of salvation from another direction by defining the salvational god as limited and (b) highlight grave difficulties confronting his doctrine in defending simultaneously the omnipotence of this god and its innocence of responsibility for evil." Augustine's account of two wills, Connolly asserts, while necessary to describe his experience, makes him subject to the critique that he has adopted the view of Manichaeans that there are competing cosmic natures that he has explicitly rejected. *The Augustinian Imperative*, 79.

32 Augustine, *Confessions*, VIII.v.

33 Ibid., I.xx.

34 Ibid., VIII.xi.

35 Ibid., XII.vi.

36 Ibid., XII.xxix.

37 This account of time is a way of responding to the question of why God did not create the world sooner. Richard Sorabji explores accounts of time that make similar responses and argues that Augustine's account is clever and original. "Time, Mysticism, and Creation," 225–30.

38 Augustine, *Confessions*, XII.xii.

39 Ibid., XII.xxii.

40 Ibid., XII.xvii.

41 Ibid., XII.xix.

42 Ibid., XIII.iv.

43 Joshua Nunziato makes a compelling case that the "creation of matter itself conditions every confession" and that confession is empowered by matter; as such, it is Augustine's very condition as a being of matter that makes his confession possible. "Created to Confess," 273. Insofar as confession is a key dimension of Augustine's conversion, Nunziato's argument affirms the significance of creatural mutability to ethical becoming.

44 Augustine, *Confessions*, XII.xi.

45 Ibid., XII.iii.

46 Ibid., VIII.xi.

47 Jean Luc Marion explores the significance of the human relation to alterity in terms of identity and individuation in creation. Humans differ from other created things that were each "created according to its kind" and thus in having self-identity; the "created thing bears a likeness to itself; it resembles itself." By contrast, with the human, "creation no longer happens according to a creature's resemblance to itself … but according to its resemblance to an other besides itself – and, moreover, to an other of maximum alterity, since it is a reference to God." Marion argues that this makes the human the kind of being that is without definition and without essence, getting its definition from otherness. *In the Self's Place*, 253–4.

48 Augustine, *Confessions*, I.i.

49 Ibid., VIII.i.

50 The idea that capacities are activated through sensorial disorganization is expressed by Rimbaud: "The Poet makes himself a seer by a long, gigantic and rational derangement of all the senses. All forms of love, suffering, and madness. He searches himself. He exhausts all poisons in himself and keeps only their quintessences. Unspeakable torture where he needs all his faith, all his superhuman strength, where he becomes among all men the great patient, the great criminal, the one accursed – and the supreme

Scholar!" "Charleville – À P. Demeny – 15 mai" in *Rimbaud: Complete Works*, 377.
51 Serres, *The Natural Contract*, 28.
52 Guattari, *Chaosophy*, 179.
53 Ibid., 182.
54 Ibid., 182
55 Ibid., 180.

3

Tamed Affect:
A Deleuzian Theory of Moral Sentiments

Jeffrey A. Bell

An admitted irony and problem confronted me as I began this chapter for a workshop and then a book on "minor ethics." Although this chapter will indeed set out a Deleuze-inspired perspective on a classical moral theory – in my case, the Humean theory of moral sentiments – doing so nonetheless presupposes something quite problematic. Gathering at a workshop to discuss one's work presupposes a common understanding of the way knowledge is produced that Deleuze, following Nietzsche, challenges. In short, these assumptions are: first, that those who gather at workshops or conferences do so with the best of intentions of working toward attaining better conclusions or insights about a certain topic, such as the possibility of a minor ethics; and, second, by subjecting one's work to critical examination and feedback, these associations will make it possible for that work to be improved. This process will draw out, promote, and refine the fullest potential of our capacities and thus facilitate the natural affinity we have for arriving, when all is going well, at the truth. If I am grossly mistaken on a basic point of Humean interpretation, for instance, my error will be called out and corrected so that, through further work, I can arrive at the best conclusions given my current abilities and knowledge. We attend philosophical associations because we want to enhance our knowledge and work, and thus we hope to leave such an experience, or to finish reading a critical review of our own work, with a more finely tuned ability to get it right. If this is indeed our motivation, then it is, as will be argued below, deeply problematic, for it accepts without criticism a common moral framework, or a common set of norms that one accepts as a standard that ought to guide one's work. Deleuze notes that it was Nietzsche who first elu-cidated this moral framework that underlies much of traditional, professional philosophy:

When Nietzsche questions the most general presuppositions of philosophy, he says that these are essentially moral, since Morality alone is capable of persuading us that thought has a good nature and the thinker a good will, and that only the good can ground the supposed affinity between thought and the True. Who else, in effect, but Morality, and this Good which gives thought to the true, and the true to thought? (DR, 132)

If our faculties are functioning well and to the best of their ability, then they will of their own reveal the truth of a subject by virtue of a natural affinity between thought and the true; and it is the true that is available for subjects of good will, intention, and morality, that is, for those who come together to seek it. Only by working together, and with the best of intentions – or so the moral presupposition of philosophy assumes – will one come to the truth. For Deleuze, how-ever, this moral presupposition is precisely what he calls the common sense "image of thought" in terms of which, he argues, "everybody knows and is presumed to know what it means to think" (DR, 131). This common sense image, Deleuze claims, presupposes "an upright nature and a good will"; that is, it presupposes thought as a faculty that is "upright" insofar as it is "endowed with a talent for truth or an affinity with the truth" in addition to a "good will" that seeks to overcome differences and contentious debate in order to arrive at a truth that is common to all. This common sense image is problematic, however, for it can only assume, without explaining, its own structure, origin, and ability. This is the sense in which the image of thought, for Deleuze, reflects what everybody knows, or what people unques-tionably think it means to know.

Given Nietzsche's and Deleuze's critiques of the moral presuppositions of philosophy, it may seem out of place here to engage with the Scottish Enlightenment figures of Adam Smith and David Hume. Rather than criticize the moral presuppositions of philosophy that take as a given the natural affinity between thought and the true, between good will and the truth common to all, Smith and Hume appear to embrace and argue for these presuppositions. Just as it is widely thought by participants at an academic conference, or the authors of a text, that others may speak up and correct one's misguided efforts in order to align them more accurately with a proper, true reading of events, Hume acknowledged the benefits of the polite culture of eighteenth-century Scotland and England. In a number of essays, for example, Hume noted that the encounter with a diverse, contrasting, and perhaps even antagonistic audience of peers could well serve to develop and refine one's sensibilities. "[W]here a number of neighboring states have a great intercourse of arts and commerce," Hume argues, "their mutual jealousy keeps them from receiving too lightly the law from each other in matters of taste and of reasoning, and makes them examine every work of art with the greatest care and accuracy."[1] "The more these refined arts advance," Hume adds in a later essay, "the more sociable men become."[2] At the frequent "improvement societies," such as the Select Society that Hume, Smith, and others attended, the very interaction and encounter with different opinions would encourage a refinement of one's own sensibilities and promote a polite culture. In short, the assumption here is that our rustic, unpolished, and prone to violent nature becomes tamed and civilized through the effort to create a shared culture within civilized drawing rooms.

Notwithstanding these apparent differences between, on the one hand, Hume's and Smith's embrace of the moral presuppositions of polite culture, and Deleuze's Nietzschean critique of those presuppositions on the other, this chapter will argue that they share a profoundly similar meta-ethics. In the first section we begin to set the stage for comparing Hume and Smith with Deleuze by sketching the risks associated with belief, in particular the risk of madness. As we will see, a similar concern haunts Smith's arguments for what he calls the "impartial spectator." For both Hume and Smith, our beliefs risk being undermined by a chaos or madness against which, on Smith's view, the impartial spectator provides a bulwark. In the second section we turn to Deleuze, and to the concept of heterogenesis, in order to provide the metaphysical basis for the risks both Hume and Smith identify. Crucial to the concept of heterogenesis, and to the normativity of heterogenesis we will identify as integral to a minor ethics, is the concept of learning. With the concept of learning we begin to sketch an account of how the chaos, the risk of madness, comes to be tamed, or how the affect inseparable from belief becomes a tamed affect. This theme of the taming of affect becomes prominent in the third and final section, in which we expand upon the concept of learning by way of a discussion of Deleuze and Guattari's chapter on art in *What Is Philosophy?* This section provides the arguments for what we can call a minor ethics. In this final section we also return to Hume and Smith to show that in their work there is also an implicit recognition of the minor ethics that traditional, normative ethics presupposes.

I. HUME AND SMITH

It was clear to the thinkers of the Scottish Enlightenment, in particular Hume and Smith, that the good will of the participants cannot simply be presupposed but is itself the result of a process. In fact, for Hume the polite culture of eighteenth-century Scotland and England was only possible as a result of a general taming of the more violent, agonistic impulses of human beings. Andrew Sabl has recently shown, in his study of Hume's *The History of England*, how Hume explored this process of the taming of violence. Sabl shows Hume's argument that the traditional barons who exercised the law themselves, and often violently, eventually came "very slowly to realize that they had a durable interest in giving up their 'right to oppress and tyrannize.'"[3] In addition to this propensity to "oppress and tyrannize," there is the propensity to delirium and madness. Hume was well aware of this propensity too when in the *Treatise* he noted that "a lively imagination very often degenerates into madness or folly, and bears it a great resemblance," since for the mad person "every loose fiction or idea, having the same influence as the impressions of the memory, or the conclusions of the judgment, is receiv'd on the same footing, and operates with equal force on the passions. A present impression and a customary transition are now no longer necessary to enliven our ideas."[4] In the case of madness and folly, therefore, one's faculties and will do not always work together, on the basis of customary expectations and habits, in order to uncover an essential truth, for instance, regarding the truth common to all tokens of a certain type. To the contrary, the violence of madness is such that an impression will involuntarily assert itself regardless of whatever customary transitions and habits may have been formed. We may assume that we possess knowledge, given the stability and force with which a given belief is held – and for Hume this is indeed his standard account of what establishes our beliefs, such as the belief in necessary connection. However, in the case of madness we may hold a belief with comparable force and stability, yet this belief may be completely anomalous and not arise through the usual process. Madness thus poses a perpetual risk and challenge to the security of our beliefs. It is for this reason, among others, that Deleuze argues that reason is not a faculty already equipped to grasp the rules and norms of science and morality; rather, "[u]nderneath all reason lies delirium, and drift" (DI, 262). In other words, if we take reason to be a state of calm, cool reflection, or a stable state established over time, the mistake is to forget that beneath this stability is the ever-present risk of delirium. Moreover, it is this delirium and folly, or the strength and power of affect that becomes recognized as a problem only as this affect is tamed, that is the condition which makes possible the cooperative enterprise of polite culture and the rational doctrines that emerge in its wake. It is this aspect of Hume's work that drew Deleuze to his early study of Hume; thus, far from being an opponent to the Deleuze–Nietzsche critique of the moral presuppositions of philosophy, Hume emerges as a key advocate.

The same can be said of Adam Smith, though this is not as widely recognized. In *The Theory of Moral Sentiments* (1759), Smith provided one of the most influential moral treatises of the eighteenth century.[5] As a student of Francis Hutcheson, who is often viewed as the father of the Scottish Enlightenment, Smith was a central figure in the intellectual life and culture of eighteenth-century Scotland. Although he is better known for his book *The Wealth of Nations* (1776), and thus for his pivotal role in the founding of economics, Smith's *Theory of Moral Sentiments* is equally important though unfortunately often overlooked. This fact is noteworthy because *The Wealth of Nations* famously maintains that one can let markets function on their own and simply let individuals pursue their own self-interest, on the basis that as individuals pursue their own self-interest, the "invisible hand" of the markets will guide nations to greater wealth than if one attempted to predetermine their economic fate. Smith certainly did stress the role of the invisible hand, which served in part to argue against the mercantilist mindset then prevalent among European nations, but what is often overlooked is the pervasive moral vision that guides his philosophy. That moral vision would lead Smith to call upon normatively guided political intervention into markets, which is precisely what many today in the name of Smith would argue against doing. It is in *The Theory of Moral Sentiments* that Smith forged his moral vision, and we must keep that vision in mind when we read *The Wealth of Nations*.

At the heart of Smith's moral theory is the concept of the "impartial spectator." Smith further develops the Humean idea that it is through active engagement with others that a polite culture can be formed which maintains differences of opinion without allowing those differences to send the group off into vulgar disputes and angry dissension. For Smith, this process becomes internalized, resulting in what he calls the *impartial spectator*, the perspective that is most likely to be maintained by people who can look upon a situation with "calm reason."[6] The passions may well get the best of us, Smith admits, or we may, as Hume recognized, succumb to delirium if we are not checked and kept within proper, tamed limits. Due to our partiality, for example, when subject to passions such as pride, anger, and jealousy, among many others, we do not look upon a situation with "calm reason" but rather with a biased, partial viewpoint for which we might provide justifications (i.e., rationalizations in the pejorative sense). The impartial spectator provides a check upon the tendency of our passions to focus on our partial interests rather than what is good from an impartial point of view. When speaking of the propriety associated with the passions of gratitude and resentment, for instance, Smith claims that "these, as well as all the other passions of human nature, seem proper and are approved of, when the heart of every impartial spectator entirely sympathizes with them, when every indifferent by-stander entirely enters into, and goes along with them."[7] If the reaction of our friend is not one that we or any other impartial spectator can enter into, then we know that the reaction lacks in propriety. If I make known my paranoia that someone is out to get me, aiming to undermine my career and reputation, and if no one else can appreciate my passions or see themselves as having similar feelings if confronted with the same circumstances, then it can justly be concluded that my passions are untamed and in need of a normative counterbalance. The impartial spectator, in other words, is the common sense basis for our moral judgments, the epitome of how we would judge our own and others' actions if we were to guide ourselves by the properly functioning faculties we hold in common with others.

For Hume, however, the common nature of these faculties – the calm habits of reason – are not to be assumed without question; rather, their very constitution and the always present risk of delirium is precisely the problem associated with these faculties. It was this problematic nature of the faculties, the problem of accounting for their very genesis and stability, that first drew Deleuze to Hume's work.

But the same is true for Smith as well. We cannot simply assume the ever present goodwill of our passions and faculties. As Smith argues, when one "suffers himself to be astonished and confounded by the judgments of ignorant and weak men," rather than polite, cultured, and impartial men, then he "discovers his connexion with mortality, and appears to act suitably, rather to the human, than to the divine, part of his origin."[8] In other words, when we do not rise above our uncultured, impetuous selves and engage with the impartial spectator, the divine side of ourselves, then the risk is a collapse into ill will rather than good will. The question, then, is how this process of generating stable faculties of good will unfolds and how it staves off the risk of delirium and ill will. Before turning to how Hume and Smith address these questions, let us bring Deleuze into the mix, for as Deleuze builds on Hume's insights he sets forth what one might call a minor ethics. This ethics, as we shall see, calls upon a normativity of heterogenesis, or a call to be open to transformation for the sake of being moral.

2. DELEUZE

According to Deleuze, we cannot resolve the problem of common sense by looking for a common truth that will overcome all differences and reconcile us once again to our "upright nature" and "good will." In his doctoral defence, published as "The Method of Dramatization," Deleuze argued that if one looks toward understanding Truth or Ideas by posing and answering a "What is this?" question, then one "prematurely judges the Idea as simplicity of the essence" (DI, 95). One prematurely assumes, in other words, that there is a common core or truth to what we seek to understand, placing us back in the throes of the common sense image of thought. If alternatively, following Deleuze, we understand the Truth or Idea as a multiplicity, and thus in terms neither of a countable one nor of a multiple of such countable ones, then a better question would be, "who? how? how much? where and when? in which case?" (DI, 96). To state this slightly differently, we ought to find ourselves within a *problem space*, such as the one in which a jealous lover finds himself when confronted with a multiplicity of signs with conflicting, irresolvable interpretations: unexplained absences, whispered conversations, shifty eyes, and so on. Deleuze evokes this very example in *Proust and Signs*, and as we will see, the problem space of the jealous lover is also a space where the moral presuppositions of common sense fail. Deleuze thus writes: "Who searches for truth? The jealous man, under the pressure of the beloved's lies. There is always the violence of a sign that forces us into the search, that robs us of peace. The truth is not to be found by affinity, nor by goodwill, but is betrayed by involuntary signs ... [T]ruth is never a product of a prior disposition but the result of a violence in thought" (PS, 15–16).[9]

For Deleuze, thought by its very nature does not have an affinity for truth, nor for good will; rather, it occurs only "involuntarily" and in response to a violence that disturbs its quiet, calm reflection. This violence, moreover, can undo thought itself. "Underneath all reason," he thus argues, "lies delirium, and drift" (DI, 262). At this point we can return to Hume, for with Hume, Deleuze claims, "if the mind is manifested as a delirium, it is because it is first of all, and essentially, madness" (ES, 83). We can begin to see why this is so, for if thought is forced upon us by involuntary signs, then those signs belie a problem space that wreaks violence upon our "upright nature" and "good will." The result is that the questions and the problematic space of a multiplicity confront us – *who? how? how much? where and when? in which case?* – and the pursuit of these questions may well undermine all that is common and familiar and unleash a madness that remains inseparable from all of our rational, well-tuned thoughts.

For example, let us say that while at a conference I happen to notice a friend in conversation with someone I do not recognize. In normal circumstances there would be nothing untoward in this particular circumstance and I would ordinarily think nothing of it and assume all is well – after all, I have been friends with this particular person for years. In the throes of madness, however, perhaps brought on by jealousy, perhaps not, I may leap to the conclusion that this friend is plotting my own demise and that he is speaking to this stranger about it. This madness may spread, and if left unchecked suddenly everything I once took to be common and familiar may take on a sinister air, as if I had suddenly fallen into a tale told by H.P. Lovecraft. This susceptibility to madness and delirium that Hume recognizes accounts for why Deleuze claims that Hume's empiricism is "a kind of universe of science fiction: as in science fiction, the world seems fictional, strange, foreign, experienced by other creatures; but we get the feeling that this world is our own, and we are the creatures" (DI, 162). At each moment, we are a short, delirious step away from a completely strange, foreign world.

This gives rise to the problem of how to account for the way madness becomes sanity, or how, as we will see below, affects become
tamed. In exploring this process, we will gain a better understanding
of how something like Smith's impartial spectator and the moral
presuppositions that found the common sense image of thought
become possible. This is precisely the problem that Deleuze takes on
in his early book on Hume, where he argues that Hume's guiding
problem was to show how a multiplicity of discrete impressions can
give rise to a systemic, unitary subject, or how "a subject transcending
the given [impressions can] be constituted in the given?" (ES, 86–7).
How can the "subject who invents and believes [be] constituted inside
the given in such a way that it makes the given itself a synthesis and
a system?" This problem is restated in *Difference and Repetition*, and,
again with reference to Hume, in terms of accounting for how, despite
the fact that repeated elements remain distinct yet the same, this
"repetition [can] change something in the case of the repeated element" (DR, 70). Hume himself recognized this problem, pointing out
in his *Treatise* that it is "certain that this repetition of similar objects
in similar situations produces nothing new either in these objects, or
in any external body."[10] Despite this, Hume continues to note that
"the observation of this resemblance [between similar objects in
similar situations] produces a new impression in the mind" and that
this new impression is the basis for the idea of necessary connection.[11]
This new idea, for Hume, is a product of the mind, or as Deleuze puts
it in *Difference and Repetition*: "Repetition changes nothing in the
object repeated, but does change something in the mind which *contemplates* it" (DR, 70, my emphasis).

What Deleuze draws from Hume – and he will continue do so
throughout his writings – is the concept of "contemplation." For
Deleuze, contemplation refers to the process whereby a series of
phenomena come to be transformed into a new entity, much as a
series of repeated phenomena become, for Hume, transformed in the
mind into the idea of necessity. Stated differently, contemplation is
the concept Deleuze uses to account for the heterogenesis of phenomena, or how a multiplicity becomes actualized as a determinate and
distinct identity. It is the concept of contemplation, along with the
concept of learning, as we will see shortly, that comes to Deleuze's
aid in addressing Hume's problem of accounting for how a multiplicity becomes a system, or how an untamed, violent affect and sign
becomes a tamed affect. In short, contemplation or learning brings

about an "incorporeal transformation" that is irreducible to the elements contemplated, to the already constituted givens, and this opens up the possibility that these givens can become a system that acts in accordance with predictable rules and norms. In *A Thousand Plateaus*, Deleuze and Guattari offer the example of a judge declaring an accused person guilty as an instance of incorporeal transformation. The guilty verdict clearly affects the person, who had been simply "the accused" prior to the reading of the verdict. After the verdict is read, that person is taken off to prison in handcuffs and his legal status will now be dramatically different. For Deleuze and Guattari, it is precisely this dramatic transformation of "the accused into a convict" that is "a pure instantaneous act or incorporeal attribute that is the expressed of the judge's sentence" (TP, 80–1). The judge's sentence, in short, effects an "incorporeal transformation" that is "recognizable by its instantaneousness, its immediacy, by the simultaneity of the statement expressing the transformation and the effect the transformation produces." Yet an incorporeal transformation cannot be effected by *anyone* with *any* utterance. A bystander outside the courtroom cannot transform the accused into a convict by shouting "guilty!" It is only a judge with a particular authority who can effectuate the transformation. It is here that the concept of *contemplation* comes into play for Deleuze, for what contemplation does is transform signs and affects into a grammar, a "plane of consistency" or problem space that is presupposed by, or implicated in, the explicated rules where, for instance, a judge can by right and law declare an accused to be guilty as charged. The problem space, in other words, is precisely the multiplicity as substantive that Deleuze argues for in *Difference and Repetition*, or the principle of sufficient reason for the norms and morals of society.

We can turn to Deleuze's use of the concept of learning[12] to show how, as with contemplation, a multiplicity of violent signs is transformed into a tamed affect or into a predictable, systematic process that forms the common sense from which we can then derive our explicit moral norms. In the case of learning to swim, for instance, Deleuze is quite clear that learning is not a matter of reproducing an already established action: "Learning takes place not in the relation between a representation and an action (reproduction of the Same) but in the relation between a sign and a response (encounter with the Other)" (DR, 22). This relation between sign and response is the manner in which a singularity or event as inflection point comes to be connected with (or communicates with) other inflection points. Thus Deleuze argues that learning to swim occurs when "a body combines some of its own distinctive points with those of a wave," or when we successfully "constitute [a] space of an encounter with signs" (DR, 23). In other words, what needs to happen as a condition for learning is that a "space of encounter," or what I have called a problem space, is constituted whereby the distinctive points of the encounter between the body and the wave, currents, and so on, come into a relationship of "consistency" whereby it then becomes possible for a new behaviour to be actualized, namely, swimming. Deleuze offers a similar example later in *Difference and Repetition* of the monkey that learns to identify the particular colour of the box in which food is hidden. Initially the monkey picks up boxes at random, but then it comes to learn that the food is hidden under boxes of a particular colour. Deleuze notes that prior to learning which coloured box the food is hidden under, "there comes a paradoxical period during which the number of 'errors' diminishes even though the monkey does not yet possess the 'knowledge' or 'truth' of a solution in each case" (DR, 164). This "paradoxical period" is the problem space – or what Deleuze and Guattari will later call "the plane of consistency" – that needs to be constituted in order for learning to occur. That which is actually learned, whether this be how to swim or the "knowledge" or "rule" associated with finding food, is precisely the "Event" within which the "ideational singularities communicate." These *ideational singularities* are the distinctive inflection points – whether of the body and waves or of colours, food, and boxes – and they are *ideational* because they are to be contrasted with the concrete givens themselves. In short, they are the events or inflection points that are inseparable from and yet irreducible to these givens. The ideational singularities then come to be hidden within the event or the learning they make possible, and the event that is actualized draws them together, at once, into the very incorporeal transformation that is the Event.[13]

At this point a contrast with Wittgenstein may facilitate our effort to understand the distinction between a common sense ethics and minor ethics, or, more precisely, it may allow us to highlight the relationship between a learned rule and the context, system, or problem space that makes such learning possible. What have we learned, to follow Wittgenstein's example, when we have learned to apply the predicate "is a metre in length"? The use of this predicate, as

Wittgenstein makes clear in his *Philosophical Investigations*, presupposes a transformation that cannot itself be identified with the predicate – or it presupposes a learning that is not to be identified with the rule or predicate that comes to be learned and known. As Wittgenstein puts it, there is "one thing of which one can say neither that it is one metre long, nor that it is not one metre long, and that is the standard metre in Paris."[14] Here Wittgenstein is stressing the incorporeal nature of measurement, or the fact that what is crucial to the standard metre in Paris is something that is not to be confused with the corporeal body that exists in Paris, for the body itself, common sense would seem to tell us, is indeed a metre in length.[15] Wittgenstein is indeed making a distinction, but it is not between corporeal bodies and incorporeal processes; rather, he is alerting us to the distinction between the standards, rules, and grammar of a language and that which is the result or consequence of these standards. As Wittgenstein puts it: "It is one thing to describe methods of measurement, and another to obtain the results of measurement."[16] To understand what someone means when she says something is a metre long, therefore, is not for Wittgenstein a matter of pointing to something that is a metre long; rather, and more importantly, it is a matter of having the ability to use the standard of measurement in practice and to explain this use to someone else. It is here that the importance of learning looms large in Wittgenstein's work – hence, we find yet another area of convergence between Deleuze and Wittgenstein.

To learn the meaning of a word, for Wittgenstein, is to learn the word's use, or as Wittgenstein puts it: "The understanding of a language, as of a game [is] like the understanding or mastery of a calculus, something like the ability to multiply."[17] Learning, however, is not simply a matter of training, of being able to reply mechanically and by rote in accordance with accepted practices. Instead, it involves the grasp of a word's place within a grammatical system. "A sign," Wittgenstein claims, "does its job only in a grammatical system."[18] A piece of carved wood on a chessboard is just a piece of wood unless seen by way of the rules of chess. If one were to add a paper hat to one of the pieces and say, "Now this piece is elevated in stature by virtue of this hat," this action would be meaningless unless incorporated into the rules of chess in such a way that others recognized the place of this innovation within the system of rules.[19] A philosophical problem arises when one identifies a rule to account for a given practice and then either excludes other rules that may equally well account for the practice or forces a rule upon practices to which it may not apply. Whether a given rule applies or not, it is nonetheless the case for Wittgenstein that language, if it is to exist at all, be systematic: "If rule became exception, and exception rule; or, if both became phenomena of roughly equal tendency, then our normal language-games would thereby lose their point."[20] What a person learns, therefore, when he learns the meaning of a word, is how to use this word within a grammatical system, a system of rules and expectations whereby my explanation of the meaning of the word will match what others expect.[21] The normative command associated with learning, therefore, is "do as I do."

For Deleuze, by contrast, learning is not a matter of representing and reproducing the actions of another, a normative "do as I do"; rather, it is an encounter with a series of distinctive points and events that need to be drawn into a plane of consistency if a new, learned behaviour is to emerge. For Wittgenstein, a systematic grammar is always already presupposed. The rules, conventions, and institutions of a culture form the bedrock upon which explanations end; as Wittgenstein puts it in the *Blue Book*, eventually our explanations "strike rock bottom, that is we have come down to conventions."[22] For Deleuze, a grammar is not presupposed but needs to be constituted, and it is the problem of how a system comes to be constituted that is an essential concern to Deleuze's project, one with which he grappled from the beginning.

3. AFFECT: FROM ART TO ETHICAL LIFE

We can gain a clearer understanding of Deleuze's contribution to a project of minor ethics, and in turn bring our earlier discussions of Hume and Smith back into the mix, by turning to Deleuze and Guattari's discussions of art in *What Is Philosophy?* It is not an unusual move for an ethicist to turn to art in the process of developing a moral theory. Aristotle, for example, made significant use of art in laying forth the fundamental principles of his theory of virtue. Aristotle argues, for example, that "we often say of good works of art that it is not possible either to take away or to add anything, implying that excess and defect destroy the goodness of works of art, while the mean preserves it; and good artists, as we say, look to this in their work."[23] From here Aristotle concludes that "if virtue, like nature, is more precise and better than any art, then virtue would be aiming at the mean," or, that in creating our life as well as we possibly can we will aspire, like the artist who avoids excess and defect, to aim at the mean. For Deleuze and Guattari, by contrast, the "work of art" is not that which hits the mean if done well, but rather nothing other than "a being of sensation" that "it exists in itself" (WP, 164). This "being of sensation" is "a bloc of sensations, that is to say, a compound of percepts and affects." However, the being of sensation is not to be confused with the perception of the artwork or with the feelings and emotions of the viewer. The being of sensation is insepa-rable from these perceptions and feelings, and the task of the artist is to extract from these perceptions and feelings a bloc and compound of percepts and affects, a being of sensation. This is no easy task, for "the artist's greatest difficulty is to make [the bloc or compound of percepts and affects] stand up on its own." The artist's task is not to represent a model or adequately portray a possible or actually existent life or state of affairs, or even a dramatic transition between states of affairs; to the contrary, the artist's task – and one that is exceedingly difficult – is to extract a life and being of sensation from the model and from the possible or actually lived states of affairs, and it is this life that is, in the end, preserved in itself. Sensations and feelings, the materials within which and through which artworks circulate, are the medium through which the artist attempts such extractions. As Deleuze and Guattari put it: "By the means of the material, the aim of art is to wrest the percept from perceptions of objects and the states of a perceiving subject, to wrest the affect from affections as the transition from one state to another" (WP, 167/158). Francis Bacon's triptych paintings, for instance, are not accurate representations of the subject he is painting, but neither are they completely removed from the subject; rather, these paintings extract a process of move-ment, a transitional state from one canvas to the next, as well as on a single canvas as evidenced by the twisting, exaggerated contortions of the figure. What Bacon is doing here, according to Deleuze and Guattari, is an example of what artists do when they extract a life and being of sensation from the subject they are painting.

When art accomplishes this, the resulting "percept," Deleuze and Guattari claim, "is the landscape before man, in the absence of man" (WP, 169/159). The percept is thus beyond the relationship between a perceiver and an object and expresses a reality that is able to "stand up on its own." Similarly, in extracting an "affect" from the transitional states from one state to another, one moves beyond or before the Spinozist theory of joy and sorrow wherein the affects of joy and sadness are how humans feel as an effect of a transition either from lesser to greater power (joy), or from greater to lesser power (sadness). The *affects* extracted by the artist are instead the "nonhuman becomings of man, just as percepts ... are nonhuman landscapes of nature." The artist then works to create a being of sensation that is a reality that stands on its own and is independent of the human relationships, all the while being inseparable from such relationships and the material that actualizes the being of sensation.

We can now return to the problem of minor ethics, or the relationship between minor ethics and the ethics of common sense. If the moral task Aristotle leaves us with is to aspire, in each of our actions and passions, to aim at the mean, for Deleuze and Guattari it is to extract affects and percepts, or the life inseparable from our lives as lived. We should, in short, follow Virginia Woolf's lead and "[s]aturate every atom," "eliminate all waste, deadness, superfluity," everything that adheres to our current and lived perceptions, everything that nourishes the mediocre novelist, and keep only the saturation that gives us the percept (WP, 172).[24] "It must include nonsense, fact, sordidity: but made transparent"; "I want to put practically everything in; yet to saturate."

Let us unpack Woolf's answer by focusing on the notion of *saturation*. Understood in its usual sense, a solution of a particular substance is saturated, for instance, when no more of that substance can be dissolved in the solution. This point of maximum concentration, or saturation point, is a state at the edge of a phase transition, and the addition of more of the substance into the solution can initiate the transition in the form of a precipitate such as crystallization. It is this point of maximum concentration, or what Deleuze and Guattari refer to as "a life" in *What Is Philosophy?*, that conditions the processes of actualization and individuation, or our lives as actually lived. In learning to swim, for example, the point of saturation occurs as the elements that need to be brought together (arm and leg motions, currents of water, etc.) achieve a point that then becomes actualized when one "gets it," when the transition from problematic state to actualized learning of a skill occurs. With respect to Hume and Smith, it is this process that accounts for the taming of affects, or the manner in which the relation between affects and impressions can be brought from the brink of chaos to a state of order and predictability. In the context of art – and returning to Deleuze and Guattari's reading of Woolf – a text is saturated, or on the brink of chaos, not because it accurately portrays a scene from a life as lived, but rather because it saturates such a scene with the instability that comes with the point of saturation, and it is this unstable state at the edge of chaos that allows for the possibility of new affects. As Deleuze and Guattari put it: "A great novelist is above all an artist who invents unknown or unrecognized affects and brings them to light as the becoming of his characters" (WP, 174); and it is the point of saturation that is the condition for the becoming of characters and for the actualization of "unknown or unrecognized affects."

To be moral from the perspective of a minor ethics, therefore, will not entail following established norms and rules, nor will it involve aiming at the mean between excess and defect. Rather, it will entail confronting the problem space or unstable state at the edge of chaos that simply is life, the condition for our lives as lived, that is, the condition for the possibility of affects that are tamed and that follow rules. As Deleuze makes this point in his *Logic of Sense*, the moral imperative we are to follow is to be worthy of the "event":

> Nothing more can be said, and no more has ever been said: to become worthy of what happens to us, and thus to will and release the event, to become the offspring of one's own events, and thereby to be reborn, to have one more birth, and to break with one's carnal birth – to become the offspring of one's events and not of one's actions, for the action is itself produced by the offspring of the event. (LS, 149–50)[25]

This moral command, if we dare call it such, echoes Seneca's claim that the motto for the Stoics is to "live according to nature."[26] For Deleuze and Guattari, however, to "become worthy of what happens to us" and "to become the offspring of one's own events" is not a matter of allowing our nature to predetermine our fate. Our nature, in short, is not a set of predetermining laws. To the contrary, the event to be released is precisely the incorporeal transformation, the multiplicity, and the problem space that every such transformation implicates. Deleuze and Guattari should be seen, therefore, echoing Wolff's command that we saturate ourselves, that we push ourselves to the life implicated in our lives as lived. To clarify this final point, let us return, in conclusion, to Deleuze's Humean theory of moral affects, and to this theory add a point of comparison with Smith's concept of the impartial spectator.

4. THE ROLE OF MINOR ETHICS

As was discussed above, for Hume, on Deleuze's reading, our lives
are not automatically lined up with the truth. Hume does not presuppose that our faculties are predisposed to reveal the nature of reality
as it is, that is, under the conditions that they are functioning properly
and that we enter a situation with good will and good intent. The
participants at an academic conference, or the readers of the text at
hand, may well come along and correct the misguided efforts of this
author, and in doing so realign my thoughts so that they more accurately line up with the text and the issues being discussed. Hume
himself recognized the widespread acceptance of this process as it
played itself out in the intellectual culture. But as we have also seen,
this ability to provide the feedback necessary to create the stable, calm
habits of reason and of polite culture is not a presupposition Hume
accepts unquestioned, given that he also recognizes the risks of delirium that confront the polite discussants around the table. Moreover,
what needs to be done is to engage in what we will call a *minor ethics*.
If we think of a *major ethics* as the ethics of common sense, the ethics
where normative values and claims are taken to be held, at least in
principle, in common and for the sake of the common good, then a
minor ethics will be an ethics that is presupposed by major ethics.
For instance, Hume readily admits in his *Enquiry Concerning the
Principles of Morals* that ethics (and he has in mind the social virtues
of benevolence and justice) increases in importance as its benefits and
utility to the community come increasingly to be known. As Hume
puts it:

> But again suppose, that several distinct societies maintain a kind
> of intercourse for mutual convenience and advantage, the bound-
> aries of justice still grow larger, in proportion to the largeness of
> men's views, and the force of their mutual connexions. History,
> experience, reason sufficiently instruct us in this natural progress
> of human sentiments, and in the gradual enlargement of our
> regards to justice, in proportion as we become acquainted with
> the extensive utility of that virtue.[27]

What is key in this passage, however, is not that justice comes to serve
the common interests, but rather the process of "gradual enlargement
of our regards to justice." What comes to be established as a result

of this process is an agreement that establishes a normative guide to behaviour, but this agreement is not predetermined, and what precisely becomes the focus of established norms is itself indeterminate as the process unfolds and is subject to transformation as new encounters enter the scene. Where we need to be careful is in assuming that Hume should be read here as addressing a coordination problem in a manner akin to contemporary rational choice theory, where the goals for maximizing advantage are taken to be known and the actors are rational and know that others are similarly engaged in maximizing their own advantage. Much has been made along these lines of Hume's famous example of two rowers. "Two men," Hume argues, "who pull the oars of a boat, do it by an agreement or convention, tho' they have never given promises to each other."[28] What the rational choice perspective presupposes in cases such as this, and in the many other cases where Hume's moral theory is understood to be a coordination problem with respect to maximizing utility, is that there is a common framework whereby the actors have already settled on a common goal or aspiration. The rowers, for instance, have an already established desire to row straight ahead as quickly as possible, rather than off to one side or the other as would occur if they were not in sync. In other words, Hume's moral theory is being read as a common sense moral theory, a major ethics as opposed to a minor ethics. As Hume develops his understanding of the process that generates the normative values of a major ethics, he does not presuppose the common framework in laying out the process. Moreover, as Sabl has shown, Hume's interest in history involved precisely those times when common conventions and values were not in place and needed to be generated and stabilized. In the terms used above, Hume viewed those historical circumstances in which common conventions or a common sense ethics were lacking as problematic states that were presupposed by and essential to the processes that generated, in the manner of learning discussed earlier, the determinate values and standards that did become the established, major ethics.

One finds a similar argument in Smith's early essay, "The History of Astronomy."[29] In his argument for the emergence first of philosophy, and then later astronomy, Smith emphasizes the need for the philosopher to develop "a nicer ear, and a more delicate feeling" for the discordances and gaps in the connections between things so that they can then think through the chains that ultimately bridge these gaps. "Philosophy," Smith says, "by representing the invisible chains which

bind together all these disjointed objects, endeavors to introduce order
into this chaos of jarring and discordant appearances, to allay this
tumult of the imagination, and to restore it ... to that tone of tran-
quility and composure, which is both most agreeable in itself, and
most suitable to its nature."[30] The risk, as it is for Hume, is that the
"tumult of the imagination" will not be tamed, that one will succumb
to folly and passion – in short, that we will revert to our "wild nature
and passion"[31] rather than develop and refine our impartial, divine
selves. To establish connections, therefore, what is presupposed is a
lack of connections, the discordant gaps that are open, consequently,
for a multiplicity of responses or solutions to the problem these discordances present. In the case of astronomy, for instance, and as Smith
sets forth its history, this discordant phenomenon emerged most clearly
with the retrograde motion of the planets. As Smith puts it, as one
observes the regular motion of the planets across the sky, this "progressive movement of the Sphere ... is every now and then shocked,
if one may say so, and turned violently out of its natural career by
the retrograde of usual motion, the fancy feeds a want of connection,
a gap or interval, which it cannot fill up, but by supposing some chain
of intermediate events to join them."[32] Astronomy emerges as the
discipline that provides the explanations and connections that bridge
the gap and thus satisfies the "want of connection" engendered by
the chaotic, problematic state.

Stating these arguments in terms of the Deleuzian theory of moral
sentiments put forth here, and returning to the theme of minor ethics, we can understand a minor ethics as a meta-ethics, or as that
which traditional, normative (major) ethics presupposes. We need
to be careful not to impose a new normative standard that calls for
change for change's sake, for an ethics of problems and transformation at all costs. Although problematic states are inseparable from
major ethics and are the conditions for the possibility of transforming
ethics, of becoming better so to speak, they are not in themselves a
new ethics. We should thus not call for major ethics to be supplanted
with minor ethics. As Deleuze and Guattari argue in their key last
line from the "Smooth and Striated" chapter in *A Thousand Plateaus*:
"Never believe that a smooth space will suffice to save us" (TP, 500).
In other words, one should engage with problematic (smooth) spaces,
but they will not save us unless there are also striated spaces – unless,
that is, there is a normative, major ethics. As this was put in *Anti-
Oedipus*, in reference to Proust and the artist: "More than vice ...

it is madness and its innocence that disturb us. If schizophrenia is the universal, the great artist is indeed the one who scales the schizo-phrenic wall and reaches the land of the unknown, where he no longer belongs to any time, any milieu, any school" (AO, 69). What is left unsaid, or perhaps goes without saying, is that the great artist scales the schizophrenic wall without becoming schizophrenic! Similarly for minor ethics, we are to develop a taste for problems and multiplicities, and in doing so allow for the transformation of normative judgments, but all the while without becoming immoral. To put this in terms Smith and Hume would recognize, the possibility and threat of madness, delusion, and savagery forever threaten to subvert the impartial spectator or our best attempts to act on behalf of the common good, returning us to the state of a partial, impetu-ous actor whose unpredictable behaviour is precisely the problem that remains inseparable from every normative ethics. The common sense and good will that allows for the affinity between truth and morality, between what we judge to be true and correct and what we judge to be morally right and proper, is thus made possible by a multiplicity of diverging passions and affects that have become moderated, tamed, and thereby capable of becoming subordinate to the normative rules of ethics. The rules that emerge are, however, themselves products of a more fundamental process, one that is integral to the transformation of rules. By presupposing the multi-plicity of diverging passions, the diversity of what it means to be human, the divine impartial spectator Smith calls upon may well change, may well come to view matters differently. The rules of eth-ics, in other words, presuppose a problem space, a life, that forever threatens to undermine and transform these very rules. An ethics always presupposes a minor ethics.

NOTES

1 Hume, *Essays*, 120.
2 Ibid., 271.
3 Sabl, *Hume's Politics*, 66. Sabl is citing Hume's *History of England*, 1:463.
4 Hume, *Treatise*, 1.3.10.9; SBN 123. Citations for the *Treatise* are by Book, Part, section, and paragraph number followed by the page number from the Selby-Bigge/Nidditch edition (SBN).
5 Adam Smith, *The Theory of Moral Sentiments*.

6 The reference here is to John Locke, who was a key influence on nearly all the intellectuals of England in Scotland during the eighteenth century. In his *Second Treatise*, Locke argues that although we have a right by nature to punish those who have wronged us, we may not do so "according to the passionate heats, or boundless extravagancy [of our] own will," but must instead limit ourselves "to retribute to him, so far as calm reason and conscience dictate, what is proportionate to his transgression, which is so much as may serve for reparation and restraint" (Ch. 2, Sec. 8). Failing to do this would initiate a cycle of vengeance and lead to a state of war.

7 Smith, *The Theory of Moral Sentiments*, 69.

8 Ibid., 131.

9 Deleuze, *Proust and Signs*. Hereafter PS.

10 Hume, *Treatise*, 1.3.14.18; SBN 164.

11 Ibid.

12 Learning, as I have argued elsewhere, does a tremendous amount of work in Deleuze and Guattari's philosophy, especially in *What Is Philosophy?*, but it was already being employed in *Difference and Repetition*. See Bell, *Deleuze and Guattari's What Is Philosophy?*

13 In *What Is Philosophy?*, Deleuze and Guattari draw from the work of Raymond Ruyer as they explain how a concept is able, all at once, to draw all the elements together. "The concept," they argue, "is defined by the inseparability of a finite number of heterogeneous components traversed by a point of absolute survey at infinite speed" (WP, 13). Ruyer's point is that the visual field has a point of absolute survey that is inseparable from the field yet draws it all together at once as a point of survey. As I sit and type on my computer, the visual field is present, including all the elements of the visual field such as the desk, coffee cup, a window with rain beating on it, bookshelves to the left, and so on. All these elements are brought together as one in the visual field by a point of survey that is not outside the visual field but is capable of moving from point to point within it. Mary Beth Mader has a very helpful discussion of this point in *Sleights of Reason*, 23–30.

14 Wittgenstein, *Philosophical Investigations*, 25.

15 When the Académie des Sciences first defined the meter, they created sixteen standard meters. The only one that remains, so far as we know, exists as a small shelf of marble beneath the arcade at 36, rue Vaugirard.

16 Wittgenstein, *Philosophical Investigations*, 88.

17 Wittgenstein, *Philosophical Grammar*, 50.

18 Ibid., 21.

19 Wittgenstein, for instance, offers the example of "bububu" in
Philosophical Investigations, 18. Wittgenstein rhetorically asks: "Can I
say 'bububu' and mean 'If it doesn't rain I shall go for a walk'? – It is only
in a language that I can mean something by something." In other words,
it is only in a language game where a community of speakers recognize
"bububu" as a move in this game; otherwise, you would simply be utter-
ing nonsense.

20 Ibid., 56. Wittgenstein then follows up this point with an example that
echoes Kant's example of cinnabar from his first *Critique*, in which Kant
argues: "If cinnabar were now red, now black, now light, now heavy, if a
human being were now changed into this animal shape, now into that one,
if on the longest day the land were covered now with fruits, now with ice
and snow, then my empirical imagination would never even get the opportunity to think of heavy cinnabar on the occasion of the representation of
the color red; or if a certain word were attributed now this thing, now to
that, or if one and the same thing were sometimes called this, sometimes
that, without the governance of a certain rule to which the appearances are
already subjected in themselves, then no empirical synthesis of reproduction
could take place." *Critique of Pure Reason*, 229 [A100–A101]. Wittgenstein
makes a similar point when he argues: "The procedure of putting a lump of
cheese on a balance and fixing the price by the turn of the scale would lose
its point if it frequently happened that such lumps suddenly grew or shrank
with no obvious cause." *Philosophical Investigations*, §142.

21 In their book on Wittgenstein, G.P. Baker and P.M.S. Hacker argue that
there are three criteria for understanding the meaning of an expression.
First, one uses the expression correctly; second, one can give a correct
explanation of the meaning of the expression; and finally, one responds
appropriately to someone else who uses the expression. *Wittgenstein*, 40.

22 Wittgenstein, *The Blue and Brown Books*, 24.

23 Aristotle, *Nicomachean Ethics*, 1747 [Bk. 2, Ch. 6].

24 Deleuze and Guattari are citing Woolf, *The Diary*, vol. 3, 209–10.

25 Deleuze, *The Logic of Sense*. Hereafter LS.

26 See Seneca, *Epistles*, 23.

27 Hume, *Enquiry*, III.ii; SBN 192.

28 Hume, *Treatise*, 3.2.2.10; SBN 490.

29 A. Smith, *Essays*.

30 Ibid., 20.

31 Smith explicitly refers to the savage as one who is guided by wild nature
and passion: "But a savage, whose notions are guided altogether by wild

nature and passion, waits for no other proof that a thing is the proper object of any sentiment, than that it excites it" (ibid., 24). This largely echoes Hume's arguments in the *Treatise*, cited earlier, where a person suffering from madness, folly, and delusion allows a single instance to have the force and strength of an impression that has the weight of history, custom, and repetition behind it.

32 Ibid., 34.

Repetition and Affirmation

Jay Lampert

Cahiers du Cinéma: There is a good deal of blood in *Pierrot*.
Godard: Not blood, red.

Godard, Godard on Godard

It's not blood, it's red.
It's not a figure, it's a colour.
It doesn't keep you safe, it keeps you colourful.
It never actually takes place, it's only ever virtual.
It never passes to action, it's only in thought.
It's not negative, it's infinitive.
It doesn't mean anything, it's in-significant.
It doesn't have good intentions, it doesn't have any intention, it has intensity.
It's not what's real, it's what's affirmed.
It's not a good thought, it's an image of thought.
It's not an image of justice, it's just an image.
It's not here, it's elsewhere.
It has no effects whatsoever, it's a quasi-cause.
It's not better, it's something different.
It doesn't improve peoples' lives concretely, it's an abstract machine.
It's not what an organic body can do, it's what a body without organs can do.
It's not even really what a body can do, it's an incorporeal enunciation.
It doesn't add anything, it's an object = X.
Its objects are neither in this world nor out of it, but in another possible world.

It's not the Good, it's the outside.

It doesn't care, it's cosmic.

It doesn't judge for the best, it decides.

It doesn't benefit the greatest number, the number of its beneficiaries is an irrational number.

It doesn't affirm what the dice say when they land on the table, it affirms what the dice don't say while they're on the way up.

It's not a commitment to the future, the future is the empty form of time.

4

A Memorandum for Past Millennia: Excising the Plague from Lucretius's *De rerum natura*

Ryan J. Johnson

In 1984, Harvard University asked Italo Calvino to deliver the next Charles Eliot Norton Lectures. After working on them obsessively for a year, Calvino died the day before he was to travel to Boston. Fortunately, he had already written out all but one of the six planned lectures,[1] which were framed as meditations on Lucretius. These are the titles of the five completed lectures: (1) "Lightness," (2) "Quickness," (3) "Exactitude," (4) "Visibility," (5) "Multiplicity."[2] The last lecture – worked out but unwritten – was titled (6) "Consistency." These are the names of concepts that fill Deleuze's oeuvre. This chapter follows the structure of Calvino's lectures – each section corresponding to each of Calvino's titles – in order to offer one take on minor ethics.[3] As the title of Calvino's lectures is *Six Memos for the Next Millennium*, we now begin *A Memorandum for Past Millennia*.

As we move through the six sections of this chapter, we will unfold several intertwined claims. Section (1) explains the origin of Gilles Deleuze's fantasy about writing a heterodox "memorandum" concerning the final scene of Lucretius's *De rerum natura*: he believed that the final scene, the depiction of the "Plague of Athens," was a counterfeit writing slipped into the text by the Christians in order to defame the great thinker of atoms. Seeking to realize this fantasy will lead us to propose a rewriting of that part of Lucretius's text with help from a powerful writing procedure provided by Louis Wolfson. Section (2) surveys the disagreement in Classical studies as to whether the final scene of *De rerum natura* is counterfeit or not. Section (3) argues that the atomistic assemblage model of materiality corroborates Deleuze's contention that the final scene was indeed counterfeit, as opposed to the organic model that some classicists inexactly use to claim that the final scene is appropriate and intended. Section (4) further motivates Deleuze's contention by displaying three moments in the fraught history of the reception of atomism and by locating Lucretius in what Deleuze sees as "a secret link" connecting him to Hume, Spinoza, and Nietzsche. Section (5) introduces Wolfson's idiosyncratic procedure for writing and translating, including Deleuze's claim that Wolfson's literary task was to continuously rewrite *De rerum natura*. Section (6) is where we deploy the Wolfson procedure in order to realize Deleuze's fantasy by rewriting the ending of *De rerum natura* so that it makes the final scene more consistent with the affirmative nature and character of Epicurean-inspired Lucretian atomism.

In sum, the Deleuze–Lucretius encounter initiates one movement of a minor ethics by providing a transformational exercise that aims to cultivate a joyful orientation toward singular things through the *creation of acts*. While major morality seeks equilibrium and consensus in deed and proclamation, a minor ethics follows the lines of disequilibrium and divergence as they shudder and stutter *in action*. Put differently, from the perspective of major morality, the minor voices sound like nonsense; from the perspective of a minor ethics, though, supposed nonsense is seen to contain the genetic material for producing novel possibilities for the practices of acting, writing, and talking. A significant implication of this practice – of attuning ourselves to what appears as nonsense in order to pick up from it the emergence of sense – is that the objects of ethical consideration are opened so as to include singularities normally excluded or covered over by the proclamations of major morality. As we will see, using the Wolfson procedure on Lucretius's plague scene is a concrete example of such attunement.

I. LIGHTNESS

Lightness is opposed to heaviness, not darkness. Deleuze once remarked in an interview about his fantasy to write "a memorandum to the Academy of the Moral Sciences in order to show that Lucretius's book cannot end with the description of the plague, and that it is an invention, a falsification of the Christians who wanted to show that a maleficent thinker *must* end in terror and anguish" (D, 15).

Rather than brushing this aside as a silly fantasy, we take it completely seriously. Perhaps Deleuze really was convinced that the gruesome scene of the Plague of Athens was secreted into the end of *De rerum natura* by the Christians in order to defame that eminent Epicurean as an unredeemable, hedonistic, debauched, and savage pagan. Since this is indeed a very bold claim, we should, at this early stage in our story, forefront a few initial reasons for at least sympathizing with it.

The most obvious reason to agree with Deleuze is that the plague scene is inconsistent with the nature and character of the Epicurean ethics that Lucretian atomism so powerfully espouses. Lucretius's take on Epicureanism openly advocates for the cultivation of a life of joy, pleasure, and immanence that emerges from overcoming the fear and pessimism derived from transcendent mythologies and metaphysical beliefs. The true Epicurean life then arises through the shaping of desire and the creation of hedonic acts. Deleuze describes his understanding of the ethics of *De rerum natura* like this: "Naturalism as the philosophy of affirmation; pluralism linked with multiple affirmation; sensualism connected with the pleasure in the diverse; and the practical critique of all mystifications" (LS, 279). The nature and character of such an ethics seems clearly inconsistent with the fear-inducing gloom, doom, and agony of the plague scene. While that final scene dovetails nicely with the Christian story of the judging and punishing transcendent force that promises to destroy the decadent and sensualistic materialisms of the Greco-Roman pagans, it is directly opposed to Lucretian ethics. This inconsistency between the final scene of *De rerum natura* and the rest of Lucretius's text, along with the deliberate slander of the Christian church (which we will reveal below in (4) "Visibility") will ultimately enjoin us to rewrite it so that the entire text is more internally consistent.

Another reason to take Deleuze's fancy seriously is that it was not the first time he had advocated for the reconsideration of the end of a text in order to make it more consistent with the rest of its story. In *Kafka: Toward a Minor Literature*, Deleuze and Guattari question the placement of the execution scene that closes Franz Kafka's *The Trial*. They argue that since there is no evidence that it was actually written at the end of the text, it is very difficult, if not impossible, to determine where exactly it fits. For them, it is a "premature, delayed, aborted ending," mainly because it is inconsistent with the rest of its story (K, 44). "The idea of ending with K's execution," Deleuze and

Guattari argue, "is contradicted by the whole direction of the novel and by the quality of 'unlimited postponement' that regulates *The Trial*" (K, 44). Most interestingly for us, Deleuze and Guattari see the inconsistency in Kafka's text as equal to the inconsistency in Lucretius's:

> The imposition of K's execution as the final chapter seems to have an equivalent in the history of literature – the placement of the famous description of the plague at the end of Lucretius's book. In both cases, it is a question of showing that at the last moment, an Epicurean can do no more than submit to agony, or that a Prague Jew can only assume the guilt that is operating within him. (K, 44)

Deleuze is clearly attuned to the consistency or inconsistency of a text, and it is distinctly obvious to him, given the nature and character of Lucretius's variation on Epicurean ethics, that the final scene of *De rerum natura* has no place in his text, just as it is with Kafka's *The Trial*.

For now, we can formulate our task: *to escape the gore and agony of the plague and reconstruct the nurturing environment of Epicurus's Garden*. In taking up this task we capture the ethical moment in the Deleuze–Lucretius encounter: by realizing Deleuze's fantasy of writing the memorandum to the Academy, we will see how Lucretian atomism affirms the joy and immanence that courses through the rest of the text and through almost all of the minor tradition. As Calvino observes, *De rerum natura* expresses "literature as an existential function, the search for lightness as a reaction to the weight of living."[4] Wolfson's procedure will untether Lucretian atomism from the heaviness of the plague so that it returns to the lightness of Epicurus' Garden.

2. QUICKNESS

We should not move too quickly too soon, but instead consider what the more conservative, slow-moving scholarship of antiquity says about the end of *De rerum natura*. Some classicists sense a conflict, while some are not so worried. Still others are so convinced that it is meant to be there that they whip up very un-Epicurean interpretations to justify it.

First there is A.A. Long, who argues that it is "plausible to suppose that Lucretius has not left his work completely as he intended; and there are other reasons for thinking that the poem lacks final revision."[5] Without suggesting that the Christians slipped in that defamatory passage, Long agrees that there is good reason to think that Lucretius did not intend to end the text as it now ends. Other scholars cannot contain the speed of their own argument. Edith Foster says that "it seems possible that Lucretius' larger aim was to undermine Academic and/or Stoic foundations ... even though he perceived its unfriendliness to his philosophy and [the] aggressiveness of the changes Lucretius undertakes."[6] Similarly, Peta Fowler notes not only that "the ending of a work is notoriously liable to textual corruption" in ancient literature in general, but also that Lucretius's ending in particular "is not constituted by the conclusions drawn from the argument – that is, it is not an 'internal ending' – but rather it is one imposed by the fictitious social framework."[7] She even goes so far as to call it a "'skewed' kind of ending"[8] and to offer the unconvincing suggestion that "Lucretius is in effect testing the readers' responses to the Epicurean 'message' of the poem."[9]

David Sedley is convinced that the final scene was intentional: "book 6 returns in its finale to the theme of death, with a grim passage on the great Athenian plague: whether or not this, as we have it, is in its finished form, there can be little doubt that its location at the close represents the author's own architectonic plan, especially as it closes a book which has opened with a hymn of praise to Athens as the cradle of civilization."[10] The "architectonic" that Sedley envisages in the overall structure of *De rerum natura* is the move from Athens as the birthplace of Epicurean philosophy to the end of Athens in the plague scene – that is, from the cradle to the grave, albeit an entirely horrific, fuming mass grave.[11] Joseph Farrell also sees the structure of the text in terms of the life cycle of an organism: "Book 6 illustrates this contrast [between birth and death]. The poem celebrates Athens as a parent that gave 'fruitful progeny' (*frugiparos fetus*, I) to mortals and that 'remade life' (*recreauerunt vitam*, 2) when it 'gave birth' (*genuere*, 5) to Epicurus. This contrast endows the book with an organic shape modeled on that of the human lifespan."[12] To all of this, I have a question: While every life begins with a birth and ends with a death, does this really mean that every life must end with the pestilent stench of rotting, festering corpses? Most go out with a sigh or a whimper. Even if the structure of *De rerum natura* is the lifespan of an organism, this does not make the final scene appropriate to the rest of the text or to the heart of Epicureanism.

In contrast to them all, Deleuze skips by this slow-moving scholarship, moving far too quickly for the classicists, for he is being carried by that gust of wind left in the wake of those swift minor thinkers. These are thinkers, Deleuze writes, "of a fragile constitution, and yet shot through with an insurmountable life" (D, 15). Speed is their measure.

3. EXACTITUDE

Speed and exactitude are a pair in atomism. Atomism is much more akin to an *assemblage model of materiality*, similar to what we see in Spinoza and Deleuze. Attention to exactitude alerts us to this. For Calvino, exactitude means three things: (1) "a language as precise as possible," (2) "an evocation of clear, incisive, memorable visual images," and (3) "a well-defined and well-calculated plan."[13]

(1) Lucretius employs *a language as precise as possible*. For Deleuze, Lucretian language clearly avoids organicism as a model for understanding the nature of things. On his reading, atomism thinks of nature as "the principle of the diverse and its production."[14] Key here is that the principle of the diverse makes it impossible to unify the infinite number of atoms into an organic whole. Instead, to see nature as the production of the diverse means that nature can only be "an infinite sum, that is, a sum that does not join its own elements."[15] There is nothing in atomic physics that embraces all of the material elements of Nature at once, into a single world or organic whole. As Deleuze says, "*Phusis* is not a determination of the One, of Being or of the Whole," figures that Lucretius considers mythical "fixations of the mind, speculative forms of belief in the *fatum,* and theological forms of a false philosophy."[16] In atomism, nature is not collective, but distributive; the laws of nature (*foedera naturae,* as opposed to the supposed *foedera fati*) distribute bodies that are non-totalizable. In this sense, nature is not predicative, but conjunctive; it is expressed by "and" rather than by "is."[17] Atomism speaks of this atom and that atom, of that atom and this atom – on and on across the infinite expanse of the atomic multiverse. The exactitude of atomic metaphysics is a conjunctive theory of singular things: this *and* this *and* this *and* so on. It is not coincidental, we could argue, that the text just ends, mid-sentence, with a conjunct.

(2) Lucretius also aims for *an evocation of clear, incisive, memorable visual images*. Given this precise metaphysics of *and*, atomic nature is presented in terms of forms of composition and decomposition, of

conjunctions and disjunctions. Everything emerges through images of material shocks and fundamental encounters, of grand harmonies and jolting disharmonies, of gaining and breaking rhythm.[18] Deleuze savours this imagery of the swirling, falling clouds of atoms constantly banging against each other. For him, atomic nature is like a "Harlequin's cloak made entirely from coloured patches and empty spaces, plenitudes *and* void, beings *and* non-being, each one positing itself as unlimited while limiting the other."[19] Deleuze also uses this imagery when speaking of Hume's account of nature, where "one sees a very strange world unfold, fragment by fragment: a *Harlequin's* jacket or patchwork, made up of solid parts *and* voids, blocs *and* ruptures, attractions *and* divisions, nuances *and* bluntness, conjunctions *and* separations, alternations *and* interweavings" (D, 55, my emphasis). This is what allows Deleuze to claim that Hume's empiricist atomism, like Lucretius's atomism before him and Bertrand Russell's logical atomism after him, succeeds in "breaking the bonds imposed by the form of the judgment of attribution, for making possible an autonomous logic of relations, and discovering a conjunctive world of atoms and relations" (DI, 163). The clear and incisive imagery of multiple combinations of singular things swirling about the void, similar to a Harlequin's coat, is another example of the exact imagery of Lucretius's language.

(3) Finally, *De rerum natura* expresses a *well-defined and well-calculated plan.* Deleuze thinks that Epicurus and Lucretius enact the first truly noble deeds of philosophical pluralism through their principle of material production. Rather than follow the order of the organism, atomic naturalism is organized in terms of power (*puissance*), albeit a power that is distributed to all atoms, one by one. This democratic distribution of power precludes the possibility of gathering everything together *all at once*, while also preventing unification into a holistic combination that could completely express nature *at one time*. To claim that atoms, taken together, form a whole is to fail to understand the principle of the diverse and its production. To think that the existence of a material diversity must arise from an organic whole, a One, rests on the belief that anything can be born from anything, that something can come from nothing, that the atomic elements supposedly forming a whole are contraries capable of transforming into one another.[20] Perhaps most of all, philosophers who use the model of the organism find it difficult to account for the existence of void; this led them to turn it into a concept that captures everything. The result is

that the one organic whole becomes an artificial and unnatural fiction, always susceptible to corruption, destruction, and, most of all, *plague*. Seeing nature as an organic whole prevents the understanding that there are beings *and* there is the void, and that both exist. Such organic philosophers replace the diversity of the diverse with the identical or the contradictory, often both at once.

Since atomism does not conceive of nature as an organism, however, Lucretius understands that there are simple beings in the void *and* that there is void in composite beings.[21] It is a matter of conjunctions *and* disjunctions. Death is not a horrifying act of destruction, but simply a disjoining and rearranging of bodies. Like birth, death is the part of the same continuous flux of atoms and void, just with a different ratio of motion and rest. The atomic nature of things is exact: it is the production of diversity through non-totalizable combinations and permutations of corporeal and incorporeal heterogeneities.

4. VISIBILITY

Let us now look at three moments in the history of the reception of atomism. Doing so will allow us to make visible the underhanded ways in which both harsh and sympathetic critics have inserted words in the mouths and texts of the ancient atomists.

(1) *Ancient anti-atomism.* Reaching back to the very beginning of atomism, we find one of the first expressions of a generalized anti-atomist attitude in Diogenes Laertius, who offers a long list of slanderous attempts to attribute shocking words and writings to that advocate of atoms.[22] Epictetus called "him a preacher of effeminacy and showers abuse on him."[23] Timocrates, a former member of Epicurus's Garden, said that "Epicurus vomited twice a day from over-indulgence," that "Epicurus' acquaintance with philosophy was small and his acquaintance with life even smaller," and that his texts are repetitive and impetuously polemical. According to Timocrates, Epicurus called the members of Plato's Academy "the toadies of Dionysius," called Aristotle a "profligate, who after devouring his patrimony took to soldiering and selling drugs," and called "Pyrrho an ignorant boor."[24] From the very beginning, people have been trying to make the atomists say things they never said. Interestingly, after listing all this slander, Diogenes provides his own assessment of people who say such things about Epicurus: all "these people are stark mad."[25]

Later in Rome, Cicero, Lucretius's near contemporary, wrote several highly critical assessments of Lucretius and Epicureanism. The first book of *De finibus*, for example, depicts Cicero's easy deflation of several Epicurean positions, as proposed by a hapless Roman atomist named Torquatus.[26]

At the end of the fourth century, St. Jerome circulated a biographical story about Lucretius's supposed madness and suicide. "Titus Lucretius," he wrote, "was driven mad by a love potion, and when, during the intervals of his insanity, he had written a number of books, which were later emended by Cicero, he killed himself by his own hand in the forty-fourth year of his life."[27] With the decline of the Roman Empire and the rise of the Christian Church, the smear campaign reached a new level of intensity, as the Christians carried out a vicious and widespread assault on atomism like none before. Philo of Alexandria, for example, often characterized the serpent tempter from Eden as an out-of-control Epicurean.[28] Later, Dante condemned Epicurus to the sixth circle of hell, the realm of heresy, where he is seen trapped in flaming tombs.[29] For sake of space, we are skipping over the long tradition in the Christian Church of censoring and manipulating pagan texts. But the clearest example of this is the not so mysterious disappearance of almost every copy *De rerum natura*. For centuries, scholars had assumed that it was lost, like so many other ancient texts destroyed by the Church. Fortunately, in 1417 the great Italian book hunter Poggio Bracciolini discovered it in a German monastery.[30]

The point is that the history of reworking, defaming, attacking, or falsely attributing words to the atomists is long and twisted. Many people have tried to erase atomism from thought and text. Given this history, it is not much of a leap to think that the Plague of Athens scene might also have been secreted in without anyone noticing.

(2) *Epicureanism in early modern Europe.* The discovery and reintroduction of *De rerum natura* in the fifteenth century may have sparked the Scientific Revolution, at the centre of which was the idea that the world is composed of atoms and void. Yet even amid this scientific fervour, the dominance of Christianity forced early modern philosophers and scientists to reduce, if not eliminate, the atheism, hedonism, mortality of soul, and all that was consistent with atomic metaphysics. What followed were centuries of reworking Lucretius's text by cutting out those parts that were at odds with Christian ethics. Let us cite a few famous examples. Francis Bacon developed a

reorganized atomism so as to make room for divine providence.[31]
René Descartes offered a corpuscular model of the universe while
simultaneously arguing for the immortality of the soul.[32] Pierre
Gassendi, the most important figure in the revival of atomism, slipped
in an omnipotent creator, excusing his amended atomism by pointing
to an old adage: mixed in with every false opinion is some truth.[33]
Isaac Newton also contributed to this grand reworking: "the philosophy of Epicurus and Lucretius," he wrote, "is true and old, but was
wrongly interpreted by the ancients as atheism."[34] In one of the most
prominent passages in scientific writing, Newton reworks Lucretian
atomism so that it more comfortably fits with Christian dogma: "It
seems probable to me," he writes,

> that God in the Beginning form'd Matter in solid, massy, hard,
> impenetrable, moveable Particles, of such Sizes and Figures, and
> with such other Properties, and in such Proportion to Space, as
> most conduced to the End for which he form'd them; and that
> these primitive Particles being Solids, are incomparably harder
> than any porous Bodies compounded of them; even so very hard,
> as never to wear or break in pieces; no ordinary Power being
> able to divide what God himself made one in the first creation.
> While the Particles continue entire, they may compose Bodies
> of one and the same Nature and Texture in all Ages: But should
> they wear away, or break in pieces, the Nature of Things,
> depending on them, would be changed.[35]

Almost all the major scientific figures in early modern Europe rei-
magined Lucretian physics by subtracting from it an Epicurean ethics.
A grand inconsistency between atomic physics and ethics ensued.
This strongly suggests that if even those most enthusiastically sup-
portive and receptive of atomic physics had little concern with rewriting the main text of this tradition to insert an inconsistent ethics, then
the Christian church, the arch-anti-atomists, would have done much
the same.

(3) These might be the most famous words attributed to Epicurus:
"Death is thus nothing to us, nor does it pertain to us at all [*nil igitur
mors est ad nos neque pertinent hilum*]."[36] The reasoning for this
bold assertion is that, for the Epicureans, all life involves sense-
experience (being strict materialists, they view body and soul as material); and since death is the privation of sense-experience, we never

experience death. Put precisely: "when we exist, death is not yet present, and when death is present, then we do not exist."[37] If life and death are mutually exclusive, death plays no part in our experience. This perspective on death forms the second part of the Epicurean *tetrapharmakon* (four-part cure): "(1) Don't fear god, (2) *Don't worry about death*; (3) What is good is easy to get, and (4) what is terrible is easy to endure."[38] In his "Letter to Menoeceus," Epicurus explicitly condemns tragic pessimism: "much worse still is the man who says it is good not to be born, but 'once born make haste to pass the gates of Death.' For if he says this from conviction, why does he not just die?"[39] From his metaphysics to his ethics, Epicurus undeniably advocates a distinct way to understand and engage death, and this *never* includes the sort of fear or pessimism that arises from that horrid scene of pestilence of Book 6 in *De rerum natura*.

Lucretius stresses this idea when, after offering thirty arguments for the mortality of the soul,[40] he concludes: "Therefore death is nothing to us." The power of this point is echoed as late as Spinoza: the "free man thinks nothing less than of death, and his wisdom is a meditation on life, not on death."[41] Almost all of Book 3 of Lucretius's text is dedicated to this atomic principle.[42]

The main cause of the non-Epicurean attitude toward death is the power of superstition, religion, and especially myth. This is one reason why Deleuze sees such a clear connection between Lucretius and Spinoza. He writes:

> Spinoza knows, *like Lucretius*, that there are no joyful myths
> or superstitions. *Like Lucretius* he sets the image of a positive
> Nature against the uncertainty of gods: what is opposed to
> Nature is not Culture, nor the state of reason, nor even the
> civil state, but only the superstition that threatens all human
> endeavor. And *like Lucretius* again, Spinoza assigns to philoso-
> phy the task of denouncing all that is sad, all that lives on
> sadness, all those who depend on sadness as the basis of their
> power. (EP, 270, my emphasis)[43]

For Deleuze, Lucretian atomism inaugurates the philosophical "enterprise of 'demystification,'" which generates "a secret link between Lucretius, Hume, Spinoza, and Nietzsche" (LS, 279; cf. N, 6).[44] Yet despite this clearly visible position, prominent voices in Epicurean scholarship try to reorganize what we see of the Epicurean position by attributing clearly un-Epicurean aims to Lucretius. For example, Monica Gale argues that the plague is an Epicurean myth comparable to Plato's Myth of Er.[45] Such a skewed attribution seems wildly inconsistent with all of Epicureanism.

In sum, from Plato's desire to burn Democritus's texts to the early modern scientists' reworking of atomism to the strange optics of contemporary scholarship, the continuous attempt to conceal and obscure the true spirit of ancient atomism is evident. In writing this memorandum, we make visible these murky attempts to alter or expunge atomism from history.

5. MULTIPLICITY

Now for the most Deleuzian theme of all. The concept of multiplicity connects with *the Wolfson procedure* through Wolfson's lifelong experiences with schizophrenia.[46] In response to his schizophrenic experience and the appalling treatments he underwent, Wolfson developed a translinguistic procedure for scattering phrases from one language into a multiplicity of different languages. In order to rewrite the ending to *De rerum natura*, we are going to put this procedure, itself a technique for and of multiplicity, to work.

But we must first understand how the procedure works. For Wolfson, it is an intricate process for translating from English into four foreign languages (German, French, Hebrew, and Russian) that Wolfson developed due to some complicated associations that arose between his actual mother and his mother-tongue English. Our use of this procedure, however, will operate somewhere between a few different registers: between Lucretius's Latin, Deleuze's French, and our English.[47]

Wolfson's procedure, according to Deleuze, moves in two directions at once. In one direction, it "moves toward an *amplified procedure*" (CC, 9). It is amplifying in the sense that it multiplies the possible associations among words through how they sound or look when written. This part of the technique is a way of opening up to a very free association among words by analyzing a word or phrase into its phonetic or graphemic parts. For example, the English word "early" becomes associated not merely semantically with the French *tôt*, but also with other French words that express the consonants *R* or *L,* such as *suR-Le-champ, de bonne heuRe, matinaLement, diLigemmment, dévoRer L'espace,* or *à La paRole.* What counts in these amplifications are the phonetic or graphemic atoms; phonemes or graphemes are extracted and then distributed through other languages.

In another direction, it "moves toward an evolved procedure" (CC, 9). It is evolving in the sense that Wolfson builds out new phrases from those component phonemes in various directions. For example, Wolfson spends about forty pages thinking about the phrase "vegetable shortening," which he found on the labels of the food items his mother used to throw at him. Having extracted the consonants *SH*, *R*, *T*, and *N* from "shortening," he pushes these through different languages in various ways. The Wolfson procedure manipulates these sounds so that *SH* in "shortening" is repeated, thus becoming "*shshshortening.*" He then divides these repeated *SH*s into three individual units, and then replaces them with homophones from different languages. The first of the three *SH* sounds is replaced with *N* (as in the Hebrew *chemenn*), the second *SH* becomes a *T* (as in the German *Schmalz*), and the third becomes an *R* sound (as in the Russian *jir*). "Shortening" could thus become something like *chemennschmalzjirening.*

For Deleuze, both of these movements involve "rules of transformation"[48] and "rules of inversion" (CC, 9).[49] However chaotic this procedure may seem, the overall gesture should not be too unfamiliar. In short, it is a process of, first, cutting up words into atoms and then, second, inverting them so that a new meaning is produced. Put differently, Wolfson's technique dissolves linguistic phrases into their component parts in terms of their physical properties rather their semantic meanings. Put one more way, the qualitative meanings of sentences are converted into distinct quantitative determinations à la atomism.

This is a clearly atomic procedure, one that echoes a classic atomic move that Pierre Gassendi calls "the similitude of letters."[50] Democritus used it first. Later, after Plato and Aristotle attacked it, Epicurus rehabilitated it.[51] According to Aristotle's formulation, the differences among atoms are like the differences in letters: "*A* differs from *N* in shape, *AN* from *NA* in arrangement, and *Z* from *N* in position."[52] In essence, it is an association between the ways in which the atomic and the linguistic worlds are produced through the same combinatory processes: *atoms are to composite individuals* as *letters are to words and sentences*. The idea is that a set of basic parts can produce both atomic and linguistic worlds through various combinations and permutations. The composite bodies of the atomic world and the meaningful words of the linguistic world are both the temporary results of the same ever-changing combinations of basic elements. Wolfson

inverts this classic atomic procedure: he dissolves language into phonetic atoms and builds up from there. A sort of foreign language is
extracted through the familiar mother tongue, that is, the language
of atoms is unearthed from within the language of humans. Deleuze
notices that "letters (especially consonants) are constantly falling from
these words," dissolving into bodies and void (CC, 15).

In this sense, Wolfson comes close to Democritus's famous quip:
"by convention, sweet; by convention, bitter, by convention, hot, by
convention, cold ... but in reality, atoms and void."[53] There is not, in
reality, a maternal language in the sense of a complete, fixed, and
steady organic whole. Instead, English is composed of a multiplicity
of other hisses, barks, "gurglings in his throat and gratings of his
teeth," which are themselves made of various emissions of atomic
conjunctions and disjunctions, as is every language" (CC, 12).[54] Like
the account of nature in atomic theory, language is not, for Wolfson,
"the formation of formally legitimate totalities" (CC, 11). Language
is not an organic whole, Deleuze writes, but "a combinatorial, a
panoply of all possible disjunctions, but one whose particular characteristic is to be inclusive and ramified to infinity," like the multiplicitous sum of Lucretian atomism (CC, 12).

It takes an operation like Wolfson's to provoke an encounter with
the infinite variety of atomic combinations, which he often calls his
"*tour de babil*" (CC, 11). Wolfson reveals the atoms in words and
words emerging out of atoms. The two are susceptible to the same
rules of transformation or translation, albeit in different directions.
Deleuze notices this "profound equivalence ... between the foreign
words of transformation and the formulas or unstable atomic link-
ages" (CC, 14). Wolfson, the schizophrenic, dissolves language into
bodies; he topples fixity and stasis into movement and change. Amid
these swirling atoms in void, he builds a meaningful world back up,
free of the obsessive fear of the body and tongue of his mother.

This is why Deleuze identifies Wolfson as the one who most clearly
takes up the Lucretian task: "He is continually rewriting *De rerum
natura*. He evolves in things and in words" (CC, 17). The cancerous
body of his mother is a "crowd of atoms," as is the meaning of the
word "mother." In the marvellously alliterative title of his second
book, we see the two movements of amplification and evolution
operating in the Wolfson procedure: *Ma mère, musicienne, est morte
de maladie maligne à minuit, mardi à mercredi, au milieu du mois de
mai mille au mouroir Memorial à Manhattan.*

6. CONSISTENCY

As this is now the sixth and final section of our story, it is time to combine the spirit of Calvino with the desire of Deleuze through the mechanism of the Wolfson procedure in order to rewrite the final stanzas of Lucretius's classic text. The effect, if successful, will bring a higher level of consistency to the entirety of *De rerum natura*, one that is not there when the Plague of Athens scene closes the text.

But what right do we, philosophers of the new millennium, have to rewrite this classic text? In what sense can we assume that we will be able to finally solve a two-thousand-year-old scholarly quandary? Perhaps a different, while still audacious, strategy is more appropriate.

To understand this different strategy, consider the style of philosophical writing into which Lucretius's text falls: didactic poetry. It is very common for ancient didactic poems to conclude with a *provocation to the reader*, a call to take up the mission of the text in one's personal life.[55] We see examples of this in the *Homeric Hymns* ("Demeter," "Delian Apollo," "Pythian Apollo," "Hermes," etc.), in Nicander's *Theriaca,* in Maniliius's *Astronomicon,* in Grattius's *Cynegeticon*, and many more. If *De rerum natura* follows the ancient tradition of didactic poetry, then a new ending to the poem could take the form of an instigation to the reader to go out and *do* something. This is much more consistent with Epicureanism in that it opens up a little space to enjoin the reader to go out and cultivate lives of joy, pleasure, affirmation, sensuality, and diversity, rather than the gruesome, excruciating pessimism expressed by the plague scene.

Yet whatever the above argument might make for rewriting the final scene, I do not think it would be consistent with or faithful to Epicureanism if we wrote a final and conclusive ending to the poem. Instead, we are going to follow the ancient tradition of didactic poetry and conclude with an injunction. The ending of *this* chapter compels you, our reader, to write the ending of Lucretius's *De rerum natura*. I am not going to do the work for you, but instead leave you with this provocation: *Follow the Wolfson procedure and rewrite the ending for yourself*. But do not be nervous, for I will not leave you high and dry. I will now give you more step-by-step instructions for how to undertake this rewriting:

First, dissolve the Latin of *De rerum natura* into the phonetics of your language.

Second, translate the new line, written in your language, back into English.[56]

Third, repeat this for the remaining lines in the text.

In essence, the Wolfson procedure is a combination of two things: (1) a *calque*, sometimes called a "loan translation," which is when a word or phrase is borrowed from another language through literal, word-for-word translation; and (2) "what is known in French as *traducson*, or translation according to sound."[57] The clearest example of this is Luis van Rooten's *Mots D'Heures: Gousses, Rames*:[58]

Humpty Dumpty	*Un petit d'un petit*	A child of a child
Sat on a wall.	*S'étonne aux Halles*	Was surprised at the Market
Humpty Dumpty	*Un petit d'un petit*	A child of a child
Had a great fall.	*Ah! degrés te fallent*	Oh, degrees you needed!
All the king's horses	*Indolent qui ne sort cesse*	Lazy is he who never goes out
And all the king's men	*Indolent qui ne se mène*	Lazy is he who is not led
Couldn't put Humpty	*Qu'importe un petit*	Who cares about a little one
Together again.	*Tout gai de Reguennes.*	All happy with Reguennes.

The left verse is the well-known Mother Goose nursery rhyme in plain English. The middle verse is the result of an English-to-French homophonic translation, that is, the nursery rhyme as it would sound if the English verse were spoken by someone with a very strong French accent. Even the manuscript's title (*Mots D'Heures: Gousses, Rames*) is the result of the same way of pronouncing the English "Mother Goose's Rhymes" with a very strong French accent. It is similar to a *mondegreen*.[59] The right verse is the translation of the French in the middle verse back into English, but this time with new set of meanings.

After deploying this procedure, the words are exactly the same yet entirely different. Here's how: the linguistic meanings of the English words are dissolved into the materiality of the French pronunciation. This is a dispersal of meaning into phonetic atoms and spaces. When they are translated back into English, there is a different starting point – *matter, not meaning* – thus moving along that same metaphysical-ethical continuum mentioned above.

The point of it all is not to determine the true meaning of the text. After all, we will never know whether Lucretius really intended to include the plague scene as the closing scene or not. But it does not matter. What matters, instead, is the injunction to the reader to *do something*. In fact, what it means to "do something" might be considered one meaning of a "minor ethics."

In *What Is Philosophy?*, Deleuze and Guattari define philosophy as the *creation of concepts* (WP, 1–12), art as the *creation and extraction of percepts or affects* (WP, 163–78), and science as the *creation of functions or logical prospects* (WP, 117–20, 135–46). Could ethics then be defined as the *creation of acts*, with a minor ethics the creation of acts in a minor sense? I leave you now not with a rewritten or corrected version of Lucretius's Book 6, but with a task, a provocation to act, in the tradition of ancient didactic poetry: take the Wolfson procedure and use it. Whatever language you speak or read, run the Wolfson procedure through your mother tongue.

The result should be a new final scene of *De rerum natura*, one that could, on the face of it, look like utter nonsense. Since this is a chapter in a volume on ethics, this might strike some readers as strange, if not unhelpful. What does nonsense have to do with ethics, after all? In response, our aim is to reveal a foreign language within a mother tongue so as to uncover the material forces subtending major moral norms. To use a famous Deleuzian phrase, Wolfson makes language stutter, and the same could be said for major morality (CC, 107–14). This stuttering scatters sense into nonsense and thereby unbends the supposed language acts heralded by major morality. A minor ethics attunes to the divergent movements of singular things concealed beneath moral codes and molar modes. Major morality, by contrast, seeks to fix the full articulation of universal moral principles so that one might judge actions and intentions through reference to transcendent values and norms.

In a sense, we might think of the Wolfson procedure as initiating a *minoritization of language, a becoming-minor of words* that corresponds to a minor ethics. A minor use of language follows not a "formal or superficial syntax that governs the equilibriums of language, but a syntax in the process of becoming, a creation of syntax that gives birth to a foreign language within language, a grammar of disequilibrium" (CC, 122). A minor language is then not outside the major language, but is instead an *outside within* the major. Such an *outside within* is encountered through the splintering of sense into pure sonic atoms, *prima facie* nonsense, provoked by the Wolfson procedure. In the same way, a minor ethics is not opposed to major morality but is simply the *outside within* the molar morality. Put more pragmatically, it is similar to a micro-historical ethics.[60] We call it a micro-ethics because it engages ethical questions from the perspective of seemingly minor events or affects that provoke the proclamations of molar morality even though they are not acknowledged as such. Examples include Nietzsche's consideration of the moral effects of food: "Do we know," he writes, "the moral effects of foods? Is there any *philosophy of nutrition*? ... There is so much in them to think about!"[61] Another example would be the invention of the cotton gin and the formation of American anti-black racism. Though major ethics might not consider the formative influence of food or agronomic technology, micro-ethics like we see in Lucretian atomism attunes us to encounters with the singular things *outside yet within* speaking and acting.

With atomic ethics in mind and the Wolfson procedure in hand, the remaining task is for you, our reader, to create acts by revealing the genetic singularities subtending your own language and morals. As Epicurus taught his followers to construct forms of relations that produced multiple affirmations of joy and pleasure – in short, to cultivate a Garden – we can use the Wolfson procedure to construct new Epicurean Gardens. Go out into your own worlds, your own linguistic domains, among the silent assemblages of bodies in which you are embedded, and act. To be concrete, use the Wolfson procedure on the most common moral prescriptions so as to attune to the supposedly non-moral atomic forces subtending major morality. For example, take Kant's Categorical Imperative and run the Wolfson procedure. What will happen is that hidden relations and genetic conditions contained in them will be let loose so that new forms of relations among singularities might emerge, ones previously unseen from the perspective of major morality like Kantian deontology.

Become-Epicurean; become-minor; become-molecular. Respond singularly to the scattered singular beings – the flocks of atomic particles – glimpsed at the limit of thought and language by applying and adapting the Wolfson procedure. Cultivate your Garden. Initiate a minor ethics, an ethics of atoms or singularities. After all, Lucretian ethics is not a generalized doctrine of universal truths but a joyful orientation from and toward singular things. A minor ethics, like Lucretius's atomism, is not something you simply say or think; it is something you *do*.

NOTES

1 Joseph Farrell agrees: "For the record, if I were asked to recommend a single meditation on the subject of Lucretius and modernism, my preference would be for Italo Calvino's marvelous *Six Memos for the Next Millennium*." "Lucretius and the Symptomatology of Modernism," 50n5.

2 Calvino, *Six Memos*.

3 We should also not forget that *De rerum natura* is also divided into six books. References to Lucretius's *On the Nature of Things* are as DRN followed by the book and line numbers.

4 Calvino, *Six Memos*, 26.

5 Long, "Roman Philosophy," 197.

6 Foster, "The Rhetoric of Materials," 115.

7 Fowler, "Lucretian Conclusions," 113, 115.

8 Ibid., 115.

9 Ibid., 120. Given that the Epicurean operation is about cultivation and nurturing, as when one grows a garden, it seems strange for Lucretius to switch to a strategy of a direct and competitive challenge.

10 Sedley, "Epicureanism in the Roman Republic," 43.

11 We note that the Plague scene was a depiction of the second year of the Peloponnesian war (430 BCE), though Epicurus was not even born for several decades (341 BCE). If Sedley's argument is true, then Epicureanism arose not in the fresh womb of Athens but in the overstuffed graves of post-plague Athens.

12 Farrell, "Lucretian Architecture," 79.

13 Calvino, *Six Memos*, 55–6. I have reordered this list so that it is the inversion of Calvino's, though there is no indication that Calvino was wedded to this order.

14 Deleuze, "Lucretius and Naturalism," 245.

15 Ibid., 245.

16 Ibid., 246.

17 Ibid., 246.

18 Lucretius, DRN, 1.633–4.

19 Deleuze, "Lucretius and Naturalism," 246.

20 See Lucretius, DRN, Bk. 1, for the critique of Heraclitus, Empedocles, and Anaxagoras.

21 Regarding the nothingness that eats away at pre-Epicurean concepts, see ibid., Bk. 1, 657–69, 753–62.

22 Laertius, *The Lives*, 10.3–8.

23 Ibid., 10.6–7.
24 Ibid., 10.7–9.
25 Ibid., 10.9.
26 The irony, of course, is that much of what we know about Epicureanism comes from Cicero.
27 Jerome's *Chronicle* as quoted in DRN, x.
28 Erler, "Epicureanism in the Roman Empire," 62.
29 Dante, *The Inferno,* 10.13–15.
30 Greenblatt, *The Swerve,* 44.
31 Bacon, *The Works,* 168–9.
32 Descartes, *Philosophical Writings,* vol. 1.
33 Gassendi, *Selected Works,* 398.
34 Newton, *Unpublished Scientific Papers,* 312–17.
35 Newton, *Opticks,* 375–6.
36 Lucretius, DRN, 3.380.
37 Epicurus, "Letter to Menoeceus," in *The Epicurus Reader,* 126.
38 Philodemus's *Herculaneum* Papyrus, quoted in *Hutchinson's "Introduction"* to ibid., vi. (my emphasis).
39 Epicurus, "Letter to Menoeceus," 126–7.
40 Lucretius, DRN, 3.417–3.829.
41 Spinoza, *Ethics,* IV.P67.
42 For extensive discussion of this, see Wallach, *Lucretius and the Diatribe.*
43 Against this, Farrell argues that, in at least some respects, "Lucretius appears not so much as a proto-Enlightenment thinker as he does a proto-fundamentalist religious fanatic … Lucretius expresses the religious sensibility of one who finds salvific message in the teachings of a great man." "Lucretius and the Symptomatology," 47.
44 Elsewhere Deleuze writes: "Not since Lucretius has the critical enterprise which characterises philosophy been taken so far (with the exception of Spinoza). Lucretius exposes the trouble of the soul and those who need it to establish their power – Spinoza exposes sorrow, all the causes of sorrow and all those who found their power at the heart of this sorrow" (NP, 190). James Jope also argues in "The Didactic Universe" for this position, even using the term "demythologization."
45 Gale, *Myth and Poetry,* 225.
46 Deleuze sees similarities among Wolfson, Raymond Roussel, and Jean-Pierre Brisset. For more on this, see Foucault's comparison of these three in his preface to the new edition of Brisset, which appears in *Dits et écrits,* 2:13–24.

47 In addition, it operates between Epicurus's Greek and Lucretius's Latin, between Lucretius's original text and the Christian's insertion of the plague, between Lucretius and Deleuze, and in the folds of the various translations of *De rerum natura*.

48 For example, "from *d* to *t*, from *p* to *b*, from *v* to *b*."

49 Deleuze, *Essays Critical and Clinical*; hereafter CC. "[Since] the English *wire* is not sufficiently invested by the German *Zwirm*, the Russian *provloka* will be invoked, which turns *wir* into *riw*, or rather *rov*."

50 Gassendi's adaptation of the similitude of the letters and its afterlife throughout the seventeenth century is treated at length in Selcer, *Philosophy and the Book*.

51 Lucretius, DRN, 1.196–8, 823–9, 907–14; 2.688-99, 1013–22.

52 Aristotle, *Metaphysics*, in *Complete Works*, vol. 2, 1.4985b4-20.

53 Sextus Empiricus, *Against the Professors*, 7.135.

54 It is no coincidence that Deleuze says that the Wolfson "procedure operates in a void" (CC, 11).

55 "There is a clear tendency for didactic works to end with a formal conclusion – a *quod erat demonstrandum* or injunction to further study." Fowler, "Lucretian Conclusions," 126. Surprisingly to me, others read this injunction as a sort of challenge. Voula Tsouna writes that "the uncontrollable and chaotic circumstances in which horrible pain and death occurred have a therapeutic purpose. They constitute the final test as to whether the readers have truly internalized the teaching of the poem and can look upon even these deaths without anxiety and fear. If they can, Lucretius' poetic art has performed its miracle. If they cannot, the readers should return to the poem and reflect on it again." "Epicurean Therapeutic Strategies," 259. This strikes me as utterly un-Epicurean, if not borderline sadistic.

56 Since most of this book is written in English, I am speaking to those readers who have a significant facility with English.

57 Jean-Jacques Lecercle, "Louis Wolfson," 103.

58 Rooten, *Mots D'Heures*.

59 A *mondegreen* is a mishearing or misinterpretation of a phrase due to close-homophony such that new meaning is produced; the famous example of a *mondegreen* is the lyric from Jimi Hendrix's *Purple Haze*: Jimi sings, "'Scuse me while I kiss the sky," though many people heard, "'Scuse me while I kiss this guy."

60 Important examples of micro-history include Carl Ginzburg's *The Cheese and the Worms*; and George R. Stewart's *Pickett's Charge*.

61 Nietzsche, *The Gay Science*, 34 (§7, my emphasis).

5

Kierkegaard and the Logic of Sense

Henry Somers-Hall

Long live the stagecoach horn! It is the instrument for me for many reasons, and chiefly because one can never be certain of wheedling the same notes from this horn. A coach horn has infinite possibilities, and the person who puts it to his mouth and puts his wisdom into it can never be guilty of a repetition, and he who instead of giving an answer gives his friend a coach horn to use as he pleases says nothing but explains everything.

Søren Kierkegaard, *Repetition*

My aim in this chapter is to explore how we might understand the relation of Deleuze's early works to ethics and to develop the connections between this way of understanding Deleuze and the work of Søren Kierkegaard. I will claim that we can view both figures as arguing that the sense or meaning we take from the world, and the metaphysical structure we ascribe to it, is secondary to an ethical stance we take in the face of a world of becoming. As such, the central preoccupation of both Kierkegaard and Deleuze is how we make sense of an existence that is necessarily temporal. As we shall see, recognizing the importance of temporality involves a move away from the traditional resolution of the problem of sense that operates by making temporality an accidental aspect of a world. In the first half of this chapter, I explore this claim in relation to Deleuze's reading of Plato, tying his claim that Plato is essentially developing an ethical rather than metaphysical doctrine with the claim that "the task of modern philosophy has been defined: to overturn [*renversement*] Platonism" (DR, 59). My emphasis in this section is on how

Deleuze, rather than "overturning" Platonism by simply rejecting the priority it gives to Forms or essences over appearances, the *renversement* of Deleuze's reading *inverts* the relation to show how the search for essence is in fact grounded in an ethical decision, or "selection," in the world of appearances/simulacra itself. As such, both Plato and Deleuze can be seen as presenting different trajectories for making sense of a world of becoming, either by grounding it in a transcendent, atemporal realm or by seeing it as an intensive field of processes. In the second half of this chapter, I will argue that Kierkegaard's philosophy rests on a claim – similar to the one we find in Deleuze's work – that we need to develop a logic of sense in response to a world of becoming. I will conclude that Deleuze's reading of Kierkegaard is limited by its focus on the theological aspects of his thought and that Kierkegaard provides a sophisticated and complementary taxonomy of the ways in which we try to make sense of our existence in a world of becoming by developing diverse ethical postures.

I. THE LOGIC OF SENSE

I want to begin by asking the question: What is a "logic of sense"? In his review of Jean Hyppolite's *Logic and Existence*, Deleuze claims that "we find [the] substitution of sense for essence already in Plato, when he shows us that the second world is itself the subject of a dialectic that makes it the sense of this world, not some other world" (DI, 16). Accounts of Plato often begin from the claim that the world we find around us – the world of appearances – is a copy of a real world of eternal Forms or Ideas. Plato presents a number of arguments for the need for an eternal realm of truths beyond the sensible world. First, we can note that many of the properties we find in the world are contradictory. Nothing is simply beautiful, for instance, as at various moments in its existence its appearance will change. At some point something may be beautiful whereas at some other point it may not be. The *same* object therefore exhibits contrary properties.[1] Similarly, Plato notes that a lot of the concepts we have are never encountered in the world around us. For instance, we have the concept of a circle, but when we look around the world we in fact do not sensibly encounter any actual perfect circles. Because of the nature of the world, things always manifest imperfections, yet we nonetheless have an idea of beauty, for instance, that goes beyond the imperfect beauty we find in the world.[2] At the heart of this account is the claim that the world as we encounter it is in a state of flux.

What makes it possible for us to talk coherently about objects in the world, or to have an idea of beauty or of geometrical forms that do not exist concretely in the world as do most things we encounter, is that there is a realm of perfect instances of these entities that form a model for the world we find around us.[3] Now, the typical way of reading Plato on this model is metaphysical. Philosophy is an attempt to move beyond the realm of appearances to the realm of the Ideas themselves. The analogy of the cave is the classic example of this model of Plato where we aim to enter into relationship with Ideas themselves. For Deleuze, this reading of Plato leads to the development of the Western metaphysical tradition. With the notion that the objects of the world have a rational ground, we open up the possibility of tracing out and specifying the nature of the objects of the world in rational, atemporal terms: "representation runs through and covers over the entire domain, extending from the highest genera to the smallest species, and the method of division takes on its traditional fascination with specification which it did not yet have in Plato" (LS, 259). This project culminates in the projects of Leibniz and Hegel, which, rather than attempting to extract the rational from the field of becoming, hold that becoming itself is simply a confused expression of the rational.[4]

For Deleuze, to understand Plato in this way, as operating in terms of a distinction between Ideas and copies, is to read Plato anachronistically from the perspective of the tradition he instituted. "This distinction operates completely within the world of representation" (LS, 262). Seeing Plato as operating in terms of this distinction between Ideas (or essences) and appearances leads to a narrative whereby Platonism is overcome in the nineteenth century with the emergence of the German Idealist tradition that reorients philosophy towards appearances. In the *Critique of Pure Reason*, for instance, Kant reconceives the major categories of metaphysics as modes of synthesis of appearances themselves, and argues that positing them as a ground for appearances is the result of a "transcendental illusion." "[N]othing is more natural and seductive than the illusion of taking the unity in the synthesis of thoughts for a perceived unity in the subject of these thoughts."[5] Hegel similarly argues in the *Science of Logic* that essence is simply the process of the movement of appearance itself.[6] Deleuze's claim is that these revisions to the essence/appearance schema do not really go beyond Plato because they fail to "bring to the light of day" the "motivation" for Plato's institution of this distinction (LS, 253). Seeing Plato as attempting to return us to the Ideas rests on a failure to recognize that the real distinction for Plato is not between the Ideas and the empirical objects that participate in them. Rather, for Deleuze, at the heart of Plato's thought is "a will to select and to choose" between different notions of copies themselves. Once we recognize this, our conception of Platonism becomes reoriented towards *sense* rather than *essence*. With this reorientation, we move to a position whereby an ethical decision precedes our understanding of the structure of the world. "The model–copy distinction," Deleuze writes,

> is there only in order to found and apply the copy–simulacra distinction, since the copies are selected, justified and saved in the name of the identity of the model and owing to their internal resemblance to this ideal model. The function of the notion of the model is not to oppose the world of images in its entirety but to select the good images, the icons which resemble from within, and eliminate the bad images or simulacra. (DR, 154–5)

So how does this reorientation take place? Well, when we look at the Platonic dialogues, we frequently find at their heart the question that defines representation for Deleuze, the question, "What is x?" Thus, the *Laches* asks the question, "What is courage?," and the *Euthyphro* asks the question, "What is piety?" These questions appear to fit naturally into the Aristotelian tradition, in that they ask for a definition of the essence of a particular kind. In fact, however, Deleuze claims that this structure of definition is ironic and that it covers over a more fundamental question of selection. In the *Statesman*, for instance, the Eleatic visitor asks for a definition of the "statesman," and defines statesmanship as "knowledge of the collective rearing of human beings."[7] Discovering this definition, however, does not resolve the question at the heart of the dialogue, since there are a number of figures who meet this definition: "merchants, farmers, millers and bakers."[8] "Difference is not between species, between two determinations of a genus," Deleuze notes of this model, "but entirely on one side, within the chosen line of descent" (DR, 72). What Plato is trying to do, according to Deleuze, is not to define a particular class of individuals (and thus to answer the question of representation), but rather to trace the genealogy of the subject in question – to distinguish between the statesman and the pretender in terms of their origin.[9] The aim of the project is therefore not to determine the characteristics of a class, but to assess the validity of a claim. "It permits the construction of a model according to which the different pretenders can be judged. What needs a foundation, in fact, is always a pretension or a claim" (LS, 255). At the heart of the Platonic method is therefore not a taxonomy of essence, but a more existential question of distinguishing the well-founded from that which lacks foundation. The visitor makes this project explicit in the *Statesman* when he describes the project of determining statesmanship by analogy with the separating out of unalloyed gold from rocks and minerals by the use of "smelting and testing." Thus, we separate off "those things that are different from the expert knowledge of statesmanship, and those that are alien and hostile to it" so that what remains are those "precious and related to it."[10] How do we therefore distinguish the statesman from the merchants, farmers, millers, and bakers, or Socrates from the sophist? It is through the introduction of a myth. In the *Statesman*, it is through the incorporation of a myth into the structure of our inquiry that we are able to resolve the question of which of the various contenders is in actual fact the statesman. Myth provides an archetype by which to properly separate the pure gold of the statesman from the mixed elements of the other figures; myth provides a model to determine what the statesman should be. Now here we arrive at the question of selection, and the selection that Plato introduces is between different kinds of copies. There are two ways in which something can be a copy of or resemble something else. Something can resemble the way something *is* (in which case it is an *icon*), or, like the manner in which sculptors may employ tricks of perspective, it can resemble the way something *appears* (in which case it is a *phantasm*, a term rendered in Latin as *simulacrum*). The true statesman resembles the Form of the statesman in the first of these senses, since the form itself cannot be given in appearance, as it is not spatiotemporal. The pretender only resembles the *appearance* of the Idea, not the Idea itself. The problem, therefore, is to distinguish those candidates who bear a true likeness from those who merely appear to do so.

Deleuze takes this distinction between different forms of resemblance to be the essential feature of Platonism, rather than the one between model and copy, and it is a distinction that is key to Deleuze's own early philosophy. In effect, Deleuze reads Plato as attempting to make sense of the world of appearances by relating it to the Idea. The focus is on giving meaning to the Heraclitean world of becoming by positing a realm of Ideas that makes possible discriminations in *this* world. Thus, at the heart of Plato's thought, for Deleuze, is in fact something like an empiricism. We can see the radicality of this reading through the fact that Plato here moves beyond Spinoza. On Deleuze's reading in *Difference and Repetition*, Spinoza privileges substance over modes: "Spinoza's substance appears independent of the modes, while the modes are dependent on substance, but as though on something other than themselves" (DR, 40). For Plato, on the contrary, Ideas emerge from the need to make sense of categories such as beauty that we encounter in the world of appearance. They allow us to cut up the world of appearance according to its natural articulations. In the *Republic*, for instance, Plato describes the eternal Ideas of numbers as "compulsory for warriors because of their orderly ranks and for philosophers because they have to learn to rise up out of becoming and grasp being, if they are ever to become rational."[11] In this sense, Plato inaugurates the process we find at the heart of Aristotle's work, which Deleuze identifies as "the extraction or cutting out of generic identities from the flux of a continuous perceptible series" (DR, 34). Thus, on Deleuze's reading, the notion of an Idea in Plato's philosophy is related to an ethical question of selecting among different ethical attitudes (cf. LS, 361).[12] In essence, Deleuze's claim is that metaphysics is introduced simply because it is needed to provide a test or method of selection that will lend coherence to the ethical claims.[13]

For Plato, the Idea presents the ground for the sense of things. As Deleuze puts it, "the Idea is not yet the concept of an object which submits the world to the requirements of representation, but rather a brute presence which can be invoked in the world only in function of that which is not 'representable' in things" (LS, 59). Deleuze notes at the opening of the *Logic of Sense*, for instance, that Plato seems to suggest in the *Cratylus* that there might be "two languages and two sorts of 'names,' one designating the pauses and rests which receive the action of the Idea, the other expressing the movements, or rebel becomings" (LS, 2).[14] In the *Cratylus* itself, these two accounts of names are related to a Platonic account and one is grounded in a Heraclitean understanding of the world, suggesting that the model of representation is not yet established. This notion of an Idea as the non-representable ground of things fits with Deleuze's own account of the Idea as an n-dimensional, virtual multiplicity that gives the genetic conditions of things, while not itself being thing-like (DR,

182-3). There is thus a parallel between the structure of Plato's meta-physics and that of Deleuze's. In both cases, we are confronted by a world of appearances that we make sense of by reference to the underlying conditions that transcend it (albeit with a very different notions of transcendence).

If it is the case that "with Plato, a philosophical decision of the utmost importance was taken: that of subordinating difference to the supposedly initial powers of the Same and the Similar, that of declar-ing difference unthinkable in itself and sending it, along with the simulacra, back to the bottomless ocean" (DR, 127), is there a similar though inverted philosophical decision at the heart of Deleuze's thought? For Plato, the Idea allows us to institute a test of selection, and there is a parallel test for Deleuze: the eternal return. At the heart of Nietzsche's eternal return for Deleuze is the aim of determining whether something orients itself towards the world in terms of a "sedentary" or a "nomadic" distribution (DR, 36–7).[15] The eternal return allows us to distinguish two ways of understanding the ground of the world. At the heart of it is the question asked by the demon: "This life as you now live it and have lived it you will have to live once again and innumerable times again; and there will be nothing new in it, but every pain and every joy and every thought and sigh and everything unspeakably small or great in your life must return to you, all in the same succession and sequence."[16] Only that which is "not separated from what it can do" (DR, 37) can truly will the repetition of everything that makes it what it is. Those who cannot affirm this do not have their ground in the affirmative field of differ-ences, but are instead grounded in the sedentary distribution, the kind of distribution favoured by Plato – they are in effect the figures who, like Plato, attempt to rise up out of the flux of becoming to grasp being. The fact that they make a distinction between what can be done and what is done (i.e. that they posit agency) means that as agents they are not the same as their actions and that they see actions as derivative of a prior field of subjects. On that basis, we can posit the return of the subject without necessarily the return of their actions. *Contra* Nietzsche, we can affirm our own return without having to affirm the whole of our past. On a metaphysical level, rather than an ethical one, we can interpret the sedentary distribution in terms of a separation that is not between subjects and actions but rather between subjects and properties. This becomes the basis for the kind of account of determination we find in the philosophy of Aristotle, with determination operating through the attribution of one of two opposing predicates to an abstract subject.

Instead, for Deleuze's Nietzsche, what returns is the nomadic distribution. Taking up the eternal return, what the test selects is a prejudicative relationship to the world, prior to the distinction between subjects and actions: it is the intensive, nomadic distribution that returns as the field of processes from which subjects emerge: "Eternal return cannot mean the return of the Identical because it presupposes a world (that of the will to power) in which all previous identities have been abolished and dissolved" (DR, 41). In doing so, it unfolds a certain conception of being and thus calls into play the Deleuzian conception of an Idea as the genealogical origin of the world of intensity that is founded in process and becoming rather than being. For Deleuze, the eternal return is explicitly related to the Heraclitean world view.[17] The eternal return is therefore a test that allows us to show that our orientation to the world is in terms of the virtual tendencies that map the field of intensities, rather than the structures of representation that will emerge from the Platonic emphasis on permanence. Once we have accepted the mode of orientation towards the flux of intensity, or appearance, which surrounds us, the twin structures of the "virtual" and "actual," which allow us to formulate a test in terms of non-representational tendencies, come into play.[18] In this sense, if we accept Deleuze's account of his philosophy as a reversal of Platonism, the distinction between virtual and actual that we find in his philosophy emerges from a primary ethical decision and is introduced in order to explicate and give coherence to a life built on that ethical decision.

Deleuze's discussion of Plato's metaphysics, and his own inversion of it, presents to us a fundamentally existential rather than metaphysical question at the heart of *Difference and Repetition*. Thrown into a world of intensities, we face a fundamentally ethical decision of which orientation to adopt. Plato's test of descent from the Ideas orients us to the world of intensities by imposing a logic of stability that relegates change to the accidental. Deleuze's test of descent from the structure of the virtual orients us to this same world of intensities by positing permanence as a transcendental illusion. For Plato, the aim is "to rise up above becoming to grasp being,"[19] while for Nietzsche it is to recognize the truth that "everything recurs is the closest approximation of a world of becoming to a world of being."[20] In each case, however, the structure of the metaphysics we adopt follows from the ethical decision we take when we are thrown into a world that is fundamentally at odds with our structures of discourse and representation. Metaphysics makes possible the formulation of a coherent test of selection and, with it, a coherent orientation toward life. At the heart of these two models are also two different conceptions of repetition. Do we see repetition in terms of the return of the soul from the realm of Ideas (metempsychosis), as in Plato's model, or do we see it in terms of the instantiation of a field of intensity in different empirical situations? These questions move us away from a logic of essences toward a logic of how one is to *make* sense of the world.

2. KIERKEGAARD AND SENSE

While Deleuze shows that a logic of sense makes existential orientation a priority over metaphysics, we are still left with the question of what an ethics of sense grounded in a nomadic distribution would look like. While Deleuze's later work with Guattari does develop an ethics, it also moves away from the logic of sense we find in Deleuze's earlier works. It is also notoriously difficult to determine the form an ethics of sense might take in these early works.[21] In this section I look at how an ethics of sense might function by turning to the work of Kierkegaard. I will begin by exploring Kierkegaard's own relationship to Plato to show how irony plays an important role in his understanding of Socrates as a thinker of sense before showing how the interplay of the temporal and the eternal shows a similar orientation to the world as we find in Deleuze's work. I will conclude by looking at the limitations of Deleuze's critique of Kierkegaard.

In *Repetition*, Constantine Constantius explicitly relates the question of Platonic anamnesis to that of repetition:

> Say what you will, this question will play a very important role in modern philosophy, for repetition is a crucial expression for what "recollection" was to the Greeks. Just as they taught that all knowing is a recollecting, modern philosophy will teach that all life is a repetition ... Repetition and recollection are the same movement, except in opposite directions, for what is recollected has been, is repeated backward, whereas genuine repetition is recollected forward. Repetition, therefore, if it is possible, makes a person happy, whereas recollection makes him unhappy – assuming, of course, that he gives himself time to live and does

not promptly at birth find an excuse to sneak out of life again, for example, that he has forgotten something.[22]

The question of how one is able to repeat is thus a central question for Kierkegaard, but the key question here, just as it is for Deleuze, is not simply whether one *can* repeat, but rather "the possibility and meaning of repetition."[23] As Kierkegaard notes, this question is fundamentally related to time. Constantine writes that "when the Greeks said that all knowing is recollecting, they said that all existence, which is, has been."[24] Recollection is a way of fixing existence outside of time, in an eternal past. *Repetition* opens with an account of Constantine's attempt to repeat his previous visit to Berlin, which is frustrated by the minor changes that have taken place. He arrives on the wrong day, takes a different seat in the stagecoach, and discovers that his landlord has married. While at first such changes are renounced ("otherwise everything repeated itself"[25]), it quickly becomes apparent that the absolute repetition of his past experiences is impossible (and in fact Constantine Constantius's own name is a failed repetition of this sort). Repetition is not only physically impossible but also philosophically impossible: "A Greek would choose to recollect without being troubled by his conscience. Modern philosophy makes no movement. In general, it merely makes a commotion. To the extent that it makes a movement, it is always within the sphere of immanence. Repetition, on the other hand, is transcendence."[26] Here, the terms "immanence" and "transcendence" point to a fundamental resonance between Deleuze and Kierkegaard: the metaphysics of the encounter. For both Kierkegaard and Deleuze, thinking in modern philosophy is construed as operating within the sphere of a representation of the world, merely drawing out the implications of a set of postulates underlying an "image of thought" that covers over the true nature of thinking. Genuine thinking needs to break from this sphere:

> Do not count upon thought to ensure the relative necessity of what it thinks. Rather, count upon the contingency of an encounter with that which forces thought to raise up and educate the absolute necessity of an act of thought or a passion to think. The conditions of a true critique and a true creation are the same: the destruction of an image of thought which presupposes itself and the genesis of the act of thinking in thought itself. (DR, 139).[27]

As such, despite differences in terminology, Kierkegaard's use of *immanence* refers to modern philosophy's (principally Hegel's) immanence to an image of thought, while *transcendence* implies an encounter that forces us beyond this image. It correlates with the movement Deleuze makes when he calls for an encounter that moves us from the transcendent image of thought to the immanent plane of non-representational thinking. Now, transcendence for Kierkegaard should here be read as the claim that repetition is not possible purely in terms of actuality – that it requires a reference to another ontological plane, much as it does for Plato and for Deleuze.[28] As such, despite antithetical terminology, we find laid out the same method for arriving at genuine thought. Physical repetition, therefore, seems to be impossible. At the point that he visits the theatre to watch a farce, where no repetition is possible due to the novelty of each performance, Constantine writes what I consider to be one of the keystones for interpreting Kierkegaard:

> My unforgettable nursemaid, you fleeting nymph who lived in the brook that ran past my father's farm and always helpfully shared our childish games, even if you just took care of yourself! You, my faithful comforter, you who preserved your innocent purity over the years, you who did not age as I grew older, you quiet nymph to whom I turned once again, weary of people, weary of myself, so weary that I needed an eternity to rest up, so melancholy that I needed an eternity to forget. You did not deny me what men want to deny me by making eternity just as busy and even more appalling than time. Then I lay at your side and vanished from myself in the immensity of the sky above and forgot myself in your soothing murmur! You, my happier self, you fleeting life that lives in the brook running past my father's farm, where I lie stretched out as if my body were an abandoned hiking stick, but I am rescued and released in the plaintive purling![29]

At the heart of this passage is a recognition that making sense of life requires reconciling two different moments: *time*, which imperceptibly and blissfully "slip[s] by, like the running water that murmurs and disappears," and *eternity*. Constantine suggests the possibility of giving up eternity by slipping back purely into time. In his journals, Kierkegaard himself brings up this metaphor of the babbling brook, but rejects this solution, claiming that the temptation of the babbling brook is a temptation of the "muddled heads" of "nature worshippers."[30]

As well as the rejection of the life of temporality, there is also the recognition that traditional philosophy both denies time and falsifies the eternal itself. The key figure in this regard is Hegel, whom Kierkegaard and Deleuze both charge with bringing about a "false movement" through a play with and on words. Referring to Hegel's repetition of the Greek claim that essence is "that which has been," rendered in German as *das Wesen ist gewesen*,[31] Kierkegaard writes that "a later age would perhaps be surprised to see that what are regarded as discarded witticisms once played an important role in logic, not as incidental explanations and ingenious remarks but as masters of movement."[32] As Kierkegaard notes, Hegel replaces movement with logical transition, effectively falling foul of a transcendental illusion whereby time is misconceived according to a representation of time. As such, Hegel falsifies experience by reducing the question of a logic of sense to the other of its terms: the eternal. He "makes no secret of the fact that things indeed do not happen quite that way in the world and yet conceals the consequence of this for the whole of logical immanence by permitting it to drift into logical movement."[33] Kierkegaard here makes three points against Hegel. First, that logical transition is not equivalent to the kind of movement we find in time. As he puts it in his *Concluding Unscientific Postscript*, "misled by repeated talk about a continual process in which opposites combine in a higher unity and then again in a higher unity etc., people have drawn a parallel between Hegel's doctrine and that of Heraclitus: all flows and nothing abides. This, however, is a misunderstanding, because everything that is said in Hegel about process and becoming is illusory."[34] The point here is not that Hegel's account is incomplete, but rather that Hegel falsifies the world by giving it a false sense:

> I remember once having heard a speculator say that one must not give undue thought to the difficulties beforehand, because then one never arrives at the point where he can speculate. If the important thing is to get to the point where one can begin to speculate, and not that one's speculation in fact becomes true speculation, it is indeed resolutely said that the important thing is to get the point of speculating.[35]

As such it is a misreading of Kierkegaard to see his work as developing a supplement to or completion of the Hegelian project,[36] as some recent commentators have done.[37] Second, Kierkegaard notes that transition brings even this false movement into philosophy as a simple presupposition. The transition between categories is prior to the categories themselves. Finally, transition itself cannot be explained in logical terms, since it is not itself a category of logic. As Kierkegaard notes: "One can see how illogical the movements must be in logic."[38] Just as with Deleuze's critique of Hegel, therefore, Kierkegaard claims that Hegel replaces temporality with a representation of temporality. By operating purely in the realm of representation, Hegel avoids the problem of the incongruity of sense and time, but only at the expense of reducing becoming to a confused representation of a rational world.[39] As such, Kierkegaard prefigures Deleuze's claims that sense requires a second distribution to operate in relation to becoming, and that philosophy has tended to cover over the problem of sense by reducing the two terms to one plane.

Each of these projects, the project of giving up the eternal to live entirely in time, or of giving up time to fall into the eternal or conceptual, therefore operates by rejecting the interrelation of time and the eternal. For Kierkegaard, therefore, the problem of philosophy is how to relate together these two categories. As Kierkegaard notes, the key problem is their incommensurability. In this manner, there is something of an existential reworking of the Kantian problem of combining concepts and intuitions in Kierkegaard's work.[40] The problem of living a meaningful life is that of reconciling time and the eternal, or of giving sense to time.[41]

To give a brief sense of how this account plays out, I want to turn to the *Concept of Irony* and Kierkegaard's account of Socrates. In this text, Kierkegaard takes up Schleiermacher's distinction "between the [Socratic] dialogues in which the dialogical is the main element and the tireless irony at times disentangles, at times tangles, the disputation and the disputants, and the [Platonic] constructive dialogues, which are characterized by an objective, methodical style."[42] The Socratic dialogues are the early dialogues, which tend to be aporetic in character; whereas the Platonic dialogues propound a definite doctrine, and as in the case of the *Statesman* I mentioned in relation to Deleuze, they do not necessarily include Socrates, or if they do, they do not include him in his individuality. Together with these two sets of dialogues, we have two conceptions of irony. In the later dialogues, we have the notion of irony as essentially a stylistic device. Readers who focus on these dialogues, such as Hegel, tend to downplay the role of irony.[43] Kierkegaard writes that "as a rule, irony is understood ideally, is assigned its place as a vanishing element in the system, and is therefore treated very briefly. For this reason it is not easy to comprehend how a whole life can be taken up with it, since, after all, the content of this life must be regarded as nothing."[44] In the early dialogues, however, irony is central to Socrates's method. This is tied to the fact that the early dialogues end inconclusively. As Kierkegaard notes, however, the inconclusive ending is not even a negative conclusion. "Even skepticism always posits something, whereas irony, like that old witch, continually makes the very tantalizing attempt to eat up everything first of all and thereupon to eat up itself."[45] As such, while Platonic thought is grounded in knowledge, Socratic irony conceives of sense in a manner different in kind from knowing.[46]

So what is the purpose of this kind of irony? Well, much as Deleuze sees the aim of Plato's method as giving sense to the world by introducing the eternal realm of Ideas against which a selection can be made in this world, Socrates's ironic method is, for Kierkegaard, a way of introducing the notion of the eternal while avoiding the flight away from appearances that we find, for instance, in non-ironic philosophers such as Hegel. Kierkegaard talks of Socrates as hovering above the world to get a bird's-eye view of it through the dialectical method, but through irony preventing the move away from giving sense to this world towards what Deleuze would call a metaphysics of essence. Here is Kierkegaard's summary of the ironist's method:

> But it is precisely this hovering that is so very significant; it is the attempted ascension that is accomplished only when the whole realm of the ideal opens up, when this staring into oneself allows the self to expand into the universal self, pure thought with its contents. The ironist, to be sure, is lighter than the world, but on the other hand he still belongs to the world; like Mohammed's coffin, he is suspended between two magnets.[47]

In effect, therefore, the early Socratic dialogues introduce the eternal into the world, in the form of metaphysical speculation, in such a way that the incommensurability between it and the world of appearance is maintained through a process of suspension. Prefiguring Deleuze's reading of Plato, the effect of this is to transform the eternal from a structure of essence to that which allows us to make sense of *this* world.

At the heart of Kierkegaard's project is a taxonomy of the different ways in which we can bring sense to time, just as it is for Deleuze and for Plato. Deleuze focuses on the paradigm case of Abraham in his reading of Kierkegaard. Here, Kierkegaard deals with the binding of Isaac, God's commandment to Abraham to sacrifice his only son as a test of faith. In working through how Abraham makes sense of his actions, Kierkegaard offers two alternatives. At the heart of these alternatives is the binding of Isaac as a metaphor for the incommensurability of sense (and the eternal, in the form of God) and time. Given the senselessness of God's commandment, Abraham could have renounced time, in effect taking the opposite path of Constantius in resolving the issue of incommensurability. In that case, he would have maintained simply a relation to the eternal: "[His love would] be transfigured into a love for the eternal being which, true enough denied the fulfillment but nevertheless did reconcile him once more in the eternal consciousness of its validity in an eternal form that no actuality can take away from him."[48] He renounces Isaac, and with it the sense of the world. He is an "alien in this world,"[49] in his engagements with the world, no longer at home in the world of finitude. Such a position is reminiscent of Hegel's approach, but with the caveat that it both recognizes and renounces time rather than just passing over it. The alternative is to have faith. Abraham is a "knight of faith," for Kierkegaard, and despite the incomprehensibility of the possibility of reconciling the eternal and the temporal, he believes on the strength of the absurd in their commensurability. He believes that Isaac will be returned to him, knowing that there is no rational possibility of this happening. Ultimately, as Kierkegaard makes clear in *Repetition*, repetition itself is this orientation towards the future on the basis of the absurd, or that which falls outside of the empirical, where Abraham receives Isaac back despite the senselessness of that return. Whether faith is possible, or is more a *focus imaginarius* for raising the question of sense, is open to question.[50] The important point to note is that all of Kierkegaard's examples of orienting oneself to the world – the tax collector, Abraham, Job, the knight of faith who believes he will win the princess despite the impossibilities thrown up by the contingencies of the world – revolve around giving sense to time in *this* world.[51]

3. DELEUZE'S CRITIQUE OF KIERKEGAARD

I want to conclude by turning to some of the critical remarks Deleuze makes about Kierkegaard. In *Difference and Repetition*, Deleuze notes that Kierkegaard and Peguy are "the culmination of Kant, they realize Kantianism by entrusting to faith the task of overcoming the speculative death of God and healing the wound in the self. This is their problem, from Abraham to Joan of Arc: the betrothal of a self rediscovered and a god recovered, in such a manner that it is no longer possible truly to escape from either the condition or the agent" (DR, 95). The root of this assertion is an attempt by Deleuze to remove God from Kierkegaard's interpretation of repetition. Kierkegaard describes the religious moment of faith, where time and the eternal are brought into relation as reliant on an immediate relationship between the self and God (Abraham's relationship to God is shown to be immediate by the fact that it is inexpressible through the categories of representation). Deleuze's criticism is that this relationship between self and God, in which man is reconciled with the world on the strength of the absurd, is still too closely tied to the concept of identity and essence, albeit an essence that falls outside of the law. In effect, at heart, the relation of Abraham to God is something like Kant's relation between the transcendental unity of apperception and the transcendental object, each of which is also unknowable and extra-categorical, but which reaffirm the transcendental grounds for repetition as reliant on constituted centres of subjectivity and objectivity. While Deleuze's response to Kierkegaard privileges faith as the relation between sense and becoming, in fact, Deleuze's characterization of Kierkegaard here is rather simplistic. Ironically for a writer renowned for his sensitivity to the diversity of voices and languages within philosophy, Deleuze provides a literal reading of the various pseudonymous works of Kierkegaard that subordinates their different perspectives to one overarching project.[52] As opposed to the binary distinction between the sedentary and the nomadic we find in Deleuze, Kierkegaard writes that "the exuberant growth of the spiritual life is not inferior to that of nature, and the varieties of the spiritual states are more numerous than those of the flowers."[53] That is, rather than the telescopic relation of aesthetic, ethical, religious, the ways in which becoming and sense should be reconciled for Kierkegaard form something more like a field of relations that blur into one another. At the heart of his project is an anthropological taxonomy of the multitude of ways in which we struggle to make sense of living in time.[54] Both for Kierkegaard and for Deleuze, the problem of ethics is to reconcile our representation of ourselves with our existence within time.[55] Similarly, for both, the problem of ethics has a Kantian inflection, but one that derives from Kant's metaphysics rather than his ethics: the problem of bringing into relation time and representation, given the difference in kind between them. Here we find the weakness of Deleuze's own account. Whereas Deleuze distributes the sedentary and the nomadic according to a sedentary distribution, seeing essentially two modes of relating to the world, the ways in which sense is made of the world for Kierkegaard form an interpenetrating, non-hierarchical multiplicity of positions.

NOTES

1 See Plato, "Parmenides," in *Complete Works*, 129c.
2 Plato, "Phaedo," in ibid., 74a–75e.
3 See Plato, "Republic," in ibid., 508.
4 See Somers-Hall, *Deleuze's* Difference and Repetition, 43–60.
5 Kant, *Critique of Pure Reason*, 442 [A402].
6 As Hegel puts it: "Illusory being, therefore, is essence itself, but essence in a determinateness, in such a manner, however, that this is only a moment of essence and essence is the reflection of itself within itself." *Science of Logic*, §831. For an analysis of essence in Hegel's *Science of Logic*, see Houlgate, "Essence, Reflexion, and Immediacy."
7 Plato, "Statesman," in *Complete Works*, 267d.
8 Ibid., 267e.
9 Julius Moravcsik calls Plato's method the "quilt" method of division, given its lack of reliance on Aristotelian differences, though Moravcsik still sees this method as one of the determination of species or sciences. *Plato and Platonism*, 213-24.
10 Plato, *Statesman*, in *Complete Works*, 303d-304a.
11 Plato, *Republic*, in ibid., 525b.
12 Here, Deleuze's reading of Plato is very close to Jacques Derrida's in "Plato's Pharmacy."
13 The connection between the theory of the forms/Ideas and ethics is recognized in Plato scholarship, and the theory of Ideas emerges from the ethical concerns Socrates deals with in the early dialogues. For instance, C.J. Rowe notes that "the assumption [of the independent existence of the forms] simultaneously feeds from and secures a fundamental premise of arguments in the moral and political spheres: that of the objectivity of moral values." *Plato*, 83. Such accounts part company with Deleuze in not seeing Plato as making a decision for a particular kind of ethics, and by

seeing Plato as operating with a distinction between making sense of the world in terms of being and a senseless world of becoming, rather than between two attitudes of sense-making.

14 Socrates suggests that there is a "civil war" between different names, with some having their origin in an understanding of the world as a Heraclitean flux, and some in terms of stability. He writes that the "name-giver might have made a mistake at the beginning and then forced the other names to be consistent with it. There would be nothing strange in that. Geometrical constructions often have a small unnoticed error at the beginning with which all the rest is perfectly consistent. That's why every man must think a lot about the first principles of any thing and investigate them thoroughly to see whether or not it's correct to assume them." Plato, "Cratylus," in *Complete Works*, 436c–d. In fact, Socrates concludes the dialogue by arguing that knowledge is impossible if we assume that the world is flux.

15 For a more detailed account of the distinction between sedentary and nomadic distributions, see Somers-Hall, *Deleuze's* Difference and Repetition, §1.6.

16 Nietzsche, *The Gay Science*, §341.

17 "When Nietzsche says that hubris is the real problem of every Heraclitean, or that hierarchy is the problem of free spirits, he means one – and only one – thing: that it is in hubris that everyone finds the being which makes him return, along with that sort of crowned anarchy, that overturned hier-archy which, in order to ensure the selection of difference, begins by sub-ordinating the identical to the different" (DR, 41). Deleuze expands on this claim in *Nietzsche and Philosophy* (NP, 22-5). Deleuze also notes that while Heraclitus is close to Nietzsche, "he only had a foreboding of the meaning of the eternal return" (NP, 201).

18 Returning to Plato's distinction between two kinds of image-making, Deleuze in these early works favours the simulacrum over the icon. In this regard, he takes up Maurice Merleau-Ponty's claim that sense also involves perspective and directedness, thus uniting its various French acceptations: "The only way we have of knowing what a painting is and what a thing is, is by looking at them, and their signification is only revealed if we look at them from a certain point of view, from a certain distance, and in a certain direction [*sens*], in short, if we put our involve-ment with the world at the service of the spectacle. 'The direction of a stream' would be meaningless if I did not take for granted a subject who looks from a certain place toward another. In the world in itself, all direc-tions and all movements are relative, which amounts to saying that there

are none at all." Merleau-Ponty, *Phenomenology of Perception*, 453.
Kierkegaard also notes the necessity of perspective. For instance: "If someone who wanted to learn to dance were to say: For centuries, one generation after the other has learned the positions, and it is high time that I take
advantage of this and promptly begin with the quadrille—people would
presumably laugh a little at him, but in the world of spirit this is very
plausible." Kierkegaard, *Fear and Trembling*, 46. Deleuze moves away
from a logic of sense in his collaborations with Guattari, a move that can
be tied to his explicit rejection of the importance of the simulacrum.

19 Plato, "Republic," in *Complete Works*, 525b.

20 Nietzsche, *The Will to Power*, 617.

21 For instance, see Badiou's claim that Deleuze presents an ethics of ascetism;
    Deleuze and the Clamor of Being, 17.

22 Kierkegaard, *Repetition*, 131.

23 Ibid., 150.

24 Ibid., 149. This Platonic notion of the real as pastness carries on in
    Aristotle, where his term essence, *to ti ên einai*, could be more literally
    translated as "the what it was to be" for a thing; see Marc Cohen,
    "Aristotle's Metaphysics." For a full analysis of the development of the con-
    cept of essence in Greek thought, and its influence on the development of
    philosophy, see the first chapter of Miguel de Beistegui, *Truth and Genesis*.

25 Kierkegaard, *Repetition*, 151.

26 Ibid., 186.

27 For Deleuze's theory of the encounter, see Somers-Hall, "Feuerbach and
    the Image of Thought." Kierkegaard makes this need for an outside clear
    in *Fear and Trembling*, where infinite resignation is seen as "a purely
    philosophical movement that I venture to make when it is demanded,"
    whereas faith is seen as something "over and beyond human powers" (48).
    Similarly, in the aesthetic, it is only through a contingent relation to
    another that the world can take on sense. This is true of the contraction
    of temporality into a moment in the seducer's diary, and similarly, in the
    realm of sin, the merman is only saved through the intervention of Agnes
    (ibid., 98).

28 Here, Kierkegaard is prefiguring the claim that opens *Difference and
    Repetition* that "repetition is not generality" (DR, 1). As Deleuze notes,
    understanding repetition in terms of actual states of affairs in fact reduces
    it to "extreme resemblance" (DR, 2). For both, true repetition involves a
    relation beyond actuality, and orients us to the future.

29 Kierkegaard, *Repetition*, 166.

30 Kierkegaard, *Journals and Papers*, 86.

31 Hegel, *Science of Logic*, §807.

32 Kierkegaard, *The Concept of Anxiety*, 12.

33 Ibid., 30.

34 Kierkegaard, *Concluding Unscientific Postscript*, 812.

35 Kierkegaard, *The Concept of Anxiety*, 83.

36 Just as Deleuze argues that Plato differs from later philosophers of repre-
    sentation such as Aristotle or Hegel, Kierkegaard argues that Plato has
    an understanding of the problem of making sense of time that is lost in
    Hegel's reduction of movement to a logical category: "Plato fully recog-
    nized the difficulty of placing transition in the realm of the purely meta-
    physical, and for that reason the category of the moment ... cost him so
    much effort. To ignore the difficulty certainly is not to 'go further' than
    Plato. To ignore it, and thus piously to deceive thought in order to get
    speculation afloat and the movement in logic going, is to treat speculation
    as a rather finite affair." Ibid., 82–3.

37 Michael Burns writes that "Kierkegaard offers a thoroughly systematic
    account of the grounds of reality and subjectivity and uses this systematic
    account to clear the space for a rigorously existential account of the lived
    experience of actuality. To use a metaphor, while music possesses a system-
    atic structure, simply knowing advanced musical theory will not lead an
    individual to instantaneously produce beautiful melodies. Instead, the indi-
    vidual subjectively appropriates the systematic structure of music, and in
    the space between the ideality of this structure and the reality of their
    contingent and free subjectivity, something new emerges." *Kierkegaard and
    the Matter of Philosophy*, 66–7. Such a reading is prefigured by Jean-Paul
    Sartre in "Kierkegaard: The Singular Universal." Burns's account relies on
    sidelining Kierkegaard's focus on temporality, and on the categories of the
    aesthetic. It is in these two areas in particular that Kierkegaard explores
    the claim that non-dialectical structures are either transposed into repre-
    sentation by dialectics, or are treated as unstructured immediacies.
    Similarly, Burns downplays the role of pseudonyms in Kierkegaard's
    thought. The reading offered here instead argues that Kierkegaard prefig-
    ures Deleuze in developing an account of structure that is different in kind
    from representation.

38 Kierkegaard, *The Concept of Anxiety*, 13.

39 In this manner, I take many of Kierkegaard's pseudonyms, such as A in
    Either/Or, to be taking up the idea of immediacy as that which is prior to
    the mediating functions of representation, and showing that, *contra* Hegel,
    the immediacy has its own form of determinacy, and thus can form the
    basis for a form of life. As such, I take it in a much more positive sense

than does, for instance, Stephen C. Evans in *Kierkegaard: An Introduction*, 68–89. This difference hinges in large part on whether one gives weight to the independent perspectives of Kierkegaard's pseudonyms, or, as with Evans, sees them as largely inessential when considering Kierkegaard's overall position.

40 Deleuze takes this difference in nature between the faculties as "one of the most original points of Kantianism." *Kant's Critical Philosophy*, 22. Hereafter KCP.

41 This need to reconcile sense and becoming is at the heart of Kierkegaard's use of pseudonyms, since to believe that the different attempts at reconciliation that Kierkegaard develops can be related together in the form of a direct representational discourse is to presuppose that sense can be understood as representation. As such, I reject here what Roger Poole calls in "The Unknown Kierkegaard" the "blunt" or "literalist" reading of Kierkegaard.

42 Kierkegaard, *The Concept of Irony*, 53.

43 Michael Inwood notes that, for Hegel, irony is roughly another word for dialectic, thus once again reducing the Socratic project to a precursor of Hegel's own thought. *A Hegel Dictionary*, 147.

44 Kierkegaard, *The Concept of Irony*, 166.

45 Ibid., 56.

46 Kierkegaard contrasts the Platonic and Socratic readings of the *Protagoras* and argues that Socratic irony prevents a reading of recollection as the retrieval of knowledge in this dialogue (ibid., 60). Cf. Deleuze's *Difference and Repetition*, where Deleuze similarly shows the priority of learning over knowledge (and their difference in kind) in his project of escaping the image of thought (DR, 164–7).

47 Ibid., 152.

48 Kierkegaard, *Fear and Trembling*, 43-4.

49 Ibid., 41.

50 See, for instance, Kierkegaard, *Fear and Trembling*, 44, where Silentio presents an account of a figure who fails to achieve even infinite resignation, which bears a strong resemblance to Kierkegaard's own relationship with Regine.

51 Kierkegaard, *The Concept of Anxiety*, 151–4, provides a taxonomy of ways in which we might fail to make sense of temporality. Thus, alongside seeing this interrelation in terms of metaphysics, or in terms of a fall into senseless becoming, Haufniensis introduces the idea of seeing the eternal as the limit of the temporal, or of integrating both moments through the imagination. Haufniensis makes explicit in these analyses that the eternal

is to be understood as repetition, thus reiterating that sense is a way of orienting oneself to the future in *this* world.

52 There is a further irony that the reading of Kierkegaard implicit in Deleuze's work, with its subordination of a variety of different pseudonyms to a single underlying schema, in fact mirrors Badiou's reading of Deleuze, where, "in starting from innumerable and seemingly disparate cases, in exposing himself to the impulsion organized by Spinoza and Sacher-Masoch, Carmelo Bene and Whitehead, Melville and Jean-Luc Godard, Francis Bacon and Nietzsche, Deleuze arrives at conceptual productions that I would unhesitatingly qualify as monotonous, composing a very particular regime of emphasis or almost infinite repetition of a limited repertoire of concepts, as well as a virtuosic variation of names, under which what is thought remains essentially identical." Badiou, *Deleuze and the Clamor of Being*, 14.

53 Kierkegaard, *The Concept of Anxiety*, 127.

54 Kierkegaard's taxonomy is spread across his pseudonymous works, all of which explore from different perspective how one might formulate a logic of sense. Kierkegaard's *Concept of Anxiety*, 151–4, provides a summary of many of the ways in which one might attempt to reconcile time and the eternal.

55 For both, this problem is formulated in terms of the categories of the past and the future, with the past signifying representation and the future as becoming that falls outside of our categories of representation. This is evidently clear in Kierkegaard's claim that "it is perfectly true, as the philosophers say, that life must be understood backwards. But they forget the other proposition, that it must be lived forwards." Kierkegaard, *Papers and Journals*, 161. Similarly, Deleuze's analysis of *Hamlet* sees Hamlet, whom Deleuze sees as a symbol for the reconciliation of time and representation, as caught between his knowledge of what he should do to avenge his father and his inability to make this act actual. Here, the representation of what he should do is likewise understood in terms of the past in contrast to the horizon of the future: "they are in the past and live themselves as such so long as they experience the act as too big for them" (DR, 112). For a more detailed reading of Deleuze and *Hamlet*, see Somers-Hall, "Time Out of Joint," 56.

6

Amor Fati in Nietzsche, Shestov, Fondane, and Deleuze

Bruce Baugh

I. THE FALL

I can recall it so clearly and vividly that it is as if it were happening before my eyes, right here, right now. It is a sunny day, hot but not too hot, a perfect day for taking down the storm windows on my old house – even if it is Father's Day and I promised my daughter I would take it easy. I've undone three of the four wing nuts holding the storm window in place and am descending from the top rung of the step ladder to the next rung down so that I can remove the remaining one. As my weight shifts, so does the ladder; it begins to tip. There is nothing I can do to halt its downward progress, nothing I can grab hold of. There is just enough time for me to make an effort to land feet first, which – to my relief and slight amazement – I succeed in doing. Sprawled on the ground, I raise myself to a sitting position. I shift my left leg, but my right foot won't budge. A sprain? I make a greater effort. My right foot does not respond in the slightest. It is then that I notice my foot sticking out at a peculiar angle to the rest of my leg, as if it were no longer attached. And so it begins.

I had sustained a spiral fracture of my right tibia. A steel plate was inserted to hold together the two fractured halves. For the next three months, I spent my time on the living room couch or in bed, with pillows under my right leg to raise it up, or seated at the dining room table with my broken leg propped on a chair. I could read, listen to music or the radio, or watch shows on a laptop, but not much else. There was nothing terribly unpleasant in all this. But the forced inactivity – not being able to walk, not leaving the house unless it was for a medical appointment – was driving me crazy. The plan had been to go to Europe that fall to walk in the footsteps of Kierkegaard, Rousseau, and Coleridge, part of a research project on walking and philosophy. My surgeon told me otherwise: "You will be doing your philosophizing at home."

While feeling miserable about all this, I thought about Friedrich Nietzsche's idea of "the eternal return." I had taught a course on Nietzsche the previous semester; thoughts of the eternal return and "tragic affirmation" sprang readily to mind. Could I will the eternal return of my fall and everything that followed in its wake? Was that not for Nietzsche the ultimate ethical test: that in order to will oneself, to *affirm* oneself entirely and unreservedly, in order to overcome *ressentiment* toward oneself and the past, one had to be able to will the eternal repetition of one's life, right down to the last detail, with not a single thing changed? Could I *will* the infinite repetition of my fall? At that moment, lying on the couch, my world narrowed down to a single floor of my house, I didn't think I could.

The thought of failing Nietzsche's "test" only exacerbated my depression, and it was my depression – my frustration, irritation, boredom, sadness – that struck me as being the most difficult thing to "affirm" and "will" eternally. Was it necessary to will *everything*, down to the last detail, including the suffering and depression? Certainly, that seems to be what Nietzsche requires: "My formula for greatness in a human being is *amor fati*: that one wants nothing to be different, not forward, not backward, not in all eternity. Not merely bear what is necessary, still less conceal it ... but *love* it."[1] Just in case it seemed that I could wriggle out of willing the negative aspects of my predicament, Nietzsche continues that *amor fati* is "a Yes-saying without reservation, even to suffering, even to guilt, even to everything that is questionable and strange in existence ... Nothing in existence may be subtracted, nothing is dispensable."[2] No way out, then; in order to affirm my life and myself – to not succumb to negativity and *ressentiment* – I would have to will and to love *everything*.

But had I understood Nietzsche? According to Gilles Deleuze, "every time we interpret the eternal return as the return of the identical or the same, we replace Nietzsche's thought with childish hypotheses ... Nietzsche explicitly denies that the eternal return is a circle that causes the same to return" (NP, xi). Perhaps, then, Nietzsche's *amor fati* would not amount to mere resignation to "things as they are," a servile submission to necessity that would seem to betray the spirit of creative freedom – "we free spirits!" – that animates Nietzsche's philosophy. Certainly, Lev Shestov (Léon Chestov) and Benjamin Fondane saw Nietzsche's *amor fati* as bowing down to the inevitability of fact, a breakdown of Nietzsche's otherwise salutary attempt to overcome idealism in philosophy. If "love of fate" is love of necessity (*anankē*) in the form of logical necessity and causal determinism, then it seems to be nothing more than the acceptance of the world as it is, or in Nietzsche's words, a "lying in the dust before *petits faits*," merely "seeing what is," instead of creatively and artistically *fashioning* one's existence according to one's *own* law and will.[3] "*One thing is needful. –* To 'give style' to one's character – a great and rare art! It is practiced by those who survey all the strengths and weaknesses of their nature and then fit them into an artistic plan ... It will be the strong and domineering natures that enjoy their finest gaiety in such constraint and perfection under a law of their own," a law that conquers nature and reshapes it instead of accepting and serving it.[4] If *amor fati* is loving the raw facts as they present themselves, then it is mere servility and the surrender of the commanding artistic will in the face of factual necessity.

If, however, fate has to do with the necessity of the whole of existence as *becoming*, then love of fate is "the radical repudiation of the very concept of *being*"[5]: not willing the repetition of isolated and static facts, but the return of *difference*, of the entire interconnection of intensities and potencies underlying actualities that allow for a different and contrary actualization, or for what Deleuze calls a "counter-actualization." For Deleuze, in the eternal return "each intensity wills itself" through all the other intensities, and one wills oneself "as a fortuitous moment, the very fortuity of which implies the necessity of the integral return of the whole series" of intensities (LS, 299–300/347–9). Nietzsche declares: "One is necessary, one is a piece of fate, one belongs to the whole, one *is* in the whole ... *But nothing exists apart from the whole!*"[6] Necessity and fate no longer come from outside, as the external necessity of facts or causal determinism. *Amor fati* would have nothing to do with the servile acceptance that whatever is and has been also *must be*, eternally, or with resignedly accepting whatever happens – "just one more form of *ressentiment*" (LS, 149/174) – but willing "something *in* that which happens, something to come [*à venir*]": the returning (*revenir*) of becoming (*devenir*) through the future (*l'avenir*). It is as returning through the future that the whole of becoming can be willed. "It is in this sense," Deleuze notes, "that *Amor fati* is one with the fight of free men" (LS, 149/174). Well, maybe so. How would that help me will the eternal return of my fall? What does it mean to "love fate" and to affirm one's existence "without reservation"?

In what follows, I will explore these ideas as they are dealt with by Nietzsche, Shestov, Fondane, and Deleuze to see to what extent these ideas can serve as the basis for an ethics, for an *art of living*. It may help distinguish what Deleuze calls "an ethical vision of the world" (EP, 23–51/255–72) from morality. Morality is a system of rights and duties based on rules that are valid for everyone and on the basis of which we can judge acts as right or wrong, good or evil, from a supposedly universal or objective point of view. Once "God is dead,"[7] however, this objective and universal point of view disappears and the moral system collapses. In its place arises an ethical vision of life according to which goodness is defined as whatever increases a living being's powers of acting, and what is bad (weak, servile, base) is whatever decreases one's powers of acting (EP, 254-7/234-6). Rather than universal moral laws that apply to everyone in the same way, the "law" that governs an individual being follows from its drive to persevere in existence, what Spinoza calls its *conatus*. The "good life" is one that involves a maximum of encounters with other beings that enhance the living being's powers of acting, and it is this drive toward the maximization of one's capabilities and powers that establishes the "norms of life" for a particular individual or group (EP, 268/247).

In the ethical system, rather than establishing transcendent ends that are independent of my capacities and needs, it is reason that establishes laws of cause and effect and that makes it possible to determine in advance whether an encounter or experience will lead to an increase or decrease in my power of acting. This "minor reason," as Fondane calls it, serves to *satisfy* our needs rather than *commanding* us through categorical imperatives. "Reason's only commandment," Deleuze advances, is to experience a maximum of joys in order to increase my power of action and to help me come into full possession of my own power (EP, 269/248, 272/251). What sort of encounters will produce joy is something that varies among individuals. Each person must experiment in order to determine the nature and limits of her powers and to discover which sorts of encounters increase or decrease them (EP, 317/296). This, then, is the "art of living" that constitutes ethical life: to come more fully into possession of one's powers through encounters and experiences that maximize one's powers of acting and living.

There is an ethical imperative here: to go to the limit of what you can do (EP, 269/248). What is *right* is not a matter of logical or rational necessity, such as Kant's Categorical Imperative (act in such a way that you could will that the rule of your action could serve as a universal law), which is itself based on reason's command that we be logically consistent. Rather, it is a matter of vital or existential necessity: what is "right" for you is something you can and must will as your own law, as a law that follows from the necessity of your own nature. It is impossible, on this view, to establish either the right or the good independently of the needs and capabilities of a particular individual. The good for an individual consists in maximizing one's powers of existing and acting; the right is whatever action promotes that good. The ethical question involved in *amor fati* is quite simply this: does willing the eternal return promote or diminish one's vital capacities? Does it help one to come into one's own power, or does it, on the contrary, alienate one from one's powers? Is it a necessity *for me*?

We must distinguish among different senses of "necessity." There is, on the one hand, rational or logical necessity, which is equivalent to the impossibility of something being other than it is. For Aristotle, this is the root, fundamental sense of necessity.[8] It is the opposite of contingency: something that is, but that could be otherwise. An example of logical necessity would be that something cannot both be and not be in the same respect at the same time; that would amount to a contradiction, and contradictions are necessarily – in the sense of logical necessity – false. An example of contingency would be an outcome that would have been different had the conditions leading to it been different, such as the results of the 2016 US presidential election, since it would involve no contradiction to conceive of Hillary Clinton or Bernie Sanders having been elected instead of Donald Trump.

To universal, rational necessity we can contrast vital or existential necessity. A vital necessity is something that is necessary for life and that will vary according to the life form involved. For example, oxygen is a vital necessity for humans but not for anaerobic microbes. What is *necessary for* a certain species to live is contingent and variable. Beyond the necessities common to entire species, there are those necessities that pertain to a specific individual: those factors without which one would not be the person one is, and that have to do with one's singular capacities for acting in and responding to one's environment. What is "necessary" for the existence of an individual also determines that individual's capacities and how those capacities can be most fully actualized. In the ethical vision of the world, the ethical "law" demands commanding oneself so that one functions to the maximum of one's capacities. But this "law" and the "necessity" on which it is based vary from one living being to another; each vital necessity is a contingent necessity, contingent on one's actual physical and mental composition and the state of the world. Vital necessities are neither universal nor eternal in the manner of logical necessity. Rather than contingency and necessity being radically opposed, as they are in the case of rational necessity, they are inextricably linked: with respect to one's existence, certain factors are both necessary and contingent.

The whole question of necessity requires separate treatment.[9] Here, I will focus on whether *amor fati* amounts to surrendering to logical necessity and sacrificing freedom, or whether, on the contrary, it involves willing the conditions without which one would not be the person one is, and as such amounts to an affirmation of one's existence and one's capacities. Only by affirming oneself and one's existence can one realize the ethical vision of the world that commands us to go to the limits of what we can do. Self-denial, including the denial of the past that has made one what one is, cuts one off from oneself and one's powers.

Shestov, Fondane, and Deleuze all take seriously Nietzsche's call for a "transvaluation of all values" as well as his critique of "slave morality." Deleuze himself was influenced by Shestov, not least by Shestov's insistence that we substitute *jubere* (commanding, creating) for *parere* (obeying) as the basis of ethics and philosophy (NP, 105/92). Fondane, Shestov's leading interpreter in the 1930s and 1940s, took Nietzschean tragic affirmation perhaps as far as it can go in his theory of poetry ("the poet affirms all of reality"). But despite some striking similarities between Fondane and Deleuze, it seems that Deleuze was not aware of Fondane's work.[10] All three agree in refusing any notion that whatever has occurred in the past could not have turned out any differently than it did; all three seek to overturn the logical necessity that would constrain one's abilities to live and act. Their disagreement concerning Nietzsche's doctrine of *amor fati* has to do with just what kind of necessity is affirmed in loving fate. For Shestov and Fondane, this amounts to the servile acceptance of an unalterable past and of a rational and universal necessity external to the living being's vital necessities. For Deleuze, on the contrary, *amor fati* involves affirming combinations of forces that have the capacity to undo whatever in the past acts as a constraint on freedom; it is an affirmation of possibility over against brute actuality.

2. NIETZSCHE ON THE ETERNAL RETURN
AND *Amor Fati*

Nietzsche provides an account of his discovery of the idea of the eternal return, "the fundamental conception" of *Thus Spoke Zarathustra*, calling it "the highest affirmation that is at all attainable," dating it "August, 1881": "It was penned on a sheet with the notation, '6000 feet beyond man and time,'" written beside "a powerful pyramidal rock" at Lake Silviplana, near Sils Maria, Switzerland.[11]

Imagine, says Nietzsche, that a demon said to you: "This life as you now live it and have lived it, you will have to live once more and innumerable times more; and there will be nothing new in it, but every pain and every joy and every thought and sigh and everything unutterably small or great in your life will have to return to you, all in the same succession and sequence." Then the question is whether "you desire this once more and innumerable times more," whether you could will "this ultimate eternal confirmation and seal" of your existence.[12]

Nietzsche himself was torn between being elated and being crushed by what he sometimes called his "most abysmal thought," "the hardest, most terrible insight."[13] In a note written while composing *Zarathustra*, Nietzsche avers: "I do not want life *again*. How could I endure it? Creating. What makes me stand the sight of it? The vision of the Overman who *affirms* life. I have tried to affirm it *myself* – alas!"[14] Yet, he has Zarathustra say: "'Was *that* life?' I will say to death. 'Very well! Once more!'"[15] It is clear that the vision itself was something that enraptured him: "like lightning, a thought flashes up, with necessity, without hesitation regarding its form – *I never had any choice* ... Everything happens involuntarily in the highest degree but as in a gale of a feeling of freedom, of absoluteness, of power, of divinity," resulting in "a depth of happiness in which even that which is painful and gloomy does not seem something opposite but rather conditioned, provoked, a *necessary* colour in such a superabundance of light."[16]

When even what is painful and gloomy is grasped as *necessary* to an overall pattern that brings joy, it is then that the eternal return is no longer an objection to existence "but rather one reason more for [Zarathustra] being the eternal Yes to all things."[17] However, "the sum of the conditions of *my* existence" prescribes an "ought," a *personal* necessity rather than a categorical imperative, "only if I *want* [*will*] *myself*."[18] If I can will myself as a whole, and will the sum of the conditions of my existence, then I can will the eternal return and carry my Yes into "all that is terrible and questionable" in existence,[19] especially insofar as "in the great economy of the whole, the terrible aspects of reality (in affects, in desires, in will to power) are to an incalculable degree more necessary than that form of petty happiness which people call 'goodness.'"[20] *Amor fati* is Dionysian affirmation of the necessity of existence as an interconnected whole.

It is not a matter of *accepting* oneself as one is, then, but of *willing* all the aspects of one's existence as necessary to one's life as artistically conceived and shaped, according to the artistic necessity of the *belonging together* of these elements when one gives style to one's character. "Power ... which reposes in *itself*, fatalistic, a law among laws: *that* is what speaks of itself in the form of great style."[21] *Amor fati* is not, then, powerlessness before the facts – of what is and what has been – but the expression of a vital power that wills itself and its own conditions; it affirms an internal necessity, "a law among laws" valid for oneself alone. It is a matter of composing into oneself "what is fragment and riddle and dreadful chance" so that even the apparently arbitrary and fortuitous take on their necessity in relation to the whole of one's life.[22] This internal necessity of the individual, encompassing the conditions of her existence, extends outward into the totality of what exists such that it is at one with fate itself: "A spirit thus *emancipated* stands in the midst of the universe with a joyful and trusting fatalism, in the *faith* that only what is separate and individual may be rejected, that in the totality, everything is redeemed and affirmed."[23]

None of this has anything to do with the mechanical necessity of determinism or universal logical necessity. Fate is derived from the internal necessity of one's nature when this nature affirms and wills itself by composing itself into an artistically conceived whole, in relation to which "external" circumstances take on their own necessity: "If it had not been for that, then I would not be the person who I am." That is why Nietzsche can write: "I was not permitted to want anything differently. – *Amor fati*. – Even Christianity becomes necessary: only the highest form of the most dangerous, the one that was most seductive in its No to life, provokes its highest affirmation – me."[24]

This gives us a way of understanding the second of Nietzsche's expositions of the eternal return in *Thus Spoke Zarathustra*, where the doctrine of the eternal return is explicitly linked to the redemption of the past. If *amor fati* is indissolubly linked to willing the eternal return as the only way to fully and unreservedly will oneself – if it is indeed "rooted in a triumphant Yes said to *oneself*" as "self-affirmation" and the "self-glorification of life"[25] – then willing oneself and willing the conditions of one's own existence as one's own law requires willing one's past. It seems that I would, in a way as yet to be determined, have to will the eternal return of my falling off a ladder and breaking my leg. The apparently fortuitous event of my fall must be grasped as integral to my life, as indispensable and even "providential": "either immediately or soon after it proves to be something that 'must not be missing' ... precisely for *us*."[26]

Moreover, I would have to will *the whole past* of which my past is but a part, a part inseparable from the whole that produced it: "For the individual, the 'single man,' as people and philosophers have hitherto understood him, is an error: he does not constitute a separate entity, an atom ... – he constitutes the entire *single* line 'man' up to and including himself."[27] *Amor fati* requires willing the whole past, including the whole of human history, with all its catastrophes, atrocities, and injustices. To affirm my own existence, I would have to affirm the Second World War and the Holocaust, among other horrors. Wouldn't such an "affirmation" be tantamount to the most extreme and narrow egoism?

Nietzsche seems unequivocal on this point: "the will's antipathy toward time and time's 'It was'" is "the spirit of revenge"[28]; "To redeem the past and to transform every 'It was' into an 'I willed it thus!' – this alone I call redemption."[29] Zarathustra teaches that one must "create the future, and to redeem by creating – *all that was past*": one creates "the past of mankind" by willing it, by affirming it, by making it inseparable from willing the future.[30] One thus "says Yes to the point of justifying, of redeeming all of the past."[31] Creating and willing the future is thus bound up with willing and creating the past, no longer as "fragment and riddle and dreadful chance," but brought together and composed into something beautiful according to artistic necessity.[32] Willing and loving the past, then, is not willing and loving the *petits faits* taken in isolation, but the *necessity* that binds them together as "the complex of causes in which I am entangled" and which will recur eternally, and me along with them.[33]

In the second exposition of the eternal return, "The Vision and the Riddle" in *Zarathustra*, Zarathustra speaks of a gateway behind which "a long eternal lane runs *back*" infinitely such that "all things that *can* happen *have* already happened, been done, run past," and another long lane runs infinitely forward into the future; the "Moment" is a gateway where these two opposed paths run up against each other.[34] If whatever *can* have happened *has* happened, then the Moment itself "must have been here before," and must return again eternally, "for all things that *can* run *must* also run forward again along this long lane." In short, everything that *can be* (as futural possibility) *has been* (as past actuality), and reciprocally, everything that *has been* (in the past) will also recur (in the future). The same necessity that binds together the whole of interconnected causes also makes each recurrence of the whole resemble all the others: "I shall return, not to a new life or a better life or a similar life: I shall return to this *identical and self-same life*, in the greatest things and the smallest."[35]

Admittedly, it is Zarathustra's animals – his eagle and his serpent – who offer the phrase "this *identical, self-same life*," but unlike the Dwarf's interpretation of the eternal return ("Time itself is a circle!") or the animals' earlier statements ("the wheel of existence rolls for ever" and "Existence begins anew in every instant"), Zarathustra does not repudiate it, but rather remains silent. Zarathustra even concludes with the same *image* Nietzsche used in *The Gay Science*: even the spider in the moonlight recurs. It would seem, then, that even the *petits faits* return, and that *amor fati* – contrary to the interpretation I have been arguing for – does indeed amount to resignation to the facts, only worse: the *petits faits*, instead of being mere "fragments of chance," have become eternal and taken on an *eternal necessity* akin to that of a-temporal logical and mathematical truths. In that case, *amor fati* seems to amount to the claim that we "must love and adore things as they are – we must affirm the *eternity* of fact that transforms every contingency ('it was') into necessity ('it had to have been')." This hardly seems to be a doctrine for free spirits, for strong and dominating natures. On the contrary, it seems to be an *idolatry of fact*, a submission to that which is.

3. NIETZSCHE BEFORE SHESTOV AND FONDANE

It is just this conversion of a contingent occurrence into something eternal and necessary that strikes Fondane and Shestov as both morally questionable and metaphysically suspect. A contingent past occurrence *becomes* an eternal truth because, as Aristotle notes, the "one thing [that] is impossible even for God: to make what has been not to have been."[36] Even though empirical facts, when they arise, are the contingent results of a chance conjunction of forces, once they have been, it is impossible for them to have been otherwise. Before Socrates was poisoned in 399 BCE, things could have turned out differently; once this event has occurred, however, it becomes as eternal and unshakeable as the *a priori* truths of mathematics. Shestov objects: "This truth has already lived too long in this world, almost 2000 years. But to promise it immortality, an existence outside of time, which no forgetfulness could destroy: who has taken upon himself the right to make such promises?"[37] It is reason that decrees that the past cannot be undone, and that a contingent fact, once it has occurred, rises to the status of an eternal and necessary truth, "apodictic, immutable," and ineluctable.[38]

Nietzsche's eternal return seems to perform the same operation of "eternalizing" the contingent and transforming chance into necessity. Yet, Fondane says, Nietzsche is the last person from whom one would have expected this. It was Nietzsche who denounced "theoretical man, *Homo philosophicus*" as a *décadent*, the product of weary and atrophied instincts,[39] and who stated that "man does not live by knowledge, but by instincts, strength, will to power; his body is more important to him than his reason."[40] "There exist men, 'Hyperboreans' as Nietzsche calls them, who cannot resign themselves" to rational necessity; "they sense that by not resigning themselves, they play their chance."[41] Nietzsche's *amor fati*, the adoration of necessity, is a retreat to a traditional philosophy "of *resignation* and *edification*, a disguised but active morality of negation"[42] of the sort that he opposed with all his strength. Although Nietzsche hated all those "who taught Duty, the categorical imperative, laws, necessity, reason, *which enchained man anew at the very moment when he should have become free and equal to the gods,*"[43] he was "possessed" by the "strict method of truth" that prevented him from "incurably soiling his intellectual conscience" by flouting reason.[44] Objectivity, disinterestedness, obligation, and necessity: Nietzsche unmasked these as *moral* duties to obey and accept.[45] Yet Nietzsche remained too much of a philosopher to discard knowledge's demands altogether. With his precept to love fate and necessity, Nietzsche has sacrificed the will to power to the idol of Logic[46] and made himself rational truth's *sacrificial animal*.[47] For Fondane, Nietzsche's is the *tragic* sacrifice born of the lucidity of someone torn apart by his own contradictions, unable to believe in objective truth and ethical or logical necessity, but still bound by the duty to *know*.[48]

Amor fati, the adoration of necessity, marks a submission to the demands of a reason that Nietzsche did not believe in, and all in order to obtain the banal pacifications and beatitudes of the rational philosophy that decrees that whatever is must be as it is.[49] It is no different than the advice one always gets "when you break a leg, when you face adversity, when you have lost a loved one, when you are ready to join the Foreign Legion or drown yourself … 'Now, there, my friend! Be philosophical!', which means: 'Accept it! Resign yourself!'"[50]

Now, Nietzsche denounces those who falsify reality. He wants to affirm the whole of existence, "all that is questionable and terrible in existence,"[51] "life even in its strangest and sternest problems."[52] But Fondane, a poet himself, also claims to affirm the whole of reality: "poetry is an affirmation of reality" and of "the full reality of our acts, of our hope, of our freedom," which makes poetry "a need, not a pleasure, an act, not a relaxation."[53] But, Fondane adds, "*reality begins only where the intelligible comes to an end.*"[54] Poetic experience is "participation" in a reality given in spontaneous sensory experience as an immediately "felt presence, an affective fusion"[55] prior to the division between subject and object.[56] Poetic experience constitutes a "restitution" of a reality obscured by the "signs, abstractions and categories" produced by our "logical mentality,"[57] a restoration taken up by existential thought,[58] which "begins precisely where rational thought ends."[59] What falsifies and negates reality, according to Fondane, is rational, representational thought: a reason that has ceased to serve the ends of the living being and instead has made itself master. Normative, "major" reason fits reality and experience into its immutable Procrustean bed, establishing moral and epistemological norms valid for all times and all people, disregarding differences among living beings and their circumstances as of no account.

Existential thought rejects "the coercive and normative authority" of the intellect.[60] It opposes "inert and immutable" concepts by a return to "the quick, mobile, infinitely adaptable instincts of the living being."[61] Reality, then, is not "the reality principle,"[62] based on the moral repression of instincts rather than metaphysical requirements;[63] nor is it the reality principle's allied concepts of causal determinism and stable things. The reality aimed at by existential thought is not beholden to "the principle of sufficient reason" that makes "that which is" into something immutable and eternal.[64] The apparent inertia and immutability of facts – that things just are what they are – is merely an illusion produced by the intellect. In that case, affirming *reality* is not at all affirming *things as the intellect says they are*. Poetic experience affirms difference, mutability, metamorphosis: a non-static, dynamic reality of desolidified, despatialized beings rather than the "objects" of representational thought.[65]

Rather than loving rational necessity, in order to affirm reality one *must* revolt *against* it.[66] This "must" is neither logical nor moral: it is a vital requirement of the living being. There exists a *"minor* reason"[67] whose function is to help the body deal with the external world in ways not adequately dealt with by instincts, a sort of "innate knowing" that can "almost instantaneously discover the relations *necessary for the life of the organism"*[68] but that does not take these relations to be constitutive of reality or as eternally and apodictically valid. Minor reason is allied with minor ethics: it is a matter of discovering relations that will enable the living being to increase its creative and active powers, relations that constitute the good for *that* living being but not for other living beings differently constituted. If Nietzsche's *amor fati* amounts to accepting and loving rational necessity and causal determinism (products of major Reason), and with them "the horrors of existence ... not because they are good or perfect in themselves but solely because they are given and ineluctable,"[69] then it would indeed seem that Nietzsche was unable to sufficiently free himself from the norms of logic and knowledge to attain the "new dimension of thought" beyond "the domain of [rational] justifications, demonstrations and proofs" that his critique of morality and reason had promised.[70] This brings me to Deleuze.

4. DELEUZE ON IRRATIONAL NECESSITY AND *Amor Fati*

Deleuze is categorical that *amor fati* is not acceptance of the ineluctability and eternal necessity of "things as they are," but love of a different sort of necessity altogether, "an irrational necessity" of "the unity affirmed of multiplicity," the multiplicity of forces that are intertwined in a single process of becoming and that constitute "the differential element" from which phenomena emerge. Love of fate affirms "the whole of chance at once" rather than its probabilistic, causally determined fragments (NP, 29–31/32–6; LS, 180/211). One affirms the irrational necessity resulting from a multiplicity of forces that come together through chance and contingency but that take on the character of necessity in relation to the resulting whole insofar as these constituent parts are indispensable to the whole. This is not at all the affirmation of a logical necessity according to which everything that has happened cannot be other than it is. "Affirmation conceived of as acceptance, as affirmation of that which is … is a false affirmation," the affirmation of the ass who takes on the burden of reality and does not know how to say "no" to negativity and *ressentiment* (NP, 181–5/208–12). True affirmation affirms difference and distance, multiplicity, will to power (DR, 54–5/ 75–7), "a world in which all previous identities have been abolished and dissolved" in a becoming that "has no identity, no resemblance, no equality" (DR, 41/59, 241/311).

The eternal return is not cyclical repetition – that is, not the return of the identical – but rather the return of becoming and of the will to power, which stand higher than any identity (DR, 6–8/14–16, 242/311). "The eternal return is a power [*puissance*] of affirming, but it affirms everything of the multiple, everything of the different, everything of chance, *except* what subordinates them to the One, the Same, Necessity" (DR, 115/152; cf. DR, 126/164–5). It is a thought *contrary* to any necessity based on identity or the negating and exclusionary principles of reason or logic, which are themselves, as Nietzsche and Fondane had argued, founded on moral requirements, the "categorical imperatives" of major reason (DR, 6–7/14, 127/167, 243/313).

Rather than affirming the rational necessity of the identical, *amor fati* affirms *the necessity of chance* beyond the causal determinism and finality that eliminate chance (NP, 27–9/31–2, 36/41, 194/222). "Chance is the putting into relation of forces" (NP, 53/60) in syntheses that differentiate them from other forces (NP, 50/56–7) and that together constitute the irrational necessity of the whole "intensive system" of differences: "a world of differences implicated in one another, a *complicated*, properly chaotic world *without identity*" in which "difference relates the different to the different": "the shimmering world of metamorphoses, of communicating intensities, of differences of differences" (DR, 57/80, 117–19/154–7, 241/311, 243/313). Forces are put into relation to one another in a system of intensive differences that has its own internal necessity, in the manner in which a living being has an internal necessity consisting of the relations of its vital forces and capacities, even if those relations arise from a chance concatenation of events and circumstances. Willing this internal, vital necessity, then, is "necessity said of the fortuitous itself" (LS, 300/348–9) – not the rational necessity of causal determinism (based on the identity of terms and the equality of cause and effect), logic, or morality, but the necessity of chaos, a "chaosmos" that has its own "chao-errance," its own co-inherence of forces that stands higher than the coherence of rational thought, the latter being that of the stability and identity of things, selves, and qualities (LS, 264/305; DR 243/313, 299/382). Identity, sameness, stability of things, qualities, selves, and events require a levelling off and cancelling of differences, a mistaking of degrees of similarity (which involve variation) for strict equivalence and identity. This is consequentially both a denial of reality (difference, becoming) and a will to stasis contrary to the maximization of one's capacities for living, acting, and existing. The negation of difference, Deleuze argues, is the expression of "reactive" forces that seek to conserve life and existence just as they are; this is the very contrary of the affirmation of life, the essence of which is difference and becoming. In all this, Fondane would agree.

In affirming the eternal return, then, I would not have to affirm the eternal repetition of my falling off a ladder and breaking my leg. Believing in the return of things and facts *in their identity*, Deleuze notes, amounts to a speculative belief in *fatum*, the false philosophy according to which the future is foreordained and the past is immutable: the *fatum* of logical and deterministic inevitability (LS, 267/309). Willing the eternal return, by contrast, amounts to willing the return of *becoming as such*: the return of the forces generative of actual things and events, but freed from actualized results, independent of the facts and the deterministic laws governing them. As I can only will forwards – that is, I can only will the future (*l'avenir*) – willing the eternal return involves willing the return (*revenir*) of becoming (*devenir*) from out of the future (*l'avenir*).

For Deleuze, only as futural can becoming take on the status of something that can be willed, and that can indeed constitute an ethical demand that replaces Kant's Categorical Imperative: I must will the return of the becoming that was and is the necessary condition for me to affirm the "necessity of chance" that I am (NP, 27–9/32–3, 68–72/77–8). Instead of willing the maxim of my action as a universal law valid for anyone (no matter their capacities and condition), the imperative becomes: whatever you will, will it in such a way that you also will its eternal return (NP, 68/77). This is what is required in order to will oneself entirely, without reservation, without wishing away anything within the concatenation of forces that one is. If you cannot will the eternal return of an action, then you cannot will it wholeheartedly, which is to say, there is something in you that wills the contrary and that puts you at odds with yourself, diminishing your powers of acting. You can only will the eternal return of what you can will without self-opposition.

Affirming eternally, rather than being resigned to the inevitability of what has been, amounts to releasing and unburdening the living being (NP, 185/212). We can only will the eternal return of active forces of becoming. Negativity and reactive forces do not return: the will to nothingness implicit in them cannot be affirmed, and when subjected to the eternal return, they instead will their own destruction, returning only as transmuted into the active forces of creative destruction and Dionysian metamorphosis (NP, 65/74, 69–71/78–81). Anything that negates difference and becoming – the same extended body, the same self – does not return (DR, 243/313; cf. NP, 71/80). "Only affirmation returns – in other words, the Different, the Dissimilar" (DR, 299/382). The eternal return affirms the creative chaos of metamorphoses (LS, 300–1/348–9, 266/307) that undoes and counter-actualizes its embodied and stable actualizations (LS, 61–4/77–81, 168/196). Rather than submission to *les petits faits*, willing the eternal return subverts the facts and undoes their supposed necessity.

What returns is difference itself, "impersonal individualities and pre-individual singularities" (DR, 299/382; cf. LS, 297/345, 300/348): not constituted things and selves, but the intensive forces that constitute them and destroy them in a process of becoming without beginning or end. Pre-individual singularities are forces that enter into relations so as to constitute the individual as the co-inherence of these mutually implicated and influencing forces. They are mobile, fluid, constantly changing and entering into new relations with one another; the existing individual, the Self, is only their surface effect, the relatively stable form that these singularities and forces take for a certain period of time. As long as the changes of these singularities take place within this relatively stable form, then we say that an identical self persists. But only becoming and *natura naturans* (the will to power) return; *natura naturata*, or actualized potentiality, does not (cf. LS, 63/79, 151–3/177–9, 168/196).

Zarathustra, then, in willing the eternal return as the "selective ordeal" that destroys identity (DR, 243/313, 298/381; LS, 178/209; NP, xi) must will his own destruction (DR, 299/381–2). This can be the source of a new anxiety: not the "great disgust" that Man recurs eternally, but terror before the abyss of unlimited becoming in which the self is "dissolved" before returning to itself as an impersonal singularity (degree of power) implicated in all the other singularities (LS, 299/347–8). For Deleuze, then, rather than being acceptance of what is, affirmation wills an eternal return of becoming that counter-actualizes and undoes what is and has been, including one's own self. This is the death of the individuated self, but it is also the undoing of everything that, when taken in isolation, can be regarded negatively: war, a wound, death (LS, 149/174). In willing the eternal return, I will not the eternal repetition of my broken leg, but rather its *destruction*. My broken leg – as a stable, constituted fact – will not return, and neither will I. Willing and affirming the return of becoming is willing and affirming becoming-other, for becoming is the contrary of the stasis of remaining the same.

5. CONCLUSION

Can Deleuze's solution satisfy us? For Deleuze, the death of the self allows one "to be reborn, to remake one's birth, and break with one's carnal birth" such that one becomes "the son of the event," a being who wills both becoming as a whole and life as singularities that exceed their incarnations (LS, 149–53/175–9). Willing becoming as a whole – and thereby willing the necessity of chance – "no longer leaves any room for the accidental"; the accidental is tied to what befalls particular bodies (such as a broken leg) rather than to the irrational necessity of *the whole* of becoming (LS, 151/177). There can then be no room for *ressentiment*; by eliminating the accidental, one overcomes the bitterness that comes from wishing that things could have turned out differently. Instead of submission to the facts, *amor fati* in Deleuze's hands takes on the quality of insurrection and revolution: the dissolution of what has been in the name of potentialities yet to be realized.

Yet is this really very different from Stoicism's advice to "be philosophical" and to bear one's misfortunes patiently? Émile Bréhier notes that in Stoicism, everything "happens in conformity with universal nature, and we speak of things [such as disease or misfortune] as contrary to nature only in connection with the nature of a particular being separated from the whole."[71] Grasped in relation to the whole – "a sort of universe of forces, of active divine thoughts"[72] – nothing is accidental. "Everything happens through universal reason, the will of God or fate ... Stoic resignation is ... a positive, joyous acceptance of the world as it is."[73] Epictetus says that "the philosopher's goal is to bring the will in line with events, so that nothing happens contrary to our wishes."[74] Similarly, Deleuze seeks to overcome *ressentiment* by aligning his will with the necessity of the whole, however differently "the whole" (as a system of differences or intensities) or the "necessity" (as the resonances among intensities) may be from that of classical Stoicism (the whole ordered according to the divine *logos*). To will oneself through the eternal return is to will oneself "as a fortuitous moment, the very fortuitousness of which implies the necessity of the integral return of the whole series" (LS, 300/348). Of course, Deleuze and Nietzsche reject the idea of there being any grand plan (a cosmic teleology) that would make the breaking of my leg necessary and justified.[75] Yet, affirming the whole requires affirming the necessity of all the parts in relation to one another: one would not will anything to have been other than it was. "Affirmation" still comes perilously close to "acceptance."

On the other hand, Deleuze's "counter-actualization" returns to the generative–destructive powers of becoming as a whole in order to undo constituted things, bodies, and qualities. It is a matter of liberating life's pre-personal singularities and potentialities, as "mobile individuating factors" (DR, 41/60), from their imprisonment in stable bodies and things. Fondane wants to remove the "screen" interposed by the intellect in order to regain the dynamic reality of change and metamorphosis that existed prior to the intellect's spatialization and solidification of processes into things and qualities.[76] Deleuze argues similarly that "the conditions of real experience differ in kind" from the understanding's categories (DR, 68/94). Thought opens directly onto difference when it holds in contempt "all the mediations and reconciliations of the concept" (DR, 58/82; cf. 86/117)[77] and instead apprehends "directly in the sensible that which can only be sensed, the very being of the sensible: difference, difference of potential, difference of intensity" (DR, 56–7/80). Both Deleuze and Fondane reject the stable self and proclaim, with Rimbaud, "JE est un autre" (DR, 58/82, 86–7/116–17). Liberation from the self is necessary in order to gain access to and affirm reality.

Regaining the full reality affirmed by the poet is achieved by what Fondane calls "affective participation" in the real[78] or by what Deleuze calls the "necessary destruction" carried out by the poet, "who speaks in the name of a creative power capable of overturning all orders and representations in order to affirm Difference in the state of permanent revolution of the eternal return" (DR, 53/75). Poetic affirmation – destruction comes at the price of "the dissolved self" (*le moi dissou*) and the subordination of rational necessity either to the needs of the living being (Fondane), or to life itself understood as pre-personal singularities (Deleuze). Following Deleuze's interpretation, in affirming myself and my life, then, I do not will the eternal return of my falling off a ladder and breaking my leg *as such*, taken in isolation, but rather the return of the powers and potentialities that generated what happened and which, in returning, can unmake what happened. My leg and its break, in their being-identical, do not return; every identity is dissolved. But I am dissolved as well. Does this really help?

The advice to overcome suffering through the destruction of the self has more to do with Arthur Schopenhauer's overcoming the "suffering self" (*leidige Selbst*) by destroying its individuality than with Nietzsche's Dionysian affirmation.[79] Destroying the self in order to liberate impersonal singularities seems like just another renunciation in the name of some universal: impersonal life, Stoic reason, and so on. Willing the eternal return in order to will the dissolution of both my broken leg *and myself* does not seem to provide what I was looking for. I sought a way of willing *myself* – even eternally – that takes into account my broken leg in all its reality, without seeking to diminish either it or the life of which it is a part.

No doubt, by referring us to the impersonal vital forces constitutive of our being, Deleuze frees us from the limits of the constituted self and from constituted group identities. A "minor" politics diverges from the majoritarian norms that bind people into groups that are based on the exclusion of the other, and instead harnesses the creative power of individuals to create new forms of life and society more responsive to the particular needs and capacities of individuals (cf. TP, 105–6, 469–70). Similarly, a "minor ethics" for the individual would enable the overcoming of stable and fixed identities in order to liberate the vital and creative powers that stand at the basis of the self, and by liberating these powers, allow for a metamorphosis, a self-transformation that is indispensable to extending to the limit one's capacities for living and acting. But that approach, however noble, does not provide a solution to my problem. That problem, to repeat, is to determine how I can affirm the eternal return of the incident of breaking my leg, an incident that is now an integral and ineliminable part of the life that is mine. To affirm myself and my life, I must will that incident eternally. Being able to overcome myself, I can make myself anew and give birth to myself non-carnally. Yet perhaps none of this will enable me to will the eternal return of my life such as I have lived it, with nothing left out or altered.

Fondane offers a hint of a solution: "Being freed from all forms and all obstacles, entering into a fluid world in which everything communicates, inter-penetrates, overlaps – where everyone commands and no one obeys. But would that be an emancipation of our self [*moi*]? Yes, but ... perhaps it's an exaggeration to say that we have gotten rid of the self. No, the self itself has become FREE."[80] I must be able to will *myself*. *Amor fati* would be less the *dissolution* of the self in the eternal return than willing the irrational necessity of the self as a combination of forces: willing the self as "one law more," as fate, as a personal necessity, as "great style," and at the same time as emancipated from the categories and concepts of the intellect that block access to reality. I would will the forces constitutive of me and the incidents in my life as parts of a whole that takes away their accidental character and imparts to them a necessity derived from the internal necessity of my own being, the individual and individuating "law" that relates me directly to the irrational necessity of the whole not as something indifferent and the same for all, but as *my own* necessity, my personal fate.

Granted, this hypothesis of willing the self in the eternal return – even as free and emancipated – is contrary to Deleuze. But Deleuze's interpretation is not necessarily correct, nor would it matter if it were. It is a question of what can help me to will myself unreservedly and will "the sum of the conditions of *my* existence,"[81] of liberating my becoming and will to power, not willing my own entire destruction. For Nietzsche, tragic affirmation means being strong enough to "conceive reality *as it is*,"[82] not breaking free from actuality through recourse to the virtual powers and forces immanent in it. Creative affirmation is indeed inseparable from destruction,[83] but it is only the negative and established values that are destroyed in order to clear a path for "the tremendous, unbounded Yes-saying and Amen."[84] Rather than dissolving both myself and my broken leg in pre-individual singularities, I need to relate my broken leg to the irrational necessity that brings together all the elements of my own being. One's internal necessity ("one law more") is in turn inseparable from the necessity of the greater whole that one calls "fate." To will oneself is to will one's conditions of existence, and thereby to will the necessity of the greater whole without which those conditions would not be. Perhaps it is Nietzsche himself who provides a solution:

Did you ever say Yes to one joy? O my friends, then you said Yes to *all* Woe as well. All things are enchained and entwined together, all things are in love. If ever you wanted one moment twice, if ever you said, "You please me, happiness, instant, moment!," then you wanted *everything* to return! You wanted everything anew, everything eternal, everything chained, entwined together, everything in love ... *For all joy wants – eternity!*[85]

In this way, one can utter "a triumphant Yes said to *oneself*," a "self-affirmation, the self-glorification of life."[86] Being able to say Yes to one joy means saying Yes to the whole of one's life, broken legs and all. And because "one is a piece of fate, a part of the whole," the necessary interconnectedness of every episode in one's own life is enchained and entwined with the necessity *immanent* in existence as a whole that Nietzsche calls "fate" (and not a transcendent finality – "design, will or purpose" – imposed from without).

Are there joys to which I can say Yes, that is, that I can will eternally? Certainly. Can those joys be conceived of as existing apart from all the other incidents in my life? Only through a process of abstraction that deprives that joy of its meaning. Joys do not exist in isolation: to will one joy is to will the entire chain of entwined events that constitute a life and make an event joyful *to* the person who experiences it. Without *this* life, without the necessity that binds it together, events would either lose their affective significance or would be attributed a significance which is that of "anyone" according to currently accepted norms. *This* joy is inextricably a part of *this* life: mine, not anyone else's, not "universal reason," not some anonymous and impersonal life. I can no more will a joy in isolation than I can will my broken leg in isolation, or will light without shadow. My broken leg, willed according to an artistic necessity by which I try to compose the relations among events in my life, can become "a *necessary* color" – necessary to my artistic conception of my life, a law that I give to myself, and not the result of bowing down before the *petits faits* of existence. Willing the eternal return, as Deleuze says, requires willing the whole of chance, not the "fragments of chance" considered apart from the whole to which they belong (see NP, 27–9/32–3). The necessity pertains to the interconnected whole that makes each fragment "a piece of fate"; without this necessary interconnection, each fragment remains a *petit fait*, a brute given. But the interconnected whole in question is that of "the sum of the conditions of *my* existence," as Nietzsche says, related to my own vital necessities and discoverable through minor reason, not the indifferent whole discovered through an impersonal form of reason and its scientific determinism. Only the whole that is *mine* is one that I can will, and will artistically by taking the relations among elements not as given and as having to be accepted as fact, but as relations posited by the artistic will that expresses the law of my being. In so doing, I overcome the *ressentiment* that separates me from my own powers of acting and existing. And that is just what minor ethics demands: that I will myself, overcome *ressentiment*, and affirm the whole – including its most terrible and questionable aspects – in order to realize fully my powers as a living being.

For me to affirm one joy by willing its eternal return, then, I must also will the eternal return of breaking my leg. It is not a question of whether, all things considered, the broken leg was worth it according to a rational calculation of all the pains and pleasures in my life. It is rather that my broken leg cannot be separated from the interconnectedness and immanent necessity of events that make that life *mine* and allow me to conceive of events artistically as "necessary colors." Willing the eternal return of one joy, then, is equivalent to unlimited self-affirmation. *Amor fati*, on this reading, is not submission to external necessity, whether conceived of as causal necessity or logical necessity, or to *petits faits*, but the willing of the internal necessity of one's own existence, one's own "ought," the law of one's being that expresses itself in great style. Through this affirmation, I can overcome my *ressentiment* toward the past and affirm myself, not simply such as I have been, but such as I must have been to become the person I am now, with a life of events and incidents connected not by chance or determinism, but through an inner necessity that has been reconceived artistically.

Such self-affirmation is part of the "art of living" that seeks to maximize one's vital capacities. It is a self-affirmation and a self-commanding through a law that belongs to my own manner of being and is valid for myself alone, discoverable through the "minor reason" that discovers relations necessary *for* the individual living being; the law of my being is not a universal norm to be followed by everyone.

As such, willing of myself as an irrational whole with its own irrational necessity remains part of a minor ethics, not a majoritarian ethics that would seek to impose one norm for everyone based on a reason that sacrifices individuals and their needs. I must will myself because this is a *vital* necessity, a necessity for me that is contingent upon how I am constituted (physically, mentally, vitally, historically) and my relations to the changing world around me, but an inner necessity which is also transformed by how I compose and affirm the elements that constitute my own, inner law such that I can grasp each element as a "necessary color" in the composition of the whole. In that respect, what Deleuze says about the eternal return being "selective" holds good: "Only affirmation returns" (DR, 199/382). *Amor fati* is the artistic affirmation of the internal necessity of the composition of one's own life. Only when we transfigure the *petits faits* of our lives into necessary elements of an artistically conceived whole can we, like Zarathustra, say, "Was *that* life? ... Very well! Once more!"[87]

NOTES

1 Nietzsche, *Ecce Homo* in *Genealogy of Morals* and *Ecce Homo*, 258 ["Why I Am So Clever," §10].
2 Ibid., 272 ["The Birth of Tragedy," §2].
3 Nietzsche, *The Twilight of the Idols*, 82 ["Expeditions of an Untimely Man," §7]. "To study 'from nature' betrays subjection, weakness, fatalism – this lying in the dust before *petits faits* is unworthy of a *complete* artist."
4 Nietzsche, *The Gay Science*, trans. Kaufmann, 232 [§290].
5 Nietzsche, *Ecce Homo*, 273–4 ["The Birth of Tragedy," §3].
6 Nietzsche, *Twilight*, 65 ["The Four Great Errors," §8].
7 Nietzsche, *The Gay Science*, 181 [§125].
8 Aristotle, *Metaphysics*, 5.5.1015a20-1015b9.
9 See Baugh, "Private Thinkers, Untimely Thoughts."
10 See ibid.
11 Nietzsche, *Ecce Homo*, 295 ["*Thus Spoke Zarathustra*," §1].
12 Nietzsche, *The Gay Science*, 273–4 [§341].
13 Nietzsche, *Ecce Homo*, 306 ["*Thus Spoke Zarathustra*," §6]. Nietzsche's reference is to Zarathustra's confession that his "most abysmal thought" is that "Man recurs eternally! The little man recurs eternally! ... That was my disgust at all existence!" *Thus Spoke Zarathustra*, 236 ["The Convalescent," §2].

14 Cited by Kaufmann in "Introduction" to Nietzsche, *The Gay Science*, 19.

15 Nietzsche, *Zarathustra*, 326 ["The Intoxicated Song," §1].

16 Nietzsche, *Ecce Homo*, 300–1 ["*Thus Spoke Zarathustra*," §3, my emphasis].

17 Ibid., 306 [§6].

18 Nietzsche, *The Gay Science*, 20.

19 Nietzsche, *Ecce Homo*, 331 ["Why I Am a Destiny," §5].

20 Ibid., 329 [§4]; see also *Twilight*, 49, 93, 121.

21 Nietzsche, *Twilight*, 85 ["Expeditions of an Untimely Man," §11].

22 Nietzsche, *Zarathustra*, 216 ["Of Old and New Law – Tables," §3].

23 Nietzsche, *Twilight*, 114 ["Expeditions of an Untimely Man," §49].

24 Nietzsche, *Ecce Homo*, 343 ["Appendix: Variants from Nietzsche's Drafts," 4(d)].

25 Nietzsche, "Epilogue" to *The Case of Wagner* in *The Birth of Tragedy and The Case of Wagner*, 190–2.

26 Nietzsche, *The Gay Science*, 224 [§277].

27 Nietzsche, *Twilight*, 97 ["Expeditions of an Untimely Man," §33].

28 Nietzsche, *Zarathustra*, 162 [II: "Of Redemption"].

29 Ibid., 161.

30 Ibid., 214–6 [III: "Of Old and New Law – Tables," §3].

31 Nietzsche, *Ecce Homo*, 308–9 ["Zarathustra" §8].

32 Nietzsche, *The Gay Science*, 223 [§276].

33 Nietzsche, *Zarathustra*, 237–8 [III: "The Convalescent," §2].

34 Ibid., 178–9 [II: "Of the Vision and the Riddle," §2].

35 Ibid., 237–8 [III: "The Convalescent," §2].

36 Aristotle, *Nicomachean Ethics*, 1139b6-10.

37 Chestov, *Athènes et Jérusalem*, 31–3. All translations of Shestov and Fondane's work here are my own, unless otherwise noted.

38 Fondane, *La Conscience Malheureuse*, 56–7.

39 Ibid., 44.

40 Fondane, "Nietzsche," front page.

41 Fondane, *La Conscience Malheureuse*, 44.

42 Ibid., 48.

43 Ibid., 92.

44 Ibid., 111–12. See Nietzsche, *Human, All Too Human*, 60–1 [§109].

45 Fondane, "Nietzsche."

46 Fondane, *La Conscience Malheureuse*, 65, 72.

47 Ibid., 89.

48 Fondane, "Nietzsche."

49 Fondane, *La Conscience Malheureuse*, 64, 79.

50 Ibid., 47.

51 Nietzsche, *Twilight*, 49 ["Reason in Philosophy," §6].

52 Ibid., 121 ["What I Owe the Ancients," §5]; see also 93.

53 Fondane, *Faux traité d'esthétique*, 108-9.

54 Ibid., 85.

55 Fondane, *La Conscience Malheureuse*, 62.

56 Fondane, *Faux traité*, 90.

57 Fondane, *La Conscience Malheureuse*, 61-2, 69.

58 Ibid., 67.

59 Fondane, "Léon Chestov," 278.

60 Fondane, *La Conscience Malheureuse*, 60.

61 Ibid., 68.

62 Ibid., 63.

63 Ibid., 64.

64 Ibid.

65 Fondane, *Faux traité*, 90.

66 Fondane, *La Conscience Malheureuse*, 67.

67 Ibid., 41n.

68 Ibid., 58 (my emphasis).

69 Fondane, "Léon Chestov," 244-5.

70 Fondane, "Nietzsche."

71 Bréhier, *The History of Philosophy*, 2:50.

72 Ibid., 2:51.

73 Ibid., 2:61.

74 Epictetus, *Discourses*, 107.

75 See Nietzsche, *The Gay Science*, §109 and §285; and Deleuze, NP 25-7/29-31.

76 Fondane, *La Conscience Malheureuse*, 61-2, 69.

77 Cf. Fondane, *Faux traité*, 25-6, 34, 47.

78 Fondane, *La Conscience Malheureuse*, 62.

79 Schopenhauer, *World as Will and Representation*, vol. 1, 241-2.

80 Fondane's unpublished note in Monique Jutrin, *Avec Benjamin Fondane*, 76.

81 Nietzsche in letter to Paul Rée, quoted by Kaufmann in his "Translator's Introduction" to Nietzsche, *The Gay Science*, 20.

82 Nietzsche, *Ecce Homo*, 329 ["Why I Am a Destiny," §5).

83 Ibid., 327-8.

84 Ibid., 306 ["Zarathustra" §6).

85 Nietzsche, *Zarathustra*, 331-2 [IV: "The Intoxicated Song," §10].

86 Nietzsche, *The Case of Wagner*, 190-2.

87 Nietzsche, *Zarathustra*, 326 ["The Intoxicated Song," § 1].

7

Kant's Conception of the Will:
The Minor Categorical Imperative

Saša Stanković

I. THE MEANING OF MINOR ETHICS

There are several reasons why Deleuze thinks of Kant as a "major" thinker. Most primarily, Deleuze argues that Kant, in order to provide a coherent account of metaphysical knowledge, subsumes the operations of all the faculties of cognition under the faculty of understanding. Thus the operation of the *imagination*, as the schematizing of synthesized appearances, and the operation of *reason*, as the thinking of unconditioned ideas, contribute to knowledge only if each is brought under the rule of concepts. This is not to say that concepts provide metaphysical knowledge on their own, but rather that the faculty of understanding "legislates" in the interest of knowledge, guiding the operations of other faculties toward that "common" purpose.[1] To imagine or to think beyond what can be understood would thus be to produce representations that are epistemically unintelligible. Such representations do not amount to knowledge in any meaningful sense. It would seem that Deleuze here is merely concerned with the traditional relationship between knowledge and reality, epistemology and metaphysics. But we can understand Deleuze's ethical project as an attempt to rethink the nature of knowledge itself, to free if from the dictatorship of the understanding, so that we can face a different type of reality. Thus in *Difference and Repetition*, Deleuze defends the "free floating use of the faculties."[2] He speaks of the "*sentiendum*" and the "*cogitandum*" as respectively that which can only be sensed and that which can only be thought. If we unhinge the faculties of sensibility and reason from the faculty of understanding, we are in fact faced with new metaphysical realities.[3] Behind Deleuze's open concern with knowledge and metaphysics lies an ethical commitment to the principles of affirmation and experimentation. To insist on the legislative primacy of the faculty of understanding in the interest of knowledge means, according to Deleuze, to close oneself off from the creative impetus of life. It means to deny the power of genesis. On the other hand, to live ethically is to open oneself to a reality beyond the conceptual.

We can see Deleuze's point by considering the way in which he deals with Kant in *Difference and Repetition*. Deleuze invokes Kant, against Descartes, at key stages of his argument in order to demonstrate that Kant puts the *cogito* into a state of crisis. Specifically, according to Deleuze, Kant's claim that the subject can only know itself under the form of intuition – that is, in time – problematizes the transcendent nature of rational subjectivity. If the subject can only be known in time, then it is not ontologically separated from its object. Instead, it is permeated and immersed in it. The self dissolves into the world and loses its identity, becoming an other to itself: "A Cogito for a dissolved self: the Self of 'I think' includes in its essence a receptivity of intuition in relation to which *I* is already an other" (DR, 58). Properly speaking, what Deleuze designates as "difference" is what this dissolved self contemplates, and he understands this contemplation to be a form of "repetition." It would seem then that Kant allows for a type of engagement with the Outside that Deleuze considers to be ethical. However, despite what Deleuze attributes to Kant as an achievement, Deleuze maintains that Kant fails to reap the rewards of his own insights. Over and against his critique of the transcendence of Descartes's *cogito*, Kant's insistence on the hierarchical organization of the faculties amounts to a reinstitution of transcendence, this time within the immanence of subjectivity itself. Kant does conceive of a self that is immanent in its own representations, but he upholds transcendence within immanence when he ties representations to a single conceptual centre.[4] According to Deleuze, Kant's critical philosophy amounts to a tragic attempt to immerse the self within difference while at the same time conceiving of knowledge as recognition, and thus reducing difference to identity through the concept itself. Thus in the final analysis, despite his best efforts, Kant's self never actually faces difference. In this sense, Kant is incapable of thinking of ethics.

Deleuze's analysis of Kant's work is meant to demonstrate the failures of his critical philosophy, and specifically to show how critical philosophy is infected by traditional moral commitments. Kant's most important critical goal is to free philosophy of traditional metaphysical ideas of freedom, God, and the immortality of the soul while at the same time providing a coherent account of metaphysical knowledge, a new science of nature, and a new science of morals. In this sense, Kant presents his critical enterprise as the overcoming of "dogmatism." On the other hand, Deleuze claims, as long as Kant conceptualizes his account of knowledge in terms of the subordination of faculties to a single legislative centre, he thereby upholds the value of transcendence. "Kant merely pushed a very old conception of critique to the limit, a conception which saw critique as a force which should be brought to bear on all claims of knowledge and truth, but not on knowledge and truth themselves" (NP, 89). A real critique, for Deleuze, unhinges the faculties from their hierarchical centre, upsetting the ground of the very possibility of knowledge. A true, immanent critique must bring us face to face with the creative forces of life, and not merely with the terms through which life is represented. Kant fails to do this, according to Deleuze, because even when he releases the dissolved self into the pool of difference, he reins it in by means of the faculty of understanding and the identity of the concept. In this sense, even though he seems to abandon traditional concepts such as God, he cannot really proclaim with Nietzsche that "God is dead," because his own faculty of understanding assumes the same place that God had occupied in traditional metaphysical accounts. It is this commitment that allows Kant to think only as far as morality. As Deleuze says, one does not actually need the traditional concept of God in order to judge life from a transcendent standpoint. Kant's account of knowledge will do just as well: "the power of judgment of God," Deleuze writes, "is nothing other than the power to organize to infinity" (CC, 130). It is not a surprise that all of the traditional metaphysical ideas end up haunting and eventually repopulating Kant's critical system. Kant cannot understand ethics in terms of creation because he never faces the power of creation.

Deleuze thinks that "minor" thought is primarily concerned with the overcoming of judgment in the name of a different relationship to life. "Herein, perhaps lies the secret: to bring into existence and not to judge. If it is so disgusting to judge, it is not because everything is of equal value, but on the contrary because what has value can be made or distinguished only by defying judgment" (CC, 135). The point is not to judge life in the name of values that transcend life, but rather to create within life and to produce values by means of this creation, values that are of life. But how can one create within life if one never faces it or only ever mediates this relationship through the security of the concept and identity? *Contra* Deleuze's characterization of Kant as *the* "major" thinker, in this chapter I present Kant as a "minor" thinker. I do not do so by directly challenging Deleuze's account of Kant's conception of knowledge. Largely, I think that Deleuze is right about that. Instead, I think that if we look at Kant's moral philosophy directly, we actually see just the example of the sort of ethics that Deleuze has in mind. In fact, when we look at Kant's moral philosophy of the will, we see that Kant is advocating for the sort of relationship between the will and nature that Deleuze thinks characterizes ethics.

There are two conditions that characterize major moral philosophy as opposed to minor ethics. It begins with the presupposition of objective value to which we must submit our agency, the activity of our will. This presupposition itself has an important effect. First, as soon as we posit the existence of the objective value, we require a theoretical account that both investigates that value and also tests the activity of our will against it. Second, the activity of the will must be mediated by the theoretical account legitimating its objective value. In short, this philosophical approach places a premium on theory. Third, this approach undermines the activity of the will, because it thinks of it as a moral faculty that can function only to the extent that it be submitted to judgment. It cannot think of the will as fundamentally active and creative. The will follows or loads itself with objective value over and against subjective or relative values. Now, there is certainly a way of thinking about Kant's moral philosophy along these lines, especially when we think of the categorical imperative.

We can say that the objective value in Kant's work takes the name of "humanity." In the *Groundwork of the Metaphysics of Morals*, Kant supposes that something about human beings has an absolute worth, not one that we happen to assign to them, but rather one that we recognize as the ground of determinate laws. "But suppose there were something the *existence of which in itself* has an absolute worth, something which as *an end in itself* could be a ground of determinate laws; then in it, and in it alone, would lie the ground of a possible categorical imperative, that is, of a practical law."[5] Kant then reveals that "humanity" is such an absolute worth and that the "practical imperative" that guides the activity of the will is as follows: "*So act that you use humanity, whether in your own person or in the person of any other, always at the same time as an end, never merely as a means.*"[6] Allan W. Wood explains Kant's conception of humanity as a "'self-sufficient,' 'independent,' or 'selfstanding' (*selbstständig*) end, in contrast to an 'end to be produced.' It is an end in the sense of something for the sake of which we act."[7] In this sense, Wood claims, the value of humanity does not succeed action, but precedes it. "In the claim that rational nature is an end in itself, rational nature is not being thought of as a state of affairs to be produced by an action. Instead, an 'end in itself' is something already existing whose value grounds even our pursuit of the ends produced by our actions." For this reason, Wood argues that Kant's practical philosophy does not begin with action. Instead, it begins with the value of humanity that determines action. "[T]his value is to motivate obedience to a categorical imperative – a principle that rationality constrains us without presupposing any end to be produced."[8]

Kant certainly does not think that we can find out about the value of humanity through experience. However, he does think that reason recognizes the value of humanity and ushers in a moral philosophy that devises a test to limit and guide the activity of the will. This test is the test of universalizability. We are, Kant argues, to act only on the maxims that can become the universal law. Thus reason recognizes an objective value and demands that we acknowledge that value through action. Hence the notion of the Categorical Imperative. "There is therefore only a single categorical imperative and it is this: *act only in accordance with that maxim through which you can at the same time will that it become a universal law.*"[9] In this sense, the Categorical Imperative is a conceptual test for the will. Each time we are about to act, we must ask ourselves whether our maxim can become the universal law. If it can, then the action is permissible. If it cannot, then the action is forbidden. Thus we have the two components of major moral philosophy. We have the recognition of value, and the submission of the will to the test that stays true to that value. Each time we act on maxims that can become the universal law, we demonstrate respect for the dignity of humanity.[10]

In this chapter I would like to upset this way of thinking about Kant's moral philosophy by thinking of it along the lines of minor ethics. Deleuze often explains his conception of ethics beyond morality in relation to Spinoza. Whereas morality posits values to which the will submits, ethics begins from the activity of the will that creates values from its own forces: "we neither strive for, nor will, neither want, nor desire anything because we judge it to be good: on the contrary, we judge something to be good because we strive for it, will it, want it, and desire it."[11] But ethics beyond morality does not mean, Deleuze insists, the abandonment of all values. "Beyond Good and Evil, at least this *does not* mean: beyond good and bad."[12] Instead, it means the foregrounding of the activity of the will that creates values. In this sense we can say that minor ethics challenges the two moments of major moral philosophy. The first moment begins from the activity of the will rather than from the given value. And the second moment is the creation of value from the perspective of the activity of will. These two moments necessitate the overcoming of conceptual judgment at the ground of ethics. There is nothing to be theorized about and tested. Instead, we are first to become active, and only if we become active can we be creative. Hence ethics is primarily about practice.

In this chapter I argue that Kant's moral philosophy follows the pattern of minor ethics. I claim that Kant begins with the concern of the activity of the will and not with the objective value of humanity.[13] Kant's main question in moral philosophy is this: how can the will be active and not merely follow values? His answer to this problem is universality. Thus, on my interpretation, universality does not name merely a conceptual test. Instead, it is the practical activation of the will beyond all value. The concern for the value of humanity comes only second. In this sense, we must take Kant's successive presentation of the two formulations of the Categorical Imperative, universality and then humanity, quite seriously. Humanity is not a given, determinate value. It is rather the value that the active will creates for itself beyond all values. It is also, I claim, the value that the will creates in relation to the Outside, mirroring Deleuze's concern with the openness of the will to the creative forces of life. This is why Kant associates the universal law formula with the universal law-of-nature formula. Kant's moral self is immersed in nature, and precisely through this immersion it creates the value of humanity. This makes the value of humanity also the value of nature, the value of "people to come" or a "new Earth."

2. KANT'S CRITIQUE OF VALUE

To begin to see the minor interpretation of the Categorical Imperative, it is important to understand why the major interpretation – the one that begins with the objective value of humanity and then proposes universality as the conceptual test that limits and guides the activity of the will – does not work well with some of Kant's most basic commitments in practical philosophy. How does Kant understand practical philosophy? If theoretical knowledge attempts to represent its object, practical philosophy attempts to *make* its object. Thus, when Kant introduces his conception of *a priori* knowledge in the *Critique of Pure Reason* he claims that "this cognition can relate to its object in either of two ways, either merely **determining** [*bestimmen*] the object and its concept (which must be given from elsewhere), or else also **making** the object **actual** [*wirklich machen*]. The former is **theoretical**, the latter **practical** cognition of reason."[14] The essence of theoretical knowledge is that it determines its object "discursively," that is, by means of concepts. This does not mean that with theoretical knowledge we create the object *ex nihilo*. Instead, we constitute it by providing the categories that unlock the background against which the object appears. This point distinguishes Kant's transcendental idealism from traditional forms of idealism. Contrastingly, practical knowledge does in fact create its object *ex nihilo*. That is its sole point: to actualize (*wirklich macht*) its object. My point here is not to say that practical knowledge is akin to traditional idealism, since what Kant means by practical knowledge is not concerned with epistemic issues of representation, experience, and perception. My claim is that practical knowledge is concerned with the actualization of the object that does not involve anything already given. I think that the major interpretation of the Categorical Imperative misses the fact that practical philosophy is not about recognizing the value of anything. It is about production.

What does actualization entail? Kant does not settle this question, let alone substantially discuss it, in the *Critique of Pure Reason*, where he first introduces this distinction. However, Kant organizes his main work in moral philosophy around this topic. Early in the *Groundwork* Kant wonders why we have been given the capacity to reason on the proposition that the end of life is the achievement of happiness. To answer this question, Kant denies the idea that the goal of life is the achievement of happiness and claims that the task of reason is to produce the good will:

Since reason is not sufficiently competent to guide the will surely with regard to its objects and the satisfaction of all our needs (which it to some extent even multiplies) – an end to which an implanted natural instinct would have led us more certainly; and since reason is nevertheless given to us as a practical faculty, that is, as one that is to influence the *will*; then, where nature has everywhere else gone to work purposively in distributing its capacities, the true vocation of reason must be to produce [*hervorbringen*] a will that is good, not perhaps *as a means* to other purposes, but *good in itself*, for which reason was absolutely necessary.[15]

Kant here distinguishes between two possible uses of reason. In the first case, reason guides the will in relation to objects that already exist and that may satisfy our happiness. It does not, however, succeed in this. In the second case, reason produces (*bringt hervor*) the will irrespective of the existence of any objects. In other words, reason in the latter case produces its object, namely the good will itself. I understand Kant's *wirkilich machen* in terms of his *hervorbringen*. The production of the good will is the primary concern of Kant's practical philosophy.[16]

Here I think Kant undermines an important idea in the history of moral philosophy, namely, that reason recognizes the abstract object of the good and then uses that object as the standard for the activity of the will, conforming and submitting to it. For Kant, to the contrary, reason is practical. It produces the good will. In this sense, the "good" of the "good will" cannot be some abstract object that the will instantiates by conforming and submitting. It is rather a quality that is inseparable from the will itself, from willing itself. I explain the good will in terms of the will that is active, the will that can will as opposed to the will that cannot will, because it succeeds some objective value. This will that is active is also the will that is creative and creates values rather than one that simply submits to them. Stephen Engstrom hits on this notion of the practical good: "'Good' will be taken to signify what can be practically cognized. For it to be good to do something is just for it to be practically knowable that the thing in question is to be done. Just as 'the true' and 'the real' can be used to pick out the object of theoretical knowledge, so 'the good' refers to the object of practical knowledge."[17] I will begin by explaining why the good will that reason produces cannot be the will that is good in the sense that good is some objective value to which the will conforms and submits in order to be good. In this way I will undermine the major interpretation and prepare for the minor one.

In the *Groundwork*, Kant argues that the will does not have "moral worth" if it is motivated in a particular way, that is, if the "good" is sought in the effect of its action or if the will "borrow[s] its motive from this expected effect."[18] It is important to recognize that Kant here aims at something more ambitious than the mere critique of consequentialism. In other words, Kant's point is not merely that a good will is constituted independently of the action that it performs. Instead, his main point is that the principle on which the will acts cannot borrow its motive *at all* from this hoped for effect. Kant's radical claim is therefore that no material principle, in the sense of having content, can be the ground of a will that is to be called "good." Kant's aim is to overcome any specific value that a will may have at its ground prior to the activity of willing. For example, if the will was motivated by the supposed goodness of telling the truth, that will could not be called "good." For that will to be good, Kant famously claims, it would have to be motivated by a formal principle that lacks all positive content rather than a material principle, such as "tell the truth," which is inseparable from its content.

Kant's critique of value is linked to his account of receptivity. Kant conceptualizes the faculty of sensibility in practical knowledge differently than he does in theoretical knowledge. In theoretical knowledge, the faculty of sensibility is the capacity to receive representations in the intuitions of space and time "as principles of *a priori* cognition."[19] In terms of practical knowledge, Kant is not interested in the representation of objects, but rather in the determination (*Bestimmung*) of the will to act. For this reason also he does not think of moral sensibility as the intuition of objects, but rather as an emotional disposition toward them, that is, as feeling: "here sensibility is not regarded as a capacity for intuition at all but only as feeling (which can be a subjective ground of desire), and with respect to it pure practical reason admits no further division."[20] Specifically, Kant thinks of the faculty of sensibility in practical knowledge in terms of the feeling of pleasure. Thus for Kant, the object can only become the ground of the will if we receive that object on the basis of the feeling of pleasure.

Thus Kant's point is not only that material principles cannot furnish practical laws because they are all empirical,[21] but also that all such empirical principles are premised on the promise of pleasure at the realization of the object:

> By "the matter of the faculty of desire" I understand an object whose reality is desired. Now, when desire for this object precedes the practical rule and is the condition of its becoming a principle, then I say (*first*) that this principle is in that case

always empirical. For, the determining ground of choice is the representation of an object and that relation of the representation to the subject by which the faculty of desire is determined to realize the object. Such a relation to the subject, however, is called *pleasure* in the reality of an object.[22]

Essentially, Kant cannot understand how a will can be good if its principle of volition aims at pleasure, no matter how "good" the grounding object may appear. In this regard it is critical that we recognize that Kant makes no distinction among the grounding objects of the will. Whatever that object may be – whether it is an object of sense, understanding, or reason – that will can only ever be interested in the pleasure of the realization of that object:

> However dissimilar representations of objects may be – they
> may be representations of the understanding or even of reason,
> in contrast to representations of sense – the feeling of pleasure by
> which alone they properly constitute the determining ground of
> the will (the agreeableness, the gratification expected from the
> object, which impels activity to produce it) is nevertheless of one
> and the same kind not only insofar as it can always be cognized
> only empirically but also insofar as it affects one and the same
> vital force that is manifested in the faculty of desire, and in this
> respect can differ only in degree from any other determining
> ground.[23]

Essentially, Kant's critique amounts to the claim that any moral system that presupposes a set of values that a will supposedly ought to follow is only a convoluted version of hedonism. Such moral systems always only foreground "the dear old self."[24]

Here then we have the first notion of why the *good* of the *good will* in Kant's moral system cannot be the objective value that limits and guides the activity of the will. Kant's point is that if we posit any such good at the ground of the will, the will must receive it, but then its activity will only ever be co-opted by the promise of pleasure and self-interest. Kant's point is that he cannot see how a will can be moral in such a case, that is, if it only ever wills from pleasure, if it only ever cares about self-interest. In other words, Kant cannot see how morality can be coincidental with hedonism. This point, I think, undermines the idea that Kant's moral philosophy can be easily dismissed as major philosophy that begins with the presupposition of objective values. Specifically, it problematizes the claim that the ground of Kant's moral philosophy is the value of humanity that limits and guides the activity of the will. On the positive note, Kant's critique of value establishes an important relationship with Deleuze. In fact, Kant's emphasis on the problems of pleasure and self-interest for the purposes of the activity of the will bear strong resemblance to Deleuze's concern with the flow of desire.

For Deleuze, ethics begins with the concern for the flow of desire in relation to life and the power of creation. For Deleuze, ethics is about difference and repetition. Desire is therefore the first moment of ethics, and there can be no grounding of desire. The real problem for Deleuze arises when we mediate the flow of desire through the categories of the self. One of the main ways of doing this constitutes the capture and the ossification of repetition through pleasure. In this case, we do not draw difference from the world, but rather become enamoured with one of its forms in order to mechanically repeat it over and over again. In this case, we get the "eternal return of the same." Thus, for example, I can relate to the power of sexual difference through experimentation but I can also get caught in pleasure and give up the power of desire in favour of mere self-satisfaction. In that case, I always seek something I lack. Desire disappears, and I die a spiritual death. Something similar can happen with drugs, where I die a physical death. We have an analogous situation in Kant. It is certainly the case that the problem with the material determination of the will is that it turns morality into hedonism. But if we think of the main goals of practical philosophy, the real problem of the material determination of the will is the undermining of willing itself. When some value determines the will, I give up the will for pleasure, for self-interest. The good that I could have created becomes the object I lack and the activity of the will becomes nothing but blind temptation and empty fulfilment. This is the real problem. When some value determines the will, it destroys the will. The will cannot will. It disappears under the pressure of pleasure. The will has been enslaved by self-interest. Thus I claim that while Deleuze might be right about the static nature of knowledge in *Critique of Pure Reason*, and the inability to face the power of the creation of life, it is also true that Kant thinks that we must not box the will into a category. I think that the connection is even closer than that, because Kant's solution to this problem will be the universalization of the will, which will relate us to nature in the way in which the flow of desire occurs only in relation to difference, to the Outside.[25]

Deleuze for his part may not see Kant's point about universalization. Before I explain how Kant's minor ethics works, I want to look closely at Deleuze's critique of universalization. Deleuze recognizes some of the elements of Kant's minor ethics, perhaps even Kant's abolition of value at the ground of the will. However, Deleuze seems to think that despite this fact, Kant has not managed to provide a minor ethics. Universality, Deleuze thinks, is not the process whereby we activate the will. Instead, while it may not itself be a value, it certainly *upholds* traditional values. Deleuze's criticism of universalization invokes the problems of transcendence and closure we noted above. For this reason, Deleuze thinks, while the will may have been freed from value, it does not become genuinely active. Universality brings the will back to all the same values that used to be ground of the will. In this sense, what we have here is the will that apparently freely creates the same old value. There has never been a more compromising critique. However, I believe that Deleuze was tempted into this interpretation through his appreciation of Nietzsche. In other words, Deleuze could not fully appreciate Kant's notion of universalization because he was influenced by Nietzsche's critique of Kant in terms of value. On the other hand, I believe that when Deleuze saw Kant's critique of value, he should have also seen his points concerning universalization, the activation of the will, and the opening of the will for creation of new values.

3. DELEUZE'S CRITIQUE OF KANT'S MORALITY

Nietzsche does not provide a systematic critique of Kant's moral philosophy. Nevertheless, his opposition to Kant is clear and suggestive. Nietzsche recognizes that it was Kant who initially freed philosophical discourse from dogmatic metaphysics. However, the problem, Nietzsche thinks, is that Kant returns to dogmatism by means of the Categorical Imperative. "Kant ... helped himself to the 'thing in itself' – another very ridiculous thing – and was punished for this when the 'categorical imperative' crept into his heart and made him stray back into his cage. Yet it had been his strength and cleverness that had broken open the cage!"[26] Nietzsche goes on to associate the overcoming of metaphysics with the freedom of the will. In other words, Nietzsche thinks that a will becomes truly free, the free spirit, only when all values collapse. On the other hand, the problem with Kant is that even though he points to the possibility of this overcoming of the metaphysics of values, the Categorical Imperative, Nietzsche thinks, betrays this possibility. Thus, Kant initially seems to overcome morality in the name of ethics, but then sacrifices this ethics at the altar of morality. Nietzsche is likely pointing to the fact that Kant's moral project secures the validity of precisely those metaphysical ideas that he finds problematic in the *Critique of Pure Reason*, namely, freedom, God, and the immortality of the soul.

Kant himself acknowledges something along these lines. For example, Kant thinks that the Categorical Imperative, and specifically the universal law formula, demonstrates the validity of transcendental freedom because when I act on the mere representation of the law, I act rationally, and, furthermore, acting rationally means acting beyond all sensible determinations that hold true of my existence as a natural being:

> Since the mere form of a law can be represented only by reason and is therefore not an object of the senses and consequently does not belong among appearances, the representation of this form as the determining ground of the will is distinct from all determining grounds of events in nature in accordance with the law of causality, because in their case the determining grounds must themselves be appearances. But if no determining ground of the will other than that universal lawgiving form can serve as a law for it, such a will must be thought as altogether independent of the natural law of appearances in their relations to one another, namely the law of causality. But such independence is called *freedom* in the strictest, that is, transcendental sense. Therefore, a will for which the mere lawgiving form of a maxim can alone serve as a law is a free will.[27]

Furthermore, on the basis of this demonstration of transcendental freedom, Kant maintains that he can also demonstrate the validity of the ideas of God and the immortality of the soul:

> Now the concept of freedom, insofar as its reality is proved by an apodictic law of practical reason, constitutes the *keystone*, of the whole structure of a system of pure reason, even of speculative reason; and all other concepts (those of God and

immortality), which as mere ideas remain without support in the latter, now attach themselves to this concept and with it and by mean[s] of it get stability and objective reality, that is, their *possibility* is *provided* by this: that freedom is real, for this idea reveals itself through the moral law.[28]

Thus, in the end, Nietzsche thinks that the Categorical Imperative actually returns Kant to metaphysics. It allows Kant to prove that, despite critical scrutiny, we really are free, and that we can postulate the existence of God and the immortality of the soul. Moreover, this return to metaphysics, Nietzsche thinks, collapses Kant's critique of morality onto itself. Just when Kant seems to liberate the will to its own activity beyond all values, he shackles that activity again, this time by means of the Categorical Imperative. Thus, after criticizing all values at the ground of the activity of the will, Kant ends up with the same set of values that characterize traditional moral systems, for example, the value of telling the truth, the value of helping out others, and so on. From Nietzsche's perspective, there has never been a more compromising critique.

Deleuze's critique of Kant is Nietzschean in spirit along these lines. Deleuze recognizes that Kant gives up all material principles at the ground of the activity of the will in favour of the formal principle. "We have seen that the faculty of desire is capable of a higher form: when it is determined not by representations of objects (of sense or intellect), nor by a feeling of pleasure or pain which would link this kind of representation to the will, but rather by the representation of form. This pure form is universal legislation" (KCP, 28). However, unlike my own argument, Deleuze does not think that Kant manages to introduce an ethics beyond morality. Deleuze is skeptical because he thinks that despite the formality of the Categorical Imperative, it compromises the activity of the will. If prior to acting, I must ask myself whether my maxim (the subjective principle) can become a universal law (the objective principle), then I am in fact providing a blueprint for the activity of the will. By doing so, however, I undermine its own activity, and thereby also I undermine its creativity. This will submits to formal principles and therefore cannot be genuinely active, and if it cannot be genuinely active it also cannot be creative. It is true that the Categorical Imperative does not posit material values at the ground of the will, Deleuze thinks, but to the extent that the will is to act on those maxims that can become the universal law, the

Categorical Imperative implies the value of universality, and while universality is not the same as God, it is suspicious how it returns us to all the divine values.

To elaborate, we can understand Deleuze's critique of Kant's moral philosophy in the context of his overall critique of the history of Western philosophy. Deleuze thinks that metaphysical philosophy and transcendental philosophy invoke the same "image of thought," which is, in the end, "a dogmatic, orthodox or moral image" (DR, 131). What is characteristic of this image of thought is its condemnation, its fear of life understood as a creative power of difference. According to Deleuze, the moralistic image of thought seeks to contain this power and subordinate it to the stability of Being and the identity of the Concept. Thus, instead, of opening ourselves up to the creative power of difference in order to think and act differently, metaphysical and transcendental philosophy presents us with the following blackmail: either you accept the reality of Being or the legitimacy of the Concept, or you submit to meaningless nothingness. "What is common to metaphysics and transcendental philosophy is, above all, this alternative which they impose on us: either an undifferentiated ground, a groundlessness, formless nonbeing, or an abyss without differences and without properties, or a supremely individuated Being and an intensely personalized Form. Without this Being or this Form, you will have only chaos" (LS, 106). Needless to say, Deleuze thinks we should reject this blackmail and rise to the task of thinking difference itself. Deleuze thinks that Kant, despite all of his revolutionary insights, fails to do precisely that.

This failure is, Deleuze thinks, influenced by Nietzsche, perfectly palpable in the Categorical Imperative. Because Kant subscribes to the image of thought, the moment that he manages to liberate the will from all material principles he faces precisely this meaningless nothingness, what we can also call the chaos of the will. Without any values, Kant must have thought, the will is capable of anything! "What disturbed us," Deleuze writes, "was that in renouncing judgment we had the impression of depriving ourselves of any means of distinguishing between existing beings, between modes of existence, as if everything was now of equal value" (CC, 134). Thus, rather than submitting to this chaos of the will, Deleuze thinks Kant chooses to ground the will, if not in material, then in formal principles. But this groundwork betrays the freedom of the will that the overcoming of material principles should have brought about in the first place. In Nietzsche's words, Kant "strays back into his cage." Even though I claim that both Nietzsche and Deleuze get Kant wrong here, I think that they conceptualize their own projects by trying not to make the mistake they have falsely attributed to Kant. They each attempt to write an ethics that actually stays true to the freedom of the will and that does not betray it to further transcendent principles, no matter how pure, empty, and formal.

I think that Deleuze's Nietzschean critique of Kant's moral philosophy is seductive. However, it is also reductive. Specifically, it fails to understand that the idea of universalizability is intimately related to the goal of practical philosophy as the actualization (*wirklich machen*) and production (*hervorbringen*) of the will, rather than recognition of value. For all of Deleuze's understanding of the formal principles of universality, he thinks that Kant animates it only in order to recognize the established values. But that certainly is unfair. But what happens when we take Kant seriously, and say that practical philosophy is not about recognizing values, but about producing the good will where the good is not some given value, but rather the ability of the will to will? Then I think we see the possibility of the minor Categorical Imperative.

4. THE MINOR CATEGORICAL IMPERATIVE

I hope to have dislodged the idea that the process of universalization is a conceptual test in relation to the objective value of humanity. Instead, I claim, universalization is the concrete process that the will must undergo in order to become active. In order to think of universalization as the animation of the will, let us think of the main problem of the material determination of the will by some value. As I have claimed, the fact is that pleasure and self-interest reign, and where pleasure and self-interest reign there can be no word of morality. Moreover, if we recognize that practical philosophy is about actualization and production of the good will, that means the problem with the material determination is not merely moralistic in that sense. The real problem, I claim, is that the will cannot will when it becomes locked into pleasure and self-interest. This will always lacks its object and compromises its activity in hopes of its achievement. This is the main problem of Kant's moral philosophy. If we focus too closely on the moralistic interpretation, we will not be able to recognize the issue from the perspective of minor ethics. The material determination of the will pacifies the will. Kant's point is that when some value determines the will to action, insofar as that will can only act on the basis of the promise of pleasure, the power of willing is sacrificed to the promise of pleasure at the possible possession of that object. Properly speaking, Kant would say there is no willing here. There is only pleasure. If we think of the will as capable of willing, we can also say that the will that is determined to act on some value relates to its own power of willing in the mode of loss. The material determination of the will is a continuous loss of the will. Furthermore, in this case, the will can only relate to its own activity in the mode of lack. To will at all thus means to lack the object of the will. In this sense, pleasure entraps the will in a state of dissatisfaction and self-alienation. If we think of morality as production, I suggest that we think of universalization less as a process whereby we can make sure to have morality that is not organized around pleasure and the self, but rather centres on the will that can will beyond pleasure and self-interest. Universalization is the process whereby we abandon values and try to animate the will beyond it so that it becomes creative.

This approach shares much in common with Deleuze. Deleuze claims that we must open ourselves to the power of creation in order to be creative ourselves. We are to draw difference in order to become creative. Something similar holds true of Kant's universalization. Kant's statement of the universal formula is fascinating. We are to abandon all values, all material, all content that might influence the will to action, and just act on the basis of the law. Kant begins by elaborating what law he has in mind. We may think that we must incorporate some law that itself has some content, for example, divine law, conscience, and so on. But that is exactly what Kant denies.ᐟ Instead, according to Kant, the law he has in mind is purely formal, and this form is universality.

> But what kind of law can that be, the representation of which must determine the will, even without regard for the effect expected from it, in order for the will to be called good absolutely and without limitation? Since I have deprived the will of every impulse that could arise for it from obeying some law, nothing is left but the conformity of actions as such with a universal law which alone is to serve the will as its principle. That is, I ought never to act except in such a way that I could also will that my maxim should become a universal law. Here mere

conformity to law as such, without having as its basis some law determined for certain actions, is what serves the will as its principle, and must so serve it, if duty is not to be everywhere an empty delusion and a chimerical concept.[29]

Now it is clear why this law must be the law of universality, because when I take the universal perspective I get rid of self-interest and therefore I get rid of pleasure. Finally, in getting rid of pleasure, I get to will for the first time. So I produce the good will. The will becomes active.

Moreover, we can make the connection between Kant's notion of universalization and Deleuze's idea that we must be open to the creative force of life. In this regard note that Kant thinks that the universal law that is to animate the will is the universal law of nature. Kant's point here is that nature is the domain of universality:

Since the universality of laws in accordance with which effects take place constitutes what is properly called *nature* in the most general sense (as regards its form) – that is, the existence of things insofar as it is determined in accordance with universal laws – the universal imperative of duty can also go as follows: *act as if the maxim of your action were to become by your will a universal law of nature.*[30]

In this regard I think that Kant comes close to those philosophers, such as Spinoza, whom Deleuze cites as his influences. Kant's idea is not that we uphold the value of nature. Instead, the idea is that we repeat the way in which nature acts. And this for Kant is the form of universalization. When we seriously open ourselves to the domain of nature, we get to will, we activate the will beyond values, beyond established categories. We draw the difference.

One issue we may encounter here is our relationship to the universal law of nature. Here the threat is that we may return to the problem of conceptual judgment. When the will acts on the universal law of nature, does it not make universality itself the value of its activity? If this is true of Kant, I think it is equally true of Deleuze. Kant for his part does everything to discourage precisely this type of interpretation. He argues that reason determines the will with the universal law of nature. However, Kant does not conceive of reason here as the theoretical faculty that transcends the will and then brings universality as a conceptual test. In fact, if that were the case then the will would have to return to self-interest and pleasure, because it would have to receive this value according to the model described above. Instead, for Kant reason is the animating, genetic principle of the will. It operates immanently within the will when the will is active. This is how Kant puts it:. "In a practical law reason determines the will *immediately*, not by means of the intervening pleasure or displeasure, not even in this law; and that it can as pure reason be practical is what alone makes it possible for it to be *lawgiving*."[31] For Kant reason is the immanent principle of the will that draws the difference from nature in order to make the will active. Note in this instance one of Kant's most famous quotations: "Everything in nature works in accordance with laws. Only a rational being has the faculty to act in accordance with the representation of laws, i.e., in accordance with principles, or has a will. Since *reason* is required for the derivation of actions from laws, the will is nothing other than practical reason."[32] Of course we can think of reason here as conceptual and theoretical. But note that Kant is saying that reason is practical here or that it is the same as the will, and that reason hijacks the universality of nature in order to make the will active. It derives actions from laws of nature. And this, for Kant, is autonomy.

We can definitely try too hard to separate Kant from Deleuze. One way to do that is to make a clear-cut distinction between moral and natural domains in Kant's practical philosophy, between freedom and determination. However, what I have demonstrated is that morality and freedom for Kant are only possible on the basis of nature in the sense that they are possible only on the basis of universal laws. The will cannot act unless it acts universally beyond all values. Thus the difference between the two for Kant can be put as follows. While nature is structured universally, it itself does not act. The free being, on the other hand, is the one who is capable of animating universality for the purposes of freedom, of hijacking nature for the purposes of freedom. We often make Kant's moral agent sound like an agent transcendent to nature. We think of freedom as separate from nature. That is not what Kant thinks. He thinks that we are immanent in nature in the sense that we only activate the vocation of rationality in and through nature. This is freedom. The will can only act on its own principles when it acts universally, that is, when it acts naturally. "Autonomy of the will is the property of the will by which it is a law to itself (independently of any property of the objects of volition).

The principle of autonomy is, therefore: to choose only in such a way that the maxims of your choice are also included as universal law in the same volition."[33]

In some sense this is where the main story of Kant's minor categorical imperative ends. We have now produced the good will. The good will is the will that can will. It is the will that is active. Kant adds a further point here that is consistent with Deleuze's ethics, namely, that the active will is the creative will. No values ground the active will, but rather the will that is active grounds and produces values. In this sense too the good will is good. It is good because it can will but it is also good because it produces the value of humanity. I do not understand humanity as the ground of the activity of the will. That goes against everything we have considered and it does disservice to Kant's moral philosophy. Instead, I close by giving a minor reading of the humanity formula. And here I remind the reader that for Kant the universal law-of-nature formula is the main formulation of the Categorical Imperative and the humanity formula is second. In short, we go from the activity of the will to the creativity of the will. There are two ways to understand the value of humanity in Kant's work, both of which are consistent with the minor reading.

When I act autonomously only on those maxims that can become the universal law, not only do I thereby overcome self-interest and the promise of pleasure, but also, in overcoming them, I demonstrate a moral concern for others. It is in this precise sense that humanity can constitute a value in Kant's moral system, namely as the achievement of practical reason or, what amounts to the same thing, of the will that autonomously acts universally. In this sense, even though the will is determined by a purely formal principle, that principle, when activated as it is in the will that autonomously acts universally, already contains matter. Matter is already in the form of the maxim that can become the universal law. And that matter is humanity. Thus actualizing the will by means of that form also brings the matter into the foreground of the will. I claim that it is only in this sense that humanity can be a value that grounds universality and autonomy. Practical reason gives itself that ground in becoming active as the autonomous, universal will. "The will is thought as a capacity to determine itself to acting in conformity with the *representation of certain laws*. And such a capacity can be found only in rational beings. Now, what serves the will as the objective ground of its self-determination is an end, and this, if it is given by reason alone, must hold equally for all rational beings."[34] Thus it is not so much that humanity is an end in itself that grounds Kant's moral system; it is rather that practical reason establishes humanity as an end in itself by exercising itself through or as the will. Humanity is the output of active will and nothing else. Finally, because universality, autonomy, and humanity essentially name the same concern of the Categorical Imperative, Kant can just as well claim that autonomy and universality are themselves the ground of morality. In other words, the will that autonomously acts universally is itself the ground of morality just as much as humanity is because those principles name what humanity is.

> For, nothing, can have worth other than that which the law determines for itself. But the lawgiving itself, which determines all worth, must for that very reason have a dignity, that is, an unconditional, incomparable worth; and the word *respect* alone provides a becoming expression for the estimate of it that a rational being must give. *Autonomy* is therefore the ground of the dignity of human nature and of every rational nature.[35]

But I think that this point about humanity can be taken further. Note here that humanity here is the value arrived at from the perspective of the will that makes the activity of nature its own. We are not separate from nature, in fact our highest vocation as moral beings has its source in the repetition of the law of nature. This point is important in relation to what humanity can mean. Take in this regard what Deleuze appreciates about Spinoza. "That individual will be called *good* (or free, or rational, or strong) who strives, insofar as he is capable, to organize his encounters, to join with whatever agrees with his nature, to combine his relation with relations that are compatible with his, and thereby to increase his power. For goodness is a matter of dynamism, power and composition of powers" (SPP, 22–3). The good in the sense of value, the good that humanity is, is the good that draws the difference from nature. I think we can link the concept of humanity to the concept of the human being who relates respectfully to nature that gives it freedom. I suggest that in Kant we can find a place for the notion of humanity that does not just include treating others as ends in themselves, but also includes the creation of humans who recognize their immanent connection with nature. Kant's ethics provides existence of a new people, a people who transform their relations to themselves and to nature. That is the good, the humanity, that the good will puts forward.

Deleuze's defends an ethics of the new, and by the new he means the forever new.

Nietzsche's distinction between the creation of new values and the recognition of established values should not be understood in a historically relative manner, as though the established values were new in their time and the new values simply needed time to become established. In fact it concerns a difference which is both formal and in kind. The new, with its power of beginning and beginning again, remains forever new, just as the established was always established from the outset, even if a certain amount of empirical time was necessary for this to be recognized. What becomes established with the new is precisely not the new. (DR, 136)

Deleuze associates "the forever new" with that which is not susceptible to the model of recognition, namely to the concept. The new value is not something that we can find out about and then help create. That defeats the purpose. Whatever we create in this monotone way will surely be that which has always already been established. I suggest that Kant's notion of humanity is "the forever new." It does not refer to some intelligible property of the human being. It does not seek recognition. There is therefore nothing to be upheld in action. Instead, there is only the perpetual activity of the will struggling to create and re-create its own foundation. That is universality in relation to nature. We take away everything from Kant when we insist that we ought to treat humanity as an end in itself as the starting point or even that we should treat nature with respect as the starting point. We are bound to create followers and skeptics. One either ends up searching for properties, and never finding them tends toward nihilism and relativism; or one submits as a matter of faith, to objectivity, and eventually returns to morality. This double bind is precisely what is forever established. What is new on the other hand is what happens silently, underneath the rumblings of identity and recognition. The good will is the beginning of all great politics.

NOTES

1 "A legislative faculty, as a source of representations, does not suppress all use of other faculties. When understanding legislates in the interest of

knowledge, imagination and reason still retain an entirely *original* role, but in conformity with tasks determined by the understanding" (Deleuze, KCP, 10).

2 "Rather than all the faculties converging and contributing to a common project of recognizing an object," Deleuze writes, "we see divergent projects in which, with regard to what concerns it essentially, each faculty is in the presence of that which is its 'own'" (DR, 41).

3 This immediate relationship between the freed faculties and new metaphysical realities allows Deleuze to develop a genetic account of the faculties. In effect, doing so means moving beyond the concept as the stable, organizing centre of metaphysical knowledge. In this sense, Joe Hughes argues that "*Difference and Repetition* rewrites the *Critique of Pure Reason* from the point of view of genesis." *Deleuze's Difference and Repetition*, 5.

4 Deleuze and Guattari note that "the *illusion of transcendence* ... comes before all others (in its double aspect of making immanence immanent to something and of rediscovering a transcendence within immanence itself)" (WP, 49).

5 Kant, *Groundwork*, 7.

6 Ibid., 80.

7 Wood, *Kantian Ethics*, 85.

8 Ibid., 85–6.

9 Kant, *Groundwork*, 73.

10 For such traditional readings of Kant's moral philosophy, see Christine Korsgaard, *Creating the Kingdom of Ends*; Wood, *Kant's Ethical Thought*; and Wood, *Kantian Ethics*.

11 Spinoza, *Ethics*, III.P9.S.

12 Nietzsche, *On the Genealogy of Morality*, I.17.

13 Andrew Reath approaches Kant along these lines in *Agency and Autonomy*. In particular, see Reath's chapters "The Categorical Imperative and Kant's Conception of Practical Rationality" and "Autonomy of the Will as the Foundation of Morality."

14 Kant, *Critique of Pure Reason*, 107.

15 Kant, *Practical Philosophy*, 51–2.

16 Stephen Engstrom's *The Form of Practical Knowledge* approaches Kant's practical philosophy along these lines.

17 Engstrom argues that the "good" is an object of practical knowledge analogously to how the "true" is the object of theoretical knowledge; *ibid.*, 14.

18 Kant, *Groundwork*, 56.

19 Kant, *Critique of Pure Reason,* 157.

20 Kant, *Practical Philosophy,* 212.

21 Kant thinks that all values can only be received extrinsically and therefore
cannot be immanently or autonomously determined. Consequently,
principles based on *received* values can only be *empirical.* Because Kant
demands that moral principles must hold with necessity, no principle that
presupposes an object at the ground of the will can be moral. "All practical principles that presuppose an *object* (matter) of the faculty of desire as
the determining ground of the will are, without exception, empirical and
can furnish no practical laws" (ibid., 155). In this sense, if telling the truth,
for example, were to become the material principle of the will, then,
according to Kant, the case of telling the truth could have no moral worth,
because the value of telling the truth in this case would only hold under
specific spatio-temporal conditions (e.g., the family, society, culture,
religion) in which one has received that value.

22 Ibid., 155.

23 Ibid., 156–7.

24 "From love of humankind I am willing to admit that even most of our
actions are in conformity with duty; but if we look more closely at the
intentions and aspirations in them we everywhere come upon the dear
old self, which is always turning up; and it is on this that their purpose
is based, not on the strict command of duty, which would often require
self-denial." Ibid., 62.

25 In a certain sense, Deleuze underestimates Kant's critique of morality.
Deleuze often animates Nietzsche as the philosopher who supposedly
completes Kant's compromising critique because, unlike Kant, so the argument goes, Nietzsche manages to conceive of critique in terms of values.
"One of the principal motifs of Nietzsche's work is that Kant had not carried out a true critique because he was not able to pose the problem of critique in terms of values" (NP, 1). In this sense, "Kant merely pushed a very
old conception of critique to the limit, a conception which saw critique as
… a force which should be brought to bear on all claims to morality, but
not on morality itself" (NP, 89). However, I suggest that this is precisely
what Kant did. He conceived of the critique of morality in terms of the
critique of values, and in that sense managed to criticize not only the false
claims to morality, but also the form of morality itself. After all, Kant criti-
cizes any morality that begins by supposing valuable objects that guide
the activity of the will. Such moral systems force the will to take endless
detours through pleasure, shackling it to the self that is insatiable in principle and susceptible to infinite analysis. What do I want exactly? Who am

I really? Psychoanalysis is the continuation of traditional morality by other means. In this way, Kant has prepared the ground for a new conception of ethics beyond morality.

26 Nietzsche, *The Gay Science*, trans. Nauckhoff, 188.
27 Kant, *Practical Philosophy*, 162.
28 Ibid., 139.
29 Ibid., 56–7.
30 Ibid., 73.
31 Ibid., 158.
32 Ibid., 66.
33 Ibid., 89.
34 Ibid., 78.
35 Ibid., 85.

Assemblage and Multiplicity

Erin Manning

An assemblage is always a multiplicity: it never moves alone. Less assemblage than assembling, it is *how* the moving happens, its togetherness always in excess of the sum of its parts.

An assemblage is an emergent collectivity orienting toward a world yet to be defined. An event, a body, a site – all of these are *agencements*. But none of these are uniquely themselves once and for all: an assemblage is ecological at its core, the multiplicity that runs through it affected by all that co-composes with its edges. There are no movements that can be repeated exactly the same way twice.

An assemblage is always protopolitical in the sense that its orientation cleaves environments in ways that produce new qualities of experience. "An assemblage is precisely this increase in the dimensions of a multiplicity that necessarily changes in nature as it expands its connections" (TP, 8). Multiplicity is not the "one more." It is the more-than.

An assemblage is always multiple, singularly so: it connects, seeds, and germinates, concretizing a set of relations while bringing the more-than of the field of relation into expression in a way that requires another iteration. An assemblage activates the potential interstices at the heart of a process, seriating expression from the interstices. This is what Deleuze and Guattari call a "collective assemblage of enunciation." Not a single articulation made by a preexisting being, but a singular quality of expression through which the world articulates itself. An assemblage is the sociality of relation.

Assemblage is a practice, and the practice is collective. There is no individual expression. No stance that pre-exists the coming-into-relation, no expression that lurks outside the force of the encounter. It is not a human practice, as though it were our task to assemble the world. *Agencement* moves the more-than of human experience into the constellations of worlding. How it does so matters. This is the work Deleuze and Guattari propose through the concept of assemblage: to become engaged with the modes of encounter activated in the assembling. To make felt how the limits of existence are crafted through the coming-into-relation of qualities of encounter. To move-with the potential of a life always more-than human. To live in the interstices of ecologies in the making.

8

Attention and Decreation as Deterritorializing Practices: Toward a Weilian Minor Politics

Sophie Bourgault

It is necessary to uproot oneself. To cut down the tree ... It is necessary not to be "myself," still less to be "ourselves." The city gives us the feeling of being at home. We must take the feeling of being at home into exile. We must be rooted in the absence of a place.

Simone Weil, Gravity and Grace

We're tired of trees. We should stop believing in trees, roots, and radicles. They've made us suffer too much.

Deleuze and Guattari (TP, 15)

Despite Deleuze's well-known claim that the *Anti-Oedipus* was "from beginning to end a book of *political philosophy*" (N, 170/230, my emphasis), the last two decades have witnessed a fair amount of debate over Deleuze's relevance for political theory. Some scholars have argued that while offering an inspiring ethics, Deleuze was too indifferent to things traditionally understood as political to have much to offer in the way of a concrete politics.[1] Peter Hallward has argued that Deleuze's predilection for the virtual (against the historical) and for the singular (against the general) makes him a poor friend for those interested in *collective* action.[2] In the eyes of some critics, there is something anti-democratic, elitist, and even *anti-political* about Deleuze's work.[3] In Philippe Mengue's view, for instance, Deleuze's "micropolitics of deterritorialization" can be read as an ethics (or better, a "style" or posture), but hardly as a responsible politics given

Deleuze's loathing of roots and stability and his distrust of democratic deliberations.[4] Mengue insists that Deleuze's work inevitably forces us to abandon all serious attempts at proposing a "theorization of State power ... and of the conditions of the legitimate relationship between historical powers."[5] Naturally, these interpretations have not gone unchallenged: Eugene Holland,[6] Paul Patton,[7] Jeremy Gilbert,[8] and Karen L.F. Houle[9] – to name but a few – have all argued distinctively that reading Deleuze as "anti-political" (or anti-democratic) hardly does justice to his work and that such a reading rests either on an overly narrow definition of the political or on an inadequate reading of the connections between ethics and politics.

The accusation of being "anti-political" is one that a number of philosophers with radical ethics have faced. In this chapter I propose to examine another philosopher who has faced such a charge: Simone Weil (1909–1943). Philosophy teacher, Marxist, Platonist, union activist, and mystic, Weil produced – despite her early death – a wealth of essays on such varied topics as factory oppression, quantum theory, colonialism, education, Greek tragedy, and totalitarianism. Weil's intellectual output has often been divided into two periods by her interpreters: an early, politically engaged period; and a later, more spiritual phase where concerns about combating working-class oppression and colonial politics seem to take a back seat, and where care for the soul, for God, and for *amor fati* predominate.[10] Partly in light of the religious preoccupations in her late work, a few scholars have described the mature Weil as disillusioned and apolitical. Others have insisted that there was something more than a resigned retreat from the political in her last essays: in these works, they argue, we have an outright *anti*-politics, captured most vividly in Weil's loathing for parties and for group deliberation. In an oft-cited essay, Conor Cruise O'Brien has argued that while Weil was a sharp analyst of nationalism and communism, she ultimately offered a highly anti-political vision: "So rigorous an enemy of the first person plural as Simone Weil is necessarily an enemy of political involvement also. And if man is a political animal, as Aristotle thought, to be rigorously antipolitical is to be antihuman as well."[11] Similarly, Susan Bickford has criticized Weil for ascribing too much importance to a *withdrawal of the self* in her ethics and her account of attention.[12] For Bickford, this can hardly be the basis for *anything substantially political*.

Naturally, a lot hangs here on how one defines "political." If O'Brien and Bickford are right to suggest that Weil did not embrace an

Aristotelian definition of the human being and did not, following Aristotle, intimately link politics to the exercise of rational *speech* (Weil's predilection was for listening over talking), Weil nevertheless had another definition of the human animal to propose that places her squarely in the tradition of political philosophy. For Weil, the human being was to be seen first and foremost as an "attentive animal." Indeed, in her *Leçons de philosophie*, she insisted that it was "attention" that distinguished the human from other animals. Weil was of the view that it was through the cultivation of attention that the individual could most meaningfully engage in creative and contemplative activities, in work, and – most critically for my purposes here – in socially responsible and transformative politics. While Joël Janiaud is certainly correct to summarize Weilian ethics as "an ethics of attention,"[13] I think that it is equally appropriate to define Weil's politics as a "minor" *politics of attention*.

In order to substantiate these claims, I propose to reread Weil's concepts of *attention* and *decreation* – two concepts recurrently identified as emblematic of Weil's apparent flight from "true" politics – through a Deleuzian lens. More specifically, I wish to read Weilian attention (and the decreative process attached to it) as a Deleuzian micropolitics of deterritorialization and nomadic practice. Following Deleuze and Guattari, the term "deterritorialization" will be used here to refer to a process or movement of "exit" that frees an entity or an individual from a particular territory or system – one that is imbued or governed by a particular coding, a set of norms, rules, laws, prejudices, and so on.[14] If Deleuzian "territories" can consist of such varied things as linguistic, conceptual, legal, scientific, and affective systems, I will be largely concerned here about political and administrative "territories."[15]

I describe attention as a micropolitical practice because it is conceived by Weil as a flight from the majoritarian; it is an uprooting characteristically geared toward the *hearing* (or *resounding*) of minor voices. As we will see below, Weil regarded attention as a kind of radically *receptive* cognitive state. She understood this hyper-receptivity as entailing at once a kind of passivity, a *waiting,* a "suspension of thought," a selflessness that requires, as we will see below, a crushing of one's egoistic desires and concerns. This loss of ego, this momentary annihilation of the self, is what Weil labelled *decreation*; and it is what she regarded as the *sine qua non* of a good ethical, spiritual, and political life. As the philosopher Iris Murdoch succinctly explains in her reflections on Weil, "we cease to be *in order to attend to the existence of something else*," namely "a person in need."[16] In its purest form, then, the ethical faculty of attention is what allows an individual to see and love alterity (the different, the marginal, the invisible, the inaudible), and, through this attending, to give the invisible a (socio-political) visibility and the inaudible a voice. In short, attention is recognition. It is for this reason that Weil regarded attentive decreation as, at once, a decisive ethical *and political* project. It is also for this reason that Weil liked to describe attention as not only the most intense, pure, *disinterested* kind of love, but also as justice itself. The attentive are the just.[17]

In the pages that follow, we will see that Weilian attention/decreation can entail two types of flights or exits: first, a flight away from the ego, its selfish or interested cravings, and its prejudices; and second, a flight away from a "we," from a "Great Beast"[18] (popular opinion and norms), from the noise and pressures of parties and large, centralized institutions and workplaces. Much like a Deleuzian nomad, the truly attentive/ethical individual must, Weil writes, "uproot [himself] socially and vegetatively"; he must "exile himself from every earthly country"[19] – an exile not necessarily in space, but in thought. Following Deleuze and Guattari's depiction of the nomad as "the Deterritorialized par excellence" (TP, 381), I will use the terms *nomadic* and *deterritorializing* somewhat interchangeably in what follows.

Despite Weil's dislike of state and bureaucratic institutions, this chapter will also indicate that for attention as a micropractice to have any significant political or emancipatory purchase, for Weil, it must take seriously (macro)reforms and measures. Even though she never used such terms, Weil would have been comfortable with Deleuze and Guattari's thesis that the "micro" and the "macro" levels of the political cannot be disentangled: "every politics is simultaneously a *macropolitics* and a *micropolitics*" (TP, 213). In short, contrary to the suggestions of O'Brien and Bickford, I wish to argue that Weil did not propose an anti-politics, but rather an *alternative vision of the political* in which the work to be done on an individual's affects, desires, and receptivity was eminently political and had to be buttressed with institutional/molar[20] measures as well as (localized) collective solidarities. As we will see, this alternative account of the political can best be unearthed from Weil's oeuvre through the lenses of a (Deleuzian) minor ethics, which can help recast her most idiosyncratic and most radical statements (often dismissed in "majoritarian"

academic forums) in a new light. More specifically, I will suggest that
it is above all Deleuze's concepts of micropolitics and deterritorialization that will allow us to elucidate Weil's alternative vision of politics
and, in so doing, offer us some fresh (if modest) intellectual resources
to reflect on what may matter most for contemporary politics.

In the first part of this chapter, we will define Weilian *attention* and
disentangle its complex relationship to will, desire, and decreation.
One of my goals here will be to underscore the degree to which there
is something joyful, profoundly active, and *affirmative* about Weil's
account of attention and decreation – something that has been insuf-
ficiently appreciated by some readers of Weil who have overemphasized the importance of passivity, negation, and suffering in her
thought.[21] If the first section is chiefly concerned with the Weilian
flight from the self's egoistic passions and unexamined, domineering
prejudices, then the second section will turn to exits from more explicitly molar/majoritarian territories: political parties and centralized,
hierarchical workplaces. In this chapter's conclusion, I will briefly
indicate that while Weilian attention can be understood partly as a
deterritorializing practice, it nevertheless takes its distance from
Deleuzian deterritorialization in numerous respects: most importantly,
I argue that it is much more *other-oriented* and that it holds on firmly
to "the sky," that is, to a thick normativity.[22]

I. EXITING THE SELF, CRUSHING THE EGO: ATTENTION, DESIRE, AND DECREATION

... by uprooting oneself one seeks greater reality.
                                        Simone Weil, *Gravity and Grace*

Weil gave her richest account of attention in the essays she penned
during the last three years of her life – three years during which she
was, effectively, in exile. (As a Jew, she had to leave Paris in 1940; she
would travel from Marseille to New York, and then to London, where
she would join the French resistance in 1942 and, shortly after, die
of tuberculosis and self-imposed starvation).[23] More specifically, it is
in her essay on school studies, published posthumously in *Waiting
for God,* that Weil offers her clearest definition of the term "attention"
and provides us with what is effectively a panegyric to it.[24] Here Weil
makes the bold assertion that the cultivation of attention ought to be
regarded as the *only* interest of school studies. Although she never

fully substantiated such a claim, Weil was convinced that if children learned to truly pay attention through, say, the patient reading of a book or the solving of mathematical problems, these skills could later on be transferred to their ethico-political lives and, most significantly, to their encounters with the marginal and vulnerable (those whom Weil referred to as "the afflicted" [*les malheureux*]).[25] In her view, looking for the truth behind a mathematical problem and attending to affliction entailed a similar cognitive and affective effort. She thought that the spirit of justice and the spirit of truth were made of the same substance, namely, attention.[26] For this reason, Weil encouraged educators to remind impatient or distracted students that one can only learn to be just if one first learns to be attentive.[27] Without attention there can be no social justice, no good politics, and no "culture" worthy of the name.[28]

We will have occasion to return to this striking claim below. But for the moment, let us consider Weil's widely cited definition of attention: "Attention consists of suspending our thought, leaving it detached, empty, ready to be penetrated by the object ... Above all our thought should be empty, waiting, not seeking anything, but ready to receive in its naked truth the object that is to be penetrated by it."[29] The close ties drawn between *attention* and *waiting* are absolutely critical to Weil's account: to attend means at once to serve (to wait on someone, on the world, on God), but also to wait (to pause, to stop). Weil insists that there can be no receptivity or openness to alterity without this patient stillness; attending properly to a *malheureux*, a book, a piece of music cannot be *rushed*. Truth or beauty should not and cannot be aggressively sought; precipitation will necessarily ruin what might be revealed.[30] "We do not obtain the most precious gifts by going in search of them," she insists, but "by waiting for them."[31] One could suggest that Weil's attentive individual has a relationship to time (and to possessive seeking) that is at base nomadic: while physically moving in territorial space, the nomad in another way "does not move," or "moves, but while seated, and is only seated while moving ... *The nomad knows how to wait, he has infinite patience.* Immobility and speed, catatonia and rush, a 'stationary process'" (TP, 381).[32]

A similar, equally paradoxical thesis is found in Weil's *oeuvre*: for her too, passive immobility is hardly something un-active. Certainly, Weil would never have used the term "speed"; she was adamant that speed was antithetical to attention.[33] Nevertheless, she thought that

attention and the radical passivity it called for were synonymous with
an effective or active power, the power to create and affirm. As we
will see, this is most critical for her unusual account of the political.
In fact, Weil challenged the positing of any strict, simplistic binary
between passivity and activity; repeatedly, we see her invoking the
notion of an "*action non-agissante*"[34] or of a "passive activity."[35] As
a philosopher with strong Pythagorean sensibilities, Weil saw nothing
strange in the idea that, at its highest level, attention could to be
regarded as a kind of harmony between opposites (i.e., activity and
passivity). Quite significantly for our purposes here, Weil associated
passivity with an *intensity* of desire (rather than its absence), a point
that has been underappreciated by some of her readers, who have
been misled by the frequent invocation of the term "passive." To *wait*
and attend "passively" upon a problem or a book, Weil insisted, was
much *more intense* (and fruitful) than purposefully and actively *searching*.[36] Indeed, to use the terms proposed by Murdoch (whose work
was profoundly shaped by her reading of Weil), attention ought to
be understood as a great "orientation, *direction* of energy not just a
[passive] state of mind."[37]

Naturally, Weil has more to say about attention than to simply
stress this dimension of patient waiting or "slowness." I consider
next two other important claims she makes about attention: namely,
that attention is tied to desire and not will; and that attention is
affirmative and creative (despite, paradoxically, being tied to destruction). Let us begin with the question of attention's link to the will.
Like other philosophers of attention, Weil was of the view that there
are different types or degrees of attention: if will might be involved
in the lower, more quotidian type of attention, it has no place in that
sustained, higher attention that she labelled "pure" or "directed"
(*attention dirigée*). In her early *and* later work, Weil was categorical:
pure attention has nothing to do with will – nothing to do with a
"tensing up of muscles," a frowning of the brow, an active search to
grasp.[38] But here her readers are confronted with some ambiguity:
for one thing, it is far from clear what *directing* one's attention
without willing might signify. Weil never fully worked out her conception of will, and she associated the term with possessiveness,
impatience, and precipitation – all of which, as we saw above, are
antithetical to attention.

More significantly, when Weil insisted that attention was not about
will, she typically qualified it with the claim that attention is a

longing, attention is love. In *Gravity and Grace,* she was explicit: "[A]ttention is bound up with desire. Not with the will, but with desire."[39] While one might be tempted to deduce from this that her account is anchored in strong emotionality, things are not that straightforward. The desire that nourishes attention – the desire that allows, say, a child to learn or a citizen to witness someone in need – is a desire for truth that Weil, as a good Platonist, understood as a kind of erotic pursuit of the Good.[40] Indeed, there is something radically Platonic and rationalist about Weilian attention (something that may, at least on certain readings, complicate any possible rapprochement between Weil and Deleuze). But what I would like to emphasize here is that despite the clear rationalist overtones of her account of attention, Weil does not leave behind immanence or the bodily. For one thing, the type of higher attention she deems so central to our ethico-political life is one "in which the whole soul *and body* participate."[41]

But more needs to be said about the nature of the desire that sustains Weilian attention. To begin with, Weil was of the view that for there to be desire (and for there to be some contact with the real, truth, or beauty), there has to be *joy.* Indeed, she insisted that without the presence of pleasure, contemplative pursuits are ineffective: "The intelligence can only be led by desire. For there to be desire, there must be pleasure and joy in the work. The intelligence only grows and bears fruit in joy."[42] This is not to diminish the difficulty or the pain that an apprenticeship in attention entails. But Weil was convinced that the most excruciating experiences can sometimes be the most rewarding and joyful; pain, indeed, can be a springboard to the affirmation of life and of necessity (a view that resonates with a Nietzschean outlook, although Weil would have shuddered at the comparison).[43] In one of her notebooks, she wrote that in order "to find reality in suffering, the revelation of reality must have come to one through joy."[44] In passages like these, one finds an erasing (or at least, a blurring) of the very distinction between suffering and joy.

Moreover, and somewhat paradoxically, Weil insists that the desire that nourishes attention must be intense yet empty. Desire must be empty in at least two senses: first, it must not be tied to any motive or longing to obtain certain things (praise, success, money, good grades, etc.). It must be a "desire without any wishes."[45] Second, and more importantly for Weil's ethics and politics, the desire that sustains attention must be empty of (socially engrained) prejudices, of egoistic passions and anxieties. Genuine attention requires us to stop projecting signifiers, preconceptions, or ambitions on those things or beings to which we attend. We have to put our "imagination" on hold, Weil argues, and try to stop our subjectivities from *imposing* meaning onto what is being attended to. In short, we must *look* at the world (and *listen*) without (pre)interpreting it.[46] What this entails, in her view, is an exit from our*selves*, a crushing of our egos. It is here that one finds a minor line of flight – one of the most idiosyncratic and disquieting dimensions of Weilian attention – if not of Weil's vision of politics altogether: attending meaningfully to the world or to another being requires, momentarily at least, a radical destruction of oneself, a *becoming* nothing, a "decreation."[47] Indeed, we must desire and consent to turn into *nothingness* in order to receive and to be able to see and appreciate what is different, what is not the same as oneself, what does not "fit" comfortably with one's existing world view, prejudices, and identity. At odds with a great deal of (majoritarian) ethical thought in the history of ideas, this self-dissolution is considered by Weil to be a highly desirable type of uprooting for a healthy ethical and political life: "All that I call 'I' has to be passive. Attention alone – that attention which is so full that the 'I' disappears – is required of me."[48] The Weilian view that in order to receive one first has to go through a process of emptying the self certainly speaks powerfully to what a minor ethics might entail at times. As Peter Zhang puts it, "becoming-minor" calls for "a clearing in the self so it can become a receiver," which "involves ego loss, ego being a hindrance against becoming."[49] Indeed, it is this Weilian attentive/decreated self that is most fit for engaging in minor politics, for witnessing and appreciating the singular, and for building more inclusive political communities. It is also this attentive self that is most likely to challenge the rigid, homogenizing, and controlling politics Weil associated with "molar" or large bureaucratic institutions – a challenge she certainly appreciated the immensity of. As Deleuze and Guattari emphasize in a passage that speaks to the trepidation – and hesitation – an attentive Weilian individual might experience vis-à-vis taking some distance from the "molar": "We are always afraid of losing. Our security, the great 'molar' organization that sustains us, the arborescences we cling to, the binary machines that give us a well-defined status, the resonances we enter into, the system of overcoding that dominates us – we desire all that" (TP, 227).

For now, however, let us look a bit more closely at why exactly decreation is considered such a meaningful ethico-political act. Weil liked to describe this process of unselfing as an exceedingly rare and highly radical act of generosity and love. But note that there is nothing sentimental here. As Murdoch rightly saw, Weilian attention is love only in the precise sense that it is the *unselfish perception* or recognition of others. Attention is, indeed, profoundly other-oriented. As Murdoch puts it: "love is the extremely difficult realization that *something other than oneself is real*."[50] This "difficult realization" that a marginalized individual matters – that a *malheureux* exists, that he is *there* with his needs and vulnerability – was something Weil considered of utmost consequence for justice. Indeed, Weil was repeatedly struck by the severe pain experienced by those with limited economic, cultural, and linguistic capital – those on the margins, the barely visible, the barely audible (the "sans-part" who do not count according to the police count, to borrow a phrase from Jacques Rancière). And it is because she was so concerned about these *sans-part*, whose voices are considered mere "noise" rather than cogent political speech, that Weil regarded attention as so critical for ethical and political life. Indeed, she claimed that no morality could ever replace attention and desire.[51] Because pure attention entails a (temporary) silencing of our prejudices, egoistic concerns, and motives, it can help us hear the dim or dissonant voices to which our "majoritarian" ears are deaf. Weil insisted that only the attentive individual can see the "invisible"; only she can hear and *comprehend* stammers and stuttering, acknowledging their existence as legitimate or genuine modes of *political speech*.[52] In an oft-cited passage, Weil explains that to attend to the excluded entails stopping and posing this very simple yet vital question of ethics (a question that, I would suggest, has too often been placed on the margins rather than at the centre of ethical thought – unlike the majoritarian question of ethics, "What is right?"): "What are you going through?" If informed by genuine compassionate concern (which Weil distinguishes from pity), this simple question has the power to offer "the recognition that the sufferer *exists*." Paradoxically, then, it is by destroying or decreating ourselves – by *fleeing from ourselves* – that we create, that we can affirm. "Through denying oneself, one becomes capable ... of affirming another through a creative affirmation."[53] It is in that sense that attention *is* recognition. One could say that attention spurs different, new capacities for receptivity, in part because it can trouble, loosen, or even crush (momentarily) our identities.

Now, Weil regarded this simultaneous decreation and creative affirmation of something/someone other than oneself as the most generous kind of love, but also as the most meaningful act of freedom (and the best route to what Murdoch summarized as "clarity of vision"). To *desire* is to consent to the real and to necessity. "There is absolutely no other free act which it is given us to accomplish – only the destruction of the 'I.'"[54] Filled with stoic overtones, Weil's account of attention/decreation is certainly pointing us in the direction of an *amor fati* (one that cannot be read, however, as minimizing the importance of a politics of social transformation). I want to underscore here that the element of consent in decreation is absolutely critical for appreciating the difference Weil draws between desirable and non-desirable types of uprooting.[55] Indeed, the destruction of the self that Weil praises and regards as the "heart" and catalyst of ethics and politics is a destruction that comes *from the self*; it is one that is consented to and desired. It is not the crushing of the self that is imposed from without; it is not the uprooting or crushing of the self that is the result of violence, conquest, rape, grave poverty, or chronic unemployment – forces that Weil regarded as uprooting the self in ways that were anything but conducive to affirmation, health, and joy.

This crucial distinction between two kinds of uprooting (one that is desired and one that is not) helps us make sense of the puzzling passage cited in the epigraph to this chapter, where Weil invites us to "uproot" ourselves. The confusion stems from the (partly correct) association of Weil's name with a *defence* of roots, most eloquently articulated in *The Need for Roots*. There Weil argued that the need to be rooted (in a city, a culture, a community, or in history) was one of the most important (if least understood) of all fundamental human needs.[56] But for Weil, being properly rooted required, first, a certain distancing or flight from one's own self, from one's prejudices and subjectivity. Being properly rooted also necessitated a flight from the "we" and from homogenous, hierarchical groups (as we will see in the next section). And in both of these processes of exiting or uprooting, *consent* has to be there – the flights must be desired. Now, what is worth underscoring here is that for Weil, a community that is properly rooted cannot be equated with some kind of political or cultural isolationism, or with a closed homogeneity: in *The Need for Roots*, she explicitly claims that what is required are "multiple roots"[57] and the *varied* (one could say, "rhizomatic") branching out and connecting with other root systems and subterranean environments.[58] Indeed, in the second part of *The Need For Roots*, Weil reminds her readers that dissimilar practices, cultures, and convictions should serve as "stimulants *intensifying* [a city]'s own particular way of life."[59]

2. FLIGHTS AWAY FROM THE "WE": WEIL ON PARTIES AND THE NOISE OF FACTORIES

Until now, my chief aim has been to explain what attention entails and why it requires a "trip" or departure away from ourselves, from our egos. Next, I look at what Weil has to say about the relationship between the attentive individual and certain groups, institutions, or "territories" that she considers most antithetical to the cultivation of attention and *most in need of* nomadic, deterritorializing practices. More specifically, we will consider attention as calling for a movement of exit from the following majoritarian systems: political parties and loud and hierarchically managed factories.[60] We will see that the Weilian attentive individual must, like the nomad, distance herself from the "we" and the undifferentiated masses; he must also muddy the old (and hierarchical) separation between manual and intellectual labour and undermine the excessively hierarchical and coded nature of centralized State structures and workplaces (cf. TP, 360–8).

Let us begin with the case of political parties. As noted above, it is Weil's proposal to abolish parties that has often informed the charge that she proposes an *anti-politics*.[61] In *The Need for Roots* and her *Note sur la suppression des partis politiques*[62] (both written when she worked for the French resistance in London in 1942), Weil delivered her most scorching critique of parties, insisting that postwar France should do away with them altogether. Her chief justification for such a radical measure was that party discipline and party rules/norms are antithetical to individual, critical thought and attention; they weigh too heavily on the mind of a party member and render impossible an attending to the vital needs of particular citizens. Weil is convinced that party discipline and the obsession parties develop with victory and fundraising are completely at odds with the quiet reflectivity, the solitude, silence, and freedom of thought that is necessary for careful political judgment and for attending to injustice, which requires attending to *singularities*. A representative cannot listen simultaneously to the voice of justice and the voice of her political party whip or leader. Weil writes: "It is impossible to examine the very complex problems of public life while being simultaneously attentive to, on the one hand, truth, justice and the public good and, on the other hand [the demands of] such groups. The human faculty of attention is not capable, simultaneously, of these two concerns. In fact, whoever cares for one abandons the other."[63] This is why Weil argued that *all* political associations and institutions should banish the "spirit of party," a spirit that renders impossible the hearing or "resounding" of minor voices – in particular, those of the *malheureux*.[64] Weil also believed that parties are groups that produce toxic "collective passions" that nourish an unhealthy, intolerant kind of patriotism – one that is too "molar" and rigid. Now, Weil did not deny that in a system without parties, elected representatives would continue to gravitate around certain constellations of projects or ideas.[65] But in her ideal constitution, these groups would be non-coercive and highly fluid, allowing individuals to come and go according to the particular issue at stake. Moreover, the practice of excommunication so prevalent in party systems would have no place; groupings would be more heterogeneous and representatives would be able to express disagreements without fear of reprisal.[66]

It is not just political parties that are the object of Weil's concern: most large, structured, and collectively codified bodies are deemed suspect. Partly as the result of her first-hand experience with union and party politics, Weil came to the (Rousseauian) conclusion that large-scale public deliberations rarely serve social justice or truth. She also objected to the Aristotelian thesis that humans have a natural and moral need for collective deliberation. Weil believed that critical thought and healthy politics cannot take place in what Deleuze and Guattari call a "majoritarian" mode; they can only arise in a "minor" mode and without too much in the way of group "communication" (anticipating, in a way, Deleuze's later provocative invitation to have more "non-communication," that is, "little gaps of solitude and silence in which they might eventually find something to say" [N, 129]).[67] In *The Need for Roots,* Weil writes that "intelligence resides only in the human being considered alone. There is no such thing as a collective exercise of intelligence."[68] In her view, majoritarian deliberations too often end up in dogmatic, intolerant thinking: the "we" undermines the "I," the group tends to undercut individual reflection.[69] Hence, the highest work of the mind will require some solitude: "Not only concrete, factual solitude, but also moral solitude." Indeed, *critical* contemplative pursuits cannot take place "in one who thinks of himself as a member of a collectivity, as one part of a 'we'."[70] In turn, Deleuze and Guattari portray the nomadic thinker also as solitary, or (to use terminology they admit is inadequate) as tending to be a "private thinker" (TP, 376–7). As such, it is not incorrect for Mengue to observe that there is, in Deleuze's account of the (counter)philosopher, a heavy dose of solitude and uprooting.[71] The same observation could certainly be made about the Weilian nomad. She herself explicitly admitted that her concern for justice and her quest for the truth required a nomadism, an uprooting, and a distancing from several institutions. As she wrote to her friend Father Perrin (in the context of a discussion of her decision to remain *outside* the Roman Catholic Church): "I do not want to be adopted into a circle, to live among people who say 'we' and to be part of an 'us' ... I feel that it is necessary and ordained that *I should be alone, a stranger and an exile in relation to every human circle without exception.*"[72]

Must this exile of the philosopher be understood geographically? Not necessarily. A Weilian nomad need not travel anywhere. Yes, certainly, Weil herself was forced into exile; and her intellectual output was no doubt shaped by her travel experiences (in Italy, in Spain, and in fascist Germany most notably). But what our minor ethics' perspective on attention reminds us of is that a truly attentive individual needs not necessarily move *in space* in order to engage in deterritorializing gestures, in careful and critical reflectivity. As Deleuze puts it in his characterization of Nietzsche, nomadism's most exemplary figure: "the nomad is not necessarily one who moves: some voyages take place *in situ*, are trips in intensity. ... [He stays] in the same place and continually evade[s] the codes of settled people."[73]

Now, what Weil says about the attentive philosopher equally applies to the factory worker, whom she considered as apt for contemplation and for contact with the Real as any philosophy professor (if not more): there is no need for him to *completely* set himself *outside* of his physical milieu in order to set out a line of flight. But in both cases (philosopher and worker), the individual needs to take a (mental) distance and to be given more opportunities for silence. "One must persuade the person that she must not let herself drown into the collective, but let the impersonal grow in her. This growth necessitates silence."[74] Note that when Weil invokes the term "silence," she means it more than metaphorically. She considered it urgent to replace overly noisy, hierarchical, and large-scale factories with small workshops where more worker autonomy could be found, and more flexible working arrangements, and a much more fluid line between home and work, and, last but not least, more silence, more peace. She urged her readers to find ways to reduce the excessive noise produced by too many machines operating in too large a space; but she also urged them to diminish the excessive noise and brutality that comes from large, hierarchical structures, where loud foremen *need* to yell in order to heighten (or maintain) discipline, control, and efficiency. Nothing could be less conducive to the cultivation or exercise of attention in a worker: "man needs warm silence, [modern workplaces] give him cold tumult."[75]

Note that another goal sought by Weil through the creation of *smaller* factories and workshops is to pave the way for a more desirable reconciliation between intellectual and manual labour.[76] Weil was convinced that to engage meaningfully in work, a worker needs to have a fair amount of control over his work pace and the organization of his milieu, but he also needs to have a solid *understanding* of the technology used. The Weilian exit or line of flight from large factories (and from large State bureaucracies for that matter) is indeed motivated by the hope of undermining hyper-specialization, and also of undermining an overly strict division and hierarchy between intellectual and manual labour.[77]

If the harsh reality of noisy, hierarchical, and inhuman factories may seem like a remote phenomenon to many twenty-first-century North American readers, one might wish to consider whether the old tumult of 1930s factories (and that of party or union politics) has not been supplanted by another kind of noise that is perhaps equally problematic for the cultivation of our capacity to attend: namely, the constant buzz of social media. Weil would certainly have been concerned by the unprecedented amount of information, stimulants, "likes," and tweets with which individuals are bombarded; and she would have interrogated the view that this constant buzz and great abundance of information will lead to more critical thinking, to more robust forms of individuality, or to the hearing and resounding of minor voices. Rather like legal theorist Cass Sunstein,[78] Weil would probably have underscored the *limited* potential of social media for increasing reflectivity or enabling a more democratic and inclusive politics. Were she alive today, Weil would have invited us to embrace another kind of "exit," another kind of flight away from the noisy "we": namely, through the intermittent turning off of some of our technological devices, and through the embracing of a more slow-paced, quieter encounter with the world.

3. CONCLUSION

Make rhizomes, not roots, never plant!

Deleuze and Guattari (TP, 24)

As we noted above, Weil's indictment of large, centralized, and hier-archical structures does not concern just parties and factories. In her "Reflections Concerning the Causes of Liberty and Social Oppression," Weil identified "centralization" as one of modernity's two main ills – one that compromised thought, justice, and human encounters everywhere that this centralization was found (be it unions, enterprises, bureaucracies, parties, or the school system). In all cases, what this centralization came down to was a deep "contempt for the individual."[79] In *Allons-nous vers la révolution prolétarienne*, she observed that the main obstacle to emancipation was the "bureaucratic machine" that "excludes all judgement and all genius [and] tends, in itself, to a totalizing power."[80] Much of her *oeuvre* (and her disquieting proposals and observations about parties, factories, and "the social") ought to be read as a passionate attempt to overturn that contempt and to ensure that the singular and the heterogeneous are not crushed by a "we," that is, by the homogeneous. In practical terms, this required various measures of *decentralization*[81]; it also required diverse deterritorializing practices to allow the individual to distance herself from majoritarian, heavily coded groups or institutions.

On the whole, then, what a Deleuzian minor ethics lens allows us to appreciate is Weil's clear preference for the *micro* over the *macro*. Indeed, I would insist that her politics (and her ethics) are both, overall, pitched in a minor mode and articulated at the micro. A fresher account of (Weilian) society and of our common world might flow from this: "From the viewpoint of micropolitics, a society is defined by its lines of flight, which are molecular. There is always something that flows or flees, that escapes the binary organizations, the resonance apparatus, and the overcoding machine" (TP, 227). Now, Weil's "lines of flight" from groups and territories might at times strike some readers as overly negative and destructive and, partly for that very reason, hardly conducive to any form of political action or solidarity. But let us note that Weil certainly did *not* think it possible to realize anything *without* the macro levels of the political. Weil was of the view that for these micropolitical "exits" to mean anything, they had to "come back" to or reconnect with what Deleuze and Guattari termed "molar organizations." Deterritorializing movements, we learn in *A Thousand Plateaus,* are typically followed by a *reterritorialization* (TP, 306). In her depictions of these more positive, affirmative moments of *reterritorialization,* Weil showed a clear penchant for the local, the horizontal, and the small over the national, the vertical, and the large.[82] Indeed, in her preference for small workshops, for fluid ideological groupings, and for local cooperatives, we can see the contours of what an *affirmative* (positive) follow-up step of what Weilian deterritorialization would consist in.

Hence, to underscore Simone Weil's preference for the local/fluid is not meant to suggest that Weil "gave up" completely on "rigid" molar institutions. For one thing, she never thought that an abolition of the state apparatus was desirable (Weil was no anarchist, despite having fought at their side in Spain). On the contrary, she thought that some majoritarian or state institutions could be improved or radically transformed by working, for instance, on the *character* of the individuals who hold positions in them. As she made clear in her late London writings, Weil was of the view that a less rigid, less alienating, and less homogeneous state bureaucracy was possible if the recruitment (and education) of civil servants was better done, specifically if *attention* and listening skills were considered to be the most vital competence an official could have. In many respects, then, Weil's political ideal is located at the juncture of the molar and the molecular. It may be appropriate to see in Weil, following Rodrigo Nunes's work on Deleuze, a "politics in the middle."[83]

This chapter has suggested that the Weilian and Deleuzian perspectives on the ethical and the political share a common invitation to break free from the confines of certain "territories" and to be nomadic, that is, to walk away from a majoritarian "we." But when we look to the ends of Weil and Deleuze's respective deterritorializations, we note one significant difference: Deleuze's efforts to become nomadic could be said to have a more self-oriented purpose. For Weil, the chief purpose of this decentring, this escape from the confines of the mental territory, was to enable us to break free from our obsessive focus on the self. As we saw earlier, Weil's attention as deterritorialization is radically other-oriented: it is chiefly to be understood as a means to hear the voices of the afflicted, a route to hyper-receptivity. It is so because it compels us to put aside the rigid identity markers and the epistemological presuppositions of our (privileged) majoritarian mode.

Indeed, that mode can render us deaf to marginal voices or unable to account for class/racial/gender markers that crisscross groups messily and, as such, "fit" nowhere in the strict binaries of the majoritarian mode and of molar institutions.

Now, if it is certainly inappropriate to charge Deleuze's micropolitics with being anti-political, his thought nevertheless seems to point *away* from attention toward *vulnerable* others. Weil's is, in this sense, more political in my view. All of this is partly tied to another fundamental (if obvious) difference between the two authors. For Weil, there is an ultimate, transcendent source for normativity – a position that Deleuze could not possibly contemplate. Weil was clearly not, to use Nietzsche's phrase, "beyond good and evil"; she held on to a thick conception of the Good and had no qualms about making strong normative, moral judgments. She would have had little patience, for instance, with the following passage in Deleuze and Guattari: "We cannot say that one of [these] lines is bad and another good, by nature and necessarily. The study of the dangers of each line ... is to make maps" (TP, 227; cf. 372). Now, this is not to suggest that there is no normativity in Deleuze's work; I rather tend to be sympathetic to Patton's view that there is indeed some nested there.[84] Yet Weil holds on much more firmly to "the sky" and locates, in that transcendent realm, the source of what is most sacred in human beings; she sought much more than to "make maps." If Weil sought to deracinate, it was not merely to plant a rhizome: it was to fix the roots firmly where she thought they truly belonged. As she observed in an essay penned shortly before her premature death: "[t]he roots of the tree are located in the sky."[85]

NOTES

1 See also Alain Badiou, "Existe-t-il quelque chose," 15–20. Some have tried to explain Deleuze's apparent indifference for politics as the result of his infatuation with Nietzsche; see Paul Patton, "Deleuze's Political Philosophy." Compare this approach with Nathan Widder, *Political Theory after Deleuze.*

2 Peter Hallward, *Out of This World,* 162.

3 For example, see Žižek, *Organs without Bodies*; and Mengue, *Deleuze.* These accounts should be compared with those of Houle, "Micropolitics"; and Buchanan and Thoburn, *Deleuze and Politics. Contra* Mengue, Patton

insists that "there is no fundamental incompatibility between Deleuze's political thought and democratic politics." *Deleuzian Concepts*, 162.

4 Mengue, *Deleuze*, 170. Cf. Véronique Bergen's insightful discussion of the *political* significance of "posture" in "La politique."

5 Mengue, *Deleuze*, 135. Editor's translation of "théorisation du pouvoir de l'État ... et des conditions d'un rapport légitime entre les puissances historiques."

6 Holland, "Nomadologie affirmative."

7 Patton, "Deleuze's Political Philosophy."

8 Gilbert, "A Deleuzian Politic?"

9 Houle, "Micropolitics."

10 See Bickford, *The Dissonance of Democracy*; and Courtine-Denamy, *Trois femmes*. While Mary G. Dietz largely challenges the idea of a strict distinction between an "early" political and a "mature" spiritual Weil, she nevertheless underscores the huge importance that the "divine" took on after 1940; *Between the Human and the Divine*.

11 O'Brien, "The Anti-Politics," 2.

12 Bickford, *Dissonance of Democracy*.

13 Janiaud, "Simone Weil et l'attention," 177.

14 At the end of *A Thousand Plateaus*, "deterritorialization" is most succinctly defined as "the movement by which 'one' leaves the territory. It is the operation of the line of flight" (TP, 508).

15 Obviously, these "exits" can take many forms and be more (or less) able to create "new earths" (AO, 131, 299, 318–19, 321, 382). Unfortunately, within the confines of this chapter I cannot enter into a detailed discussion of the various types of deterritorialization. For a succinct account, see TP, 508–10.

16 Murdoch, *Existentialists and Mystics*, 348 (my emphasis).

17 Weil, *Écrits de Londres*, 36, 177. All Weil translations from the French editions cited below are my own.

18 When Weil speaks of the "Great Beast," she has in mind Plato's depiction of the "great blob" of the *demos*'s opinions and prejudices (*Republic*, Book VI, 493a-d); see Weil, *Gravity and Grace*, 164–9.

19 Weil, *Gravity and Grace*, 39.

20 In a *Thousand Plateaus*, the term "molar" is used in contradistinction to the term "molecular" to characterize the realm of the State and of large (and highly perceptible) bureaucratic and civic institutions.

21 For example, see Susan Sontag, "Simone Weil." What Sontag sees in Weil is martyrdom, "contempt for pleasure and for happiness," "elaborate self-denials," and the "tireless courting of affliction." Ibid., 51. See also Jean Bethke Elshtain, "The Vexation of Simone Weil."

22 Naturally, countless other differences between the two authors could be highlighted here. While Weil calls for critical "exits" and uprooting, she is more appreciative of the moral importance of cultural and *historical* rooting, whereas Deleuze and Guattari offer a sustained critique of historical and cultural sedentariness or "sedimentation" (TP, 23–4). Also, Weil is more at ease with some hierarchy (hierarchy is one of the needs of the soul she lists in *The Need for Roots*, although equality is also deemed central).

23 For more details about Weil's life, see Simone Pétrément, *La vie de Simone Weil*.

24 Weil, *Waiting for God*.

25 "*Malheur*" (affliction) is a Weilian term of art; see *Waiting for God*, 67–71. Affliction entails physical suffering but also, simultaneously and more importantly, "social degradation," humiliation, and non-recognition.

26 Weil, *Écrits de Londres*, 36.

27 Ibid., 177.

28 Ibid., 160.

29 Weil, *Waiting for God*, 62.

30 Weil, *Gravity and Grace*, 116.

31 Weil, *Waiting for God*, 62.

32 Much could be said about Deleuze and Guattari's distinction between "movement" (as extensive) and "speed" (as intensive), which may strain the comparison with Weil (cf. WP, 21).

33 For a lengthier discussion about the connections between Weilian attention, speed, and what has been referred to as the "slow movement" (whether in scholarship, at work, or in life more generally), see Bourgault, "Attentive Listening and Care."

34 Weil, *Œuvres*, 885.

35 Ibid., 752.

36 Ibid., 753.

37 Murdoch, *Metaphysics as a Guide to Morals*, 503.

38 Weil, *Gravity and Grace*, 116-7. Note that Weil is not perfectly consistent here: if in most places she posits a stark distinction between will and attention, a few passages of her notebooks and *Waiting for God* suggest otherwise: see ibid., 59; and *Oeuvres complètes*, vol. 1, 390.

39 Weil, *Gravity and Grace*, 118.

40 "Love is the teacher of gods and men, for no one learns without desiring to learn. Truth is sought not because it is truth but because it is good. Attention is bound up with desire." Ibid., 118.

41 Ibid., 24 (my emphasis).

42 Ibid., 61.

43 As one can gather from her correspondence, Weil was both profoundly attracted to and repulsed by Nietzsche in whom she saw too much gloom and anxiety. If Nietzsche was Deleuze's "nomadic" thinker *par excellence* (see DI, 260) and the one he painted as an exceedingly joyful philosopher, Weil certainly had a different view. In Nietzsche, she saw "a sadness linked to the deprivation of any sense of Happiness; [he] needs to be annihilated" (*une tristesse liée à la privation du sens même du Bonheur; [il] a besoin de s'anéantir*). But notice how she justifies her refusal to read Nietzsche: "*Even when he expresses ideas that I share*, Nietzsche is still literally intolerable to me" (*Même quand il exprime des choses que je pense*, il m'est littéralement intolérable" (my emphasis); *Oeuvres completes*, vol. 7, pt. 1, 474–5 (my emphasis).

44 Weil, *Notebooks*, 291.

45 Weil, *Gravity and Grace*, 13.

46 For more on the Weilian concept of reading, see her essay on *lecture* in *Œuvres completes*, vol. 4, pt. 2; and *Gravity and Grace*, 134–6.

47 For detailed discussions of this complex Weilian notion, see Miklos Vetö, *La métaphysique religieuse*; J.P. Little, "Simone Weil's Concept of Decreation"; and Janiaud, "Simone Weil et le déracinement du moi."

48 Weil, *Gravity and Grace*, 118.

49 Zhang, "Gilles Deleuze and Minor Rhetoric," 224; cf. Braidotti, "Nomadic Ethics."

50 Murdoch, *Existentialists and Mystics*, 215 (my emphasis).

51 Weil, *Œuvres*, 754.

52 Ibid., 730.

53 Ibid., 725

54 Weil, *Gravity and Grace*, 26.

55 Ibid., 26-8.

56 Weil, *The Need for Roots*, 43–5.

57 Ibid., 43.

58 Weil would have been comfortable with Deleuze and Guattari's idea that a multiplicity must be "connected to other multiplicities by superficial underground stems in such a way as to form or extend a rhizome" (TP, 22).

59 Weil, *The Need for Roots*, 43 (my emphasis).

60 Other "territories" that are the object of her ire are the Roman Catholic church, the "media," and advertisers.

61 O'Brien, "The Anti-Politics of Simone Weil."

62 Weil, *On the Abolition of All Political Parties.*

63 Weil, *Écrits de Londres*, 139.

64 Ibid., 32, 132–4.

65 Ibid., 144.

66 Ibid., 140.

67 "Stupidity's never blind or mute. So it's not a problem of getting people to express themselves, but of providing little gaps of solitude and silence in which they might eventually find something to say. Repressive forces don't stop people expressing themselves but rather force them to express themselves. What a relief to have nothing to say, the right to say nothing, because only then is there a chance of framing the rare, and ever rarer, thing that might be worth saying. What we're plagued by these days isn't any blocking of communication, but pointless statements" (Deleuze, N, 129–30).

68 Weil, *The Need for Roots*, 25.

69 "[When] a group starts having opinions, it inevitably tends to impose them on its members." Ibid., 27.

70 Weil, *Écrits de Londres*, 17.

71 Mengue, *Deleuze*, 170.

72 Weil, *Waiting for God*, 13 (my emphasis).

73 Deleuze, "Nomad Thought," 149.

74 Weil, *Écrits de Londres*, 155.

75 Ibid., 22.

76 Weil, *Œuvres*, 271.

77 This is central for what Deleuze and Guattari call the form of "Royal science" (TP, 361–94).

78 See Ch. 1, "The Daily Me" of Cass Sunstein, *Republic.com 2.0*.

79 Weil, *Oppression and Liberty*, 113.

80 Weil, *Oeuvres*, 265.

81 Weil, *Oppression and Liberty*, 113–17.

82 Although Deleuze and Guattari very frequently insist that the distinction between the micro and macro is *not* about size (see TP, 217; N, 173), I think that it is not completely insignificant for thinking about what the distinction means (see Holland, "Nomadologie affirmative").

83 Nunes, "Politics in the Middle."

84 Patton, *Deleuzian Concepts*.

85 Weil, *Écrits de Londres*, 30.

9

Toward a Minor Ethics of the Impersonal Life: Gilles Deleuze and Roberto Esposito

Antonio Calcagno

Roberto Esposito urges us to recognize and address the challenges posed by globalization, large-scale migration, climate change, the crisis of Europe, and massive shifts in geopolitics.[1] At the core of his philosophy lies a rethinking of central ethical and political concepts, including life, politics, and the person, that he feels need to be reconceived outside of our highly governmentalized, global, liberal, and economic world. The concepts of the person and life have been deployed in Western philosophy to denote a specific realm of ownership that is proper to an individual, a realm of ownership that can be said to be increasingly governmentalized and, therefore, majoritarian, to borrow an expression from Gilles Deleuze. Esposito, drawing on Deleuze and Simone Weil, argues that concomitant with the concept of the person, we find the minoritarian concept of the "impersonal." The interplay between the concepts of the governmentalized, majoritarian person and the minoritarian impersonal may be read as manifesting a minoritarian ethics in which a realm of human existence resists majoritarian pressure while articulating itself as a care for the very becoming of life.

I understand *governmentalization* in the Foucaultian sense, that is, as the power of modern bureaucratic governments to fix and then control populations and the lives of individuals through the enforcement of certain policies, laws, and conventions. For example, health policies and access to medical services controlled by the state have a profound impact on people's physical well-being. Policies on immunization, cost–benefit analyses for determining the distribution of funds and services in hospitals, drug testing and licensing (relevant here is the case of retroviral medications to treat AIDS patients and access to such medicines in the late 1990s), the payment regimes of doctors and nurses – all of these are instruments used by governments to create populations and then control those populations via their health. Following Foucault, Esposito claims that as populations increase, governments extend their control over them through greater governmentalization with the result that people's lives – especially their physical, biological lives – become more and more subject to restrictions and decisions that are not necessarily their own and that also cannot be traced to a sole active agent who can be held responsible or accountable. For example, the decision of Italy's Salvini–Di Maio coalition government to strip, through a series of bills and bureaucratic changes, the daily subsistence allowance for migrants and refugees – and to take from them certain passes/permissions entitling them to medical assistance, temporary employment, and access to education – resulted in new groups of stateless and rightsless people seeking shelter in Italy. The effects of these disastrous decisions can be seen directly in the Calabrian town of Riace, where the mayor Domenico Lucano was arrested and townspeople and refugees were pitted against one another in an excruciating battle for survival. A once peaceful coexistence is now marked with tension and strife. Esposito also discusses in numerous places the effects that new technologies – especially prostheses, new antiviral medications, and genetic modification – have on how science conceives of and controls biological life. Technological advances have brought with them a corresponding drastic modification of the lives of large populations on whom these technologies come to bear. Through governmentalized control of scientific advances, the social and political lives of vast populations will be increasingly affected by modes of technological control of individuals' basic physical, biological lives. For example, the growing resistance to antibiotics is about to become a crisis, and when it does, it is likely that significant portions of the population will be killed by the rise of superviruses. Governments will tightly control who has access to experimental and new antibiotics, thereby controlling the basic biological lives of individuals. In this way, we will be returning to the essence of political power: the power to decide who lives and who dies.

Esposito draws upon Gilles Deleuze's essay "Immanence: A Life"[2] to articulate what he calls the "third person." Like Deleuze's "a life," Esposito's notion of the third person or the impersonal – a term borrowed from Simone Weil – offers a conception of a person's life as made up of virtualities, events, and singularities. A person's life, because of its potential to actualize itself in unforeseen ways, holds within itself the potential configuration of forces to resist the large-scale, majoritarian governmental determinations that have come to shape modern life. The person's life is inscribed in what Spinoza and Deleuze tell us is a "plane of immanence" that is actualized in subjects and objects, or what Esposito calls "bodies." If ethics is a way of thinking about how we should live with one another, what do Esposito and Deleuze, through these new concepts, offer us by way of insights into collective, personal life? I argue that we can read Esposito and Deleuze as uncovering a zone or aspect of life that can resist oppressive governmentalization, not by opposition but by virtue of life's power to create new forms of impersonal embodiment and individuation. This zone of life can thus virtually bring forward new ethical possibilities that may be described as minoritarian: new actions, bodies, collectivities, ways of being and acting, and relationships. Esposito's transindividuated, embodied person – for example, the unified voice of a people demanding justice and change – gives rise to a new form of collectivity that cuts through groups of individuals, and the virtuality that Deleuze sees as immanent to "a life" allows that new collectivity to act, to respond. The response engendered by a new collective body can respond to oppression, violence, and injustice in an ethical way by trying to preserve and save a life that is on the cusp of death, to heal a body that has been deprived of food, water, and shelter. *Life itself* calls forward a collective response to suffering, and in this sense the work of Deleuze and Esposito may be viewed as offering readers a minoritarian ethics that lies outside classical normative accounts of ethics rooted in majoritarian notions of the state, rational duty, utility, or happiness: a life, the impersonal life, makes a demand and creates the possibility of an ethical response to the social and political strictures of life.

I. DELEUZE: A LIFE

Deleuze's beautiful and moving essay "Immanence: A Life" presents a partial answer to the ever elusive question: What is life? Life is never described as a whole, systemic, organic being. What this means is that the governmentalization that names, counts, and controls has its sights on organic beings, and hence does not have control over the entire "life" of individuals. Rather, life, as Deleuze conceives it, is highly individuated and there exists a multiplicity of individuations of life (there are lives). Deleuze describes an encounter with an individual person, a person who lives in the world in a way akin to Charles Dickens's "disreputable man," "the rogue" who lies dying and who is held in contempt by everyone around him.[3] The rogue can be understood as occupying a certain place in society, a place determined by economic, social, ethical, and political structures – that is, by governmentalizing structures. The rogue never self-identifies as a "rogue"; rather, as Deleuze's description makes clear, it is *society* that views him as a rogue. Society determines that, being a rogue, he should be separated out of the usual collective structure that binds people into some acceptable form of Victorian sociality. We know he is separate from "good society" because the rogue himself, as he revives at one point in the story, has contempt for those around him; but we also know that prior to the rogue's illness, no one is near the rogue: people stay away from him.

Deleuze tells us, in dramatic terms, that as the man lies dying he is, in fact, attended to by all kinds of people. The man is lapsing into a coma, and Deleuze describes how Dickens portrays the reaction of those surrounding him: a liminal stage between social life and death emerges. "Suddenly," Deleuze writes,

> those taking care of him manifest an eagerness, respect, even love, for his slightest sign of life. Everybody bustles about to save him, to the point where, in his deepest coma, this wicked man himself sees something soft and sweet penetrating him. But to the degree that he comes back to life, his saviors turn colder, and he becomes once again mean and crude. Between his life and his death, there is a moment that is only that of a life playing with death.[4]

What becomes visible is a life, but whose life is it? What kind of life is it?

One could easily say it is the life that belongs to the dying man, the governmentalized "rogue," but it could also be the life that manifests itself in the collective activity around the dying man – a collective life, not confined to one body, but across different individuated bodies: the collective recognizes that there is *a* life at stake, and they also conjointly live the intensity of that life. We have before us the sheer man with whom everyone empathizes. Deleuze notes the life of the individual gives way to an impersonal and yet singular life that releases a pure event freed from the accidents of internal and external life, that is from the subjectivity and the objectivity of what happens: a "*Homo tantum*" with whom everyone empathizes and who attains a sort of beatitude. It is a haecceity no longer of individuation but of singularization: a life of pure immanence, neutral, beyond good and evil, for it was only the subject that incarnated it in the midst of things that made it good or bad. The life of such an individuality fades away in favor of the singular life immanent to a man who no longer has a name, though he came to be mistaken for no other. A singular essence, a life.[5]

One would be mistaken to think and to read "individuation" or "singularization" simply in terms of the oneness of identity or the self-same: the one who, in classical ethical terms, "deserves" to be treated with dignity by virtue of some property inherent to him, or who has a right to medical intervention because he is a citizen of a state with legal status; rather, in this conception and in the realm of ethical possibility, there is a relation between the *homo tantum* and those working around him. There is also the relation between the life of the man in the world and his singularity. The current social and political determinations of subjectivity and objectivity – or, for Esposito, the person and the thing – obscure a life, *the impersonal*. Deleuze tells us that "a life is everywhere":

> But we shouldn't enclose life in the single moment when individual life confronts universal death. *A* life is everywhere, in all moments that a given living subject goes through and that are measured by given lived objects: an immanent life carrying with it the events or singularities that are merely actualized in subjects and objects. This indefinite life does not itself have moments, close as they may be one to another, but only between-times, between-moments [something like Bergson's *interval*]; it doesn't just come about or come after but offers the immensity of an empty time where one sees the event yet to come and already happened, in the absolute of an immediate consciousness ... The singularities and the events that constitute *a* life coexist with the accidents of *the* life that corresponds to it.[6]

Instead of seeing "a" life as the *one of identity*, Deleuze posits a different kind of One: "The indefinite article [i.e., *a*] is the indetermination of the person only because it is determination of the singular. The One is not the transcendent that might contain immanence but the immanent contained within a transcendental field. One is always the index of multiplicity: an event, a singularity, a life."[7] The indeterminacy emerges not only in the rogue, as his usual societal place is forgotten as he moves toward death, but also in those who attend to him, as they too forget the sharp distinction between good or legitimate society and the rogue. Furthermore, there is an indeterminacy that is collective: rogue and people are joined together in a new undertaking, a new event or becoming of life that is shared among them all. Deleuze notes in *Difference and Repetition* that indeterminacy – that "fringe of determination which surrounds individuals and the relative, floating and fluid character of individuality" – is to be understood not as incompleteness but as an affirmation of power that is not confined to traditional models that privilege the centrality of the self or the I: "The error ... is to believe that this indetermination or this relativity indicates something incomplete in individuality or something interrupted in individuation. On the contrary, they express the full, positive power of the individual as such, and the manner in which it is distinguished in nature from both I and a self" (DR, 258). The rogue, then, is to be viewed not as an incomplete person, but as someone who is potentially able to become *more* through a series of new relations and the ethical care of others.

Moreover, the multiplicity Deleuze speaks of refers to a life, the singular life of the dying man; it is not a life that is confined to his rogue, disreputable life as determined by society; rather, it is a life that moves across individuals. Deleuze observes: "For example, small children all resemble one another and have hardly any individuality, but they have singularities: a smile, a gesture, a funny face – not subjective qualities. Small children, through all their sufferings and weaknesses, are infused with an immanent life that is pure power and even bliss. The indefinite aspects in a life lose all indetermination to the degree that they fill out a plane of immanence."[8] The plane of immanence is not understood as an immanence in life; rather, "the immanent that is in nothing is itself a life."[9] The immanence of a life "is not *in* something, *to* something," but rather is in itself. For Deleuze, the immanence of a life is the impersonal, that is, it refers to all that cannot be personalized, measured, or counted by a subject or governmentalized by society and biopolitical forms of power. As we will argue, the indetermination of a life that Deleuze discusses in his work may be read as similar to Esposito's idea of the impersonal. They play similar roles in releasing a dimension of life from life, thus allowing a minor ethical possibility to come into our view.

But what exactly allows the impersonal to configure itself? Deleuze tells us that the "virtualities," as events or singularities, that make up a life refer to a reality that is the "process of actualization":

> A life contains only virtualities, events, singularities. What we call virtual is not something that lacks reality but something that is engaged in a process of actualization following the plane that gives it its particular reality. The immanent event is actualized in a state of things and of the lived that makes it happen. The plane of immanence is itself actualized in an object and a subject to which it attributes itself. But however inseparable an object and a subject may be from their actualization, the plane of immanence is itself virtual, so long as the events that populate it are virtualities. Events or singularities give to the plane all their virtuality, just as the plane of immanence gives virtual events their full reality. The event considered as non-actualized (indefinite) is lacking in nothing. It suffices to put it in relation to its concomitants: a transcendental field, a plane of immanence, a life, singularities. A wound is incarnated or actualized in a state of things or of life; but it is itself a pure virtuality on the plane of immanence that leads us into a life. My wound existed before me: not a transcendence of the wound as higher actuality, but its immanence as a virtuality always within a milieu (plane or field).[10]

Because the immanence of a life is virtual, it becomes as the event becomes, and its becoming is not simply a repetition of what was prior, nor is it the extension of cause and effect. Classical ethical notions depend on the establishment of cause and effect in order to establish both guilt and responsibility, whereas Deleuze's and Esposito's concepts of a life or the impersonal do not exclusively depend on the majoritarian logics of agency and action. "A life" is marked by the newness of a process of potentiality becoming actual, a process marked by a certain intensity of duration. Here the emphasis is on a potential becoming that has ethical possibilities as opposed to the determined end result of an act. For example, Deleuze tell us that the dying rogue becomes the life of a collective as it tries to maintain life; the rogue is not simply what governmentalizing society has determined him to be as he lives in the world.

2. ESPOSITO'S IMPERSONAL

Esposito's recent essay *Le persone e le cose*[11] (*Persons and Things*) extends Deleuze's foregoing discussion of subject and object, but in relation to broader conceptualizations of persons and things. The Italian philosopher notes, like Deleuze, that there is a gap between the governmentalized determinations or actualizations of subjects and objects in political society, which are intimately related to each other, and the virtuality of a life or the "impersonal."[12] Esposito sees life as constituted by the "immunological" relation between the actual and the virtual, but one in which all actualizations and determinations of biological life are ordered by an ever more powerful political order that has at its disposal the means to make and control life through various technologies and practices. In his work *Immunitas*, Esposito carefully charts how cell biologists changed their models of cell life, pathology, and death, especially through the interventions of Xavier Bichat and Rudolf Virchow, to show the borders between the becoming of life and life in its more established forms as well as the blurred borders between living and dying.[13] For both Esposito and Deleuze, the life of the impersonal resists socio-political, governmentalized determinations and actualizations. But the resistance in Deleuze is stronger than it is in Esposito, for Esposito argues that the real transcendence that Deleuze associates with immanence is not always and necessarily possible; there are times when social and political determinations will completely destroy life rather than control its course, for example, in the concentration camps of the twentieth century. Life for the Jews had become so thoroughly depersonalized that resistance became impossible for many; they were thoroughly determined by the dehumanization of Nazi subjection and violence. There is potential, however, for other forms of life to arise in Esposito's model. Deleuze situates indeterminacy at the very core of an individual's life, in the lives of the rogue and his attendants. Indeterminacy is there, always operating. Resistance to the governmental, the arboreal, or the personalization imposed by social and political forces lies within the impersonal. Both thinkers maintain the existence of a zone of a life that is impersonal, but for Deleuze, the resistance capacities of the impersonal to governmentalization lie in virtuality, singularity, and the event, whereas for Esposito the resisting power of the impersonal lies in the body, in embodiment or incorporation, which unites both person and thing, both subject and object – an embodiment that resists the very determinations or actualizations imposed upon things and persons. What we have here are two claims about the nature of the impersonal: on the one hand, it is a life that contains virtualities, events, and singularities; on the other, the impersonal appears as a body. I maintain that Esposito's concept of body can be understood in much the same way as the virtual, as a set of collective relations that exist in the bodies attending to the body of Dickens's rogue. I also wish to argue that such a view of the body carries with it ethical implications, albeit minoritarian ones.

Esposito claims that both the concepts and the realities of persons and things have been overdetermined either by social and political realities or by philosophy, in particular, metaphysics. This has ultimately resulted in the flattening and even destruction of the full, living realities of both persons and things. The person and the thing have been largely determined by or subjected to a regime of Western legal property ownership.[14] For example, the thing is defined by an owner's use, disposal, and even destruction of the thing.[15] The relation between legal persons is conditioned by the things they use, dispose of, destroy, and enjoy. Concerning the person, Esposito notes:

This variance is an integral part of the category of person since its earliest beginnings. It has been well established that the Greek etymology of the term refers to the theatrical mask placed on the actor's face, but precisely for this reason the *persona* was never identical to the face. The word later referred to the type of character depicted in the play, but this, too, was never the same as the actor who interpreted it from one occasion to the next. The law seems to have reproduced this element of duality or duplicity at the heart of humanity. *Persona* was not the individual as such, but only its legal status, which varied on the basis of its power relationships with others. Not surprisingly, when ancient Romans referred to their role in life, they used the expression *persona habere* (literally, "to have a person"). *Persona* was not what one is, but what one has, like a faculty that, precisely for this reason, you could also lose. That is why, unlike what is commonly assumed, the paradigm of person produced not a union but a separation. It separated not only some from others on the basis of particular social roles, but also the individual from its biological entity. Being something other than the mask that it wore, the individual was always exposed to a possible depersonalization, defined as *capitis dimunutio*, which could go as far as the complete loss of personal identity. The category person, we might say is what made one part of the human race subject to others.[16]

Western philosophy has viewed the person largely as a unity or a unifying centre, be it a unity of body and soul (as in the case of someone like Thomas Aquinas), or as the lived experience of the unity of body, psyche, and spirit (as is the case in the phenomenological tradition, especially in the thought of Edith Stein). Esposito is very critical of the unifying account of personhood,[17] noting that the notion of person manifests a separation or dualism at the core of our understanding of what it is to be human. As we saw earlier, even the etymology of the word "person" reinforces a split and differentiation between the human being and the actor playing a character. In Roman law, the person acquires a legal status. Esposito tells us that personhood is something that can be taken away, for it is a possession: we *are* not persons. It is the *law* that attributes personhood, be it to human beings, corporations, and now, in some cases, to animals. Personhood can function almost like a thing insofar as it can be enjoyed or be taken away, as we saw most violently in the last century with the stripping of personhood from various human beings, including Jews, homosexuals, and the Roma.

If Esposito situates the impersonal within an originary space that arises between the living and dying of an organism, the self can be conceived neither in a substantive sense nor in identitarian terms. "Rather than a first person, that self has become a third person: not a 'he' or 'she,' but the non-person who bears both its reality and its shadow." Esposito's third person is the impersonal,[18] which is understood as a confluence, a crossing (*varco*) of various forces:

Rather than acting as a barrier for selecting and excluding elements from the outside world, [the immune dynamic] acts as a sounding board for the presence of the world inside the self. The self is no longer a genetic constant or a pre-established repertoire, but rather a construct determined by a set of dynamic factors, compatible groupings, fortuitous encounters; nor is it a subject or an object, but rather, a principle of action ... It is never original, complete, intact, "made" once and for all; rather, it constantly makes itself from one minute to the next, depending on the situation and encounters that determine its development. Its boundaries do not lock it up inside a closed world; on the contrary, they create its margin, a delicate and problematic one to be sure, but still permeable in its relationship with that which, while still located outside it, from the beginning traverses it and alters it.[19]

The third person is not conceived as stable or as a product of forces; rather, it is the site where various dynamic forces and encounters intersect.

Similarly, the thing or object has been determined not only by its legal uses and definitions centred around ownership and transmission between persons, but also by (especially) metaphysical philosophy. Esposito argues that modern philosophy has rendered the thing so abstract that it no longer has any real concrete stuff or "thingness" to it:

Persons and things face each other in a relationship of mutual interchangeability: to be a subject, modern man must take the object dependent on his own production; but similarly, the object cannot exist outside of the ideational power of the subject. Kant's separation of the thing into phenomenon and noumenon – between the thing as it appears to us and the 'thing in itself' – takes this splitting to its extreme conclusion. Never is the implication between the separation of the person and the disintegration of the thing so clearly visible as it is in this case. Each can be divided from the other only starting from what separates it from itself, inverting it into its opposite. Thus, while the person is always vulnerable to becoming a thing, the thing always remains subject to the domination of the person.[20]

Esposito makes two important claims here. First, the doubling and bifurcation we saw happening with the person now reappears in the thing. The concept of the thing is not conceived as a unifying placeholder or container; rather, it separates things from persons, even though they both become objects, and the concept of the thing is separated from its real, thingly content. Second, things can become persons and persons can become things. Furthermore, things can become subjected to the will and desires of persons, and things can come to subject persons. Undoubtedly, capitalism – in both its modern and its neoliberal, globalized forms – attests to this easy relation of identity between persons and things.

Given the determinations over time of things and persons, subjects and objects, one has to ask: Is there something that is not a thing or not a person? This is Esposito's central question in *Persone e le cose*.[21] Elsewhere I have argued that Esposito does not account for the particularity of the body, the lived experience of the body, which fortifies and singularizes relations between persons as well as the very singularity of the experience of personhood itself.[22] The dialogue with Deleuze that I wish to undertake here, however, proposes another challenge.

In his earlier works, *The Third Person* and *Terms of the Political*, we read that the impersonal, or what even earlier he called "the negative self," is to be understood as that which resists and that cannot be contained by the historical, legal, social, and political, governmentalized determinations of the person. The impersonal or the third person is an in-between, an originary space, one that exists between human social and political construction, ultimately exceeding our thinking and action:

> The impersonal is situated outside the horizon of the person, but not in an un-related way; rather, the impersonal sits on the confines or borders of the personal. More precisely, it sits on the lines of resistance that carve out a territory that impedes or, at least, contrasts with, the functioning of its excluding *dispositif*, that blocks its reifying exit. It is not its frontal negation – as would be the case for an anti-personal philosophy – but its alteration, an outward turning, of an exteriority that revokes its cause and reverses the prevailing sense.[23]

Esposito's concept of the impersonal delineates a mechanism built into the very structure of life that not only resists reification but also simultaneously pushes us to think outside the logical, normative, and grammatical confines we have created. This means that the person is not just defined by what the law, for instance, views as a person, namely as a property owner, someone who has the right to mobility, and so on. Part of what allows the person to become lies outside the final products and performative declarations of governmentalizing law. The life or becoming of a person also lies in the impersonal, in that realm of becoming in which the body becomes or starts to take shape as an individuation, which exists prior to the law and upon which the law is ultimately dependent.[24]

In his more recent work, the impersonal also acquires embodiment, as the body is that which exists between the person and things and which is never defined by law. Esposito argues that the body, the living and lived body, though subject to more and more governmentalization by biotechnologies, still manages to resist the depersonalization of persons and the metaphysical abstraction that has happened to real things. In fact, the body, understood as a genuine site of resistance, can bring together persons and things, but it is also the locus that exceeds biopolitical governmentalization and cannot be completely subject to it. The living body, and even the "body politic," can resist governmentalization for various reasons. First, the body is a living entity in its own right and has built into it the very immunological paradigm of birth, death, sickness, and resistance that Esposito attributes to all life. One never says that I am my body; rather, one has a body. Yet the body is who we are.[25] "The reason the body falls outside the great division between things and persons lies in the fact that it cannot be ascribed to one or the other."[26] Second, the law generally has no status for the body: the law concentrates on persons, and persons do not always have bodies; for example, various legal entities such as corporations are legal persons, but they do not have a body:

> While the law tends to omit the body, philosophy includes it in its framework, but in the form of the body's subordination. Without repeating the exclusionary gesture of Platonic metaphysics, and yet not entirely foregoing it, modern thought places the body under the rubric of object. The body is what the subject recognizes inside itself, as different from itself. To be able to deal with the body, the subject must separate itself from the body and keep it a distance. Descartes' position on this is exemplary.[27]

Finally, the incorporation that a body assumes, as a living being, need not always result in a single (one) individual; rather, incorporation can produce a multiplicity of bodies that transcend the individual. Nowhere is this clearer than when it comes to the relationship between the living body and technology:

Of course, our own bodies constitute the floating bridge that connects us to technical objects. This means not only the mind, from which they derive their functional and symbolic characteristics, but also the bodily signs that are deposited in them in the act of their invention. The passage from one set of hands to the next by those who have used them creates a continuous flow that goes beyond the individual to involve the "transindividual" dimension to which Simondon dedicated his greatest work.[28]

The possibility of transindividuation, which is part of the living body that exceeds the very limited notions of person and things that both philosophy and the law have given us over the centuries, becomes evident in something like the body politic. A multiplicity of bodies can unify in order to resist and combat any perceived threat. A multiplicity of bodies can unite to create something new and unexpected, for example, a new form of political organization or rule. Esposito notes:

> Something of the body politic remains outside their confines. When masses of people crowd into the public squares across half the world, as is happening today, something is revealed that exists prior even to their demands. Before even being uttered, their words are embodied in bodies that move in unison, with the same rhythm, in a single wave of emotion. As much as the Internet can function as a place for mobilization, without living bodies connected together by the same energy, not even it can be the new political subject of the future. Ever since the statement "we, the people" was first pronounced in the founding event of the first modern democracy, it has had a performative character – it has the effect of creating what it declares. Since then, every linguistic act that seeks to have an impact on the political scene requires a mouth and a throat – the breath of bodies close enough to hear what the other says and to see what everyone can see.[29]

A body can be multiple and unified; it can speak and declare. With its declarations it can make things happen and thereby define itself and the world around it. This is the power of the body politic, and this power can resist what comes to destroy it. The body is a site or a zone that incorporates and gives flesh to the impersonal.

3. TOWARD A MINOR ETHICS:
DELEUZE AND ESPOSITO

Both Deleuze and Esposito give us a body that is multiple and collective and that can extend across individuals – a body with neither individuated organs nor points of affect. Furthermore, they maintain a zone of life that is not reducible to our socio-political governmentalizing forms of personhood. "A life" and "the impersonal" are the descriptors with which we can denote the immanence or real transcendence that exceeds socio-political determination. It seems that what both philosophers have sketched is an ontological reality, albeit a virtual one, but does this ontological reality have any ethical importance or relevance? Neither Deleuze nor Esposito ever explicitly takes up normative ethical prescriptions or demands that flow from their respective philosophies, but in the aforementioned discussion we can see what Deleuze might call a minoritarian or minor possibility of ethical comportment, a stance or position in the world that is not obligatory, prescriptive, or universalizable: a demand that emerges in and through contact with governmentalized bodies.

Let us look back at Deleuze's description of Dickens's story. The "rogue" is ill: his body is weak, and he is dying. It is the body of "this" man, who signals to other bodies that "a life" is in need of attention. It would seem that the "life" shared between individuals, which exceeds socio-political determinations, is appealing for help to sustain it, to heal it, to relieve it of its suffering, but the rogue wavers between his real-world personality and the immanent life that shows itself and spreads across the bodies of those who are trying to assist. In the scenario that Deleuze describes as "a life," a collective action occurs that tries to save that life. In Esposito, we also find an attempt to save "life": he describes how today's refugees and their supporters gather in public squares to demand, articulate, and express the need for a common "we" – a *we* that calls for nourishment, security, help, and shelter in the face of the tragedy of war, economic collapse, poverty, and disease. A multitude of bodies form one body that appeals to other multitudes and bodies for help. The appeal is launched not on grounds of existing socio-political and juridical conventions, but in terms of the sheer power of life that transcends such conventions: the life of the impersonal that gives both resistance and the possibility of overcoming imminent injury, destruction, and death.

Esposito's impersonal draws inspiration from the multitude of Antonio Negri's thought.[30] Deleuze's "a life" is not so much focused on public squares or places: there is a haphazard series of relations, which can occur anywhere and at any point in time. Esposito is very partial to this configuration, whereas Deleuze's impersonal operates in a less organized fashion. Despite their different emphases, both Deleuze and Esposito speak of an affect or an intensity that may arise when the impersonal or "a life" begins to manifest itself in the world. The affect or intensity resulting from such a manifestation or activity launches an appeal for some kind of assemblage that has an ethical valence insofar as the assemblage tries to preserve, resist, or maintain the impersonal and the immanence of life itself, outside the traditional structure of cause and effect that drives most normative accounts of ethics. The immanent life of the rogue and the embodied impersonal of the multitude in the piazzas of Italy gather, relate, form new bodies, and the affect of this kind of relationality and gathering, though motivated by some urgent crisis, such as the threat of death, need not necessarily produce a result or effect that stems from the new assemblage that has arisen. We must think of the affect or the intensity of the new embodied assemblage (of "a life" or the impersonal) as launching new possibilities of becoming, a virtuality in the Bergsonian sense. This virtuality is the life that exists with and vis-à-vis socio-political and governmentalized life. The virtuality that extends from the intensity of becoming new bodies and immanence returns us to something fundamental to our existence, namely, a life that has the potential to become, to evolve creatively. The new assemblage of bodies discussed above makes a virtual appeal to preserve, save, and extend life in its impersonal and immanent forms. This appeal is ethical because its seeks to create new forms of life of persons together, mindful of the impersonal and immanent possibilities that lie within such socio-politically determined lives. There is no necessity to this appeal of the new assemblage: we may refuse it. Also, there is no guarantee that certain effects will flow from certain causes; rather, we try to save and respond to what events and singularities bring forth: the singularity/event of the rogue, and the collective bodies of the multitude of the public squares. A minoritarian ethical response to the assemblage that comes to be in and through the rogue or the refugees and their supporters in the *piazze* is the virtuality of a demand to recognize, extend, transform, and create anew the immanence of a life or the impersonal. Esposito poignantly remarks about Deleuze:

In this sense life, when it is understood in all its impersonal
power, is that which contradicts at the root the hierarchical separation of the human type (*genere*), and of the same human being,
in two superimposed or subjected substances: the first rational
and the second animal. It's no accident that Deleuze understands
the enigmatic figure of 'becoming animal' as the culmination of
the deconstruction of the idea of person, in all its philosophical,
psychoanalytical, and political tonality. In a tradition that has
always defined humanity in the separation and difference from
the animal, only to animalize again a part of humanity because
it wasn't human enough, asserting animality as our most basic
nature to rediscover breaks with the fundamental prohibition
that governs us. Contrary to the presupposed split of the disposi-
tive of the person, the animal in the human being, in each and all
human beings, means multiplicity, plurality, metamorphosis: "We
do not become animal," Deleuze affirms, "without a fascination
for the pack, for multiplicity. A fascination for the outside? Or is
the multiplicity that fascinates us already related to a multiplicity
dwelling within us?" The "becoming animal" of and in the
human being means and demands the loosening of the metaphysical knot tightened by the idea and the practice of person in
favor of a mode of being human (*uomo*) that no longer moves
toward the thing, but ultimately that coincides only with itself.[31]

Does the foregoing view of a minor ethics have any force? Can it
make or impose demands on individuals? No, it cannot. A minor
ethics, in my view, helps prepare the way for fuller ethical action,
always reminding one of the traps of more traditional majoritarian
or governmentalized forms of ethics. It is an ethics that makes possible larger bodies, bodies without organs, that can respond, can
demand, can voice, can reject, resist, fight, and can even enact
responses to various crises that confront those who suffer injustice,
violence, cruelty, and the ravages of war. In this sense, a minor ethics
helps us understand the very possibility or virtuality of an ethical
response or action, reminding us to be critical of the pitfalls of an
ethics that yields all too clear and distinct representations or pictures
of reality and the world we share. More importantly, the virtuality
of the response that we can say manifests a minor ethics of preserving
and safeguarding life that resists or lies outside of governmentalized
ethical and political conventions and institutions; it delineates an

ontic zone, a reality that lies between persons and things, subjects and objects, namely, a life or the impersonal. In the becoming of a life or the impersonal, a response becomes, it takes shape – a demand begins to be articulated across a collectivized body. In this sense, then, perhaps a minor ethics can be understood as the beginning of ethics, an ethics that has its ontic space and time, the virtuality or event of the impersonal or a life.

The minoritarian ethical response that becomes possible in the Deleuzian–Espositian views of the impersonal life is minoritarian in that it can never become a majoritarian or "royal" form of politics, for it is a distinct, discrete reality that is not fully accessible by human planning and organization: it operates as internally resistant to the "royal," for it has its own unique force of potency. A minoritarian ethics has to work and operate within a determining system; it lies in a realm that a social and political system has within itself and that cannot be determined – that is, as Deleuze suggests, it is "indetermined." Indeterminacy is constitutive of all of reality and, as Esposito insists, all politics and all life admits of the virtuality of a becoming. From a minoritarian ethical perspective, an ethical response is possible, but it cannot be determined by a given regime of politics or even an established normative system: there is only the newness, the spontaneity, that arises from a new collectivization and transindividuated embodiment, a force that desires to act, that desires to bring about a new way of being and living.

NOTES

1 Esposito, "Biological Life and Political Life," 11–22.
2 Deleuze, "Immanence: A Life," in *Pure Immanence*; also in Deleuze, *Two Regimes of Madness*. Hereafter TRM.
3 Ibid., 28 (TRM, 390).
4 Ibid.
5 Ibid., 28–9 (TRM, 390–1).
6 Ibid., 29 (TRM, 391).
7 Ibid., 30 (TRM, 392).
8 Ibid. (TRM, 391–2).
9 Ibid., 27 (TRM, 289–90).
10 Ibid., 31–2 (TRM, 392–3).
11 Esposito, *Persons and Things*.

12 Esposito's thinking about the impersonal draws not only from Deleuze but
    also from Simone Weil, Maurice Blanchot, and Jean-Luc Nancy.
13 Esposito, *Immunitas*, 134-6. See also Thomas Lemke, "*Gesellschaftskörper
    und Organismuskonzepte*," 201–3.
14 Esposito, *Le persone e le cose*, 3.
15 Ibid., 5.
16 Esposito, *Persons and Things*, 29–30/14. "Del resto tale scarto è parte inte-
    grante della categoria di persona fin dalla sua remota genesi. È noto che
    l'etimologia greca del termine rimanda alla maschera teatrale, poggiata
    sul volto dell'attore, ma proprio perciò mai coincidente con esso. Lo stesso
    personaggio è sempre diverso dall'attore che volta in volta lo interpreta.
    È come se il diritto riproducesse questo elemento di duplicità, di dopiezza,
    all'interno dell'uomo. La persona non è l'uomo in quanto tale, ma solt-
    anto il suo status giuridico, che varia in base ai rappporti di forza con gli
    altri uomini – non a caso i romani, alludendo al proprio ruolo, usavano la
    locuzione personam habere. Persona non si è, ma si ha, come una facoltà
    che, proprio perciò, si può anche perdere. Ecco perché, diversamente da
    quanto comunemente si suppone, il paradigma di persone produce non
    un'unione ma una separazione. Esso separa non solo gli uni dagli altri,
    secondo determinati ruoli sociali, ma anche il singolo individuo dalla
    propria entità biologica. Egli, essendo altro dalla maschera che indossa,
    è sempre esposto a una possibile depersonalizzazione, definita capitis
    diminutio, che può arrivare fino alla completa perdita di identità per-
    sonale. Si potrebbe dire che la categoria di persona è ciò che rende una
    parte del genere umano, ma anche di ogni uomo, soggetta all'altra."
17 Esposito, "For a Philosophy of the Impersonal," 123.
18 Esposito, *Terza persona*, 19-20.
19 Esposito, *Immunitas*, 169.
20 Esposito, *Persons and Things*, 63–4/43–4. "Il processo di dissolvimento
    della cosa, intrinseco al suo trattamento metafisico, appare ormai inevita-
    bile. La sua trasposizione in 'ente' anticipa quella costituzione in "'ggetto'
    che Heidegger pone al centro del saggio sull'Epoca dell'immagine del
    mondo. Se nel Medioevo la cosa e' Intesa come ens creatum, frutto
    dell'azione creatrice di Dio, successivamente viene interpretata come ciò
    che è rappresentata o prodotta dall'uomo. Ma entrare nel dispositivo della
    rappresentazione o della produzione significa, per la cosa, trasformata in
    oggetto, dipendere dal soggetto cosí da perdere ogni autonomia ... Torna
    a stringersi quell nodo che la separazione tra persone e cose vorrebbe
    tagliare: esse si fronteggiano in un rapporto di reciproca fungibilità: come,
    per essere soggetto, l'uomo moderno deve rendere l'oggetto dipendente

dalla propria produzione, così l'oggetto non può esistere fuori dalla potenza ideativa del soggetto. La separazione kantiana all'interno della cosa, tra fenomeno e noumeno, tra la cosa come ci appare e 'la cosa in sé,' porta questo sdoppiamento al suo esito estremo. Mai come in questo caso torna a balenare l'implicazione tra separazione della persona e dissoluzione della cosa. Ognuna può essere divisa dall'altra solo a partire da ciò che la separa da se stessa, rovesciandola nel proprio contrario. Cosí, se la persona è sempre esposta a diventare cosa, la cosa resta sempre soggetta al dominio della persona."

21 See *Persone e le cose*, 3.

22 Calcagno, "Individuated Embodiment and Action." This article was written before Esposito published his more recent work, in which he articulates a powerful concept of the body that can address many of the challenges brought forward in the aforementioned article.

23 Esposito, *Termini della politica*, 18–19. English translations are mine.

24 Esposito remarks: "It is this complex relation, which is not simply oppositional, between the personal and impersonal, that makes sense of the notion of the 'third person.' ... To work conceptually on the 'third person' is to open a passageway with the very togetherness of forces that, though they may annihilate the person – as they demanded and as they ended up doing, as evidenced by the thanatopolitics of the 20th century – push the person outside of its logical and grammatical confines." Ibid., 19.

25 Esposito, *Persone e le cose*, 89.

26 Esposito, *Persons and Things*, 118/88. "Il motivo per il quale il corpo eccede la grande divisione tra cose e perosne sta nel fatto che non è ascrivibile né alle une né alle alter."

27 Ibid., 108/80. "Se il diritto tende a cancellare il corpo, la filosofia lo include nel proprio orizzonte – ma nella forma della sua souborndinazione. Senza ripetere il gesto escludente della metafisica platonica, ma senza neanche lasciarselo del tutto alle spalle, il pensiero modern situ ail corpo nel registro dell'ogetto. Esso è ciò che il soggetto riconosce, all'interbno di se stesso, diverso da sé. Per poterne trattare, egli deve separarsene e tenerlo a distanza. In questo senso la posizione di Cartesio appare esemplare."

28 Ibid., 133–4/100. "Naturalmente il ponte mobile che si collega agli oggetti tecnici è il nostro stesso corpo. Non solo la mente, da cui essi traggono le loro caratteristiche funzionali e simboliche, ma anche i segni corporei che sono depositati in essi nell'atto della loro invenzione. Il passaggio di mano in mano, da parte di chi li ha adoperati, crea un flusso continuo che va al di là del singolo individuo per coinvolgere quella dimensione 'transindividuale' alla quale Simondon ha dedicato la propria opera maggiore."

29 Ibid., 146–7/110. "Qualcosa, del corpo politico, resta fuori dai suoi con-
    fine. Quando ingenti masse si accacano nelle piazza di mezzo mondo,
    come aggi sta accdendo, viene allo scoperto qualcosa che precede anche le
    loro rivendicazioni. Prima ancora di essere pronunciate, le loro parole
    sono incarnate in corpi che si muovono all'unisono, con il medesimo
    ritmo, in un'unica ond emotive. Per quanto possa funzionare come luogo
    di mobilitazione, senza corpi viventi saldati dalla stessa energia, neanche la
    rete può essere il nuovo soggetto della politica a venire. Fin da quando fu
    formulato, nell'evento costituente della prima democrazia moderna,
    l'enunciato 'noi il popolo' aveva un carattere performativo – produceva
    l'effetto di creare quanto dichiarava. Da allora ogni atto linguistico che
    voglia incidere sula scena politica richiede una booca e una gollla, un res-
    piro di corpi abbastanza vicini da sentire ciò che l'altro dice e da vedere
    ciò che tutti vedono."
30 Michael Hardt and Antonio Negri, *Multitude*.
31 Esposito, "For a Philosophy of the Impersonal," 133.

10

Césaire and Senghor alongside Deleuze: Post-Imperial Multiplicity, Virtual Assemblages, and the Cosmopolitan Ethics of Négritude

Simone Bignall

The Western academy often understands Négritude as a theory of African ethnicity grounding an identity politics of decolonization and so dismisses Aimé Césaire and Léopold Senghor as racial or cultural essentialists.[1] At the same time, subaltern critics often find the anti-colonial poetics expressed by these insurgent thinkers of Négritude difficult to reconcile with their apparent capitulations to a moderate politics of neocolonial compliance.[2] However, a number of authors are returning to the works of Césaire and Senghor to disrupt received interpretations of their thought. This recent thread in scholarship finds an unrealized potential in Négritude, reconsidered as a cosmopolitan ethics of decolonization that refuses to base postcolonial self-determination in state sovereignty.[3] Césaire and Senghor sought new types of postcolonial and democratic political association in the decentralized, interdependent, plural conditions enabled by the French empire itself, as a transnational form of cultural multiplicity and complex social assemblage. In doing so, they contested the presumed nature and course of decolonization. Conceived as a nationalist process of political separation and sovereign isolation, the struggle for decolonization typically proposed the postcolonial disentanglement of peoples and their consequent cultural restoration along appropriate nationalist lines. Whereas anti-colonial struggles for independence were usually accompanied by the reification of nationalist identities and strident assertions of the sovereign independence of nations, Césaire and

Senghor held that the separation of nations after their colonial entanglement would not only devolve the colonial state but also diminish
the post-colony. They believed that the colonial encounter brought
with it the potential to advance human civilization through the imbri-
cation of peoples by increasing their capacity for cultural co-implica-
tion and complexification. Indeed, they did not view the problem with
French imperialism as the fact of encounter and entanglement *per se*.
Rather, the problem was the unethical and destructive way in which
the communication of differences in the colonial encounter proceeded
as a result of the colonial administration's efforts to impose a presumed
superior (and thus naturally dominant) French culture on the diverse
peoples comprising the empire. Against this imperial framework of
colonial reduction and simplification toward cultural uniformity, and
also against the cultural separation and simplification reified by nationalist decolonization, Négritude posits both the resilience of cultural
difference and the benefits of its ethical communication for the purpose
of human social enrichment in a transnational association of co-
implicated cultures coexisting after colonization. In light of this fresh
understanding of Césaire and Senghor as pluralist thinkers in opposition to the uniformity of empire, recent scholarly attention has renewed
our appreciation of the complexity of Césaire's and Senghor's political
intentions and reassessed the potential of the inspiration they continue
to provide today for resistance to the global imperialism of Western
cultural formations.[4]

The experience of colonization influenced intellectuals on both sides
of the colonial divide. French post-structuralist "philosophies of difference" stem in part from the political conditions internal to fascist
Europe during the Second World War and to the Vichy Regime. Those
conditions generated a postwar conviction that public intellectuals
have a responsibility to confront powerful philosophies and ideologies
of assimilation, especially those enabling "ethnic cleansing." However,
these philosophies of difference arose in part "out of Africa" as well,
for instance, as a consequence of French childhoods spent in Algeria
observing colonial injustices.[5] Many of these children grew up to
become student activists and Parisienne intellectuals in support of
decolonization.

The anti-colonial influence on French post-structuralism is palpable
in an early conversation between Deleuze and Foucault on the subject
of "Intellectuals and Power," in which Deleuze expresses the importance of "something absolutely fundamental: the indignity of speaking

for others."[6] His ethical assertion, and the conversation itself, became a significant pressure point in the emerging field of postcolonial theory when Gayatri Chakravorty Spivak questioned post-structuralist methodologies for contesting power, in light of the insensibility of subaltern speech, which can only be articulated in a discursive field significantly constituted through the phenomenon of empire.[7] Political speech, then, is always already demarcated by powerful practices of representation that delimit possibilities for speaking (and hearing) an alternative regime of truth and of sense-making.

I have argued that many of Deleuze's conceptual creations can be understood as responding to this political problem by prioritizing the generative power of alterity as an affective pathway for the ethical coordination of complex orders of sense and action.[8] Here, by reading Césaire and Senghor alongside Deleuze, I aim to bring into alliance diverse conceptual resources coexisting in the mélange of the post-imperial French confederation. Like Césaire and Senghor, who invented Négritude to imagine the perseverance of cultural differences and the conditions of their ethical interaction in the political milieu of the post-imperial French confederation of nations, Deleuze proposes the concepts of "multiplicity" and "assemblage" as means to dismantle an empire of representational uniformity by theorizing a positive mode of desire as the basis for an association of differences that are mutually affective, enduring, constitutive, and resistant to assimilation.

The first section of this chapter aligns the philosophical approach of Négritude with Deleuze's constructivist image of thought, highlighting how both are concerned with the ethical communication of differences for the purpose of conceptual and structural complexification. I then use Deleuze's associated concepts of "multiplicity" and "assemblage" to consider the anti-colonial disinclination of Césaire and Senghor to embrace nationalist sovereignty, as well as their inclination toward an alternative conceptualization of postcolonial existence involving social entanglement and shared enrichment. Yet for Deleuze, the play of difference in a process of assemblage is not only constructive but also unsettling and transformative. In the final section, I interpret the political poetry of Négritude in light of Deleuze's work on "signs" that escape semantic discipline and reference his figurations of art and philosophy as catharses for a creative encounter with alterity, shocking thought into movement. Here, I rely on Deleuze's temporal philosophy to explain the ongoing transformative potential of Césaire's and Senghor's notions of liberation, transnational democracy, and pluralist solidarity. Ultimately I show how this mixed conceptual milieu allows us to understand how Négritude, like French post-structuralism, is an unmaking and reworking of the transcendent universals of imperial modernism. Négritude does this in the form of a situated alter-humanism that expresses, in the surrealist poetry of political life, the dispersed and decentred subject after empire. This anti-colonial subject seeks the joyful communication of differences for the purpose of cultural complexification. Accordingly, Négritude professes a "minor ethics" that strains toward liberty in a virtual ethos of complex interdependence, an ethos that has yet to be actualized in a post-imperial global federation of nations.

I. NÉGRITUDE, THE IMAGE OF THOUGHT, AND LARVAL SUBJECTIVITY

In his introduction to Césaire's *Discourse on Colonialism*, Robin D.G. Kelley notes that Négritude "was a vision of freedom that drew on Modernism and a deep appreciation for pre-colonial African modes of thought and practice; it drew on Surrealism as the strategy of revolution of the mind and Marxism as revolution of the productive' forces."[9] The combined influence of these intellectual, aesthetic, and political movements on Césaire and Senghor cannot be overemphasized. However, as Kelley points out, it would be wrong to think of this influence as unilateral or as "European" in origin: as if the imperial force of France alone produced anti-colonial "Africanism" as a style of humanism; as if André Breton had inculcated in Césaire a marvellous new vision of the world. Indeed, for Césaire, surrealism was less an external influence that he absorbed following his encounter with Breton, than something he recognized as an aesthetic stance or style already existing within him as a consequence of his embodiment of a particular style of French intellectualism combined with his African cultural heritage.[10] Like Senghor, he was a surrealist because he shared in surrealism's *affective* way of conceiving reality, especially the way it used poetry to convey the experience of existence as a pure field of sensation. In fact, then, Césaire and Senghor were themselves creative influences in twentieth-century artistic and political movements, and their culturalist perspectives contributed enormously to the theorization of a surrealist sensibility sharpened by the experience of empire bringing diverse cultures of significance into creative clash and disjunctive discord. Similarly, in their formal political roles and contributions to political writing, both Senghor and Césaire contributed to postwar Marxism a more nuanced understanding of the proletarian condition and of the diverse cultural characteristics of universal socialism, duly sensitive to the particularity of colonialist capitalism and to African traditions of productivity and community that were not only ante-capitalist but also anti-capitalist.[11]

The concept of "Négritude" should be understood in this light, as an insistence on the role to be played by diverse cultures allied in the ethical expression of human civilization after the systematic dehumanization wrought by European imperialism and fascism. Césaire coined the term "Négritude" in a political polemic published in 1935 and then used it again in a surrealist poem published in 1939;[12] but it was Senghor who developed the idea of Négritude as the crux of his political thought. In his writings, he states definitively that Négritude is "not racialism, it is culture."[13] Thus, he insists, "Négritude has never insisted on skin colour, but on ethnicity. As one knows, ethnicity is not only race with its physical qualities, but more culture with its civilizational values." Négritude, then, is "the awareness, defence and development of African cultural values."[14] What, then, are these "African cultural values"? For Senghor, "it is their *emotive* attitude towards the world which explains the cultural values of Africans."[15] Similarly for Sartre in *Black Orpheus*, Négritude is "a certain affective attitude towards the world."[16]

Senghor sets this affective cultural tendency against the objective form of instrumental reason as the mode of thought or thinking typical of modern European culture – a mode that supports imperial attitudes of conduct and relation. In *Prose and Poetry* (1962), he compares the culturally distinctive ways of knowing and being he believes are demonstrated by imperial Europeans and by African peoples. The European expresses

> an objective intelligence ... He first distinguishes the object from himself. He keeps it at a distance. He freezes it out of time and, in a way, out of space. He fixes it, he kills it. With his precision instruments he dissects it in a pitiless factual analysis. As a scientist, yet at the same time prompted by practical considerations, the European makes use of the Other that he has killed in this way for his practical ends. He makes a means of it. With a centripetal movement, he assimilates it. He destroys it by devouring it.[17]

Similarly, in his anti-colonial manifesto of 1955, *Discourse on Colonialism*, Césaire regards Europe's decline into fascism as a natural extension of the instrumental and objectifying mode of reason residing at the heart of imperial operations and justifying colonial conduct. Other radical black intellectuals of the time, including W.E.B. Du Bois and C.L.R. James, concurred with this analysis, as did various European intellectuals such as Hannah Arendt, Theodor Adorno, and Max Horkheimer. As Edward Said famously elaborated, colonial domination required a whole way of thinking: an imperial epistemology in which everything that was advanced, valued, and civilized was defined and measured in European terms, with the "knowing subject" of this discourse thus relying on an objectified Other, who became simultaneously denigrated and assimilated within these dominant terms of reference.[18]

Senghor provides us with an alternative African account of thought and sensibility:

> The African ... does not begin by distinguishing himself from the object [and] does not keep it at a distance. He does not analyse it. Once he has come under its influence, he takes it like a blind man, still living, into his hands. He does not fix it or kill it. He turns it over and over in his supple hands, he fingers it, he *feels* it. The African is one of the worms created on the Third day ... a pure sensory field. Subjectively, at the end of his antennae, like an insect, he discovers the Other. He is moved to his bowels, going out in a centrifugal movement from the subject to the object on the waves sent out from the Other.[19]

The strictness of Senghor's demarcation between European and African modes of reason is problematically stereotypical and simplifying, for multiple and various styles of thinking and analysis are available to all cultures and everyday human activity generally relies on affective or intuitive reason.[20] Indeed, this Senghorian imagery of the African as a "worm" or a "pure sensory field" oriented expansively outward to cautiously and gently embrace the Other who affects him, invites association with the "larval subjects" Deleuze describes in *Difference and Repetition* and in his 1967 seminar paper "The Method of Dramatisation." In these texts (and others), Deleuze compares a dominant "image of thought," which seeks to understand the Idea as essence or "objectality" and is driven by the question "What is this?," with an alternative image of thought driven by questions of conceptual composition or orchestration: *who, how much, which one, where?* (D I, 95). This is an image of thought as intuitive, affective, processual, and creative. Deleuze thus points us toward a minor tradition of the Idea *within* Western thought, suggestive as a basis for philosophical alliance between Continental European post-structuralism and the anti-colonial theorists of African Négritude. For Deleuze, as for Senghor's "African," difference (when it is adequately conceived) is not objectified as a negative or oppositional facet of a representative and defining identity; rather, it is a kind of creative force one encounters in a shared movement of affective transition. As we shall see, this understanding of difference enables a self or subject to appreciate how she might combine with the other bodies or Ideas she encounters and comes to comprehend relationally, to produce a more complex order of differential organization with a higher degree of affective power. The realization of this potential for complexification and empowerment through an understanding of relations depends on the ethical communication of the different parts comprising an emergent complex structure, such that they may combine successfully without diminishing or destroying one another's forms.[21]

In the seminar paper of 1967, Deleuze explains how his constructivist image of thought does not describe a representational system so much as a "strange theatre" in which concepts emerge through a "method of dramatization" (D I, 98). This philosophical theatre can be thought of as an "intensive field" that constitutes an "environment of individuation" (D I, 97): elemental parts or singularities encounter one another, or are drawn together, and so come into contact and communication; different parts combine to form complex unions; and as these in turn encounter forces that transform them, they may break down and reconfigure in alternative patterns of connectivity, or they may combine and develop into increasingly complex formations that are relatively enduring. In this "strange theatre" of conceptual association and composition, what matters most, then, are the force-relations that bring conceptual forms into being. In fact, the forms themselves have no essence; they are pure "differentials," which exist and are determined only with respect to one another. The "sense" or quality of a thing therefore depends entirely on its specification and organization via the forces that have taken hold of it and on the relations into which it enters with neighbouring entities (D I, 96–7, 99). For example, on this constructivist account of being, when conceived in terms of dynamic relations that confer sense and value, being "black" has a particular meaning when a person is defined in relation to her ancient ancestral civilizations, her rich cultural traditions of knowledge, art, and poetry, and her legal and social practices of non-possession or of communal ownership. Yet it means something else entirely when a black person enters into a colonial relationship, which subjects her to a new set of forces: imperial powers that construe her as racially primitive and without civility or reason, as belonging to an immoral society without proper forms of law and governance, or as lazy and incompetent, having failed to take sovereign possession of territory by mixing the land with her labour.

For Deleuze, the virtual "Idea" is actualized by processes of association and composition that depend entirely on the environmental opportunities (or impossibilities) for relationship available to its comprising elements. Individual orders of sense may combine to form a complex union when some or all of their parts are compatible; but then over time the tenure of a particular element in the merger may become impossible if a new encounter introduces a force-relation that disallows its continued presence, making it insensible as an element in the new arrangement. In this way, the nature of the individual order of sense transforms as its elemental configurations shift and morph in the context of the relations into which it enters with other composite forms it encounters. For example, Frantz Fanon conceives of himself in a given circumstance as a complex of black skin, self-loathing, inferiority, and awkwardness when he is affected by hostility, suspicion, and revulsion while experiencing racism in Paris; but when he encounters Césaire and Sartre, and develops a new set of relations (to history, to Africa, to the French, and to Paris), this experience changes important aspects of his sense of self, and he becomes individuated differently – making it impossible for him to be self-loathing anymore, or at least not in the same way.[22] In Deleuze's theatre of philosophy, the Idea is not individual, fixed, singular, and representational, but rather a dynamic multiplicity that is virtual, relational, indeterminate, and problematic and that takes a definitive form only contingently as elements cohere momentarily to determine a contextually significant or sensible existential "solution." The virtual and problematic Idea of "civilization," for example, is solved in one way by the concept of Négritude as an advanced cultural aesthetic describing the accomplishments of the African peoples; and it is solved in a different way by the concept of "blackness" as racial inferiority, informing a colonial assemblage of sense that asserts the superiority of European culture as a marker of "true" civilization.

If what matters most in the constructivist method for dramatizing conceptual forms are the force-relations that bring virtual Ideas into actual being, then the affective nature or quality of the force of association becomes of primary concern. *How* will differences relate to one another? *How* will combinations take place? For Deleuze, complex individuation relies on the "communication of differences," and this presumes something like a systemic agency of interaction and affection, a "difference operator" that "relates difference to difference." According to him, this role is filled by "an *obscure precursor*" (DR, 119, 145; DI, 97). The role of the obscure or "dark" precursor as a systemic agent of differential communication is not simply to draw whole orders into contact and one-on-one communication; more precisely, it is to advance a path highlighting potential bonds that may form between some of their respective comprising elements. These may then become swept up in new combinations of forces to produce a new complex emergence, forged "bit by bit" in a "piecemeal" and selective manner from parts of the existing structures meeting in an affective neighbourhood (EP, 237; TP, 504). The dark precursor not only highlights potential bonds but also throws into relief elemental incompatibilities between forms, particular sites of disjunction where their elements cannot combine to produce a higher order that contains them both in a new relation. Agreements can be reached when complex orders come into contact, even when the individual partners do not agree in many respects, and even where their particular differences and dispositions are strikingly incommensurable. As I have argued elsewhere, this is a suggestive framework for imagining postcolonial encounters that strive against the imposition of a dominant uniformity.[23] Such encounters will be orchestrated to create forms of association that value individual differences as productive sites for the development of a higher accord, while acknowledging and managing persistent disagreements as indications of the vital particularities that define each individual as such and that cannot be subsumed or erased by the fact of the relationship.

The work of "communicating transversals" (TP, 11) in an encounter between disparate entities or series does not seek to ascertain the universal essence of a thing they share in order to confirm its identity; rather, it proceeds by understanding and orchestrating the differential conditions under which a relationship takes shape. It is guided by affective or intuitive questions of artistic production or direction: *who, how much, when, in what way*? The "subject" that acts out this constructive drama of individuation is not a unified, coherent, fixed source of agency or intention, but rather is pre-individual, dynamic, unstable, complex, shifting. In constructivist philosophies, complex arrangements of forces bind elemental content into shifting affective assemblages; beneath the apparently stable macroforms of actualized individuals lie seething molecular processes of association and combination (TP, 272–86). The process of individuation takes place through the relational agencies of those part-forms Deleuze calls "larval subjects," those elemental combinations of content, which he considers to be "rough drafts, not yet qualified or composed" (DI, 97). Yet in their supple molecularity, it is these larval subjects, Deleuze suggests, that are "able to endure the demands of systematic dynamism" (DI, 98): rather than experiencing destruction in their entirety when confronted by an unfavourable force-relation that reduces them to the status of mere objects, they become-otherwise bit-by-bit through affective and intuitive encounters with the other.

Let's return to Senghor as an African "worm," or larval subject. Senghor says that "the person-man is an unstable tissue of forces which interact: a world of solidarities which seek to link themselves."[24] As we have seen, Senghor's view is that this intersubjective linkage takes place affectively, through intuitive intelligence involving a cautious and gentle discovery of the Other, approached sensitively as if touched by the antennae of an insect. "Négritude is intuitive reason, reason which is embrace and not reason which is eye."[25] The subjective style of Négritude correlates with intuitive reason and an image of thought as affective and creative; these are epistemological, noological, and ontological tendencies, which Senghor aligns culturally with Africa. This, however, is not an exclusive cultural attribution, since Senghor is also deeply influenced by European traditions of thought, including the creative evolutionism of Pierre Teilhard de Chardin, whose affective theory of the complexification of the "noosphere" itself draws inspiration from Bergson and Spinoza, influences that are, of course, shared by Deleuze. Négritude is, therefore, wrongly criticized as racial or cultural essentialism: the painter Pablo Picasso, the poets Paul Claudel, Charles Péguy, and Arthur Rimbaud, and the philosopher Henri Bergson have all likewise been "enrolled by Senghor under the banner of Négritude," not only because each has individually influenced Senghor, but also because for Senghor they articulate a common style, a conjoint affect, which also is expressed by Négritude.[26] For Deleuze, a set of unlikely "nuptials" joining incongruent entities always relates them to a common problem, which prompts the engagement and is itself shaped and redefined through the act of communication (D, 1–19). This explains why participants with highly disparate characters and outlooks can enjoy "a felicitous encounter. Kurosawa can adapt Dostoyevsky at least because he can say: 'I share a concern with him, a shared problem, this problem'" (TRM, 322).

Indeed, Senghor explicitly recognizes that Négritude is a "myth" rather than a factual representation of African being.[27] In Deleuzian parlance, Négritude is a fabulation: it involves a narrative individuation or dramatization of the Idea of Africaneity, which draws together a cross-cultural array of sources to respond to the problem of colonization as a process of cultural and territorial assimilation through the uniform imposition of a dominant European identity as globally superior. Négritude realigns perceptions of blackness with positive cultural affects that are very different from those experienced under colonial domination by Europe. Furthermore, I want to suggest that Négritude functions less as a positive individuation of African being than as a "difference operator": Négritude is an obscure or "dark precursor" ("dark" in a sense no doubt unintended by Deleuze) that throws into sharp relief alternative possibilities for the relationship between (colonial) subject and (colonized) other. As Senghor explains in his comparison of African and European epistemologies, because it is a form of affective and intuitive reason, Négritude is a way of knowing, a mode of individuation, and a style of relation to the other that guides the formation of social and political relations alternative in kind to those orchestrated by instrumental and objective reason as the "difference operator" of modern European colonialism. Because it describes an image of thought or a mode of knowing that approaches epistemological relations cautiously and in a way that is attentive to the affective specificity of the object – that is, it does not presume to know the Other in advance or beyond the circumstances of the knowledge relation – Négritude invites an ethical mode of relationship between Europe and Africa. This kind of relationship is best conceived not as taking place between subject-self and object-other, but rather between mutually affecting and co-defined subjectivities; it participates in the construction of an alternative differential. Négritude projects a relation of differences that is based not on hierarchy and domination, but on sensitivity and collaboration in defining a more complex union of parts. The remaining sections of the chapter will consider some political and aesthetic ramifications of this understanding of Négritude as an affective and creative philosophy concerned with the ethical communication of differences for the purpose of complexification.

2. ASSEMBLAGE AFTER EMPIRE

The lens of politics allows us to observe more clearly how Négritude promotes the ethical communication of differences in a complex assemblage of parts. Césaire was instrumental in bringing about the "departmentalization" of Martinique, Guadeloupe, Guiana, and Réunion in 1946, changing their status from "colony" to "overseas department." His vision was of a new transcontinental federation in which the former colonies would participate on an equal footing with the metropolis, constituting a cultural multiplicity in which "the point is not to see the particular fade into the universal but to go to the universal through the particular."[28] This vision contrasts markedly with the colonial mode of social assemblage, in which cultural difference is formally devalued in relation to the imperial (French) cultural identity and cultural contact is limited to the formal imposition of colonial (French) values as universally relevant and superior. Of course, in reality, the situation of colonial contact enabled a messier mixing of cultures and peoples: colonial desire tends toward an ambivalent form of satisfaction that is predicated not only on denial and annihilation of the other as an object of repulsion, but also on assimilation with and incorporation of the other as an object of fascination.[29] Nonetheless, the colonial assemblage operates as such on the basis that moral communication is unilateral and universalizing, articulated actively by a colonizing subject seeking to inform and transform a colonial public by inculcating in them an appreciation of (French) cultural values as markers of a globally superior humanity to which all may aspire. In his anti-colonial manifesto *Discourse on Colonialism*, Césaire affirms

> that it is a good thing to place different civilisations in contact with each other; that it is an excellent thing to blend different worlds; that whatever its own particular genius may be, a civilisation that withdraws into itself atrophies; that for civilisations, exchange is oxygen; that the great good fortune of Europe is to

have been a crossroads, and that because it was the locus of all ideas, the receptacle of all philosophies, the meeting place of all sentiments, it was the best centre for the redistribution of energy.[30]

But, he asks, "has *colonisation really placed civilisations in contact*? Or, if you prefer, of all the ways of *establishing contact*, was it the best?"

For Césaire, decolonization would best be achieved not through the formal independence of the colonies as new sovereign states cut loose from the empire, but rather through the reconstruction of the colonial assemblage on an alternative political and ethical basis of intercultural contact. He believed that both France and the colonies would be diminished in mutual isolation after decolonization but could mutually benefit from ongoing entanglement – so long as the transnational political assemblage of the French Republic was recalibrated to allow all of its comprising elements equitable political participation in shaping their interactions. Decolonization called for a new appreciation of cultural difference as a vital and creative force, as well as the development of a bilateral means for the ethical communication of differences (or "departments") for the purpose of transnational complexification. Césaire's vision was, of course, never realized in practice, since the French government persisted in treating "departmentalisation" as a form of cultural assimilation or a neocolonialism prolonging its political dominance and its economic power in the region.

The decolonial assemblage envisioned by Césaire is defined more abstractly by Senghor as "the Civilization of the Universal, which will be the work of all races, of all different civilizations."[31] Responding implicitly both to Sartre's claim in *Black Orpheus* that Négritude only reaches its own truth when it fades out into the universal, in a dialectical synthesis of opposites, and to the misapprehension that Négritude constrains political action within a narrow cultural identity, Césaire writes:

Provincialism? Not at all. I am not burying myself in a narrow particularism. But neither do I want to lose myself in a disembodied universalism. There are two ways to lose oneself: walled segregation in the particular or dilution in the "universal" ... My conception of the universal is that of a universal enriched by all that is particular, a universal enriched by every particular: the deepening and coexistence of all particulars.[32]

In similar terms, Senghor insists (drawing from Leo Frobenius) that to cultivate Négritude is to take part in "conciliating accord" in order to comprehend the Civilization of the Universal, which always already exists as the cultural terrains of all humanity taken in its entire diversity.[33]

Senghor's notion of the "Civilisation of the Universal" is influenced in part by his reading of Teilhard de Chardin and Bergson. He finds in their evolutionary philosophies a dialectic in which difference does not indicate a negativity opposing a primary, positive identity, and whose fate it is to be progressively assimilated; rather, difference itself is primary, positive, and creatively enduring. This kind of dialectic is best understood as Spinozian and not Hegelian in its choreography: in Deleuze's Spinozism we find a similar "affirmation of the reality of a particularity whose fate is not to be dissolved in universality but rather to find and recognise itself in that universality."[34] Thus for Deleuze and Guattari, following Spinoza, universality is not a final, ideal, or actual unity or uniformity. Instead, the universal is a primary, real, and virtual field of infinite variation; being is expressed univocally, taking form in a common process of becoming as diverse modes of existence actualize through the affective interaction of elemental parts. They therefore conceive universality in terms of a virtual plane of consistency or composition, which is "the intersection of all concrete forms" in a zone of proximity (TP, 251). The potential Civilization of the Universal is, similarly, the virtual encounter of all particular human cultures in a cosmopolitan "rendezvous of give and receive," and the universal here means "all human cultures in their convergence, as they are all different expressions of it: universality is not the nature of any given civilisation or culture, it is not, in particular, just another name for the telos of Western civilisation" imposed globally through imperialism.[35] The Civilization of the Universal thus offers global humanity an antidote to quell the historical malaise stemming from complicity between modern European humanism and colonialism, criticized scathingly by Césaire: "At the very time when it most often mouths the word, the West has never been further from being able to live a true humanism – a humanism made to the measure of the world."[36]

For Senghor, "Integral Man" is the virtual subject of the Civilization of the Universal.[37] Revised in accordance with a feminist sensibility, the "Integral Human" may be thought of as an alter-humanist self, exposed constitutively to all of the world's cultures, which in *metissage* become the common property of any particular human society and furnish elemental material for the ongoing self-constitution of distinct peoples as culturally particular groupings. Similarly, in his vision of the transnational French assemblage after empire, Césaire considers that the reformed federation will be justly comprised of metropolitan and overseas departments that interact equitably and collaborate to define the nature of their union, but at the same time remain self-determining, culturally distinct formations within the collective. In this complex assemblage of parts, French language and citizenship and the signature values of liberty, equality, and fraternity belong rightfully to all members of the transnational republic, just as Négritude as a culturally African or Antillean style of being and knowing becomes available for general use in the constitution of an enriched "French" culture after empire. The retention of their self-determined cultural distinctiveness by the peoples comprising the transnational or cosmopolitan multiplicity is necessary for the act of collaboration in a postcolonial assemblage. Without this, the participants "would have nothing to offer" one another in a process of "cultural borrowing," positive adaptation, and mutual augmentation; Senghor is deeply critical of how colonized subjects become merely "pale copies of Frenchmen, consumers not producers of culture."[38] Crucially, in promoting Négritude to affirm the continuing global relevance and resilience of African cultural values or qualities, Senghor and Césaire insist on a style of politics involving the coexistence of differences that endure despite entanglement, and they disavow political processes or structures based on the dialectical resolution of differences in a dominant register or in a hybrid form of identity. Arguably, this is where the political philosophy of Négritude departs from that of some Creole theorists, such as Édouard Glissant who is often singled out for his postcolonial use of a Deleuzian philosophy of affective becoming that emphasizes cultural hybridity and refuses original purity or natural authenticity.[39] The valorization of hybrid becomings celebrates a process of constitutive mixing that blends differences to create new forms, comprising a new assemblage that encompasses and transcends them. However, the method of hybrid composition does not guarantee the endurance of vital particularities that are incommensurable and that resist blending when diverse orders meet. Furthermore, the process can ultimately downplay the *creative* significance and positive contribution of particular differences in favour of the *created* effect that emerges as the hybrid middle ground of the constructed common identification. For Deleuze, this corresponds with a subordination of difference to identity in a philosophy of process resting on a false conception of real causation (DR). Deleuze's Spinozist writing (with Guattari) on "becoming" and "assemblage" accordingly emphasizes the piecemeal and selective nature of the formative interactions between participants in a creative encounter, while simultaneously bringing them into a process of mutual transformation *and* preserving aspects of their individual differences (EP, 237; TP, 504).[40] Similarly, we see in the work of Paget Henry,[41] Jane Gordon,[42] and Michael Monahan[43] cautious conceptualizations of Creolization that not only celebrate the creative enrichment produced when differences come into contact and hybrid relation, but also preserve a place and role for the enduring particularity of differences in the relationship.

Imperial history transformed France into a transnational federation that was a "plural polity composed of multiple cultural formations, administrative regimes and legal systems," thus "creating the conditions for an alternative federal democracy that might have been."[44] The theorists of Négritude envisaged the decolonized assemblage of peoples – initially brought together through empire – as a non-nationalist, non-statist, and radically deterritorialized multiplicity in which cultural differences were revalued and became free to interact with equal creative input in productive associations unconstrained by normative identities and sovereign state boundaries. In this way, as Gary Wilder has demonstrated in his striking critical revision of this history, they effectively disputed the conventional narrative heard during the postwar struggle for decolonization, during which anticolonial nationalism expressed the demand for liberty and self-determination through the political form of state sovereignty:

> They were not simply demanding that overseas peoples be fully integrated within the existing national state but proposing a type of integration that would reconstitute France itself, by quietly exploding the existing national state from within. Legal pluralism, disaggregated sovereignty, and territorial disjuncture would be constitutionally grounded. The presumptive unity of culture, nationality and citizenship would be ruptured ... Rather than counterpose autarchic notions of Africa, the Caribbean, or

blackness to a one-dimensional figure of France, they claimed within "France" those transformative legacies to which they were rightful heirs and attempted to awaken the self-surpassing potentialities that they saw sedimented within it. Rather than found separate national states, they hoped to elevate the imperial republic into a democratic federation.[45]

For Senghor, non-national decolonization that resists reinstating independent state sovereignty against European neocolonialism and in defence of strong territorial borders is how "local differences, being complementary to each other, will enrich the Federation and, conversely, the Federation will preserve the differences."[46] This was also how Césaire understood postcolonial "departmentalization" – as a "creative anticolonial act" in the Caribbean, a "legal and political framework that would recognise the history of interdependence between metropolitan and overseas peoples and protect the latter's economic and political claims on a metropolitan society their resources and labour had helped to create."[47] Accordingly, "they each hoped to transcend the limitations of the UN's nationalist internationalism by anticipating supranational forms of political association that did not ground citizenship in territory, ethnicity or community."[48] Preempting the Fanonian and Sartrean conceptualizations of freedom that later also influenced Foucault and Deleuze, who likewise considered liberty more as "a set of improvisational and self-constituting practices [than] a legal status or political condition," the anti-colonial theorists of Négritude sought to establish an interactive social milieu in the form of a decentralized democratic federation that would include former colonies as freely associated member-states.[49] By demanding that France "accommodate itself legally and politically to the interpenetrated and interdependent realities its own imperial practices had produced," they were arguing, then, for "a future political formation that could better serve as a framework for democratic politics on a planetary scale"[50]:

Not satisfied with securing a favourable place for their peoples within the existing international order, they sought to transcend it; rather than simply pursue sovereignty, they envisioned unprecedented arrangements for dwelling and thinking through which humanity could realise itself more fully. From the evanescent opening of the post-war moment they anticipated a new era of world history in which human relations would be reorganised on the basis of complementarity, mutuality and reciprocity. Through these novel political arrangements, humanity might overcome the alienating antinomies that had impoverished the quality of life in overseas colonies *and* European metropoles.[51]

The reorganization of the human multiplicity after Empire "on the basis of complementarity, mutuality and reciprocity" relies upon a new style of communication of differences. This is why, for Senghor,

> the struggle for Négritude must not be negation but affirmation. It must be the contribution from us, the peoples of sub-Saharan Africa, to the growth of Africanity, and beyond that, to the building of the *Civilisation of the Universal*. Négritude is part of Africanity, and as such is part of human civilisation. To see that there are parts is not to set them against each other. Or rather, it is to set these against each other so as to be able to unite them more firmly in a dynamic symbiosis of complementary parts: for it is in this that Culture consists.[52]

Instead of sovereign independence and opposition, and instead of a Hegelian movement toward the resolution of differences through transcendence and incorporation, in Senghor and Césaire we see something more like a Spinozian development of "common notions." Spinoza defines "common notions" as the shared idea that emerges when two bodies, upon meeting, understand they possess attributes in common. As a mutually developed understanding of how individual cultures can agree and be united in part, even while disagreeing and remaining distinctive in other ways, common notions reveal sites of relationship where the "dynamic symbiosis of complementary parts" takes place through deliberation and careful acts of affective transformation.[53] Similarly, Senghor and Césaire strive to appreciate not only how universal being is expressed as a process of becoming through relations of complex composition, but also how these relations can be actively directed to express being "adequately," that is, joyfully. In his reading of the Spinozist system, Deleuze explains how Spinozian Being comes into existence as elements combine to produce complex assemblages. Initially this process is happenstance, as bodies encounter one another and combine without knowing how they will affect one another or what kind of composition will ensue. When they are defined primarily by their passive encounters, bodies know themselves and others only in terms of their appearance each to the other and the accidental affects of sadness and joy caused when they meet or when they are thrown together, for example, by colonization. This, then, is the "first kind of knowledge" individuals will form as they come to understand themselves as complex formations made through relationships. At this point, beings remain inadequately conceived: they are incognizant of the ways in which they may combine actively with compatible bodies in their environment to produce combinations that are enriching. This "second kind of knowledge" arises from the gradual learning of common notions, formed when relational beings over time come to understand the nature of the community they form when they enter into relationship, when they become capable of knowing precisely how the relationship brings mutual benefit by enhancing affective powers of each through the greater complexity created by the union; and, conversely, how the relationship is in other ways potentially detrimental. Common notions enable a deeper understanding of the affective nature of combinations, of natural agreement and disagreement, and how bodies may combine well or poorly: "we enter, with common notions, into the domain of expression: these notions are our first adequate ideas, they draw us out of the world of inadequate signs" (EP, 291). Common notions lead us to the "third kind of knowledge," of oneself as part of a universal and infinitely complex field of interconnection through which being is actively and lawfully expressed as ethical becoming, moving through increasing levels of complexity and affective potentiality.

Common notions reveal "norms of composition, rules for the realisation of powers" (EP, 291). They enable a human capacity for self-realization and for creativity, since in knowing how complex relations can be actively disposed, agents can encourage and seek out encounters expected to be beneficial; and they can creatively construct and organize environments to maximize their diversity and so enhance their potential for increasingly complex and rich expressions of life. The development of common notions is the task of the Deleuzian "difference operator" as a non-human or structural agency that "relates difference to difference" by revealing how combinations may emerge, and where mutual disjunctions prohibit agreement without recourse to coercion. Considered through a Spinozian lens, the "Civilisation of the Universal" serves the joyful purpose of infinite complexification and increase of affective potentiality: it posits a world of cultural

differences engaged in non-coercive processes of shared becoming
and individuation, potentially participating in the social discovery of
"common notions" as sites of ethical encounter where mutual enrichment may occur, bit by bit.

3. CONCLUSION: SURREALISM, VIRTUAL TEMPORALITY, AND THE MINOR ETHICS OF NÉGRITUDE

Gary Wilder reads Césaire and Senghor as visionaries "seeking to
invent socio-political forms that did not yet exist for a world that
had not yet arrived."[54] Surrealism was a crucial aspect of this vision-
ary endeavour, and indeed Césaire and Senghor were first and foremost surrealist poets; their political careers developed as a consequence
of their poetic interventions in colonialism. They were interested in
the potential of surrealist expression to communicate the positive
and productive relation of differences, and also to communicate an
understanding of difference itself. Accordingly, it is important to
understand how the poetry of Négritude exemplifies how language
operates the relation of difference to difference. In the jarring discordances of its imagery, the surrealist text itself becomes what Jodie
Barker calls "the artistic milieu of the interplay of differences."[55] The
poem itself expresses the coexistence of differences, making the political poetry of Négritude an "architecture" of non-sense that is at the
same time a precise logic of sense: "a mathematical formula, based
on *unity in diversity*."[56] Like Deleuze's own "logic of sense," the
poetry of Négritude, through an unconventional orchestration of
signs and images, creates "cosmopolitan and corporeal ethical movements that do not result in unity, but emerge from and encourage
difference and diversity."[57]

As colonial subjects, Césaire and Senghor wrote in French, but in
doing so they sought to bring the French language in touch with its
Outside, its Unthought. In an interview, Césaire says that "French
was a tool that I wanted to use in developing a new means of expression. I wanted to create an Antillean French, a Black French that,
while still being French, had a black character."[58] For him, surrealism
"was a weapon that exploded the French language." Making use of
an "African image," a surrealist image, the poetry of Négritude invents
signs that escape the semantic discipline imposed by a dominant
imperial language usually expressing a European mode of reason;

now, "the object does not mean what it represents but what it suggests, what it creates. The Elephant is strength, the Spider is Prudence;
Horns are the Moon and the Moon is Fecundity."[59] The surrealist
image is an affective force of poetic sense bringing the sensation of
disjuncture. The listener experiences an unsettling encounter with
alterity, disrupting her established frameworks of sense-making, shocking thought into movement. In this way, the poem unhinges sense
from its past restrictions, liberating it for a new use, for the creation
of a future humanity perhaps unimaginable in existing structures of
comprehension and significance.[60]

Thus, as poetry and as politics, Négritude is a mode of being – a
style of thought and practice – "implicated in and responsible for
remaking the world and redeeming humanity."[61] Critics tend to read
Négritude as the celebration of an ancestral Africa, warm and inviting
like childhood: a lost unity that the colonized subject must seek out,
reclaim, and revive. But neither Césaire nor Senghor calls for a return
to an idealized pre-colonial past: their concepts of Négritude are
future-oriented. In his *Discourse on Colonialism*, Césaire writes:

> [Our] problem is not to make a utopian and sterile attempt to
> repeat the past, but to go beyond. It is not a dead society that we
> want to revive. We leave that for those who go in for exoticism.
> Nor is it the present colonial society that we wish to prolong,
> the most putrid carrion that ever rotted under the sun. It is a
> new society we must create."[62]

And, he says elsewhere, Négritude affirmed how "negro heritage was
worthy of respect, and that this heritage was not relegated to the past,
that its values ... could still make an important contribution to the
world" as "Universalising, living values that had not been exhausted."[63]

There is a complex temporality at work here, which (as Deleuze
explains) involves a use of virtual memory of the past in its entirety
to open an actual present to its potential for transformation. The
Bergsonian perspective that we cohabit with "*all* our past, which
coexists with each present" allows that past, present, and future are
multiple and coextensive levels, rather than singular and successive
moments, which interact in complex and nonlinear ways (B, 59;
cf. DR, 70ff).[64]

We also see this understanding of temporality at work in Césaire's
enduring and intense interest in Haiti, and especially in the Revolution

steered by Toussaint Louverture. Following a slave revolt in 1791, Toussaint led an organized rebellion culminating in confrontation with Napoleon Bonaparte and a final war of independence that led to the founding of the Republic of Haiti. In 1801 he issued a new constitution claiming rights to liberty, equality, and fraternity and identifying Haitians as "free and French," thus positioning the French Revolutionary doctrine of the Rights of Man over Haitian national sovereignty; this, then, was a project of general liberty rather than national liberation. In a similar way, Césaire's vision of Caribbean departmentalization was inspired by the idea of being "free and French." He wanted the colonies to be able to share equally in the French cultural values of liberty, equality, and fraternity, which he saw as the foundation of a new postcolonial political assemblage, based on the ethical communication of the differences comprising the transnational French Republic born of empire. In this way, like Toussaint had done beforehand, Césaire "takes the Declaration of the Rights of Man at its word."[65] Thus, Césaire "was prepared to accept departmentalization as a 'failure,' but only because the French failed to honour the full reach of universal rights."[66] In Césaire's play about Toussaint, we see him "bringing the writings of Toussaint out of the past in the effort to portray the revolution not as a historical impasse but as an ongoing, refractory process."[67] For Césaire, the Haitian Revolution failed in actuality but retains its virtual potential; similarly, the departmentalization of the French-Caribbean nations failed in actual fact to guarantee equal rights and participation in a transnational assemblage after empire, but its virtual potential as an unrealized promise of liberty experienced in an ethos of cultural intimacy remains available to postcolonial humanity. This virtual promise of joyful complexification after empire already exists for us as potential: an obscure precursor for future justice, which remains yet to be actualized in fact.

If Négritude is a "difference operator" that "relates difference to difference," we can now see that there are two aspects to this operation. In the first instance, Négritude is concerned with the relations obtaining between *actually existing differences*. Césaire and Senghor are interested in decolonizing – and so reforming – the nature of the engagement between the different cultures coexisting in the mélange of the French empire. Second, however, Négritude is attentive to the ethical potential of *virtual difference*, conceived in relation to an actual state of affairs or cultural relations and its permanent capacity for becoming-otherwise. This transformative or redemptive capacity is understood in part as a consequence of the virtual multiplicity of the past and its continued bearing on the lived present and the future-to-come. In this way, Négritude articulates an ethics of "becoming-minor" as a movement away from a "majoritarian" mode of experience organized on the basis of a given set of power relations that privilege a historically dominant subject (TP, 232).

Négritude describes a situated alter-humanism that expresses, in the surrealist poetry of political life, the dispersed and decentred subject after empire. However, unlike the "minor ethics" of Adorno, who finds in "damaged life" a model of self-deflation to counter the aggrandizing tendency of the colonial-fascist self,[68] Négritude promotes an ethos of mutual enrichment through the transversal communication of differences. It is this joyful quality, I have argued, that suggests the possibility of an alliance between Négritude and the idiosyncratic approach to ethics indicated in Deleuze's philosophy. In both, we find a careful emphasis on the processes and the practices of "becoming-minor" that open up alternate modes of relational subjectivation through heterodox conjunctive operations. These can confront and counteract dominant or entrenched frameworks of sense and sensibility by challenging and unsettling the habitual limits of the permissible and the punishable. Furthermore, these minor modes of affection and assemblage not only are vested with the potential to *counteract* dominant realities, but also and simultaneously contain a power to *counter-actualize* them by materializing alternative conditions of association to support the invention or the emergence of a new people-to-come. Here, "the minor is foremost an activity, a power, a tendency towards creation in its own right."[69] In racist postcolonial worlds defined by the willed erasure or disparagement of indigeneity and blackness, coupled with a domineering and oppressive constancy in the social and political imaginaries derived from the imperial centres and imposed unilaterally and universally, "the minor is a creative resistance *against conformity*" and in the service of diversity, complexity, and alterity.[70] A distant harbinger of a virtual future to come, the anti-colonial subject of Négritude seeks the molecular communication of differences – "bit by bit" – for the purpose of cultural innovation and complexification. As political practitioners in the service of decolonization, Césaire and Senghor profess a "minor ethics" of liberty in an ethos of complex interdependence unconstrained by state sovereignty, which remains yet to be actualized as the cosmopolitan democratic practices of the civilization of the universal.

NOTES

1 My sincere thanks to the editors, and to the participants in the Minor Ethics Conference held at the University of Guelph in May 2016 who gave early feedback on the ideas presented in this chapter. Thanks also to Professor Lewis Gordon and to other participants at the annual conference of the Australasian Society for Continental Philosophy at the University of Tasmania in 2017.

2 See Denis Ekpo, "From Negritude to Post-Africanism."

3 See Gary Wilder, *Freedom Time.*

4 See ibid.; and John Patrick Walsh, *Free and French in the Caribbean.*

5 See Pal Ahluwalia, *Out of Africa.*

6 Deleuze quoted here from "Intellectuals and Power" conversation, printed in Foucault, *Language, Counter-Memory, Practice,* 207.

7 Spivak, "Can the Subaltern Speak?"

8 See Bignall, *Postcolonial Agency.*

9 Kelley, "A Poetics of Anticolonialism," 14.

10 Césaire in conversation with R. Depestre in 2000, quoted from Césaire, *Discourse on Colonialism,* 83.

11 See ibid., 44; and Senghor, *On African Socialism.* Cf. Marx and Engels's text *On Colonialism.*

12 Kelley, "A Poetics of Anticolonialism."

13 Senghor, *Prose and Poetry,* 99.

14 Senghor, *Liberté 3,* 281; and *Prose and Poetry,* 96–7. All translations from the French are my own.

15 Senghor, *Prose and Poetry,* 35.

16 Sartre, *Black Orpheus,* xxix.

17 Senghor, *Prose and Poetry,* 29.

18 Said, *Orientalism.*

19 Senghor, *Prose and Poetry,* 29–30.

20 I am grateful to Professor Lewis Gordon for this point and for his advice on other aspects of the chapter.

21 See also Bignall, "Affective Assemblages."

22 See Fanon, *Black Skin, White Masks,* 109; and also L. Gordon, *Fanon and the Crisis of European Man.*

23 See Bignall, "Affective Assemblages."

24 Senghor, *Liberté 5,* 7.

25 Senghor, *Prose and Poetry,* 99.

26 Diagne, "In Praise of the Post-racial," 246.

27 Senghor, *Prose and Poetry,* 97.

28 Diagne, "Praise of the Post-racial," 245.

29 See Robert J.C. Young, *Colonial Desire*.

30 Césaire, *Discourse on Colonialism*, 33.

31 Senghor, *African Socialism*, 9.

32 Césaire's *Letter to Maurice Thorez* cited in Diagne, "Praise of the Post-Racial," 245.

33 Senghor, *Prose and Poetry*, 98.

34 Diagne, "In Praise of the Post-racial," 244.

35 Ibid., 246; Senghor, *Prose and Poetry*, 73.

36 Césaire, *Discourse on Colonialism*, 73.

37 Senghor, *Liberté* 1.

38 Senghor, "The Foundations of 'Africanité'," 75, 49.

39 Glissant, *Poétique de la relation*; see Nesbitt, "The Postcolonial Event."

40 Bignall, "Affective Assemblages."

41 Henry, *Caliban's Reason*.

42 J. Gordon, *Creolizing Political Theory*.

43 Monahan, *The Creolizing Subject*.

44 Wilder, *Freedom Time*, 5.

45 Ibid., 2, 7.

46 Senghor, *Prose and Poetry*, 64.

47 Wilder, *Freedom Time*, 21, 2.

48 Ibid., 98.

49 Ibid., 75, 2.

50 Ibid., 7, 97.

51 Ibid., 12.

52 Senghor, *Prose and Poetry*, 97; see also *On African Socialism*, 7-65.

53 See Moira Gatens, "Affective Transitions."

54 Wilder, *Freedom Time*, 3.

55 Barker, "From Parole Poétique to the Ethical Turn," 53.

56 Senghor, *Prose and Poetry*, 88.

57 Barker, "From Parole Poétique," 69.

58 Césaire, *Discourse on Colonialism*, 83.

59 Senghor, *Prose and Poetry*, 85.

60 Barker, "From Parole Poétique," 61.

61 Wilder, *Freedom Time*, 8.

62 Césaire, *Discourse on Colonialism*, 52.

63 Ibid., 92.

64 Deleuze, *Bergsonism*. Hereafter B.

65 Césaire, *Touissant Louverture*, 344.

66 Walsh, *Free and French*, 152.

67 Ibid., 20. See also Whyte, "'The Work of Men Is Not Durable'";
    cf. Foucault, "Kant on Enlightenment and Revolution."
68 Adorno, *Minima Moralia.*
69 Ford and McCullagh, "Introduction" above, 11.
70 Ibid.

Minor Ethics and the Practice of History[1]

Casey Ford

Philosophical time is thus a grandiose time of coexistence that does not exclude the before and after but superimposes them in a stratiographic order. It is an infinite becoming of philosophy that crosscuts its history without being confused with it. ... Philosophy is becoming, not history; it is the coexistence of planes, not the succession of systems. (WP, 59/58–9)

Minor Ethics involves a transhistorical investigation and deployment of concepts that is at once attentive to their past genesis and oriented toward future innovations. In taking up texts, thinkers, and ideas from the history of ethical philosophy, the project is situated with practices in the history of philosophy and aims to contribute to how we might approach anew the history of thought.[2] In this volume, we have considered the historically oriented aspect of the project in terms of two general questions. First, what happens to our understanding of a text or figure when a certain concept or set of concepts – which are operational in a text but rendered minor in the tradition of interpretation – are given a new accent or valence once assembled with heterogeneous concepts from another time and place? And second, what value do these newly activated concepts (what we have called the minor) have for destabilizing and re-enlivening the way we approach the study of ethics now? In short, our interest is in the power of the past, when major narratives are disrupted or multiplied, for changing the conceptual trajectories of our present intellectual moment.

Our project made a temporal choice. From the vantage point of concepts proximate to our philosophical present – that is, as given an inflection by Deleuze's thought – we turned to the diverse and winding history of philosophical thought, which is often represented linearly.[3] Our conviction was that doing philosophy in the present required recognizing that the forms and content of our thinking are the products of a history that is neither linear nor complete, that is, a development that is not fully determined in advance to amount to what it has become. In this sense, we have taken up the history of ideas as a *problem space* that has not been acknowledged and appreciated in the scope of its divergences. While the present necessarily involves a moment of innovation, we follow Marx's insight that when people "make their own history ... they do not make it just as they please; they [make it] under circumstances directly found, given and transmitted from the past. The tradition of all the dead generations weighs like a nightmare on the brain of the living."[4] There is no need to focus on the pessimism in this statement to recognize the central insight: no philosophical concept lacks a history or has the opportunity of occurring in a vacuum, and no present moment can ever be divorced from the complexity of the past that birthed it. But the past is neither a Sisyphean burden to be carried by any generation, nor simply a costume to be worn, as Marx notes, by those interested in dominating the present with the force and grandeur of old and tried methods.[5] What is at stake for us is the extent to which the diverse and minoritized ideas of the past can be rendered active and transformative.

In uncovering and developing minor elements of philosophical texts, the chapters in this volume have focused less on understanding texts exclusively in their specific historical and socio-cultural contexts, as many worthwhile projects in intellectual history have done, and more on the minor lines of thought that have been obscured once the history of philosophical ethics was rendered in the form of a major ethics. Much of the contemporary work in ethics given to us through majoritarian narratives presents texts and ideas from the historical tradition in ways that are useful for a certain set of normative questions and concerns in the present. For instance, Descartes's *cogito*, Kant's Categorical Imperative, and Mill's principle of utility are presented (in both teaching and scholarship) as core resources for conceptualizing ethics in terms of autonomous, rational action. The concern of minor ethics is that there are other philosophical ways of understanding past texts that major ethics covers over, alternatives to major modes of thinking and reading the history of philosophy of and for the present. Our concern is with opening up different routes of thinking and doing ethical philosophy in the future, and many resources for this work, we maintain, are nested in the intellectual past. "History can untie our minds, our bodies, our disposition to move," Howard Zinn proposes, "to engage life rather than contemplating it as an outsider. It can do this by widening our view to include the silent voices of the past, so that we look behind the silence of the present ... It can reveal how ideas are stuffed into us by the powers of our time, and so lead us to stretch our minds beyond what is given."[6]

The chapters in this volume do not strive to represent the intellectual past of ethics more completely and accurately than it has been represented until now.[7] Nor do they set out to discount or challenge the valuable objective methods of historians in the domain of events and ideas. Rather, our goal is to supplement these approaches to how the past is engaged and employed (rather than simply known). While intellectual history is not the focus of this volume, several chapters do engage strongly with the historical past in which the texts of focus were written. For instance, Bell considers the emergence of the "improvement societies" in Scotland and England as a significant social and historical phenomenon that shaped Hume's, and Smith's, assumption "that our rustic, unpolished, and prone to violent nature becomes tamed and civilized through the effort to create a shared culture within the civilized drawing rooms." Johnson engages with classical studies on the "history of reception of atomism" to support the possibility that the final scene of Lucretius's *De rerum natura* is counterfeit. Bignall draws attention to the "political milieu of the post-imperial French confederation of nations" that formed the essential context in which Césaire and Senghor invented Négritude as a concept that insists "on the role to be played by diverse cultures allied in the ethical expression of human civilization after the systematic dehumanization wrought by European imperialism and fascism." While these social-historical considerations do contribute to our knowledge of what certain philosophical ideas meant in their time and place, we also mobilize them to loosen concepts from major narratives of interpretation that have fixed them in place so that we might use them differently in the present.

Throughout this volume we have paired or conjoined figures, texts, and concepts across historical distances in terms of their conceptual resonances. This procedure contrasts with the traditional mode of considering figures or texts conjointly according to their philosophical or socio-historical influence. For instance, a reading together of Hume and Bertrand Russell, spanning three hundred years, might be justified

by the influence of the former's atomistic empiricism on the latter; or
a reading of Cicero and Marcus Aurelius might be appropriate given
the common socio-philosophical context that is the Roman world.
As a way of approaching the history of philosophy, conjoining the
internal concepts of a classical text with those of an extrinsic and
contemporary one naturally risks charges of anachronism, of reading
into the historical past the present day's intellectual interests and
interpretations.[8] For intellectual historians, this error is of course
grave, since it proceeds with the intent of understanding something
of the past only to misconstrue that past with interests and content
entirely foreign to its time and place. In the end, the anachronistic
reading comes to understand nothing new of the past except what it
already possessed in the conviction of its own present views. As well,
we must add, it sheds little light on present ideas because it has blocked
out the intellectual differences that form the labyrinth of their historical origin. In addition, to elucidate the truth of the past, Foucault
writes, history also "disturbs what was previously considered immobile; it fragments what was thought unified; it shows the heterogeneity
of what was imagined consistent with itself."[9]

Our procedure has explicitly involved conjunctures of historical
texts with concepts developed outside their intellectual, temporal,
and cultural milieux; even so, we do not believe that these readings
proceed anachronistically. This is because our goal is not to take up
historical texts or concepts as if they had a fixed position in an objective past, nor is it simply to understand what they mean in themselves
or in their contexts. Consequently, the problem at hand is not the
epistemic or hermeneutic one of bridging the gap between a present
mode of inquiry and a world of truth at a temporal distance from it.
To the contrary, our thesis is that no concept can simply be relegated
to a determinate and fixed position in history and that no text is
exhaustible by subsequent interpretations and uses. For instance,
certain aspects of Aristotle's account of how we form habits, and of
the logistical difficulties we face in overcoming them, resonate with
a number of experiential and conceptual problems outside Aristotle's
text and time, such as today's opioid crisis. In much the same way,
Augustine's struggle with the alterity of his self, gestated originally in
a religious context, can produce important resonances at a time when
humans are struggling with the ecological consequences of the human
domination of the more-than-human world. In short, an important
difference that marks our practice from others in intellectual history

is that we do not purport to take up the past in terms of uncovering and disclosing it as a final and objective truth.[10] If our practice is as much appropriative as it is interpretive, this indicates for us the inevitably double temporality of concepts themselves.

In terms of historical practice, the procedure employed throughout *Minor Ethics* is experimental and our objects uniquely conceptual. But what do we mean by "concept" as an object of historical study and engagement? Our proposition is, following Deleuze and Guattari, that the philosophical concept is more than an idea, statement, or meaning as a historical occurrence: it is foremost an "event" that constitutes a transhistorical power which, by virtue of being a *concept*, escapes and becomes effective beyond its historical place. "The concept," Deleuze and Guattari argue, "belongs to philosophy and only to philosophy" (WP, 34/37), and "philosophy is the art of forming, inventing, and fabricating concepts" (WP, 2/8). If philosophy's proper occupation is the "creation" of concepts, what role does history have in philosophy's work? Deleuze and Guattari make three significant points about the nature of the concept that are important for distinguishing the object of our philosophico-historical practice from other kinds of objects delimited by intellectual historians. First, the concept is not fully explainable through a "state of affairs" from which it has been effectuated; second, it should not to be reduced to a linguistic or semantic proposition; and third, its structure is always fundamentally open and communicative, especially to other concepts outside its internal structure and the proximate fields in which it is articulated (e.g., a text, corpus, or intellectual world). In all three of these respects, Deleuze and Guattari argue that there is an "ideality" to the concept (WP, 22/27), one that, rather that designating a fixed essence, attests to its capacity to be detached from its point of origin, to innovate beyond the objective delimitation of its significance. The concept, in short, carves a "line of flight" in and through history. Before turning to the possibilities this "concept of *concept*" (WP, 19/24) offers for historical practices, we want to consider these respective claims in relation to some of the significant methods and concerns in intellectual history.

(1) The concept is *more than* its "state of affairs," that is, it is irreducible to the facts, bodies, utterances, and contexts from which it emerged. Naturally, every philosophical concept has an extraphilosophical source: it is articulated in a particular text rather than another, composed and given a sense by the thoughts and motivations

of a certain author, and conceived in a concrete cultural and historical place. Social histories are importantly able to show that ideas are more than idiosyncratic and placeless novelties – they are also the products of interwoven social, cultural, and intellectual milieux that gave rise to certain ideas at a specific time. It *is* significant that Descartes's concept of the *cogito* emerged in an intellectual climate asserting the power of autonomous, human rationality against theological dogmas; that Leibniz's "monad" was generated through a certain intellectual cross-pollination between biological, physical, and theological investigations[11]; and that the Stoic concept of "necessity" was, in a certain respect, as Hegel asserts, suited for the authoritarian demands of Roman imperial life, a philosophy of freedom "whether on the throne or in chains."[12] "Every concept has a history" (WP, 17/23), whether it is the history of its generation in a thinker or the more all-encompassing history of its appearances in the totality of intellectual thought.[13]

However, as Deleuze and Guattari argue, the "knowledge" we might develop of a philosophical concept should not be "confused with the state of affairs in which it is embodied" (WP, 33/36; 21/26). This is to say, the concept should not be reduced to the history of its actual genesis. This is because every concept is also a "pure event," a "creation," an "act of thought" that "extract[s]" something new "from things and being" (WP, 33–4/36–7; 21/26, 36/38–9). As an ideational creation, a concept is necessarily a break from the past that announces something new and that opens itself onto a future. Equating the "concept" with an "event," which is typically understood as an objective historical happening, may seem to obscure rather than elucidate the significance of this point. However, when we distinguish between a historical *occurrence* and a historical *event* in terms of their temporal, impactful, and ontological frames, we can better understand Deleuze and Guattari's point about concepts. Any historical occurrence can be explained by antecedent conditions that led to it, but not all historical moments have the same significance or potency. Explaining what historically led to the storming of the Bastille does not explain what made that occurrence an "event" once it had occurred, nor does it explain how the event came to be commemorated, repeated, and employed in futural time (see DR, 91–2/123): the Bastille meant something quite different when invoked by Napoleon than it did for Louverture, and it may mean something else at a future conjuncture. What makes something an "event," as an accented occurrence, is not just its retrospective historical importance or flashpoint of activity, but more fundamentally its openness to the future and the power it exerts on that future; the more the event inclines toward the latter, the more it departs from its past conditions, asserting an autonomy or "ideality" from its own genesis. What makes a philosophical concept irreducibly an event is its inclination toward an outside, whether that means subsequent interpretations or the potential to encounter other problems in its field. In this sense, Deleuze and Guattari propose that we also treat concepts as "intensive," as powers, rather than terms to be represented "extensively" in their historical situation (w P, 20–1/25–6), like points on a graph that simply need to be calculated in terms of their fixed proximities or distances to other points.

(2) The concept is not simply a semantic or "discursive" statement (w P, 22/27), that is, a linguistic utterance with a meaning that must be deciphered and traced. Asserting the autonomy of the concept from its context might mean, alternatively, that we focus simply on its meaning or ideational content rather than on the social determinations or personal motivations that factored into it. The history of a concept like Descartes's *cogito* might first note the propositional context in which the "unit-idea" appears,[14] that is, in the proposition "I think therefore I am" (*cogito ergo sum*). Understanding the meaning of this proposition would then require deconstructing it and interpreting it within the internal logic of Descartes's *Meditationes*, or of his wider corpus, to trace the semantics of the terms "thought" and "existence." And this would ultimately require, as Quentin Skinner argues, rooting this singular concept and claim back in the broader linguistico-intellectual context in which it was possible to articulate it.[15] Here is situated a fundamental debate about whether to understand ideas through their social contexts or strictly through the internal coherence of ideas and texts themselves.[16] In terms of comprehensively understanding the meaning and reality of *past* ideas, both of these approaches are essential and valuable, but what they do not elucidate is the particular power that Deleuze and Guattari isolate in the philosophical *concept*.

By *concept* we do not mean the semantics of a philosophical and linguistic utterance, regardless of whether its meaning is determined in conjunction with the limitations of either a textual logic or a set of historico-cultural conditions.[17] But more importantly, the problem with equating the concept with a linguistic utterance is that it reduces the power of a concept to a determinate meaning of "reference" that is supposed to lurk behind it, defined in "relationship with a state of affairs" as "entirely extensional" (WP, 22/27). The task becomes simply a matter of representing the meaning that is intended behind an idea, or reconstructing what had to be the case for the meaning it has; in either case, the idea is rendered static, fixed to its historical circumstance, so that the scope of its meaning is fully circumscribed by the past in which it is trapped. Once this has occurred, for philosophy it matters little whether this meaning is pursued textually or into its social milieu. What is amputated from the idea is its efficacy to become different, to be efficacious, to enter into "heterogeneous" relations of thought and philosophical life (whether these are foreign concepts, new interpretations, or new social urgencies). Treating a concept in terms of its historical objectivity appears innocuous only if we forget that these kinds of risks, anticipations, and openings were the very conditions of the emergence of philosophical concepts to begin with. No philosophical concept, be it articulated historically or in the present, is reducible to this kind of stasis and fixity; these states might serve a certain historical retrospection, but they do not serve the totality of the temporal dimensions in which concepts are involved. There is a power of a concept itself, born in a particular text and of a determinate world, as a *power* of a thought beyond its origin, inclined toward a future.

(3) Every philosophical concept is ontologically always related to an outside without necessarily anticipating what the latter will be. In a temporal sense, the concept by its nature tends beyond itself as an expressive act; it inclines to be taken up, interpreted, and re-formed. The concept calls for an intellectual response yet it cannot predict what that response will be; it incites critiques or endorsements, pleads for allies and detractors so that it may move and transition away from the vanishing point of ordinary speech. Experientially, our quotidian actions or words do not carry much weight in relation to the future; we need not worry whether a remark or offhand gesture will be impactful and interpreted differently in a few generations. Philosophical concepts, by contrast, bear "irregular contours" (WP, 23/28) that never quite fit their time and place because they invite something indeterminate beyond what is being thought in their situation. And they are impotent with regard to their own endurance beyond their textual or cultural presence, whether it is in the hands of the sages who preserve them through and beyond ages of ruin, or in the eye of a student who interprets a set of propositions from a world far divorced from its origin. We are interested in the potency of a concept's

assemblings beyond its historical frame and beyond the major narratives that fix it in determinate orders of intelligibility and significance. This is one way of defining a *problematic space*, where
something's reality becomes open to variability.

What then does it mean to engage with philosophical concepts
nested in past worlds? These concepts may be at once homogeneous
and heterogeneous with the world in which we encounter them, in
the way a Humean concept might share our English tongue but
come from economic relations far removed from our own. Deleuze
and Guattari identify a "history of philosophy" as a particular task:
to "evaluate not only the historical novelty of the concepts created
by a philosopher but also the power of their becoming when they
pass into one another" (WP, 32/35–6). It must be emphasized that,
here for Deleuze and Guattari as well as for the practices that constitute this volume, it is not a matter of appropriating the alternative
potential of concepts while ignoring their semantic or social meaning.
Rather, it involves showing how a given concept has both an internal
logic (whether the scope is the idea itself, its text, or its world) and a
certain efficacy beyond itself. As Deleuze and Guattari note, every
concept has a determinate "endoconsistency" (WP, 19–20/25), that
is, a set of internal elements that constitute it, in the way Descartes's
cogito assembles a logical relation or equation between *thought* and
existence. The "novelty" is the extent to which *heterogeneous* elements
form parts of its composition (for Descartes, thought had been ontologically separated from the existence that is thought). To simply
appropriate a concept without considering the novelty of its own
consistency would be tantamount to not engaging that concept at all.
But in addition to this, every concept has a certain "exoconsistency"
(WP, 20/25), a set of "contours" by which it is capable of entering
into new conceptual relations. Every concept has a multiplicity of
"irregular" contours by which it can be connected or fail to connect
with other concepts, internally and externally, each involving possible
relations that form "bridges" with other concepts without ever constituting a fully cohesive and "discursive whole" (WP, 23/28). If they
constitute a "wall," it is a "dry-stone wall" in which "everything holds
together only along diverging lines."[18] These bridges might form a
coherence within a certain local milieu, as when Descartes's *cogito* is
logically bridged with the concept of "God" as a ground, or it may
form a problematic field with extraneous concepts, as when the *cogito*
opened the problem of the constitution of the self within which Kant

would "[introduce] time into thought" itself, "fracturing" the subject
of experience into passive and active sides (DR, 86–8/116–19).

While intellectual history assesses the development of ideas as propositional utterances in their proper textual logics or cultural contexts,
the "history of philosophy" identified by Deleuze and Guattari aims
to treat the created concept as "self-referential" (WP, 22/27). This does
not mean, however, that the concept is enclosed upon itself; rather, it
asserts a novel expression or "ideality" distinct from either essential
meaning or contextual "reality." Taking concepts seriously as "events"
means treating them as "concrete assemblages, like the configuration
of a machine" (WP, 36/39) whose functioning does not override its
possible modes of reassemblage. Of course, this does not mean that
every concept possesses an infinite potential; the *cogito* might not be
structurally conducive, for instance, to becoming with experiences in
body dysmorphia or addiction, which may demand the creation of a
new concept of the self to adequate them. Our foremost concern is
with how philosophical concepts can be approached differently *now*,
based on their contours or potencies, for the sake of thinking differently in the future. We thus in part follow R.G. Collingwood's proposal
for a "pragmatic view of history," one that, rather than treating the
past as an object of "true knowledge," pursues the "reconstruction of
an ideal object in the interests of knowing ... (and therefore [acting]
relatively to) the present."[19] There is much to be said for Collingwood
here, but we wish to take up one significant interpretation of what is
implied by his "ideal object." It means an attention to the concept as
a particular kind of historical reality that is, we maintain, transhistorical by virtue of being a concept. "There is no act of creation," Deleuze
and Guattari argue, "that is not transhistorical and does not come up
from behind or proceed by way of a liberated line ... Creations are
like mutant abstract lines that have detached themselves from the task
of representing a world, precisely because they assemble a new type
of reality that history can only recontain or relocate" (TP, 296/363).
Deleuze's infamous and often parodied methodological remark about
"taking an author from behind" (N 6/15) is less about distortion and
more about the opening of an idea up to an outside, to a renewed
becoming in non-successive history.

Readers of Deleuze and Guattari will note a certain antipathy in
their work to the project of history.[20] History, Deleuze and Guattari
tell us, "is always written from a sendentary point of view" (TP,
23/34).[21] Experientially, this means that the past tends to be

interpreted and rendered coherent from the specific perspective of a present we take to be an ossified standard of reality and thought. Politically, it means that the past becomes a material to shape in the interests of supporting an established present world.[22] Books, Deleuze and Guattari suggest, are "burdened by too heavy a cultural load" in that they trace "established concepts and words" and "the world of the present, past, and future" (TP, 24/35). Their alternative aim is a "nomadology," that is, the "opposite of a history" (TP 23/34).[23] In order to escape the tracing of the already established, they propose using books "for forgetting instead of remembering, for underdevelopment instead of progress towards development, in nomadism rather than sedenterity." The way we read and take up books, in addition to possibly making the present rigid, is crucial to finding alternatives to writing and thinking History. What we have proposed in this volume is, in part, an investigation of the minor lines of thought resting virtually in the major histories of thought that have formed and sedimented our present ways of thinking, the rhizomatic offshoots buried beneath and diverging from the trees we think we cannot escape.

One way to approach the historical texts and ideas bequeathed to us in the present is to get beyond tracing and reproducing ideas in order to assemble concepts and texts in heterogeneity. "How can the book find an adequate outside with which to assemble in heterogeneity, rather than a world to reproduce?" (TP, 24/35) In one sense, the historian inevitably becomes a nomad in relation to her own present world, venturing into the foreign, open space of the past. There is the risk, however, that this venture into the heterogeneous will only restriate or reterritorialize the past in rigid and immobile ways. One way out, we propose, is to allow historical concepts themselves to become nomadic, to partially deterritorialize them from the codes assigned to them, their boundaries of signification, and the milieux of their birth. Doing so, we believe, will allow ideas to enter into new becomings, new pairs, and "unnatural nuptials" of conceptual interaction (TP, 241/295, 273/335). In certain instances it is effective to trace the cross-historical resonances of problems, both to better understand a problem's complex source and to explore the scope of its significance beyond that origin. Bell thus recasts our understanding of the "impartial spectator" such that, in the tradition of modern epistemology and political thought, reason appears not in strict opposition to madness and irrationality but as emerging from and in response to it. As Bell shows, this has important implications for how we understand ethics because it indicates a continuous problem for normative ethics, no less than for epistemology, to account for the generation of universal and stable principles from the particular and unstable experiences of human life. In other respects, it might be necessary to fully recast the interpretation of a singular thinker's concepts and problems to better appreciate the scope of their significance in light of contemporary concerns. In this vein, Bourgault reconsiders Weil's concept of "attention" as politically (and not just spiritually) significant. This goes against the grain of dominant scholarship that reads Weil's concept as apolitical or even anti-political. Detached from this common interpretation, we are able to see the wider significance of Weilian attention for addressing contemporary phenomena that are currently depleting our capacities to attend to human suffering (such as Twitter and QAnon). In each of these distinct instances, certain historical concepts and figures are recast, rearticulated, or joined beyond their contexts. The point is not to falsify them, but to activate them for a more ethically capacitating or socially just future.

From a philosophical perspective, there are some significant problems with the way intellectual historians approach the history of ideas, just as much as there are problems with the way past is taken as mere object of knowledge rather than action. Rather than abandoning the historical occupation altogether, however, we choose to extract from it a potential for doing the history of philosophy in the minor key, that is, we choose to focus on the discontinuity, multiplicity, and heterogeneity of concepts that effect lines of flight within a major system of historical thought.[24] "The history of ideas should never be continuous; it should be wary of resemblances, but also of descents or filiations; it should be content to mark the thresholds through which an idea passes, the journeys it takes that change its nature or object" (TP, 235/288). As a practice, minor ethics is not a "method" in the sense of a regimented procedure for studying some predetermined object, one that would constitute a "striated space," in order to trace "a path that must be followed from one point to another" (TP, 377/467). It is a technique for making, within a major tradition itself, a "form of exteriority" or "smooth space" to resituate thought, "for which there is no possible method, no conceivable reproduction, but only relays, intermezzos, resurgences." We methodologically follow the aberrant and problematic, the concepts that always exist *between* things, especially in the intermediary zone between our present and another future.

There is no innocent history, no unmediated reading of the past, precisely because the point at which the past is taken up is one charged with meaning, limitation, and a concern with possibility.[25] Baugh, for instance, thus takes up ideas and problems intrinsic to Nietzsche's corpus (*amor fati* and the "eternal return") in order to chart them through a diverse and minor tradition from Nietzsche toward the demand of addressing an existential and ethical problem of living. In this course, the senses of the problem are multiplied without abandoning their historical origin and without relegating the problem to a pedantic or hermeneutic concern. By reconsidering the Western academy's casting of the Négritude movement as promoting a problematic form of cultural and racial essentialism, Bignall opens Négritude as a resource for imagining and crafting pluralist and culturally complex political communities capable of promoting the "joyful communication of differences for the purpose of cultural complexification." Rather than seeing the ideas of the past as a linear series of static facts to be known, we approach it as a virtual reserve of possible conceptual relations and problems[26] on the basis of which we are oriented in the present toward future philosophical creations. Depending on our comportment to the past, ideas may be either capacitating or stunting. It is in this sense that Foucault envisions the practice of history, à la Nietzsche, as a "curative science."[27] Were we to adopt a "perspectival knowledge [*savoir*]," historical practice could be "constructive"[28] of a new "theatre" of conceptual play and personage, a "concerted carnival,"[29] where the past and the future become stage positions in an unfolding narrative. In this practice, history might be "curative" of present problems, but the task of the historian also *curational* in assembling what the past has to offer for the problems that plague us. If there is a problem in treating history as a "pure science,"[30] it is that it potentially neutralizes the historical past as a problem space that continues to work on and through the present. The past is a problem before it is an object of knowledge; the future is a problem before the present looks to the past for a solution or a guideline; the historical present is a problem because it must decide what to do and use.

Our present is always the product of a past without being absolutely determined by it, and neither the events of the past nor the terms of the present, which may sometimes seem final or ossified, are sufficient to determine the future. We take this to be true of historical existence no less than the history of thought. The present is, or retains the potential to be, an evaluative, discerning, differentiating moment. This point of evaluation not only opens an indeterminacy of futural possibility but also reactivates or intensifies the past for the sake of the future, for thinking differently about what our present is. Any revolutionary thought, we should add, cannot simply be turned toward the world; it must also engage the concepts by which that world is and has been thought. This means parsing out how ideas and concepts have been solidified in major narratives, and what minor lines remain like "variations" and "centers of vibration" to be reactivated (WP, 20/25, 23/28). As a practice, a minor ethics intends to be both intervening and creative. What would it mean to return to the history of philosophical thought (not just of ethics, but of politics, science, economics, epistemology, etc.), not to reinterpret it along lines already demarcated in our present, but to reconstitute it intensively? How can we approach history with a sight newly charged by the conceptual limitations of our present, to take up the history of ideas geared toward the possibility of new assemblages of thinking?

NOTES

1 This postscript owes a great deal to the collaboration, ideas, conversations, decisions, and editorial work of Suzanne M. McCullagh.

2 See Introduction, n33.

3 Hegel's lectures on the philosophy of history are taken to provide an emblematic instance of approaching history as a linear, teleological, and progressive movement. He proposes that philosophy provides "Reason" to the "contemplation of history" in order to see how "the history of the world ... presents us with a rational process." *The Philosophy of History*, 9; cf. ibid., 36, for a discussion of the "divine plan" revealed in nature. However, it is an oversimplification to stress the "rational" and teleological aspects of Hegel's conception of history, since his philosophico-historical account also understands "Reason" as "infinite" (ibid.), "Spirit" as "plastic activity" (ibid., 73), and the narrative of world history as fundamentally retrospective and undeterminable of "New World[s]" and "Land[s] of the Future" like America, which, Hegel claims, "has no interest for us ... for, as regards *History*, our concern must be with that which has been and that which is" (ibid., 86–7). See n6 below for a further discussion of progress in history.

4 Marx's "Eighteenth Brumaire," in Marx and Engels, *The Marx–Engels Reader*, 595.

5 Ibid. Marx here emphasizes the way present revolutionary practices draw an important force from the "names, battle slogans and costumes" of history: "The awakening of the dead in those revolutions therefore served the purpose of glorying the new struggles, not of parodying the old; or magnifying the given tasks in imagination, not of taking flight from their solution in reality; of finding once more the spirit of revolution, not of making its ghost walk again." Ibid., 596; cf. Deleuze's discussion of these points in DR 91–2/133.

6 Zinn, *The Politics of History*, 54.

7 An interest in studying the past in terms of its objective reality – such as a historical text's social, cultural, or semantic context – is a common feature of many approaches in intellectual history as distinguished from appropriationist approaches; see our Introduction, n33, as well as our discussion below. This is given a distinct methodological value in Auguste Comte's "positivist" approach to social, scientific, and intellectual history under the banner "Order and Progress": "And now that man's history has been for the first time systematically considered as a whole," Comte writes, "and has been found to be, like all other phenomena, subject to invariable laws, the preparatory labours of modern Science are ended. Her remaining task is to construct that synthesis which will place her at the only point of view from which every department of knowledge can be embraced." *A General View of Positivism*, 34.

8 For a concise account of the problem of anachronistic readings in the history of ideas, see Quentin Skinner, "Meaning and Understanding." Skinner notes two forms of anachronistic "absurdities": those which impose concerns or values of the present on the things said in the past in the attempt to understand them, that is, based on what the "historian is *set* to expect" (12); and the valuations of past ideas based on what they did not manage to articulate according to present expectations. For our purposes, it should also be noted that Skinner recognizes that it is impossible for intellectual historical work to be done fully divorced from the vantage point of the present.

9 Foucault, "Nietzsche, Genealogy, History," 375.

10 Foucault appeals to Nietzsche's notion of "effective history" as an alternative to the "suprahistorical perspective" critiqued by Nietzsche, whose "function is to compose the finally reduced diversity of time into a totality fully closed upon itself." "Nietzsche, Genealogy, History," 379; cf. Nietzsche, *On the Advantage and Disadvantage of History*, 12.

11 See J. Smith, *Divine Machines*.

12 "As a universal form of the World-Spirit, Stoicism could only appear on the scene in a time of a universal fear and bondage, but also a time of

universal culture which had raised itself to the level of thought." Hegel,
Phenomenology of Spirit, 121 [§199].

13 Arthur O. Lovejoy argues that in order for an idea to be "fully understood,"
it must "be traced connectedly through all the phases of men's reflective
life in which those workings manifest themselves, or through as many of
them as the historian's resources permit ... [There] *is* a great deal more
that is common to more than one of these provinces than is usually recognized, that the same idea often appears, sometimes considerably disguised,
in the most diverse regions of the intellectual world." *The Great Chain of
Being*," 15.

14 Following an analogy with molecular chemistry, Lovejoy proposes that the
materials the historian of ideas is in "quest" of are "unit-ideas" as "the
elements, the primary and persistent or recurrent dynamic units, of the
history of thought." "In the whole series of creeds and movements going
under the one name, and in each of them separately," Lovejoy writes of
such notions as "God" or "Christianity," "it is needful to go behind the
superficial appearance of singleness and identity, to crack the shell which
holds the mass together, if we are to see the real units, the effective working ideas, which, in any given case, are present." Importantly for our
account is Lovejoy's insistence that the elemental parts composing larger,
dominant notions "are rather heterogeneous" and may not permit "formal
definitions." Ibid., 6–7. See Skinner's critique of Lovejoy in "Meaning and
Understanding," 35–6.

15 Skinner argues that the "understanding of texts ... presupposes the grasp
both of what they were intended to mean, and how this meaning was
intended to be taken." This means that "the appropriate methodology for
the history of ideas must be concerned, first of all, to delineate the whole
range of communications which could have been conventionally performed
on the given occasion by the utterance of the given utterance, and, next, to
trace the relations between the given utterance and this wider linguistic
context as a means of decoding the actual intention of the given writer."
"Meaning and Understanding," 48–9.

16 Reinhart Koselleck argues that while "social" and "conceptual" historical
theories share an important "analytic" difference – focusing on social conditions or events and linguistic articulations respectively – he importantly
insists that both approaches are necessary that they are mutually implicating. "Without searching for social formations together with their concepts,
by virtue of which – reflectively or self-reflectively – they determine and
resolve their challenges, there is no history, and it cannot be experienced,
interpreted, represented or explained. Society and language insofar belong

among the meta-historical givens without which no narrative and nor history are thinkable." "Social History and Conceptual History," 310.

17 Skinner's approach importantly aims to bridge this methodological disjunction: "the study of all the facts about the social context of the given text can then take its place as a part of this linguistic enterprise." "Meaning and Understanding," 48–9. While the approaches of Skinner and Koselleck offer important contributions to eliminating the opposition between the intellectual and the social conditions of a historical text or idea, we depart from these approaches in their primary concern with how to understand elements of the past (whether it is a text, a concept, or a semantic proposition) in strict terms of their historical truth-content.

18 For a discussion of this image of the irregular, heterogenous "wall" in Deleuze's thought, see McCullagh and Ford, "The Desert Below," 169–71.

19 Collingwood, *Idea of History*, 405-6.

20 While drawing from important claims Deleuze and Guattari make, this reaction also ignores Deleuze's own consistent concern with constructing minor lineages through the history of thought (be they aesthetic, scientific, political, or philosophical). The value of Deleuze and Guattari's multidisciplinary approach to history is echoed, at least in spirit, by Lovejoy in his appeal for a maximally expansive purview for studying the emergence, continuation, and development of historical "ideas." "[A]ny unit-idea which the historian thus isolates," Lovejoy proposes, should be "[traced] through more than one – ultimately, indeed, through all – of the provinces of history in which it figures in any important degree, whether those provinces are called philosophy, science, literature, art, religion, or politics." *Great Chain of Being*, 15.

21 "All history does," Deleuze and Guattari argue, "is to translate a coexistence of becomings into a succession" (TP, 430/537), to represent what is temporally multidimensional and causally heterogeneous as a simplified line of progress. If history is a system of recollection, then "[b]ecoming is an anti-memory" (TP 294/360), an immersion in what Nietzsche calls the "unhistorical" (TP, 296/362–3) in which alone becomings are germinated; see Nietzsche, *On the Advantage and Disadvantage*, 11. For Deleuze and Guattari, the concept and practice of history is thus no more than a service rendered to majoritarian thought, power, and the conquest of representing time in the image of the major: "There is no history but of the majority" (TP, 292/257) which is "one with the triumph of States" (TP, 393–4/490) and the subordination of minoritarian elements, peoples, and thoughts (cf. TP, 295/362; and D, 2/8).

22 For a further discussion of this point, see Ford, "Captured Time."

23 For a systematic treatment of Deleuze and Guattari's ontological and practical approach to the philosophy of history, see Lampert's *Deleuze and Guattari's Philosophy of History* and the response by Lundy, *History and Becoming*.

24 Foucault argues that with the refusal of the "certainty of absolutes," "effective history ... introduces discontinuity into our very being." "Nietzsche, Genealogy, History," 379–80.

25 For an account of the political uses of history, see Zinn, *The Politics of History*.

26 In this respect, we understand our approach to the history of philosophy as following Deleuze's ontological account of temporality (see DR, Ch. 2). Lampert is singular in innovatively bridging this in Deleuze scholarship, arguing for a "philosophy of co-existential time as philosophy of history" in which "history is not the past, but the circulation of events." *Deleuze and Guattari's Philosophy of History*, 2–3. This notion of time – in which the dimensions of time (past, present, and future) are understood as dynamic, enfolding aspects of one another – is not foreign to the discourse on intellectual history. For instance, see Kosseleck's remarks on historical synchrony and diachrony: "Any synchrony is *eo ipso* diachronic at the same time. *In actu*, all temporal dimensions are always meshed and it contradicts any experience to define the so-called present as perhaps one of those moments which are added together from the past into the future – or which conversely slip from the future into the past as fleeting points of transition. Purely theoretically, all histories can be defined as permanent present in which the past and the future are contained – or, however, as the lasting meshing of past and future which constantly makes any present disappear." "Social History and Conceptual History," 317.

27 Foucault, "Nietzsche, Genealogy, History," 382. "Only so far as history serves life will we serve it," Nietzsche demands, "but there is a degree of doing history [which] brings with it a withering and degenerating of life." Nietzsche, *On the Advantage and Disadvantage*, 7.

28 Deleuze and Guattari claim that "[p]hilosophy is a constructivism" with two aspects: "the creation of concepts and the laying out of a plane" of "immanence" as the "fluidity of the milieu" or "horizon of events, the reservoir or reserve of purely conceptual events" (WP, 35–6/38–9; 22/27).

29 Foucault, "Nietzsche, Genealogy, History," 386. Anticipating Deleuze and Guattari's definition of concepts as events, Foucault proposes that historical concepts "must be made to appear as events in the theater of procedures" rather than proceeding as if historical "interpretation were the slow exposure of the meaning hidden in an origin." "Nietzsche, Genealogy,

History," 378–9. This should be corresponded with Deleuze's opposition between "the theatre of representation" and "the theatre of repetition," with the latter alone, he claims, capable of producing "movement" and "something effectively new in history" (DR, 10/18-19; 91–2/123, 192/248). For an extended discussion of ideas and the process of "dramatization," see Deleuze, "The Method of Dramatization" (DI, 94–116/131–62). Regarding the relation between Foucault and Deleuze, we follow Baugh's claim that Foucault's genealogy should be seen as the "practical and historical elaboration" of the "theoretical underpinnings" of Deleuze's own work; French Hegel, 147.

30 Nietzsche, History for Life, 14.

Bibliography

Adorno, Theodor. *Minima Moralia: Reflections on a Damaged Life*. London and New York: Verso, 2005.

Ahluwalia, Pal. *Out of Africa: Post-Structuralism's Colonial Roots*. London and New York: Routledge, 2010.

Aristotle. *Nicomachean Ethics*, translated by Terence Irwin. Indianapolis: Hackett, 1999.

– *Nicomachean Ethics*, translated by H. Rackham. Cambridge, MA: Harvard University Press, 1934.

– *The Complete Works of Aristotle*. 2 vols, edited by Jonathan Barnes. Princeton: Princeton University Press, 1984.

Aurelius, Marcus. *The Communings with Himself of Marcus Aurelius Emperor of Rome Together with his Speeches and Sayings*, translated by C.R. Haines. New York: G.P. Putnam and Sons, 1916.

Bacon, Francis. *The Works of Francis Bacon*, edited by R.L. Ellis, J. Spedding, and D. Heath. London: Longman, 1861.

Badiou, Alain. *Deleuze and the Clamor of Being*, translated by Louise Burchill. Minneapolis: University of Minnesota Press, 2000.

– "Existe-t-il quelque chose comme une politique deleuzienne?" *Cités* 4 (2009): 15–20.

Baker, G.P., and P.M.S. Hacker. *Wittgenstein: Understanding and Meaning*, Part II: *Exegesis §§1–184*. Oxford: Basil Blackwell, 2005.

Barker, Jodie. "From Parole Poétique to the Ethical Turn: Moving with Léopold Sédar Senghor." *Research in African Literatures* 46, no. 10 (2015): 53–71.

Baugh, Bruce. *French Hegel: From Surrealism to Postmodernism*. New York and London: Routledge, 2003.

– "Private Thinkers, Untimely Thoughts: Deleuze, Shestov, and Fondane." *Continental Philosophy Review* 48, no. 2 (June 2015): 313–39.

Beistegui, Miguel de. *Truth and Genesis: Philosophy as Differential Ontology*. Bloomington: Indiana University Press, 2004.

Bell, Jeffrey A. *Deleuze and Guattari's What Is Philosophy?: A Critical Introduction and Guide*. Edinburgh: Edinburgh University Press, 2016.

Bergen, Véronique. "La politique comme posture de toute agencement." In *Gilles Deleuze, Félix Guattari et le Politique*, edited by M. Antonioli, P.-A. Chardel, and H. Regnauld. Paris: Éditions du Sandre, 2006.

Bickford, Susan. *The Dissonance of Democracy: Listening, Conflict, and Citizenship*. Ithaca: Cornell University Press, 1996.

Bignall, Simone. "Affective Assemblages: Ethics beyond Enjoyment." In *Deleuze and the Postcolonial*, edited by Bignall and Paul Patton, 78–102. Edinburgh: Edinburgh University Press, 2010.

– *Postcolonial Agency: Critique and Constructivism*. Edinburgh: Edinburgh University Press, 2010.

Bourgault, Sophie. "Attentive Listening and Care in a Neoliberal Era: Weilian Insights for Hurried Times." *Etica e Politica – Ethics and Politics* 18, no. 3 (2016): 311–37.

Braidotti, Rosi. "Nomadic Ethics." In *The Cambridge Companion to Deleuze*, edited by Daniel W. Smith and Henry Somers-Hall, 170–97. Cambridge: Cambridge University Press, 2012.

Bréhier, Émile. *The History of Philosophy*, vol. 2: *The Hellenistic and Roman Age*, translated by Wade Baskin. Chicago: University of Chicago Press, 1965.

Buchanan, Ian, and Nicholas Thoburn, eds. *Deleuze and Politics*. Edinburgh: Edinburgh University Press, 2008.

Burke, Edmund. *Reflections on the Revolution in France*. Oxford: Oxford University Press, 2009.

Burns, Michael. *Kierkegaard and the Matter of Philosophy*. London: Rowman and Littlefield, 2015.

Butler, Judith. *Gender Trouble: Feminism and the Subversion of Identity*. New York: Routledge, 1999.

Calcagno, Antonio. "Individuated Embodiment and Action: Interrogating Roberto Esposito's Negative Self." *MOSAIC: Journal for the Interdisciplinary Study of Literature* 48, no. 3 (September 2015): 111–24.

Calvet, Louis-Jean. *La Sociolinguistique*. Paris: Presses Universitaires de France, 1993.

Calvino, Italo. *Six Memos for the Next Millennium*, translated by Patrick Creagh. Cambridge, MA: Harvard University Press, 1988.

Canguilhem, Georges. "Machine and Organism." In *Zone 6: Incorporations*, translated by Mark Cohen and Randall Cherry, edited by Johnathan Crary and Sanford Kwinter. Cambridge: Zone Books, 1992.

Carson, Anne. *Decreation*. Toronto: Vintage Canada, 2005.

Césaire, Aimé. *Discourse on Colonialism*, translated by J. Pinkham. New York: Monthly Review Press, 2000.

– *Touissant Louverture: La Revolution Francaise et le problème colonial*. Paris: Présence Africaine, 1981.

Chestov, Léon. *Athènes et Jérusalem*. Paris: Librairie Vrin, 1938.

Chomsky, Noam. *On Language* [1975]. New York: The New Press, 1998.

Code, Lorraine. "Taking Subjectivity into Account." In *Women, Knowledge, and Reality: Explorations in Feminist Philosophy*, edited by Ann Garry and Marilyn Pearsall, 191–221. New York: Routledge, 1996.

Cohen, Marc. "Aristotle's Metaphysics." In the *Stanford Encyclopaedia of Philosophy*. http://plato.stanford.edu/entries/aristotle-metaphysics.

Collingwood, R.G. *The Idea of History: With Lectures 1926–1928*. Oxford: Oxford University Press, 1994.

Comte, Auguste. *A General View of Positivism* [1848], translated by J.H. Bridges. New York: Cambridge University Press, 2009.

Connolly, William. *The Augustinian Imperative: A Reflection on the Politics of Morality*. New York: Rowman and Littlefield, 2002.

– *A World of Becoming*. Durham: Duke University Press, 2011.

Coulthard, Glen Sean. *Red Skin, White Masks: Rejecting the Colonial Politics of Recognition*. Minneapolis: University of Minnesota Press, 2014.

Courtine-Denamy, Sylvie. *Trois femmes dans de sombres temps*. Paris: Albin Michel, 2002.

Cummins, Robert. "Functional Analysis." *Journal of Philosophy* 72, no. 20 (1975): 741–65.

Curzer, Howard J. "Aristotle's Mean Relative to Us." *American Catholic Philosophical Quarterly* 80, no. 4 (2006): 507–19.

Dante. *The Inferno of Dante*, translated by Robert Pinsky. New York: Farrar, Straus and Giroux, 1994.

Deleuze, Gilles. *Bergsonism*, translated by Hugh Tomlinson and Barbara Habberjam. New York: Zone Books, 1988; *Le Bergsonisme*. Paris: Presses Universitaires de France, 1966.

– *Desert Islands and Other Texts 1953–1974*, translated by Mike Taormima, edited by David Lapoujade. New York: Semiotext(e), 2004; *L'Île déserte: Textes et entretiens 1953–1974*. Edited by David Lapoujade. Paris: Les Éditions de Minuit, 2002.

– *Difference and Repetition*, translated by Paul Patton. New York: Columbia University Press, 1994; *Différence et répétition*. Paris: Presses Universitaires de France, 1968.

- *Empiricism and Subjectivity: An Essay on Hume's Theory of Human Nature*, translated by Constantin V. Boundas. New York: Columbia University Press, 1991; *Empirisme et Subjectivité. Essai sur la nature humaine selon Hume*. Paris: Presses Universitaires de France, 1953.
- *Essays Critical and Clinical*, translated by Daniel W. Smith and Michael A. Greco. London: Verso, 1998; *Critique et clinique*. Paris: Les Éditions de Minuit, 1993.
- *Expressionism in Philosophy*, translated by Martin Joughin. New York: Zone Books, 1990; *Spinoza et le problème de l'expression*. Paris: Minuit, 1968.
- *Kant's Critical Philosophy*, translated by Hugh Tomlinson and Barbara Habberjam. London: Athlone Press, 1984; *La Philosophie critique de Kant*. Paris: Presses Universitaires de France, 1963.
- *The Logic of Sense*, translated by Mark Lester and Charles Stivale. New York: Columbia University Press, 1990; *Logique du sens*. Paris: Éditions de Minuit, 1969.
- "Lucretius and Naturalism." In *Contemporary Encounters with Ancient Metaphysics*, translated by Jared C. Bly, edited by Abraham Jacob Greenstine and Ryan J. Johnson. Edinburgh: Edinburgh University Press, 2017.
- *Negotiations*, translated by Martin Joughin. New York: Columbia University Press, 1995; *Pourparlers*. Paris: Les Éditions de Minuit, 1990.
- *Nietzsche and Philosophy*, translated by Hugh Tomlinson. New York: Columbia University Press, 1983; *Nietzsche et la philosophie*. Paris: Presses Universitaires de France, 1962.
- "Nomad Thought." In *The New Nietzsche*, edited by David Allison. Cambridge, MA: MIT Press, 1977.
- *Proust and Signs*, translated by Richard Howard. Minneapolis: University of Minnesota Press, 2004; *Proust et les signes*. Paris: Presses Universitaires de France, 1964.
- *Pure Immanence*, translated by John Rajchman. New York: Zone Books, 2001.
- *Spinoza: Practical Philosophy*, translated by Robert Hurley. California: City Lights Books, 1988; *Spinoza: Philosophie pratique*. Paris: Presses Universitaires de France, 1970.
- *Two Regimes of Madness: Texts and Interviews 1975–1995*, translated by Ames Hodges, edited by David Lapoujade. New York: Semiotext(e), 2007; *Deux régimes de fous et autres textes: 1975–1995*. Edited by David Lapoujade. Paris: Les Éditions de Minuit, 2001.

Deleuze, Gilles, and Félix Guattari. *Anti-Oedipus: Capitalism and Schizophrenia*, translated by Robert Hurley, Mark Seem, and Helen R. Lane. Minneapolis: University of Minnesota Press, 1983; *L'Anti-Oedipe*. Paris: Les Éditions de Minuit, 1972.

- *Kafka: Toward a Minor Literature*, translated by Dana Polan. Minneapolis: University of Minnesota Press, 1975; *Kafka: Pour une littérature mineure*. Paris: Les Éditions de Minuit, 1975.

- *A Thousand Plateaus: Capitalism and Schizophrenia*, translated by Brian Massumi. Minneapolis: University of Minnesota Press, 1987; *Mille plateaux, volume 2 of Capitalisme et schizophrénie*. Paris: Les Éditions de Minuit, 1980.

- *What Is Philosophy?*, translated by Hugh Tomlinson. New York: Columbia University Press, 1994; *Qu'est-ce que la philosophie?* Paris: Les Éditions de Minuit, 1991.

Deleuze, Gilles, and Claire Parnet. *Dialogues*, translated by Hugh Tomlinson and Barbara Habberjam. New York: Columbia University Press, 1987; *Dialogues*. Paris: Flammarion, 1996.

Derrida, Jacques. "Plato's Pharmacy." In *Dissemination*, translated by B. Johnson. Chicago: University of Chicago Press, 1981.

Descartes, René. *The Philosophical Writings of Descartes*. 3 vols, translated by John Cottingham, Robert Stoothoff, and Dugald Murdoch. Cambridge: Cambridge University Press, 1985.

Dewey, John. *Art as Experience*. New York: Perigee, 2005.

Diagne, Souleymane Bachir. "In Praise of the Post-Racial: Negritude beyond Negritude." *Third Text* 24, no. 2 (2010): 241–8.

Dietz, Mary. *Between the Human and the Divine: The Political Thought of Simone Weil*. Totowa: Rowman and Littlefield, 1998.

Ekpo, Denis. "From Negritude to Post-Africanism." *Third Text* 24, no. 2 (2010): 177–87.

Elshtain, Jean Bethke. "The Vexation of Simone Weil." In *Power Trips and Other Journeys*. Madison: University of Wisconsin Press, 1990.

Engstrom, Stephen. *The Form of Practical Knowledge*. Cambridge, MA: Harvard University Press, 2009.

Epictetus. *Discourses and Selected Writings*, translated by Robert Dobbin. London: Penguin Books, 2008.

Epicurus. *The Epicurus Reader*, translated by Brad Inwood and L.P. Gerson. Indianapolis: Hackett, 1994.

Erler, Michael. "Epicureanism in the Roman Empire." In *Cambridge Companion to Epicureanism*, edited by James Warren, 46–64. Cambridge: Cambridge University Press, 2009.

Esposito, Roberto. "Biological Life and Political Life." In *Contemporary Italian Political Philosophy*, edited by Antonio Calcagno, 11–22. Albany: SUNY Press, 2015.

– *Immunitas: The Protection and Negation of Life*, translated by Zakiya Hanafi. London: Polity Press, 2011.

– *Persons and Things: From the Body's Point of View*, translated by Zakiya Hanafi. Cambridge: Polity Press, 2015; *Le persone e le cose*. Turin: Einaudi, 2014.

– "For a Philosophy of the Impersonal," translated by Timothy Campbell. *New Centennial Review* 10, no. 2 (2010): 121–34.

– *Termini della politica: Comunità, immunità, biopolitical*. Milan: Mimesis, 2008.

– *Terza persona*. Turin: Einaudi, 2007.

Evans, Stephen C. *Kierkegaard: An Introduction*. Cambridge: Cambridge University Press, 2019.

Fanon, Frantz. *Black Skin, White Masks*. New York: Grove Press, 1967.

Farrell, Joseph. "How to Be a Good Empiricist: A Plea for Tolerance in Matters Epistemological." In *Philosophical Papers*, vol. 3: *Knowledge, Science, and Relativism*, edited by John Preston. London: Cambridge University Press, 1999.

– "Lucretian Architecture: The Structure and Argument of the *De rerum natura*." In *The Cambridge Companion to Lucretius*, edited by Stuart Gillespie and Philip Hardie, 76–91. Cambridge: Cambridge University Press, 2010.

– "Lucretius and the Symptomatology of Modernism." In *Lucretius and Modernity: Epicurean Encounters across Time and Disciplines*, edited by Jacques Lexra and Liza Blake, 39–56. London: Palgrave Macmillan, 2016.

Fondane, Benjamin. *La Conscience malheureuse*, edited by Olivier Salazar-Ferrer. Paris: Verdier, 2013.

– *Faux traité d'esthétique*. Paris: Denoël et Steele, 1938.

– "Léon Chestov et la lutte contre les évidences." In *Rencontres avec Léon Chestov*, edited by Nathalie Baranoff and Michel Carassou. Paris: Non Lieu, 2016.

– "Nietzsche et les problèmes répugnants." *Le Rouge et le Noir* 8, 24 November 1937, front page.

Ford, Casey. "Captured Time: Simone Weil's Vital Temporality against the State." In *Simone Weil, Beyond Ideology*, edited by Sophie Bourgault and Julie Daigle. London: Palgrave Macmillan, 2020.

Foster, Edith. "The Rhetoric of Materials: Thucydides and Lucretius." *American Journal of Philology* 130, no. 3 (Fall 2009): 367–9.

Foucault, Michel. *Dits et écrits 1954–1988*, 2 vols. Paris: Gallimard, 1994.

– "Kant on Enlightenment and Revolution," translated by C. Gordon. *Economy and Society* 15, no. 1 (1986): 88–96.

– *Language, Counter-Memory, Practice: Selected Essays and Interviews*, translated by D.F Bouchard and S. Simon. Ithaca: Cornell University Press, 1977.

– "Nietzsche, Genealogy, History." In *Essential Works of Michel Foucault, 1954–1984*, vol. 2: *Aesthetics, Method, and Epistemology*, translated by Robert Hurley, edited by James D. Faubion, 369–91. New York: The New Press, 1999.

Fowler, Peta. "Lucretian Conclusions." In *Oxford Readings in Classical Studies: Lucretius*, edited by Monica R. Gale, 199–233. Oxford: Oxford University Press, 2007.

Frede, Michael. "History of Philosophy as a Discipline." *Journal of Philosophy* 85, no. 11 (November 1988): 666–72.

Freeland, Cynthia A. "Feminism and Ideology in Ancient Philosophy." *Apeiron* 33, no. 4 (December 2000): 365–406.

Gale, Monica. *Myth and Poetry in Lucretius*. Cambridge: Cambridge University Press, 1994.

Gassendi, Pierre. *Selected Works*, edited and translated by C. Brush. New York: Johnson Reprint, 1972.

Gatens, Moira. "Affective Transitions and Spinoza's Art of Joyful Deliberation." In *Timing of Affect: Epistemologies, Aesthetics, Politics*, edited by M. Angerer, B. Bosel, and M. Ott, 17–33. Zurich: Diaphanes Verlag, 2014.

Gilbert, Jeremy. "A Deleuzian Politic? A Survey and Some Suggestions." *New Formations* 68 (2010): 10–33.

Ginzburg, Carl. *The Cheese and the Worms: The Cosmos of a Sixteenth-Century Miller (with a New Preface)*, translated by John and Anne C. Tedeschi. Baltimore: Johns Hopkins University Press, 2013.

Glissant, Édouard. *Poétique de la relation*. Paris: Gallimard, 1990.

Godard, Jean-Luc. *Godard on Godard*, translated and edited by Tom Milne. New York: Da Capo Press, 1972.

Gordon, Jane Anna. *Creolizing Political Theory: Reading Rousseau through Fanon*. New York: Fordham University Press, 2014.

Gordon, Lewis R. *Fanon and the Crisis of European Man*. London and New York: Routledge, 1995.

Gould, Stephen Jay, and Elisabeth Vrba. "Exaptation – a Missing Term in the Science of Form." *Paleobiology* 8, no. 1 (Winter 1982): 4–15.

Greenblatt, Stephen. *The Swerve: How the World Became Modern*. New York: W.W. Norton, 2011.

Grosz, Elizabeth. "Habit Today: Ravaisson, Bergson, Deleuze, and Us." *Body and Society* 19, nos. 2–3 (2013): 217–39.

Guattari, Felix. *Chaosophy*, translated by David L. Sweet, Jarred Becker, and Taylor Adkins. Los Angeles: Semiotext(e), 2009.

Hallward, Peter. *Out of This World: Deleuze and the Philosophy of Creation*. London: Verso, 2006.

Hamilton, Alexander, James Madison, and John Jay. *The Federalist Papers: A Collection of Essays Written in Favour of the New Constitution as Agreed Upon by the Federal Convention, September 17, 1787*. Dublin, OH: Coventry House, 2015.

Haraway, Donna. "The Science Question in Feminism and the Privilege of Partial Perspective." *Feminist Studies* 14, no. 3 (1988): 575–99.

Hardt, Michael, and Antonio Negri. *Multitude: War and Democracy in the Age of Empire*. New York: Penguin, 2004.

Hegel, G.W.F. *Hegel's Science of Logic*, translated by A.V. Miller. New Jersey: Humanities Press International, 1989.

– *Phenomenology of Spirit*, translated by A.V. Miller. Oxford and New York: Oxford University Press, 1977.

– *The Philosophy of History*, translated by J. Sibree. New York: Dover, 1956.

Henry, Freeman G. *Language, Culture, and Hegemony in Modern France*. Birmingham: Summa, 2008.

Henry, Paget. *Caliban's Reason: Introducing Afro-Caribbean Philosophy*. London and New York: Routledge, 2000.

Holland, Eugene. "Nomadologie affirmative et machine de guerre." In *Gilles Deleuze, Félix Guattari et le Politique*, edited by M. Antonioli, P.-A. Chardel, and H. Regnauld. Paris: Éditions du Sandre, 2006.

Houle, Karen L.F. "Animal, Vegetable, Mineral: Ethics as Extension or Becoming? The Case of Becoming-Plant." *Journal for Critical Animal Studies* 9, nos. 1–2 (2011): 89–116.

– "Micropolitics." In *Gilles Deleuze: Key Concepts*, 2nd ed., edited by Charles J. Stivale, 88–97. Durham: Acumen, 2011.

Houlgate, Stephen. "Essence, Reflexion, and Immediacy in Hegel's Science of Logic." In *A Companion to Hegel*, edited by Stephen Houlgate and Michael Baur, 139–58. Oxford: Blackwell, 2011.

Hughes, Joe. *Deleuze's Difference and Repetition*. New York: Continuum, 2009.

Hume, David. *Enquiry Concerning the Principles of Morals*. Oxford: Oxford University Press, 1999.

– *Essays, Moral, Political, and Literary*. Indianapolis: Liberty Fund, 1985.

– *The History of England in Six Volumes*. Indianapolis: Liberty Fund, 1983.

– *Treatise Concerning Human Nature*, edited by David Fate Norton and Mary J. Norton. Oxford: Oxford University Press, 2000.

Inwood, Michael. *A Hegel Dictionary*. Oxford: Blackwell, 1992.

James, William. *Varieties of Religious Experience*. New York: Penguin Books, 1982.

Janiaud, Joël. "Simone Weil et l'attention." In *Simone Weil*, edited by Chantal Delsol. Paris: Cerf, 2009.

– "Simone Weil et le déracinement du moi." In *Simone Weil: Lectures politiques*, edited by Valérie Gérard. Paris: Éditions Rue d'Ulm, 2011.

Jope, James. "The Didactic Universe and Motional Import of Book Six of De rerum natura." *Phoenix* 43 (1989): 16–34.

Jun, Nathan, and Daniel W. Smith. *Deleuze and Ethics*. Edinburgh: Edinburgh University Press, 2011.

Jutrin, Monique. *Avec Benjamin Fondane au-delà de l'histoire*. Paris: Parole et Silence, 2011.

Kant, Immanuel. *Critique of Pure Reason*, translated by Paul Guyer and Allen W. Wood. Cambridge: Cambridge University Press, 2009.

– *Groundwork of the Metaphysics of Morals*, translated by Jens Timmermann. Cambridge: Cambridge University Press, 2012.

– *Political Writings*, translated by H.B. Nisbet. Cambridge: Cambridge University Press, 1991.

– *Practical Philosophy*, translated by Mary J. Gregor. Cambridge: Cambridge University Press, 1999.

Kelley, Robin D.G. "A Poetics of Anticolonialism." In Aimé Césaire, *Discourse on Colonialism*, translated by J. Pinkham, 7–28. New York: Monthly Review Press, 2000.

Kierkegaard, Søren. *The Concept of Anxiety*, edited and translated by Reidar Thomte. Princeton: Princeton University Press, 1980.

– *Concluding Unscientific Postscript*, edited and translated by Howard Hong and Edna Hong. Princeton: Princeton University Press, 1992.

– *Fear and Trembling and Repetition*, edited and translated by Howard Hong and Edna Hong. Princeton: Princeton University Press, 1983.

- *Søren Kierkegaard's Journals and Papers*, vol. 5, edited and translated by Howard Hong and Edna Hong. Bloomington: Indiana University Press, 1978.

Kitcher, Philip. "Unification as a Regulative Ideal." *Perspectives on Science* 7, no. 3 (1999): 337–48.

Koselleck, Reinhart. "Social History and Conceptual History." *Politics, Culture, and Society* 2, no. 3 (Spring 1989): 308–25.

Korsgaard, Christine. *Creating the Kingdom of Ends*. Cambridge: Cambridge University Press, 1996.

Kuhn, Thomas. *The Structure of Scientific Revolutions*. Chicago: University of Chicago Press, 1996.

Laertius, Diogenes. *The Lives of Eminent Philosophers*, translated by R.D. Hicks. Cambridge, MA: Loeb Classical Library, 1925.

Lærke, Mogens, Justin E.H. Smith, and Eric Schliesser, eds. *Philosophy and Its History: Aims and Methods in the Study of Early Modern Philosophy*. New York: Oxford University Press, 2013.

Lampert, Jay. *Deleuze and Guattari's Philosophy of History*. London and New York: Continuum, 2006.

Lecercle, Jean-Jacques. "Louis Wolfson and the Philosophy of Translation." *Oxford Literary Review* 11, no. 1 (1989): 103–20.

Lemke, Thomas. "*Gesellschaftskörper und Organismuskonzepte. Überlegungen zur Bedeutung von Metaphern in der soziologischen Theorie*." In *Die Ökonomie der Organisation – die Organisation der Ökonomie*, edited by Martin Endreß and Thomas Matys, 201–23. Dordrecht: Springer, 2010.

Little, J.P. "Simone Weil's Concept of Decreation." In *Simone Weil's Philosophy of Culture: Readings toward a Divine Humanity*, edited by Richard Bell. Cambridge: Cambridge University Press, 1993.

Lloyd, Genevieve. *The Man of Reason: "Male" and "Female" in Western Philosophy*. London: Routledge, 1995.

Locke, John. *Second Treatise of Government*. Indianapolis: Hackett, 1980.

Long, A.A. "Roman Philosophy." In *The Cambridge Companion to Greek and Roman Philosophy*, edited by David Sedley, 184–210. Cambridge: Cambridge University Press, 2003.

Lovejoy, Arthur O. *The Great Chain of Being: A Study of the History of an Idea*. Cambridge, MA: Harvard University Press, 1964.

Lucretius. *On the Nature of Things*. Translated by W.H.D. Rouse, revised by Martin F. Smith. Cambridge: Loeb Classical Library, 1992.

Lundy, Craig. *History and Becoming: Deleuze's Philosophy of Creativity*. Edinburgh: Edinburgh University Press, 2013.

MacIntyre, Alasdair. "The Relationship of Philosophy to Its Past." In *Philosophy in History: Essays on the Historiography of Philosophy*, edited by Richard Rorty, J.B. Schneewind, and Quentin Skinner, 31–48. New York: Cambridge University Press, 1984.

Mader, Mary Beth. *Sleights of Reason: Norm, Bisexuality, Development*. Albany: SUNY Press, 2012.

Marion, Jean Luc. *In the Self's Place: The Approach of Saint Augustine*, translated by Jeffrey L. Kosky. Stanford: Stanford University Press, 2012.

Marx, Karl, and Friedrich Engels. *On Colonialism*. London: Lawrence and Wishart, 1960.

– *The Marx–Engels Reader*, translated by Robert C. Tucker. New York and London: W.W. Norton, 1978.

McCullagh, Suzanne, and Casey Ford. "The Desert Below: The Labyrinth of Sensibility between Rancière, Deleuze, and Weil." *Journal of Aesthetics and Phenomenology* 5, no. 2 (November 2018): 157–73.

Medina, José. *The Epistemology of Resistance: Gender and Racial Oppression, Epistemic Injustice, and Resistant Imaginations*. New York: Oxford University Press, 2013.

Melamed, Yitzhak Y. "Charitable Interpretations and the Political Domestication of Spinoza, or, Benedict in the Land of Secular Imagination." In *Philosophy and Its History: Aims and Methods in the Study of Early Modern Philosophy*, edited by Mogens Laerke, Justin E.H. Smith, and Eric Schliesser, 258–77. Oxford and New York: Oxford University Press, 2013.

Mengue, Philippe. *Deleuze et la question de la démocratie*. Paris: Harmattan, 2003.

Merleau-Ponty, Maurice. *The Phenomenology of Perception*, translated by Donald A. Landes. London: Routledge, 2013.

Mill, John Stuart. *On Liberty, Utilitarianism, and Other Essays*. Oxford: Oxford University Press, 2015.

Millikan, Ruth. "In Defense of Proper Functions." *Philosophy of Science* 56, no. 2 (1989): 288–302.

Mills, Charles W. "White Ignorance." In *Race and Epistemologies of Ignorance*, edited by Shannon Sullivan Nancy Tuana, 11–38. Albany: SUNY Press, 2007.

Monahan, Michael J. *The Creolizing Subject: Race, Reason, and the Politics of Purity*. New York: Fordham University Press, 2011.

Moravcsik, Julius. *Plato and Platonism*. Oxford: Blackwell, 1992.

Murdoch, Iris. *Existentialists and Mystics: Writings on Philosophy and Literature*. New York: Penguin, 1997.

– *Metaphysics as a Guide to Morals*. New York: Penguin Books, 1998.

Nesbitt, Nick. "The Postcolonial Event: The Problem of the Political." In *Deleuze and the Postcolonial*, edited by Simone Bignall and Paul Patton, 103–18. Edinburgh: Edinburgh University Press, 2010.

Nestler, Eric J. "Molecular Basis of Long-Term Plasticity Underlying Addiction." *Nature Reviews Neuroscience* 2, no. 2 (2001): 119–28.

Nestler, Eric J., and George K. Aghajanian. "Molecular and Cellular Basis of Addiction." *Science* 278, no. 3 (1997): 58–63.

Newton, Isaac. *Opticks: Or, A Treatise of the Reflections, Refractions, Inflections and Colours of Light*, 4th ed. London: William Innys at the West-End of St. Paul's, 1730.

– *Unpublished Scientific Papers*, edited by A.R. Hall and M.B. Hall. Cambridge, MA: Cambridge University Press, 1962.

Nietzsche, Friedrich. *On the Advantage and Disadvantage of History for Life*, translated by Peter Preuss. Indianapolis: Hackett, 1980.

– *The Birth of Tragedy* and *The Case of Wagner*, translated by Walter Kaufmann. New York: Vintage Books, 1967.

– *The Gay Science*, edited by Bernard Williams, translated by Josefine Nauckhoff. Cambridge: Cambridge University Press, 2001.

– *The Gay Science with a Prelude in Rhymes and an Appendix of Songs*, translated by Walter Kaufmann. New York: Vintage Books, 1974.

– *On the Genealogy of Morality*. Translated by Maudemarie Clark and Alan J. Swensen. New York: Hackett, 1998.

– *On the Genealogy of Morals* and *Ecce Homo*, translated by Walter Kaufmann. New York: Vintage, 1969.

– *Human, All Too Human*, translated by R.J. Hollingdale. Cambridge: Cambridge University Press, 1986.

– *The Twilight of the Idols* and *The Anti-Christ*, translated by R.J. Hollingdale. London: Penguin, 1990.

– *Thus Spoke Zarathustra*, translated by R.J. Hollingdale. Harmondsworth: Penguin, 1969.

– *The Will to Power*, translated by Walter Kaufmann. New York: Random House, 1968.

Nunes, Rodrigo. "Politics in the Middle: For a Political Interpretation of the Dualisms in Deleuze and Guattari." *Deleuze Studies* 4 (2010): 104–26.

Nunziato, Joshua. "Created to Confess: St. Augustine on Being Material." *Modern Theology* 32, no. 3 (July): 361–83.

Nussbaum, Martha. "Non-Relative Virtues: An Aristotelian Approach." *Midwest Studies in Philosophy* 13 (1988): 32–50.

O'Brien, Conor Cruise. "The Anti-Politics of Simone Weil." *New York Review of Books*, 12 May 1977).

O'Donnell, James J. "Augustine's Unconfession." In *Augustine and Postmodernism: Confessions and Circumfession*, edited by John D. Caputo and Micheal J. Scanlon, 214–19. Bloomington: Indiana University Press, 2005.

Patton, Paul. "Deleuze's Political Philosophy." In *The Cambridge Companion to Deleuze*, edited by Daniel W. Smith and Henry Somers-Hall, 198–219. Cambridge: Cambridge University Press, 2012.

– *Deleuzian Concepts: Philosophy, Colonization, Politics*. Stanford: Stanford University Press, 2010.

Pearson, Keith Ansell. *Germinal Life: The Difference and Repetition of Deleuze*. New York: Routledge, 1999.

Pétrément, Simone. *La vie de Simone Weil*. Paris: Fayard, 1973.

Plato. *Complete Works*, edited by John M. Cooper, translated by G.M.A. Grube. Indianapolis: Hackett, 1997.

Poole, Roger. "The Unknown Kierkegaard: Twentieth-Century Receptions." In *The Cambridge Companion to Kierkegaard*, edited by Alister Hannay and Gordon D. Marino, 48–75. Cambridge: Cambridge University Press, 1998.

Prendiville, John G. "The Development of the Idea of Habit in the Thought of Saint Augustine." *Traditio* 28 (1972): 29–99.

Preston, Beth. "Why Is a Wing Like a Spoon? A Pluralist Theory of Function." *Journal of Philosophy* 95, no. 5 (1998): 215–54.

Ravaisson, Félix. *Of Habit*, translated by Clare Carlisle and Mark Sinclair. London: Continuum, 2008.

Reath, Andrew. *Agency and Autonomy*. New York: Clarendon Press, 2006.

Rilke, Rainer Maria. *The Selected Poetry of Rainer Maria Rilke*, translated by Stephen Mitchell. New York: Vintage, 1989.

Rimbaud, Jean Nicholas Arthur. *Rimbaud: Complete Works, Selected Letters*, translated by Wallace Fowlie. Chicago: University of Chicago Press, 2005.

Rooten, Luis d'Antain van. *Mots D'Heures: Gousses, Rames*. New York: Penguin Books, 1967.

Rorty, Richard, J.B. Schneewind, and Quentin Skinner, eds. *Philosophy in History: Essays on the Historiography of Philosophy*. New York: Cambridge University Press, 1984.

Rowe, C.J. *Plato*, 2nd ed. London: Bristol Classical Press, 2003.

Rubenstein, Mary-Jane. "Undone by Each Other: Interrupted Sovereignty in Augustine's *Confessions*." In *Polydoxy: Theology of Multiplicity and*

Relation, edited by Catherine Keller and Laurel C. Schneider, 105–25. New York: Routledge, 2011.

Russon, John. "Aristotle's Animative Epistemology." *Idealist Studies: An Interdisciplinary Journal of Philosophy* 25, no. 3 (Fall 1995): 241–53.

– "Personality as Equilibrium: Fragility and Plasticity in (Inter-)Personal Identity." *Phenomenology and the Cognitive Sciences* 16, no. 4 (2017): 623–35.

Sabl, Andrew. *Hume's Politics: Coordination and Crisis in the History of England*. Princeton: Princeton University Press, 2012.

Said, Edward. *Orientalism: Western Conceptions of the Orient*. London: Penguin, 1978.

Saint Augustine. *Confessions*, translated by Henry Chadwick. New York: Oxford University Press, 1998.

Sartre, Jean-Paul. *Black Orpheus*, translated by S.W. Allen. Paris: Présence Africaine, 1948.

– "Kierkegaard: The Singular Universal." In *Between Existentialism and Marxism*, translated by John Matthews. London: New Left Books, 1974.

Schopenhauer, Arthur. *The World as Will and Representation*, vol. 1, translated by Richard E. Aquila and David Carus. New York: Longman, 2008.

Sedley, David. "Epicureanism in the Roman Republic." In *Cambridge Companion to Epicureanism*, edited by James Warren, 29–45. Cambridge: Cambridge University Press, 2009.

Selcer, Daniel. *Philosophy and the Book: Early Modern Figures of Material Inscription*. London: Continuum, 2010.

Seneca. *Epistles, 1–65*. Cambridge, MA: Harvard University Press, 2006.

Senghor, Léopold Sédar. *On African Socialism*, translated by M. Cook. London: Pall Mall Press, 1964.

– "The Foundations of 'Africanité.'" *Critical Interventions* 3, no. 10 (2009): 166–9.

– *Liberté 1: Négritude et Humanism*. Paris: Seuil, 1964.

– *Liberté 3: Négritude et Civilisation de l'Universal*. Paris: Seuil, 1977.

– *Liberté 5: le Dialogue des cultures*. Paris: Seuil, 1993.

– *Prose and Poetry*, translated by J. Reed and C. Wake. Oxford: Oxford University Press, 1965.

Serres, Michel. *The Birth of Physics*, translated by Jack Hawkes, edited by David Webb. Manchester: Clinamen Press, 2000.

– *The Natural Contract*, translated by Elizabeth MacArthur and William Paulson. Ann Arbor: University of Michigan Press, 1995.

- *The Parasite*, translated by Lawrence R. Schehr. Baltimore: Johns Hopkins University Press, 1982.
- *Troubadour of Knowledge*, translated by Sheila Faria Glaser with William Paulson. Ann Arbor: University of Michigan Press, 1997.

Sextus Empiricus. *Against the Professors*, translated by R.G. Bury. Cambridge: Loeb Classical Library, 1949.

Skinner, Quentin. "Meaning and Understanding in the History of Ideas." *History and Theory* 8, no. 1 (1969): 3–53.

Smith, Adam. *Essays on Philosophical Subjects* [1759]. New York: Georg Olms Verlag Hildesheim, 1992.
- *The Theory of Moral Sentiments* [1759]. Indianapolis: Liberty Fund, 1976.

Smith, Justin E.H. *Divine Machines: Leibniz and the Sciences of Life*. Princeton: Princeton University Press, 2011.

Somers-Hall, Henry. *Deleuze's* Difference and Repetition. Edinburgh: Edinburgh University Press, 2013.
- "Feuerbach and the Image of Thought." In *At the Edges of Thought: Deleuze and Post-Kantian Philosophy*, edited by Craig Lundy and Daniella Voss, 253–71. Edinburgh: Edinburgh University Press, 2015.
- *Hegel, Deleuze, and the Critique of Representation*. Albany: SUNY Press, 2012.
- "Time Out of Joint: Hamlet and the Pure Form of Time." *Deleuze Studies* 5, Issue supplement (2011): 56–76.

Sontag, Susan. "Simone Weil." In *Against Interpretation: And Other Essays*. New York: Farrar, Straus & Giroux, 1966.

Sorabji, Richard. "Time, Mysticism, and Creation." In *Augustine's Confessions: Critical Essays*, edited by William E. Mann, 209–35. New York: Rowman and Littlefield, 2006.

Sparshott, Francis. *Taking Life Seriously: A Study of the Argument of the Nicomachean Ethics*. Toronto: University of Toronto Press, 1994.

Spinoza, Baruch. *Ethics: With the Treatise on the Emendation of the Intellect and Selected Letters*, translated by Samuel Shirley. Indianapolis: Hackett, 1992.
- *Spinoza: Complete Works*. Translated by Samuel Shirley. Indianapolis: Hackett, 2002.

Spivak, Gayatri Chakravorty. "Can the Subaltern Speak?" *Wedge* 7, no. 8 (1985): 120–30.

Stewart, George R. *Pickett's Charge: A Microhistory of the Final Attack on Gettysburg, July 3, 1863*. Boston: Houghton Mifflin, 1959.

Sunstein, Cass. *Republic.com 2.0*. Princeton: Princeton University Press, 2009.

Tsouna, Voula. "Epicurean Therapeutic Strategies." In *Cambridge Companion to Epicureanism*, edited by James Warren, 249–65. Cambridge: Cambridge University Press, 2009.

Turner, Dale. *This Is Not a Peace Pipe: Towards a Critical Indigenous Philosophy*. Toronto: University of Toronto Press, 2006.

Urmson, J.R. "Aristotle's Doctrine of the Mean." *American Philosophical Quarterly* 10, no. 2 (July 1973): 223–30.

Vetö, Miklos. *La métaphysique religieuse de Simone Weil*. Paris: Harmattan, 1997.

Wallach, Barbara Price. *Lucretius and the Diatribe against the Fear of Death: De Rerum Natura III, 830–1094*. Leiden: Brill, 1976.

Walsh, John Patrick. *Free and French in the Caribbean*. Bloomington: Indiana University Press, 2013.

Weil, Simone. *On the Abolition of All Political Parties*. New York: NYRB, 2014.

– *Écrits de Londres et dernières lettres*. Paris: Gallimard, 1957.

– *Gravity and Grace*, translated by E. Crawford and M. von der Ruhr. London: Routledge, 2002.

– *The Need for Roots*, translated by A. Willis. New York: Routledge, 2002.

– *Notebooks*, translated by Arthur Wills. London: Routledge and Kegan Paul, 1956.

– *Œuvres*, edited by Florence de Lussy. Paris: Gallimard, 1999.

– *Oeuvres complètes*, vol. 1: *Premiers écrits philosophiques*, edited by André A. Devaux and Florence de Lussy. Paris: Gallimard, 1988.

– *Oeuvres completes*, vol. 4, pt. 2: *Écrits de Marseille (1941–1942)*, edited by Anissa Castel-Bouchouchi and Florence de Lussy. Paris: Gallimard, 2009.

– *Oeuvres complètes*, vol. 7, pt. 2: *Correspondance familiale*, edited by Robert Chenavier and André A. Devaux. Paris: Gallimard, 2012.

– *Oppression and Liberty*, translated by Arthur Wills and John Petrie. London and New York: Routledge, 2004.

– *Waiting for God*, translated by E. Craufurd. New York: HarperCollins, 2001.

Whyte, Jessica. "'The Work of Men Is Not Durable': History, Haiti, and the Rights of Man." In *Agamben and Colonialism*, edited by M. Svirsky and Simone Bignall, 239–60. Edinburgh: Edinburgh University Press, 2012.

Widder, Nathan. *Political Theory after Deleuze*. New York: Bloomsbury, 2012.

Wilder, Gary. *Freedom Time: Negritude, Decolonisation, and the Future of the World*. Durham: Duke University Press, 2015.

Wittgenstein, Ludwig. *The Blue and Brown Books* [1935]. London: Basil Blackwell, 1958.

- *Philosophical Grammar* [1933]. Oxford: Basil Blackwell, 1974.

- *Philosophical Investigations*. Oxford: Basil Blackwell, 1953.

Wood, Allen W. *Kantian Ethics*. Cambridge: Cambridge University Press, 2008.

- *Kant's Ethical Thought*. Cambridge: Cambridge University Press, 1999.

Woolf, Virginia. *The Diary of Virginia Woolf*, vol. 3, edited by Anne Olivier Bell. London: Hogarth Press, 1980.

Young, Robert J.C. *Colonial Desire: Hybridity in Theory, Culture, and Race*. London: Routledge, 1995.

Zhang, Peter. "Gilles Deleuze and Minor Rhetoric." *ETC: A Review of General Semantics* 68, no. 2 (2011): 214–19.

Zinn, Howard. *The Politics of History*. Champaign: University of Illinois Press, 1990.

Žižek, Slavoj. *Organs without Bodies: Deleuze and Consequences*. New York: Routledge, 2004.

Contributors

BRUCE BAUGH is a professor in the Department of Philosophy, History, and Politics at Thompson Rivers University (Kamloops, British Columbia). He is the author of numerous articles on Gilles Deleuze and Benjamin Fondane as well as the book *French Hegel: From Surrealism to Postmodernism* (Routledge, 2003). His translation of Fondane's philosophical essays, *Existential Monday*, was published in 2016 (NYRB Books).

JEFFREY A. BELL is a professor of philosophy at Southeastern Louisiana University. He is the author of numerous articles and three monographs on topics in phenomenology, post-structuralism, and Deleuze. His latest book is *Deleuze and Guattari's What Is Philosophy? A Critical Introduction and Guide* (Edinburgh).

SIMONE BIGNALL is a senior researcher in the Jumbunna Research Hub for Indigenous Nations and Collaborative Futures at the University of Technology Sydney in Australia. Her book publications include *Postcolonial Agency: Critique and Constructivism* (Edinburgh 2010); *Deleuze and the Postcolonial* (with Paul Patton); *Agamben and Colonialism* (with Marcelo Svirsky); *Deleuze and Pragmatism* (with Sean Bowden and Paul Patton); and *Posthuman Ecologies: Complexity and Process after Deleuze* (with Rosi Braidotti). She is currently completing titles on *Posthuman Desire* and *Excolonialism: Ethics after Enjoyment.*

SOPHIE BOURGAULT is an associate professor of political science at the University of Ottawa. Her current research interests gravitate toward the ethics of care and hospitality, feminist philosophy, and the political thought of Simone Weil. In addition to several book chapters on Plato, Simone Weil, and Hannah Arendt, her publications include articles published in journals such as *Ethics and Politics/Etica and Politica*; *The European Journal of Women Studies*; *Recherches Féministes*; and *Frontiers: A Journal of Women Studies*. She is also the co-editor of *Simone Weil, Beyond Ideology?* (2020); *Les éthiques de l'hospitalité, du don et du care* (2020); *In Yet a Different Voice* (2020); *Cura ed emozioni* (2018); and *Le care: Éthique féministe actuelle* (2015). She was guest co-editor of special issues for *Politique et Sociétés* (2016) and for *The International Journal of Care and Caring*. She has co-edited a new translation and critical edition of some of Christine de Pizan's political writings (Hackett, 2018). Bourgault is a Research Director at the CIRCEM of the University of Ottawa; she is also the current president of the American Simone Weil Society.

ANTONIO CALCAGNO is a professor of philosophy at King's University College in London, Canada. He works in Continental philosophy and has interests in medieval and Renaissance philosophy. He is the author of *Giordano Bruno and the Logic of Coincidence*, *The Philosophy of Edith Stein*, *Badiou and Derrida: Politics, Events and Their Time*, and *Lived Experience from the Inside Out: Social and Political Philosophy in Edith Stein*. He is also the editor of the recently published volume *Contemporary Italian Political Philosophy*.

CASEY FORD received his PhD in philosophy from the University of Guelph in 2016. He was a Philosophy Fellow at Marlboro College (Vermont) from 2019–20. His research and teaching interests are in the history of philosophy, nineteenth- and twentieth-century European philosophy, ethical and social-political thought, and the tradition of ontology widely construed. He has published and presented work on Gilles Deleuze, Simone Weil, John Dewey, Jacques Rancière, Michel Foucault, Giorgio Agamben, and literature and art. With Suzanne McCullagh and colleagues, he is the co-organizer and co-founder of the City Seminar, an annual seminar in the history of philosophy for graduate and postgraduate scholars.

KAREN L.F. HOULE is a professor of philosophy at the University of Guelph, in Canada. She is the author of numerous articles on the following thinkers: Gilles Deleuze and Félix Guattari, Michel Foucault, Spinoza, Jacques Derrida, and Luce Irigaray; and on the following subjects: animality, plant ontology, micropolitics, friendship, copyright, and reproductive technology. With Jim Vernon (York University), she co-edited a book of essays on Hegel and Deleuze (2013, Northwestern). She is the author of *Toward a New Image of Thought: Responsibility, Complexity, and Abortion* (2013, Lexington Press, Outsources Series). She is the author of three books of poetry: *Ballast* (2000, House of Anansi), *During* (2005, Gaspereau), and *The Grand River Watershed: A Folk Ecology* (2019, Gaspereau), which was nominated for a Governor General's Award in 2019.

RYAN J. JOHNSON is an assistant professor of philosophy at Elon University in North Carolina. He is the author of *The Deleuze–Lucretius Encounter* (Edinburgh, 2017) and contributing co-editor of *The Movement of Nothingness: Trust in the Emptiness of Time* (Davies Group 2012), *Contemporary Encounters with Ancient Metaphysics* (Edinburgh, 2017), and *Nietzsche and Epicurus* (Bloomsbury, 2020). His next book is called *Deleuze, A Stoic* (Edinburgh, forthcoming), and he is currently co-writing (with Biko Mandela Gray) *Phenomenology of Black Spirit*, which stages a dialectical parallelism between Hegel's *Phenomenology of Spirit* and six moments in American Black Thought.

JAY LAMPERT is a professor of philosophy at Duquesne University and previously professor of philosophy at the University of Guelph. He is the author of four books on Husserl, Deleuze and Guattari, and time.

LEONARD LAWLOR is the Edwin Erle Sparks Professor of Philosophy at Pennsylvania State University. He has written prolifically on nineteenth- and twentieth-century European philosophy, especially the phenomenological tradition, Merleau-Ponty, Jacques Derrida, and Gilles Deleuze. He is the author of *From Violence to Speaking Out* (Edinburgh, 2016) and *Early Twentieth Century Continental Philosophy* (Indiana, 2011) among other books, articles, translations, and edited volumes.

ERIN MANNING is a research chair in speculative pragmatism, art, and pedagogy in the Faculty of Fine Arts at Concordia University

(Montreal, Canada). She is also the founder of SenseLab (www. senselab.ca), a laboratory that explores the intersections between art practice and philosophy through the matrix of the sensing body in movement, and a 3 Ecologies Institute collaborator. Artworks tend to explore more-than human participatory ecologies. Exhibitions include the Sydney and Moscow Biennales, Glasshouse (New York), Vancouver Art Museum, McCord Museum (Montreal), House of World Cultures (Berlin), and Galateca Gallery (Bucarest). Publications include *For a Pragmatics of the Useless* (Duke University Press, 2020), *The Minor Gesture* (Duke University Press, 2016), *Always More Than One: Individuation's Dance* (Duke University Press, 2013), *Relationscapes: Movement, Art, Philosophy* (Cambridge, MA: MIT Press, 2009), and, with Brian Massumi, *Thought in the Act: Passages in the Ecology of Experience* (University of Minnesota Press, 2014).

SUZANNE M. MCCULLAGH is an assistant professor of philosophy in the Centre for Humanities at Athabasca University. Her current research interests include the temporalities of extinction discourse, ecological justice, grace, and critical posthumanism. She has published work on the following thinkers: Gilles Deleuze and Felix Guattari, Jacques Rancière, Simone Weil, Max Scheler, and Hannah Arendt; and on the following subjects: empathy, political belonging, capacities for action, reparation ecology, education, and aesthetics. She is currently co-editing a volume titled *Contesting Extinctions: Critical Relationality, Regenerative Futures*.

HENRY SOMERS-HALL is a reader in philosophy at Royal Holloway, University of London. His primary research interests are German idealism and modern French philosophy. He is the author of *Judgement and Sense in Modern French Philosophy* (forthcoming 2021), *Hegel, Deleuze, and the Critique of Representation* (2012) and *Deleuze's Difference and Repetition* (2013), as well as co-translator of Salomon Maimon's *Essay on Transcendental Philosophy* (2009) and co-editor of the *Cambridge Companion to Deleuze* (2012) and *A Thousand Plateaus and Philosophy* (2018).

SAŠA STANKOVIĆ is currently an assistant professor at Trent University in Peterborough, Ontario. He has taught philosophy at Brandon University in Manitoba, Ryerson University, and the University of Prince Edward Island. His research interests include ethics, Kant's Critical Philosophy, and Continental Philosophy. His published work deals with issues of knowledge, freedom, and morality in Kant's *Groundwork* and *Critique of Practical Reason*. He is currently completing a book-length project about the advantages of the transcendental method for ethical philosophy, especially in the works of Kant and Deleuze.

Index